# THE CLIQUE

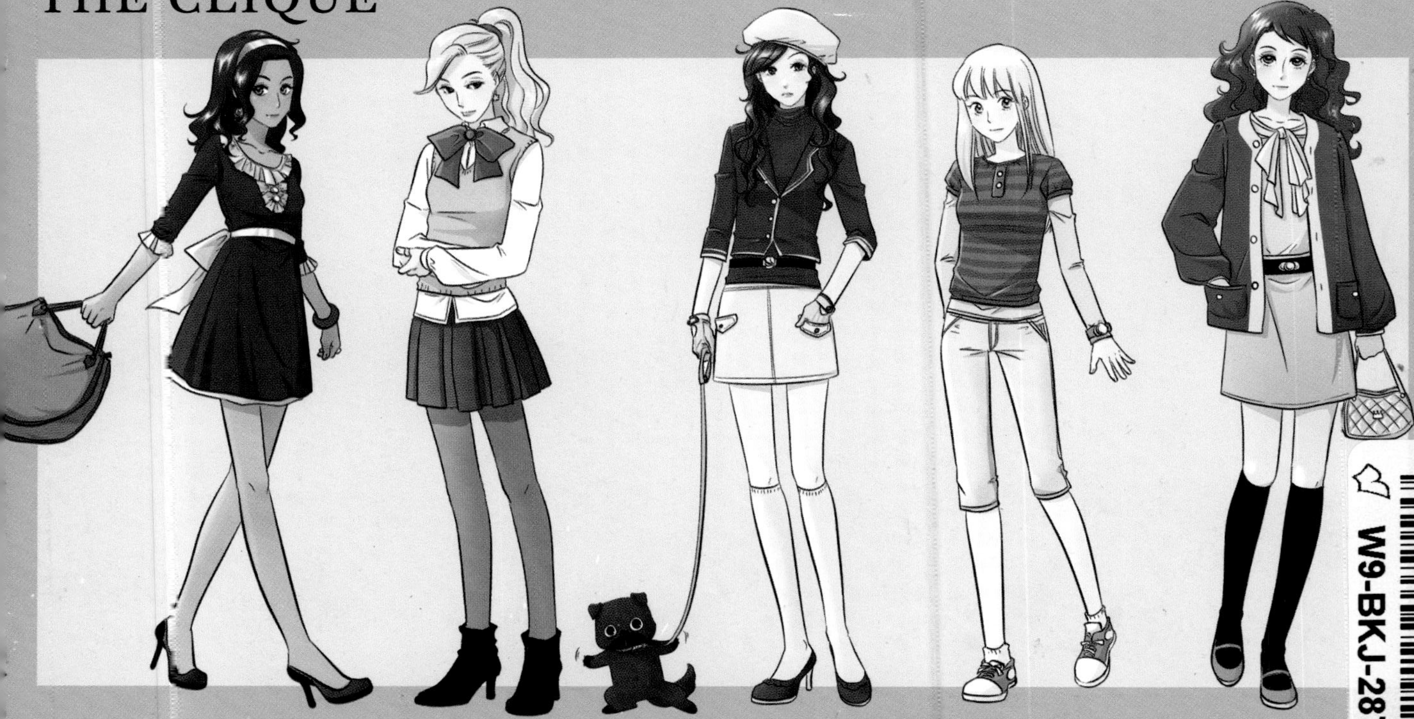
ALICIA
KRISTEN
MASSIE
CLAIRE
DYLAN

# THE CLIQUE

A GRAPHIC NOVEL BY LISI HARRISON & YISHAN LI

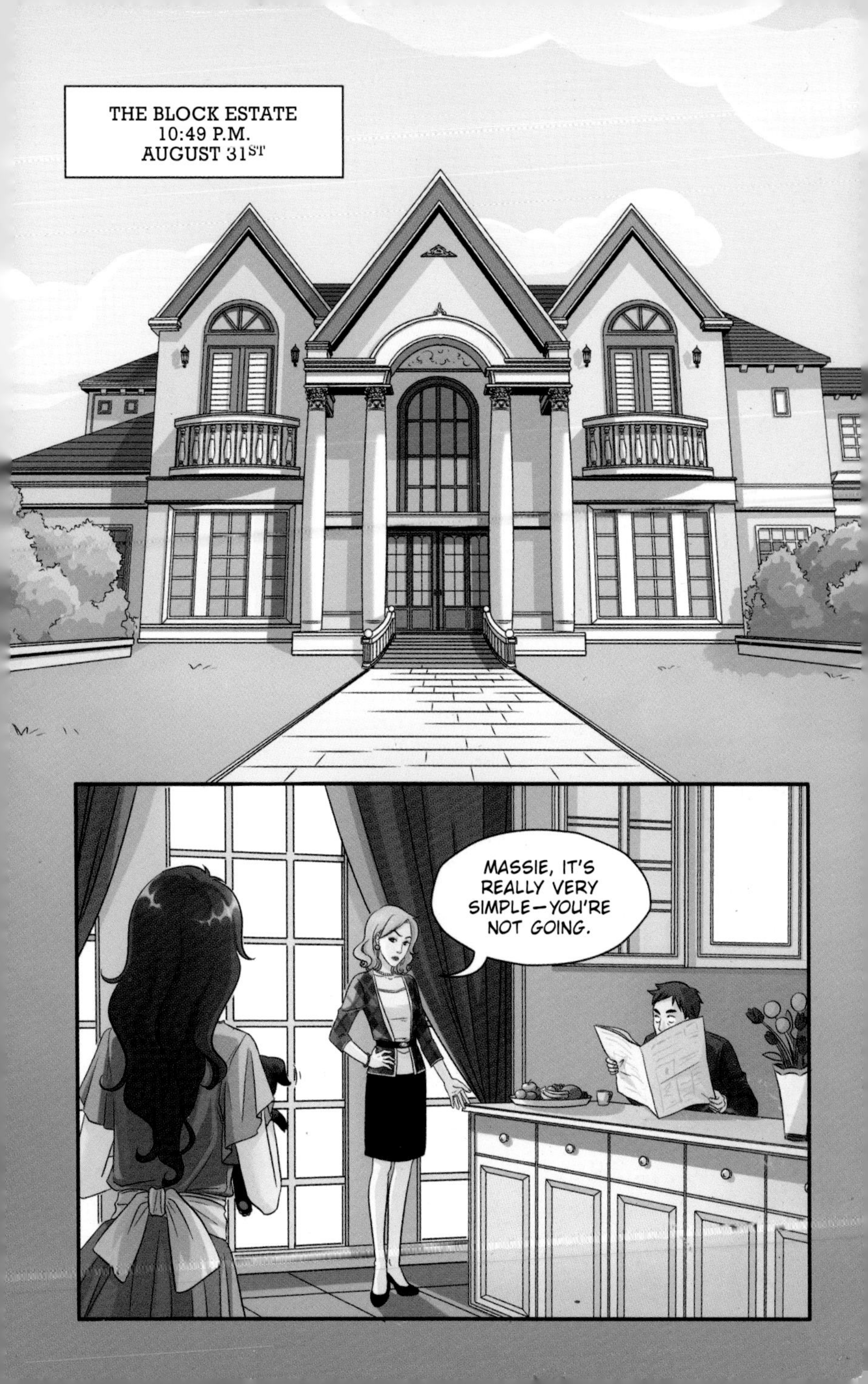
THE BLOCK ESTATE
10:49 P.M.
AUGUST 31ST
MASSIE, IT'S REALLY VERY SIMPLE—YOU'RE NOT GOING.

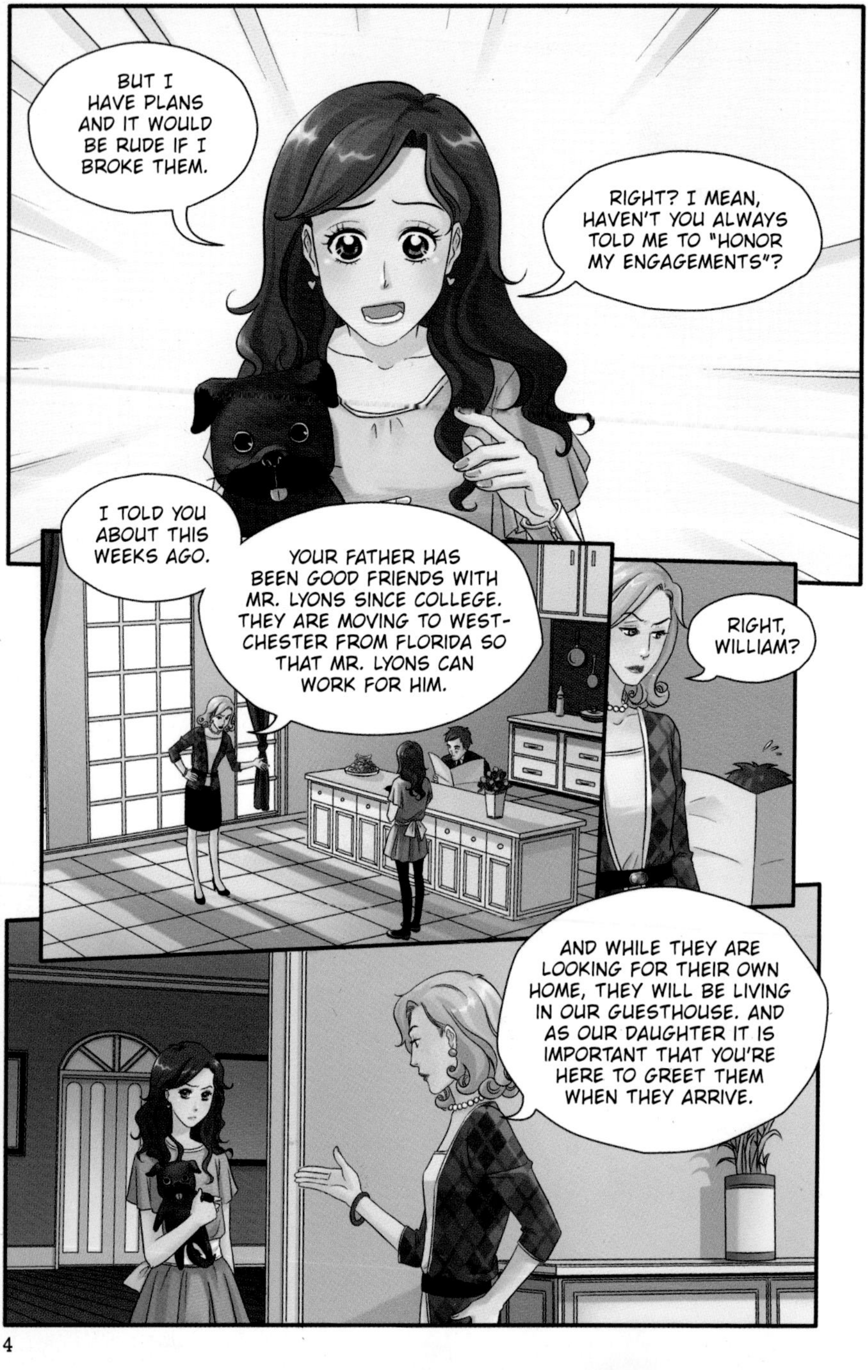
BUT I HAVE PLANS AND IT WOULD BE RUDE IF I BROKE THEM.
RIGHT? I MEAN, HAVEN'T YOU ALWAYS TOLD ME TO "HONOR MY ENGAGEMENTS"?
I TOLD YOU ABOUT THIS WEEKS AGO.
YOUR FATHER HAS BEEN GOOD FRIENDS WITH MR. LYONS SINCE COLLEGE. THEY ARE MOVING TO WEST-CHESTER FROM FLORIDA SO THAT MR. LYONS CAN WORK FOR HIM.
RIGHT, WILLIAM?
AND WHILE THEY ARE LOOKING FOR THEIR OWN HOME, THEY WILL BE LIVING IN OUR GUESTHOUSE. AND AS OUR DAUGHTER IT IS IMPORTANT THAT YOU'RE HERE TO GREET THEM WHEN THEY ARRIVE.

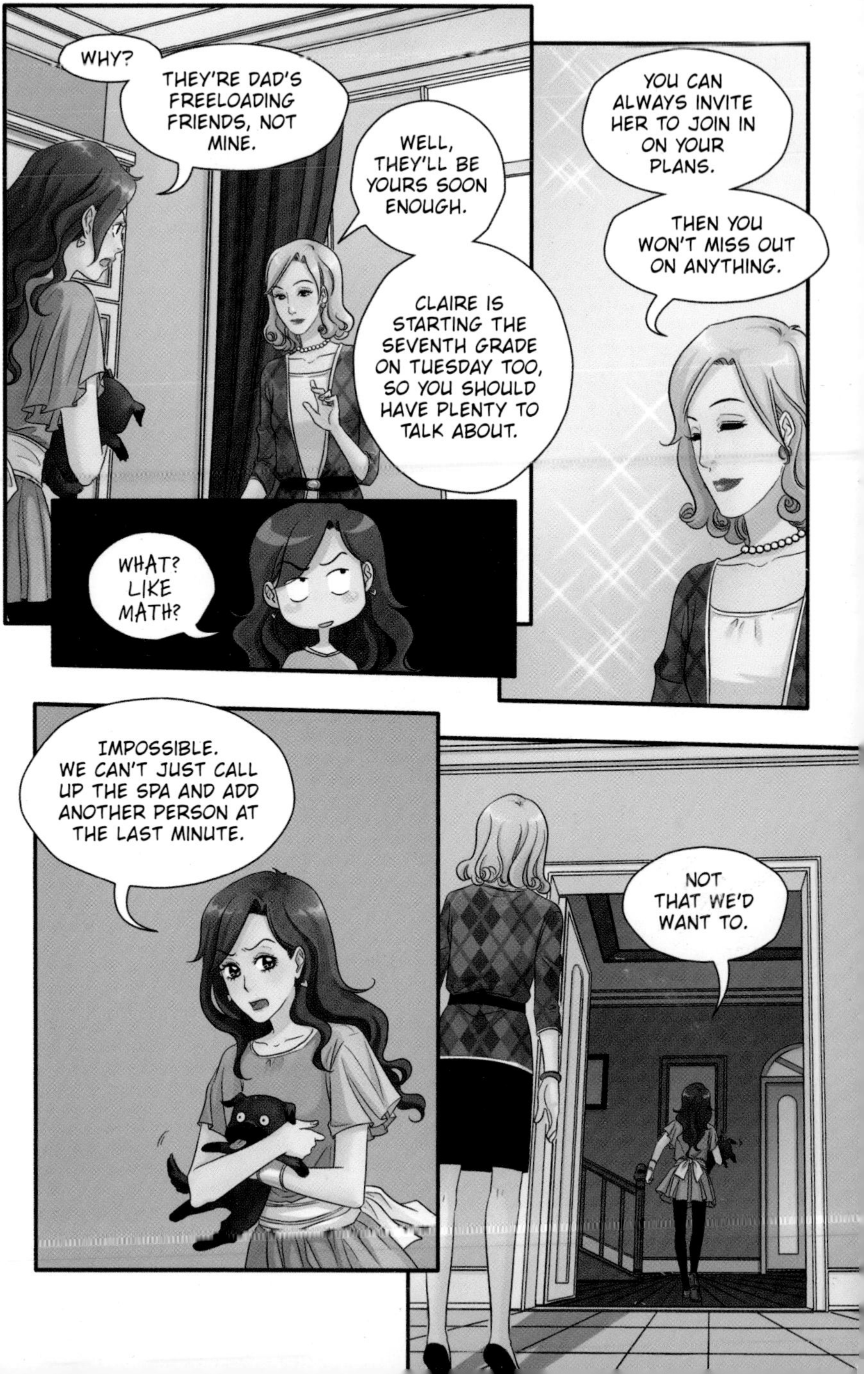
WHY?
THEY'RE DAD'S FREELOADING FRIENDS, NOT MINE.
WELL, THEY'LL BE YOURS SOON ENOUGH.
CLAIRE IS STARTING THE SEVENTH GRADE ON TUESDAY TOO, SO YOU SHOULD HAVE PLENTY TO TALK ABOUT.
WHAT? LIKE MATH?
YOU CAN ALWAYS INVITE HER TO JOIN IN ON YOUR PLANS.
THEN YOU WON'T MISS OUT ON ANYTHING.
IMPOSSIBLE. WE CAN'T JUST CALL UP THE SPA AND ADD ANOTHER PERSON AT THE LAST MINUTE.
NOT THAT WE'D WANT TO.

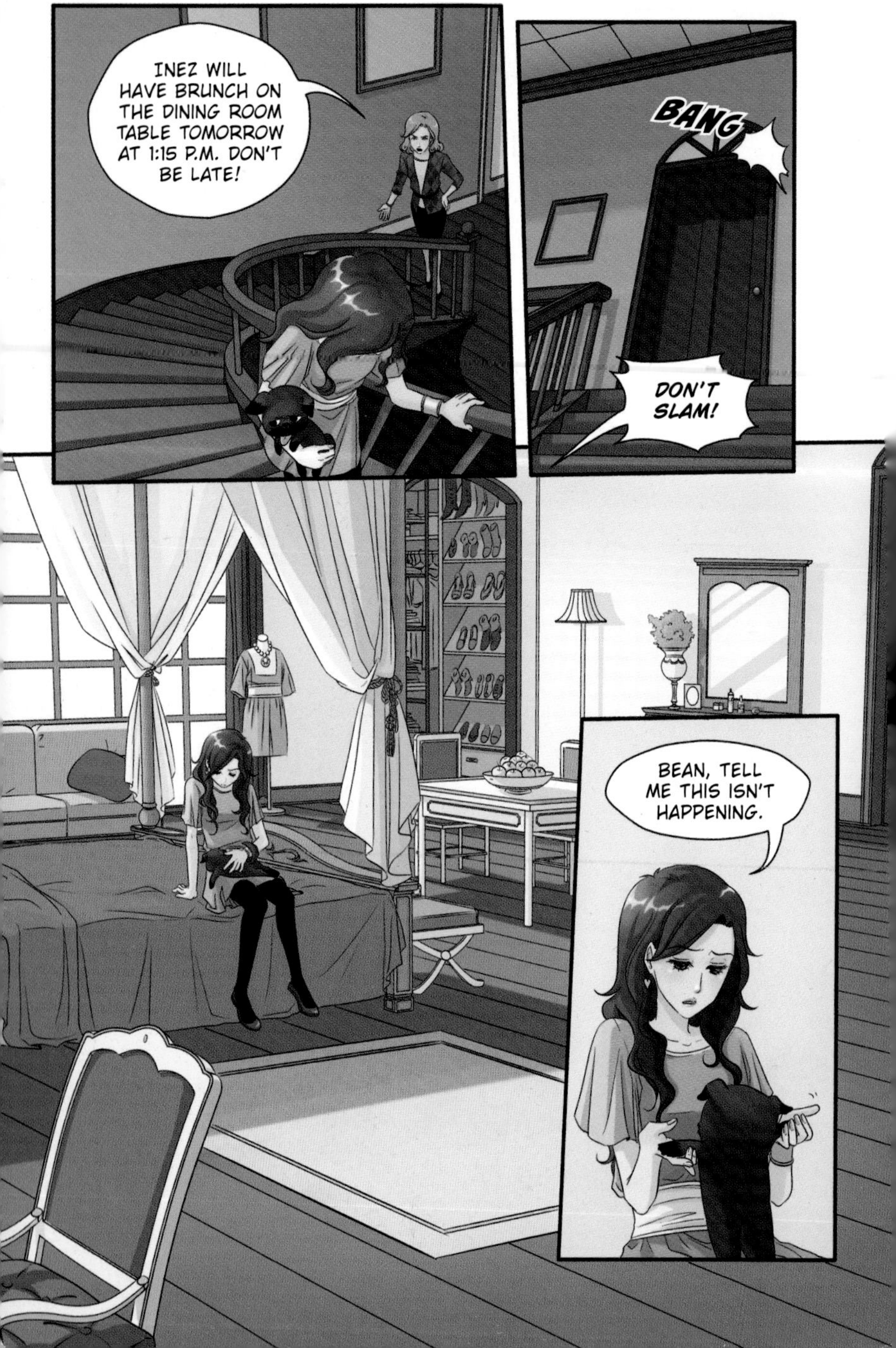
INEZ WILL HAVE BRUNCH ON THE DINING ROOM TABLE TOMORROW AT 1:15 P.M. DON'T BE LATE!
BANG
DON'T SLAM!
BEAN, TELL ME THIS ISN'T HAPPENING.

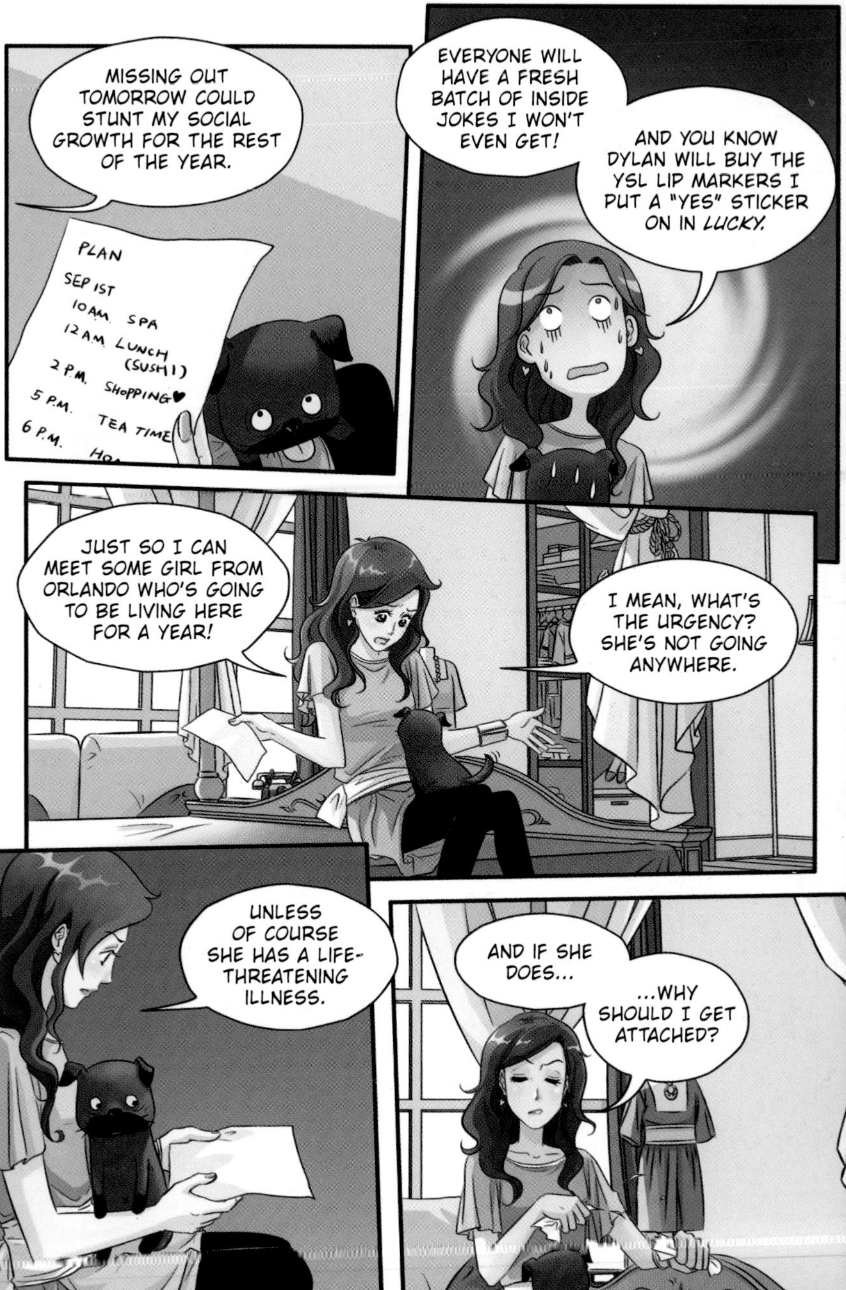
MISSING OUT TOMORROW COULD STUNT MY SOCIAL GROWTH FOR THE REST OF THE YEAR.
PLAN
SEP 1ST
10AM. SPA
12AM. LUNCH (SUSHI)
2P.M. SHOPPING♥
5P.M. TEA TIME
EVERYONE WILL HAVE A FRESH BATCH OF INSIDE JOKES I WON'T EVEN GET!
AND YOU KNOW DYLAN WILL BUY THE YSL LIP MARKERS I PUT A "YES" STICKER ON IN *LUCKY.*
JUST SO I CAN MEET SOME GIRL FROM ORLANDO WHO'S GOING TO BE LIVING HERE FOR A YEAR!
I MEAN, WHAT'S THE URGENCY? SHE'S NOT GOING ANYWHERE.
UNLESS OF COURSE SHE HAS A LIFE-THREATENING ILLNESS.
AND IF SHE DOES...
...WHY SHOULD I GET ATTACHED?

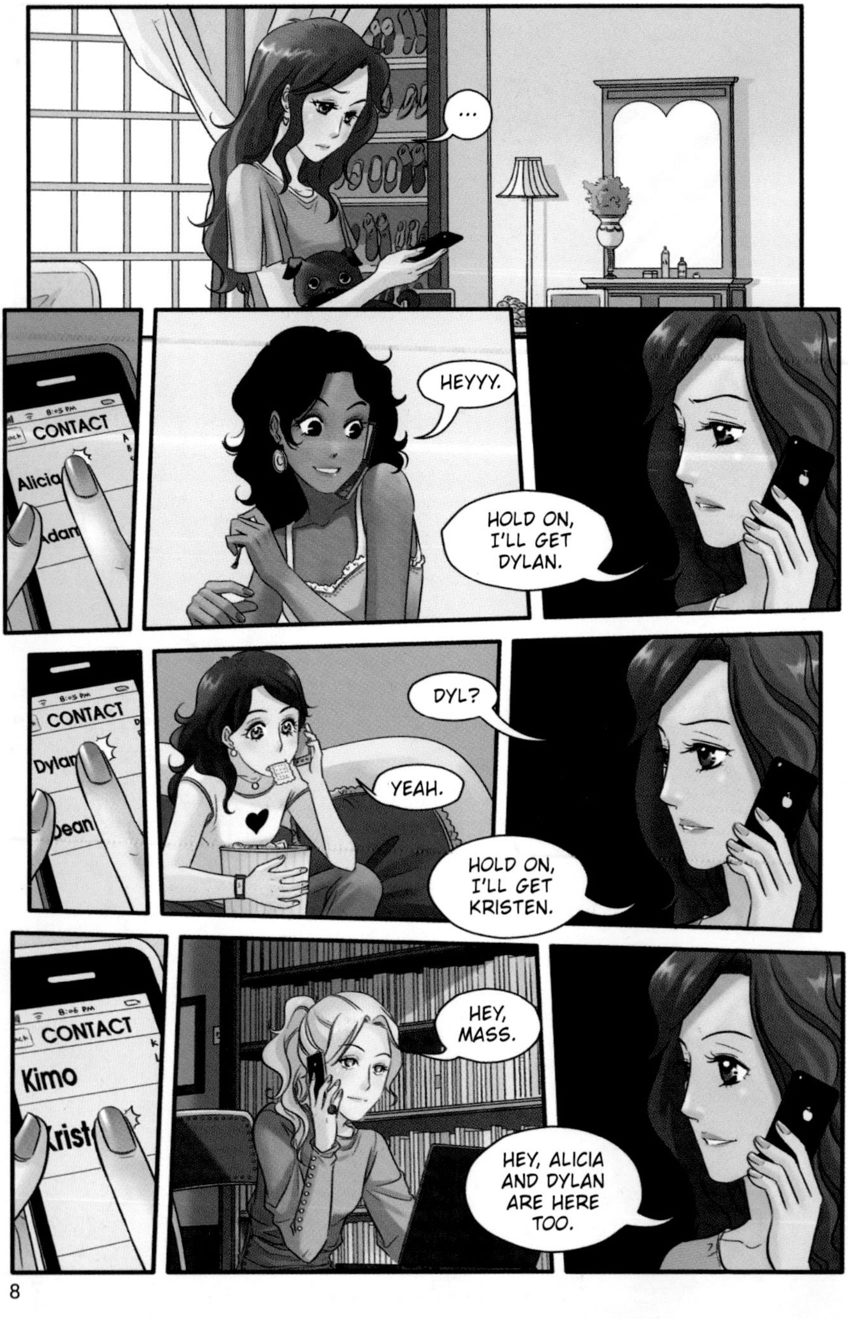
...
8:05 PM
CONTACT
Alicia
Adam
HEYYY.
HOLD ON, I'LL GET DYLAN.
8:05 PM
CONTACT
Dylan
Dean
DYL?
YEAH.
HOLD ON, I'LL GET KRISTEN.
8:06 PM
CONTACT
Kimo
HEY, MASS.
HEY, ALICIA AND DYLAN ARE HERE TOO.

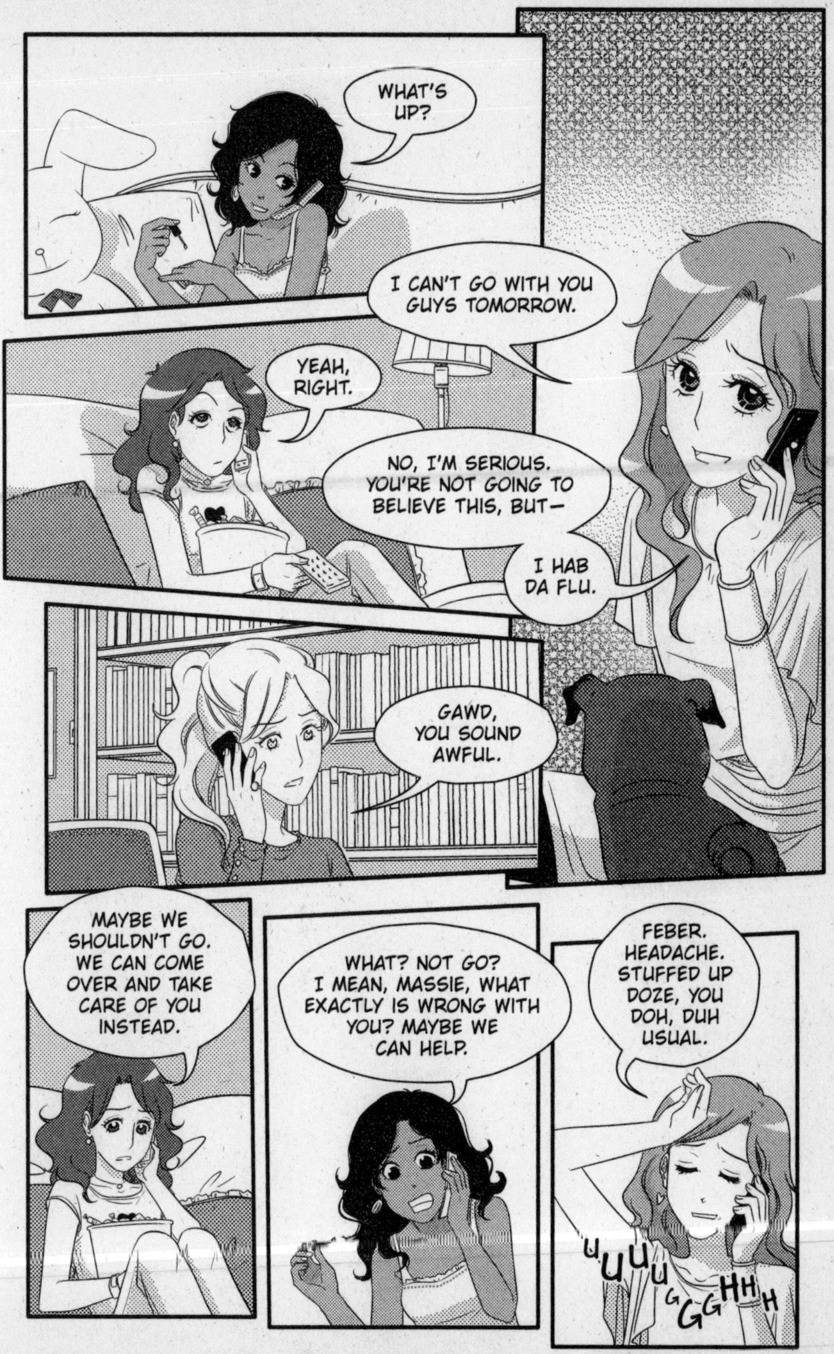
WHAT'S UP?
I CAN'T GO WITH YOU GUYS TOMORROW.
YEAH, RIGHT.
NO, I'M SERIOUS. YOU'RE NOT GOING TO BELIEVE THIS, BUT—
I HAB DA FLU.
GAWD, YOU SOUND AWFUL.
MAYBE WE SHOULDN'T GO. WE CAN COME OVER AND TAKE CARE OF YOU INSTEAD.
WHAT? NOT GO? I MEAN, MASSIE, WHAT EXACTLY IS WRONG WITH YOU? MAYBE WE CAN HELP.
FEBER. HEADACHE. STUFFED UP DOZE, YOU DOH, DUH USUAL.
UUUUUGGGHHHH

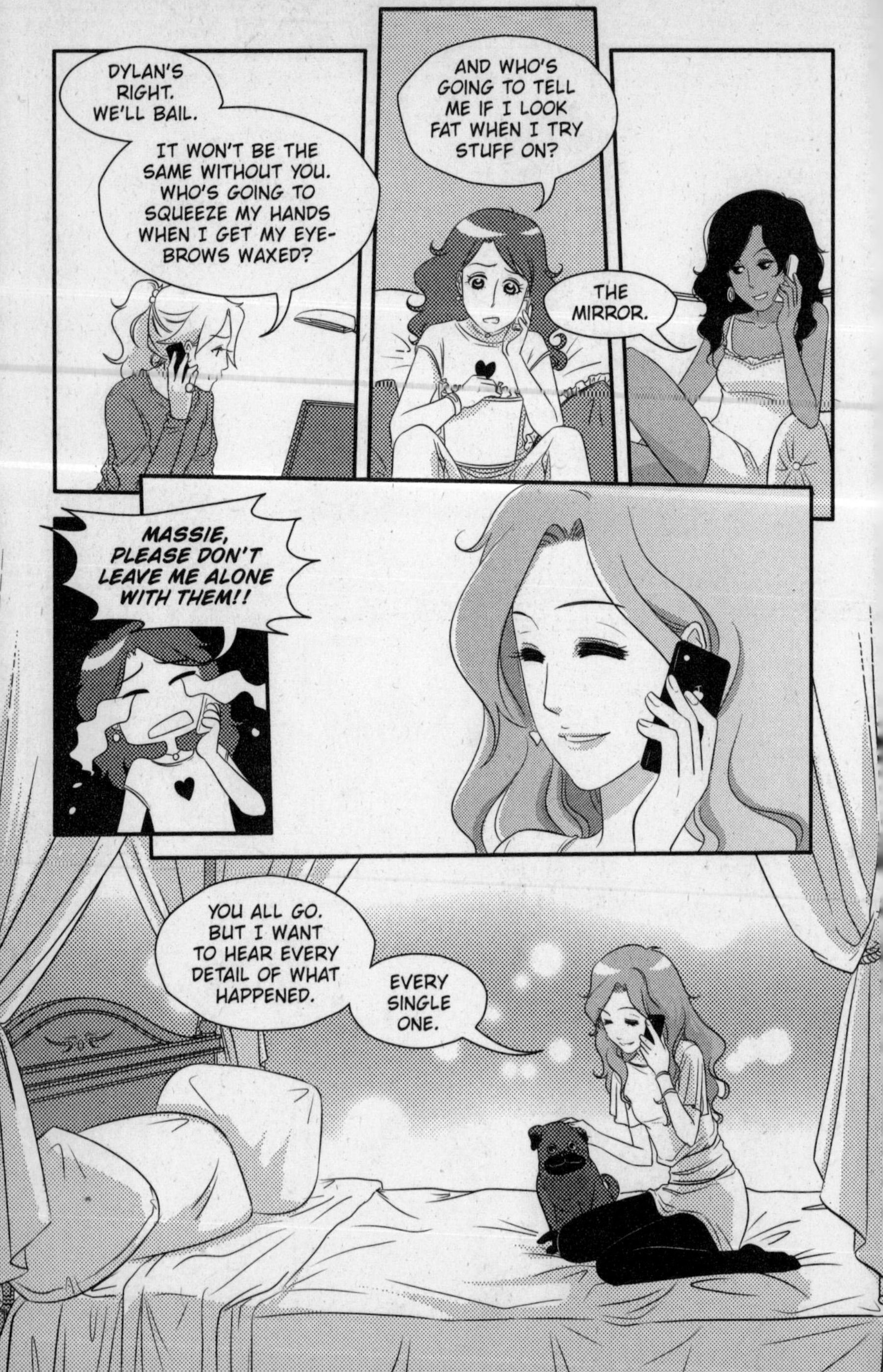
DYLAN'S RIGHT. WE'LL BAIL.
IT WON'T BE THE SAME WITHOUT YOU. WHO'S GOING TO SQUEEZE MY HANDS WHEN I GET MY EYE-BROWS WAXED?
AND WHO'S GOING TO TELL ME IF I LOOK FAT WHEN I TRY STUFF ON?
THE MIRROR.
MASSIE, PLEASE DON'T LEAVE ME ALONE WITH THEM!!
YOU ALL GO. BUT I WANT TO HEAR EVERY DETAIL OF WHAT HAPPENED.
EVERY SINGLE ONE.

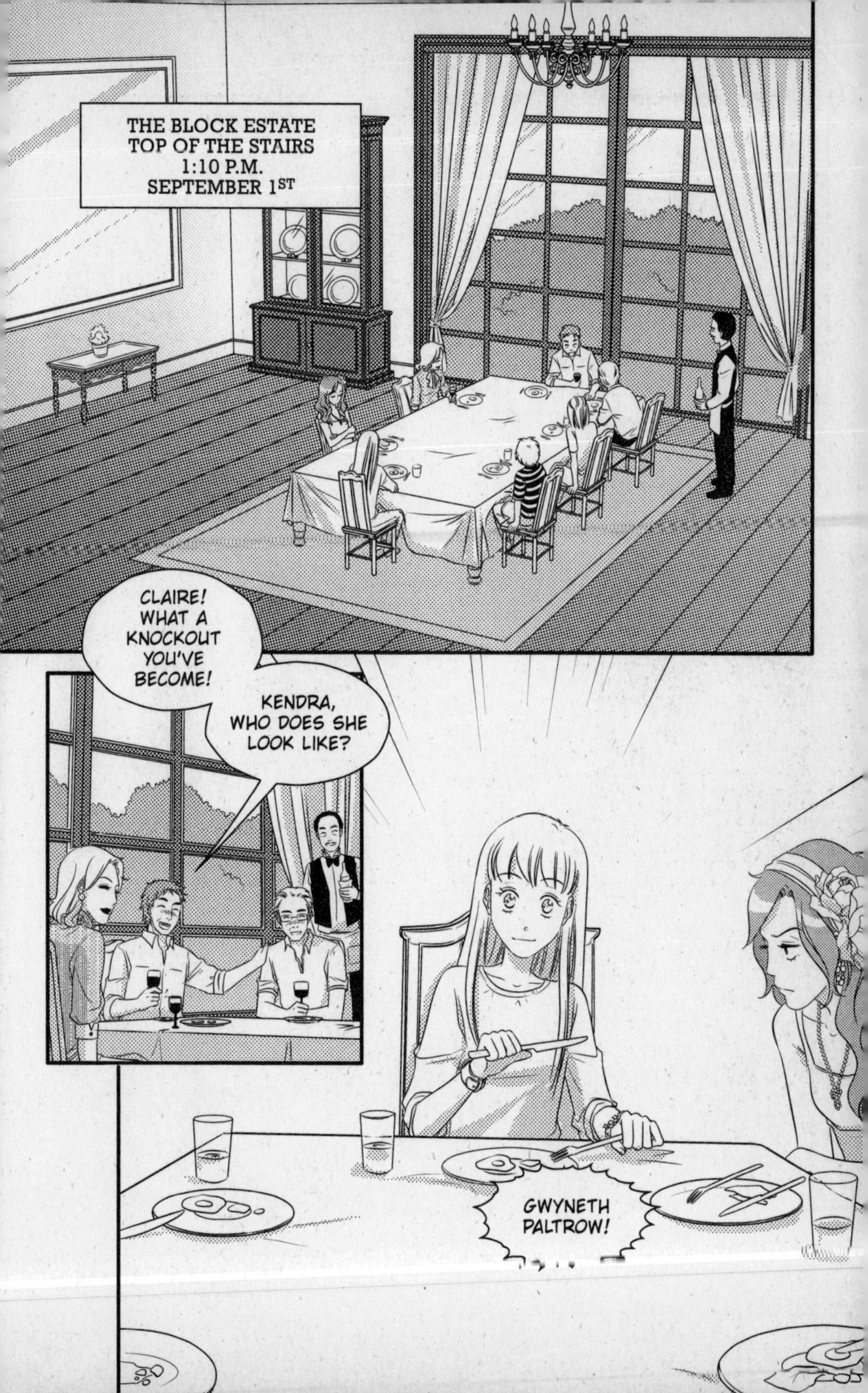
THE BLOCK ESTATE TOP OF THE STAIRS 1:10 P.M. SEPTEMBER 1ST
CLAIRE! WHAT A KNOCKOUT YOU'VE BECOME!
KENDRA, WHO DOES SHE LOOK LIKE?
GWYNETH PALTROW!

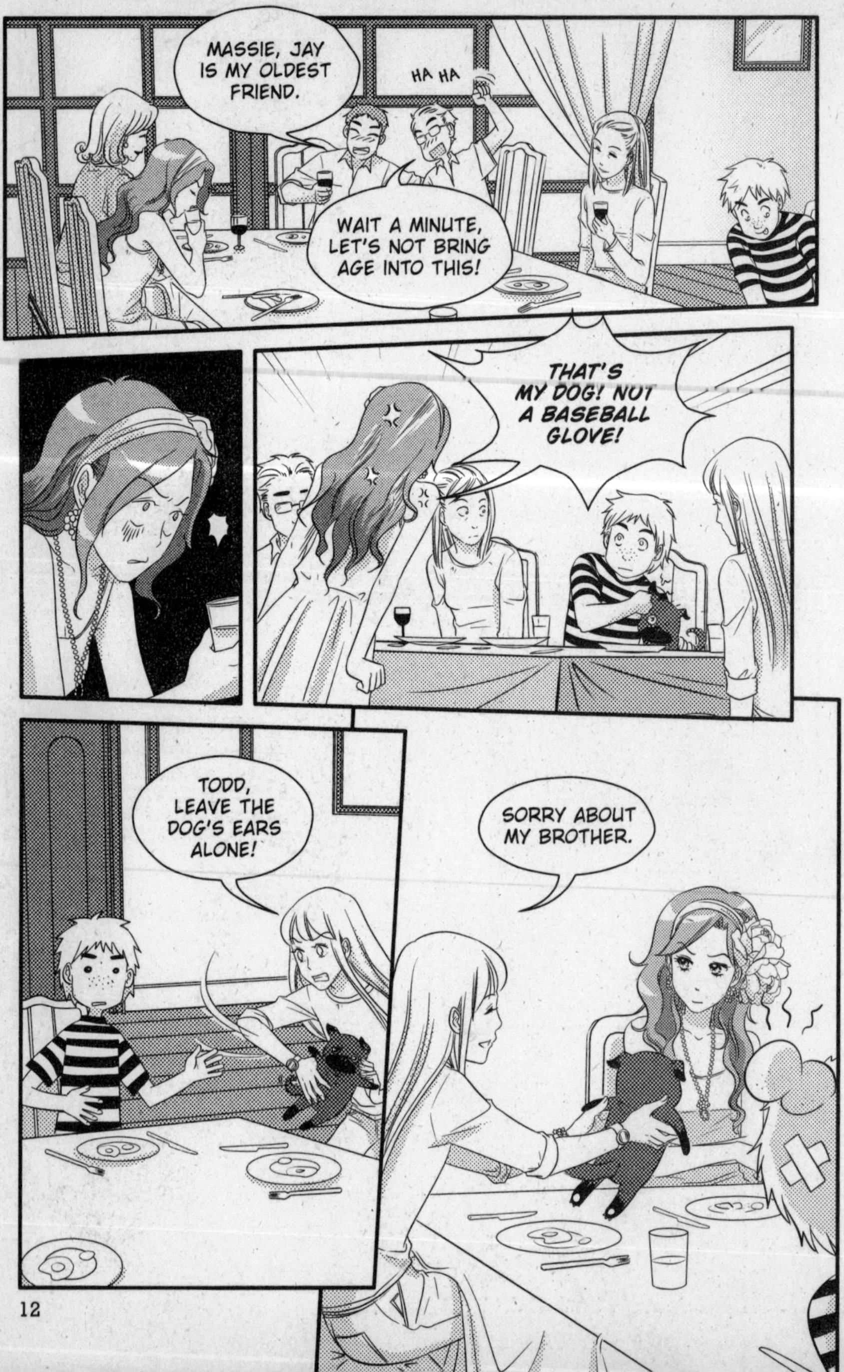
MASSIE, JAY IS MY OLDEST FRIEND.
HA HA
WAIT A MINUTE, LET'S NOT BRING AGE INTO THIS!
THAT'S MY DOG! NOT A BASEBALL GLOVE!
TODD, LEAVE THE DOG'S EARS ALONE!
SORRY ABOUT MY BROTHER.

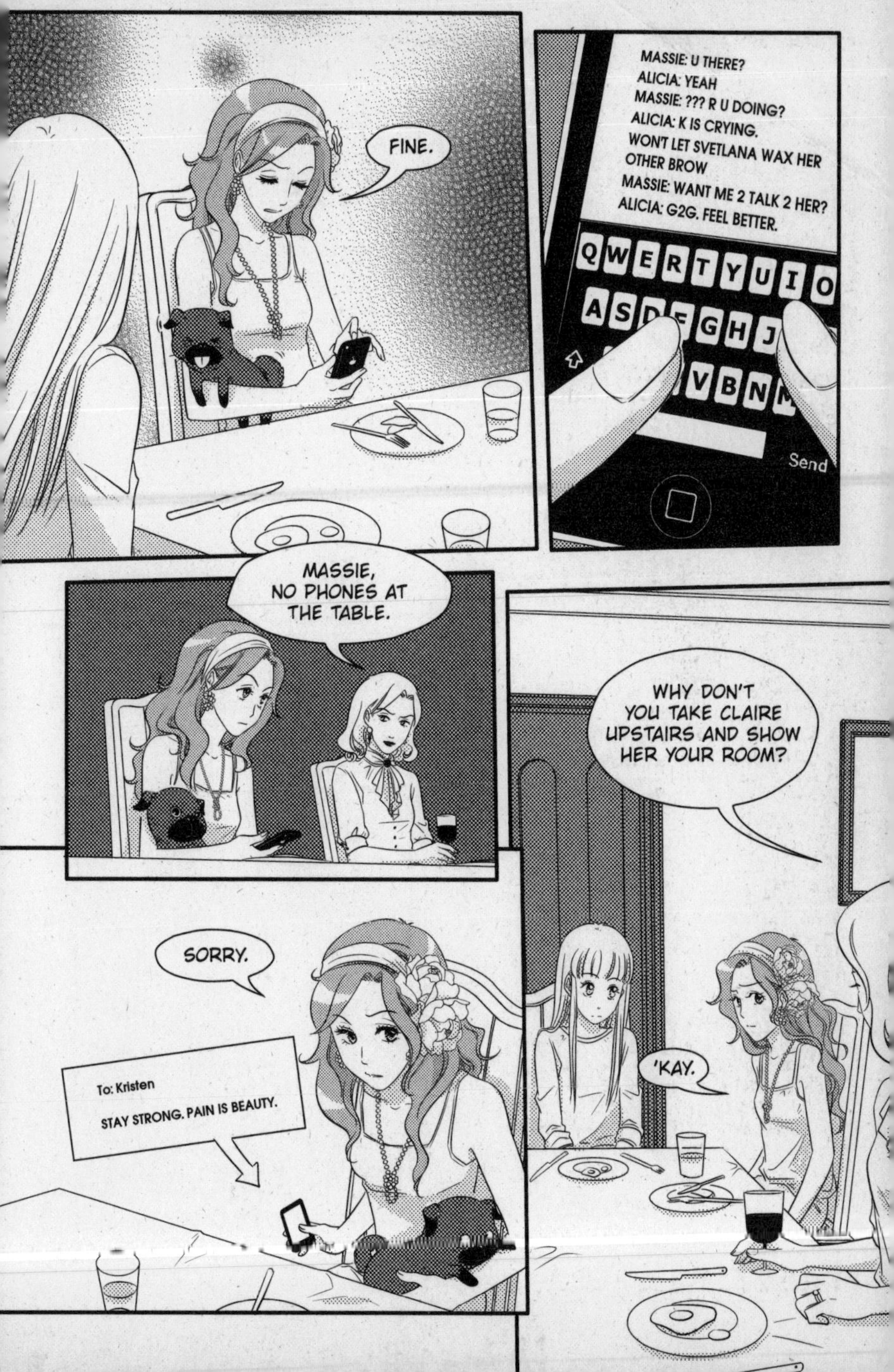
FINE.
MASSIE: U THERE?
ALICIA: YEAH
MASSIE: ??? R U DOING?
ALICIA: K IS CRYING. WON'T LET SVETLANA WAX HER OTHER BROW
MASSIE: WANT ME 2 TALK 2 HER?
ALICIA: G2G. FEEL BETTER.
Send
MASSIE, NO PHONES AT THE TABLE.
WHY DON'T YOU TAKE CLAIRE UPSTAIRS AND SHOW HER YOUR ROOM?
SORRY.
To: Kristen
STAY STRONG. PAIN IS BEAUTY.
'KAY.

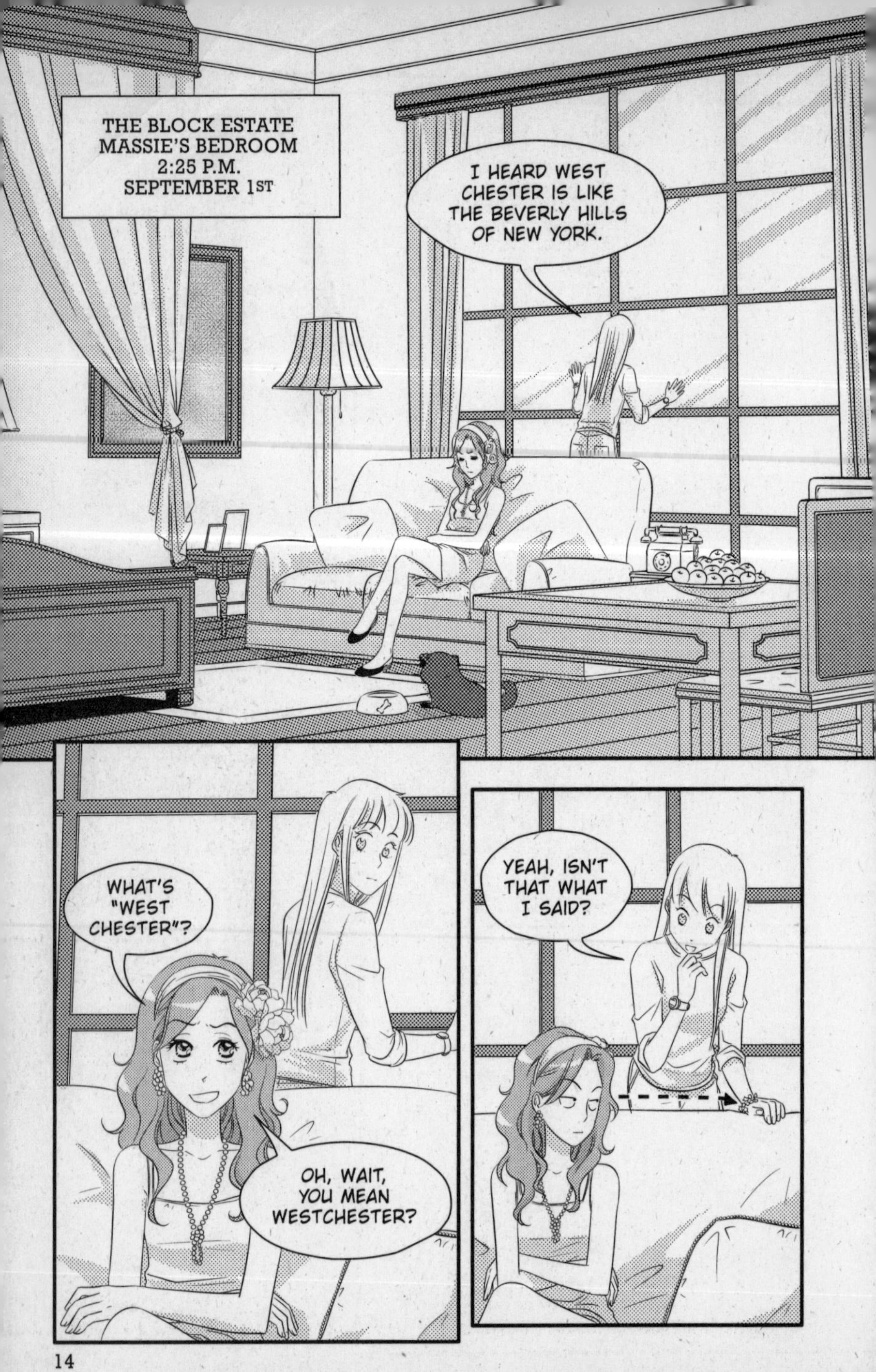
THE BLOCK ESTATE
MASSIE'S BEDROOM
2:25 P.M.
SEPTEMBER 1ST
I HEARD WEST CHESTER IS LIKE THE BEVERLY HILLS OF NEW YORK.
WHAT'S "WEST CHESTER"?
OH, WAIT, YOU MEAN WESTCHESTER?
YEAH, ISN'T THAT WHAT I SAID?

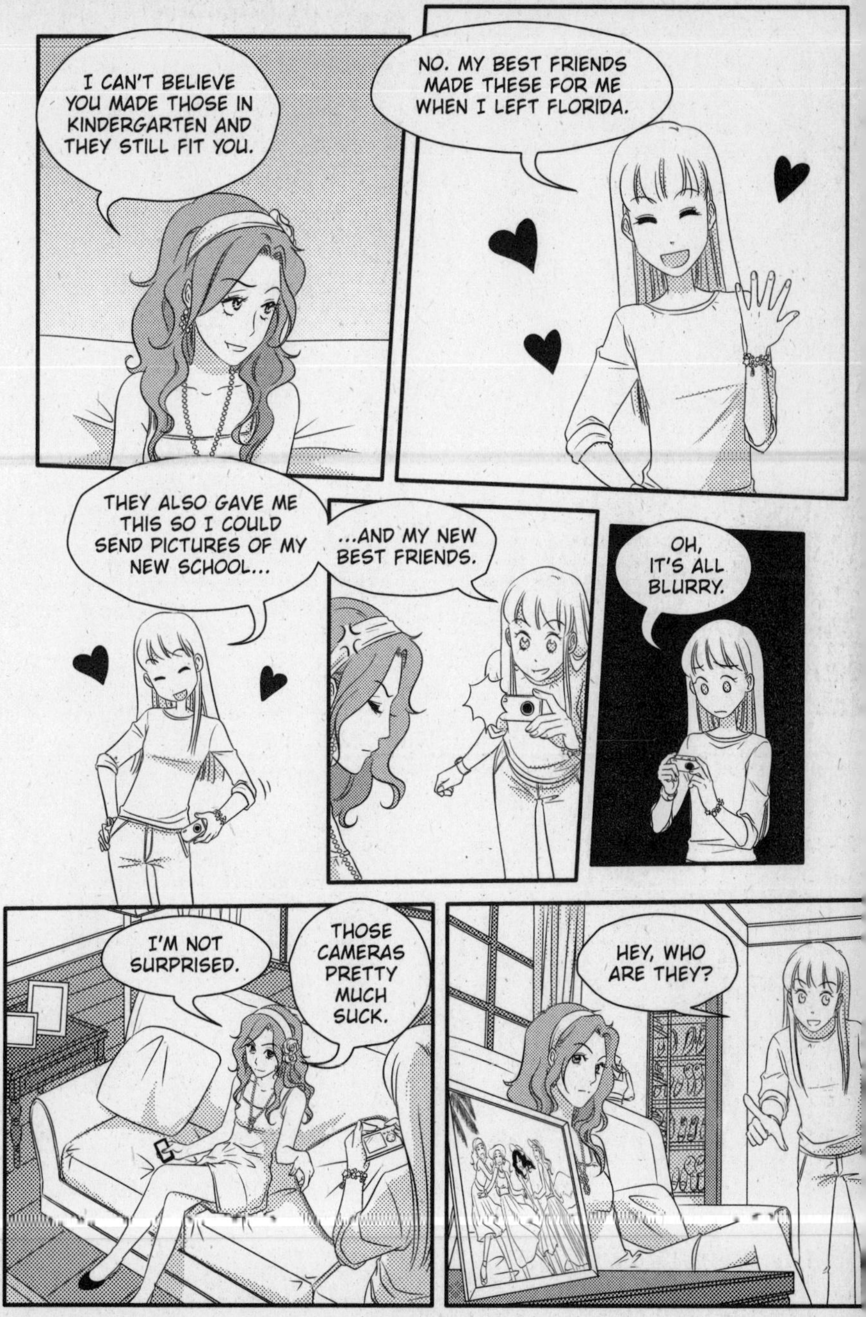
I CAN'T BELIEVE YOU MADE THOSE IN KINDERGARTEN AND THEY STILL FIT YOU.
NO. MY BEST FRIENDS MADE THESE FOR ME WHEN I LEFT FLORIDA.
THEY ALSO GAVE ME THIS SO I COULD SEND PICTURES OF MY NEW SCHOOL...
...AND MY NEW BEST FRIENDS.
OH, IT'S ALL BLURRY.
I'M NOT SURPRISED.
THOSE CAMERAS PRETTY MUCH SUCK.
HEY, WHO ARE THEY?

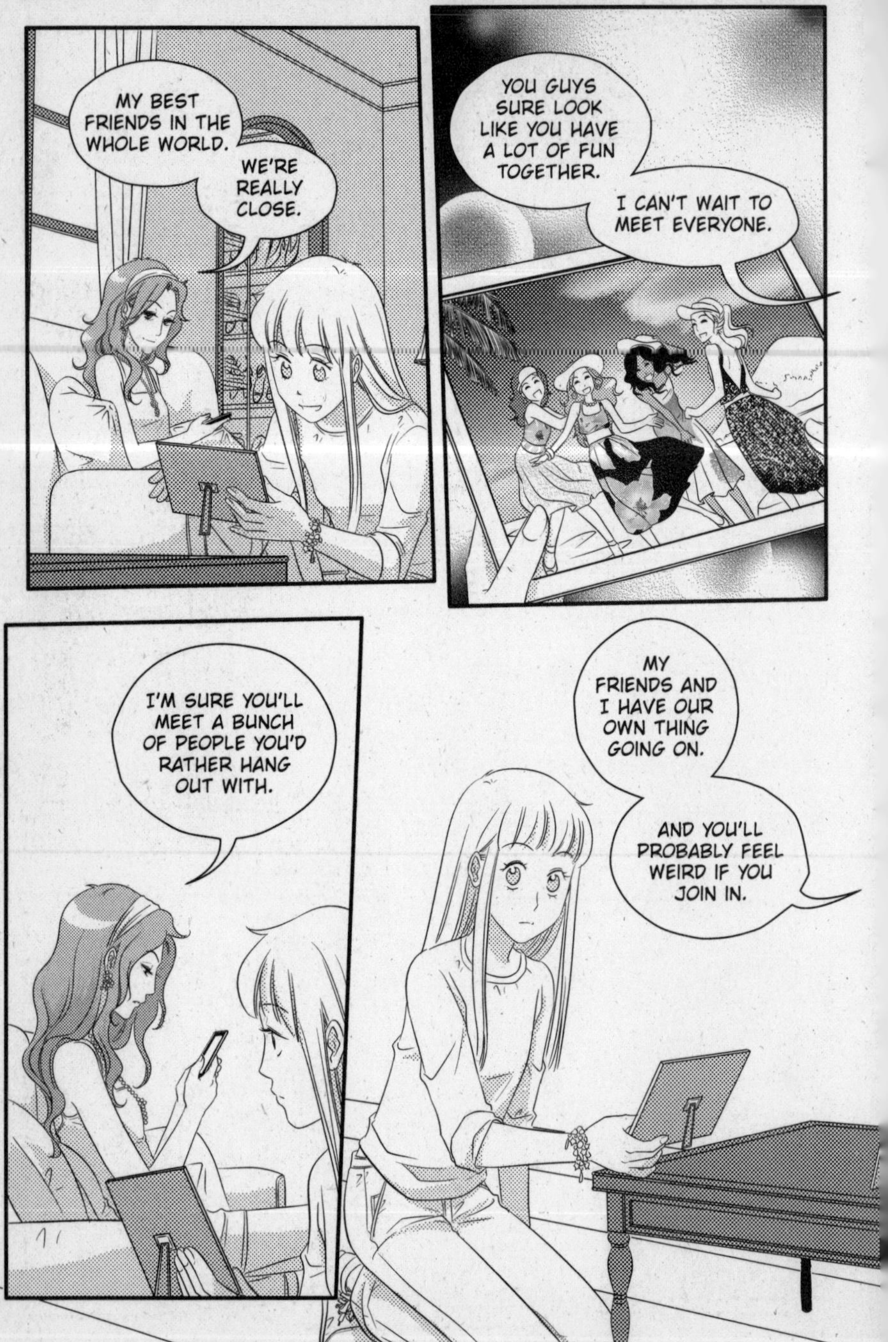
MY BEST FRIENDS IN THE WHOLE WORLD.
WE'RE REALLY CLOSE.
YOU GUYS SURE LOOK LIKE YOU HAVE A LOT OF FUN TOGETHER.
I CAN'T WAIT TO MEET EVERYONE.
I'M SURE YOU'LL MEET A BUNCH OF PEOPLE YOU'D RATHER HANG OUT WITH.
MY FRIENDS AND I HAVE OUR OWN THING GOING ON.
AND YOU'LL PROBABLY FEEL WEIRD IF YOU JOIN IN.

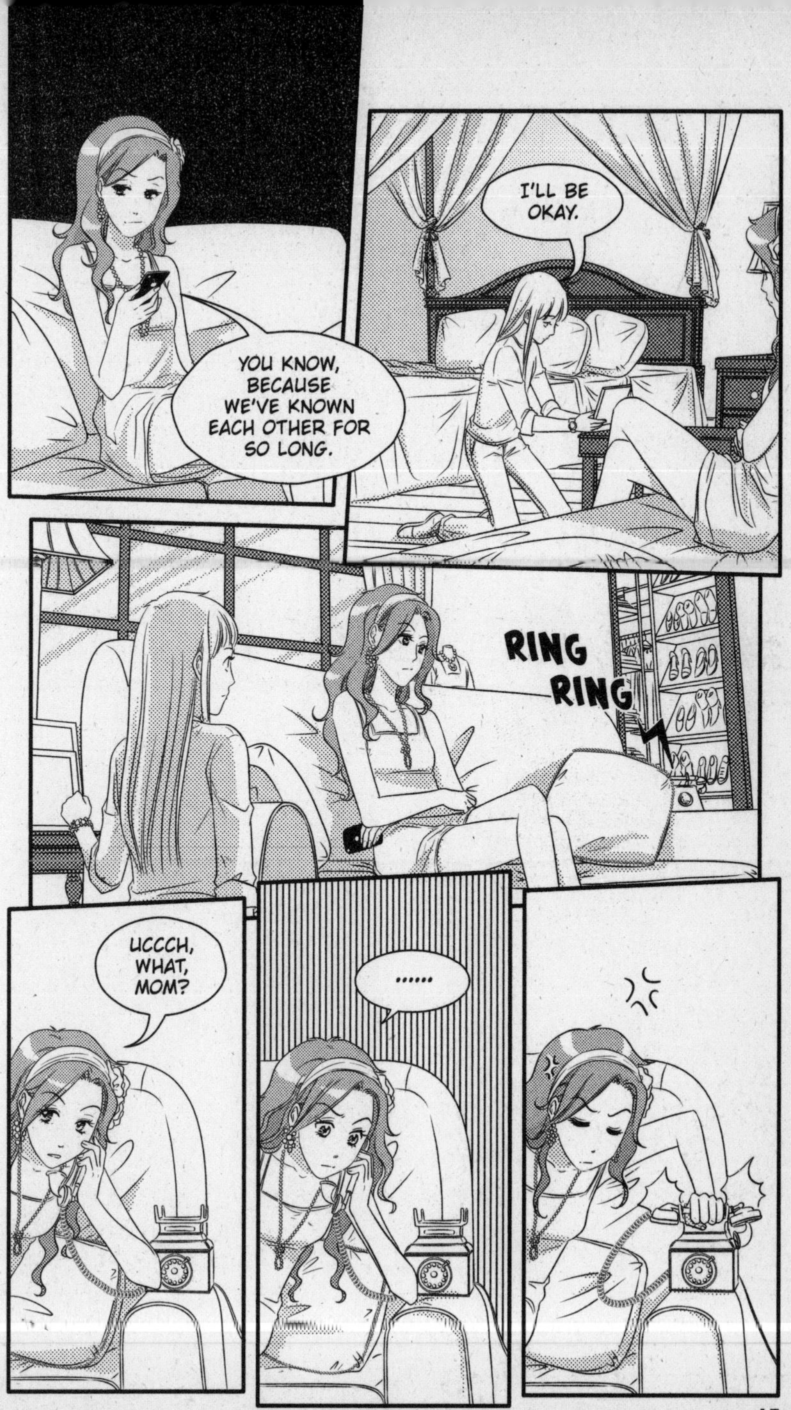
YOU KNOW, BECAUSE WE'VE KNOWN EACH OTHER FOR SO LONG.
I'LL BE OKAY.
RING RING
UCCCH, WHAT, MOM?
......

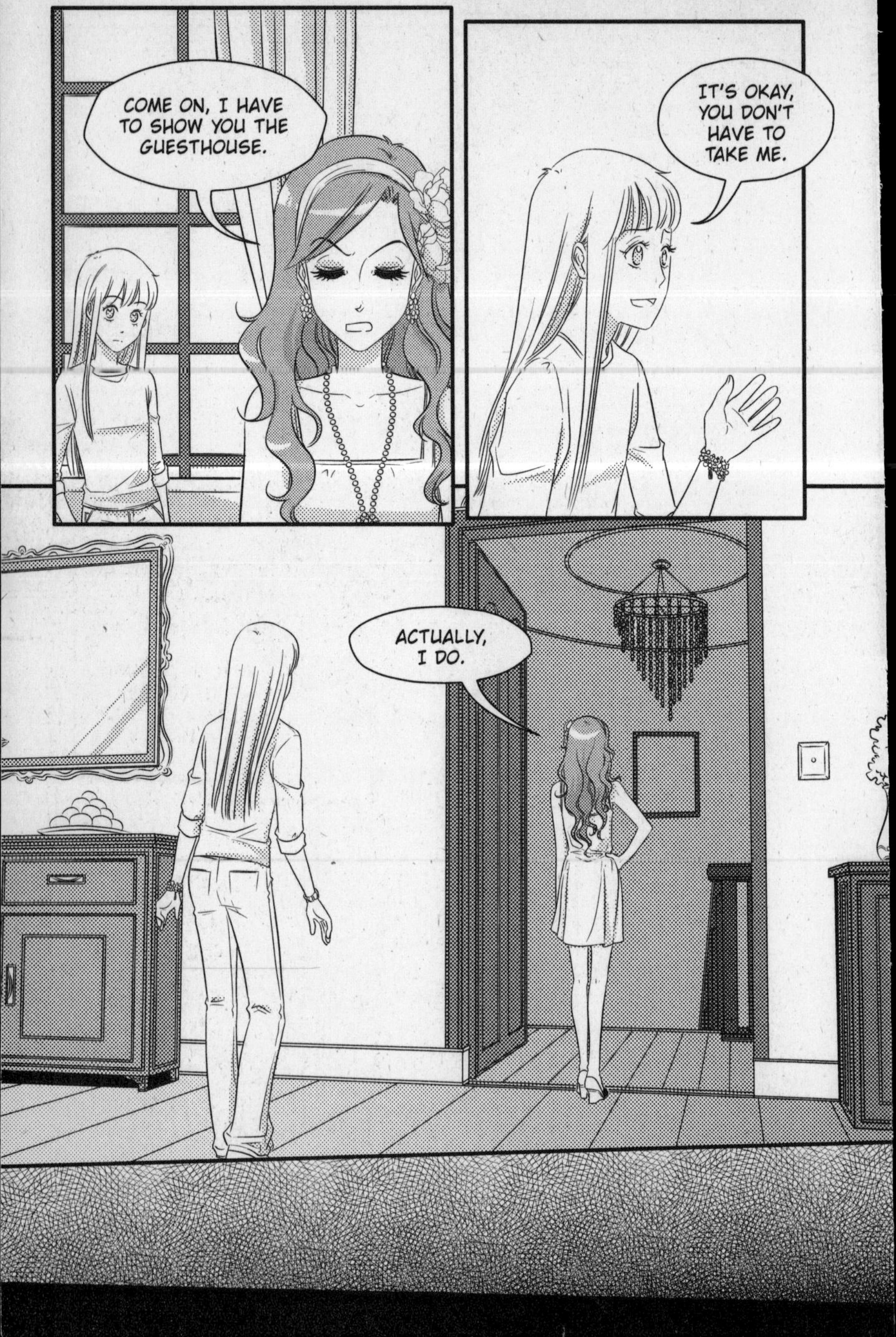
COME ON, I HAVE TO SHOW YOU THE GUESTHOUSE.
IT'S OKAY, YOU DON'T HAVE TO TAKE ME.
ACTUALLY, I DO.

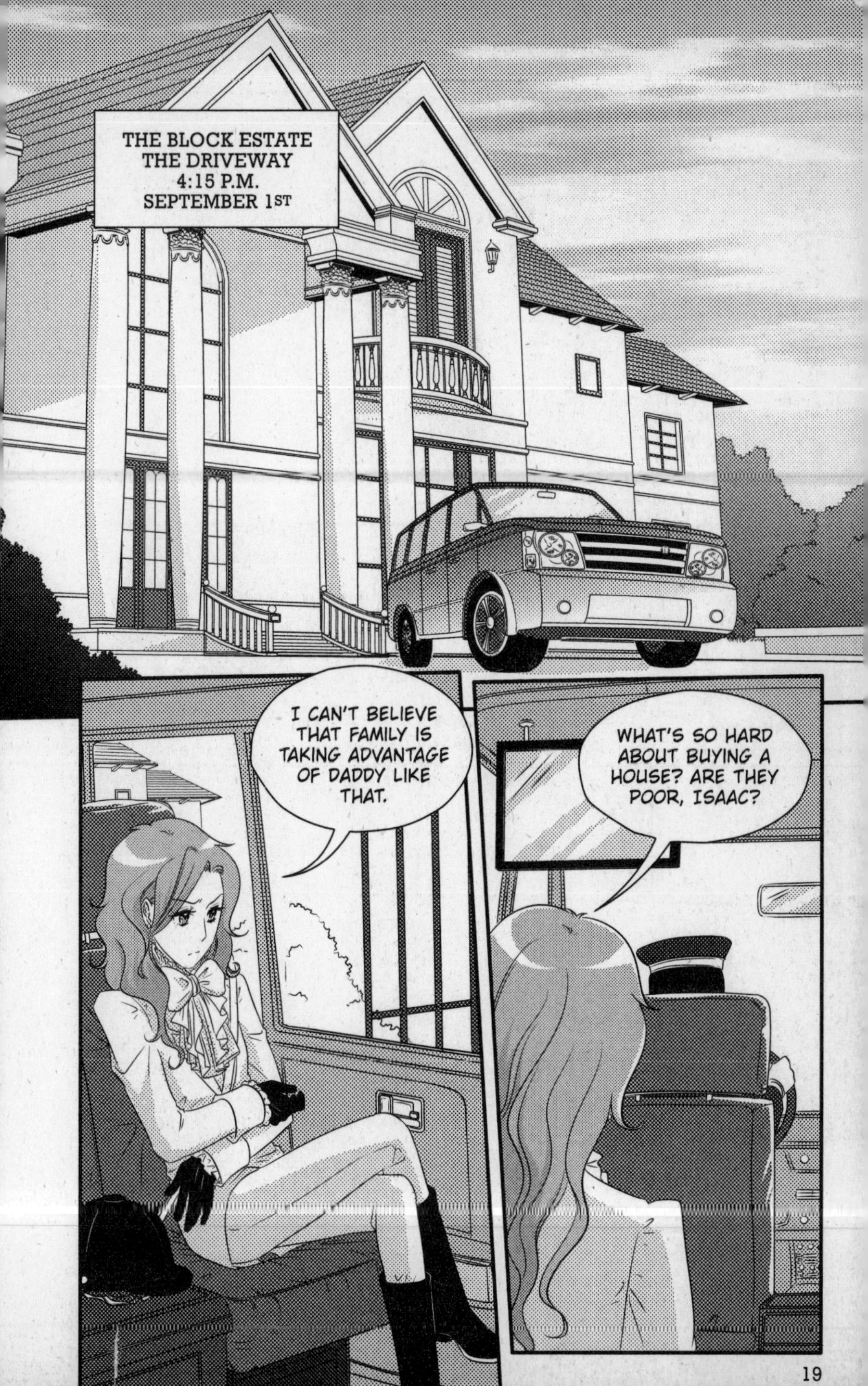
THE BLOCK ESTATE
THE DRIVEWAY
4:15 P.M.
SEPTEMBER 1ST
I CAN'T BELIEVE THAT FAMILY IS TAKING ADVANTAGE OF DADDY LIKE THAT.
WHAT'S SO HARD ABOUT BUYING A HOUSE? ARE THEY POOR, ISAAC?

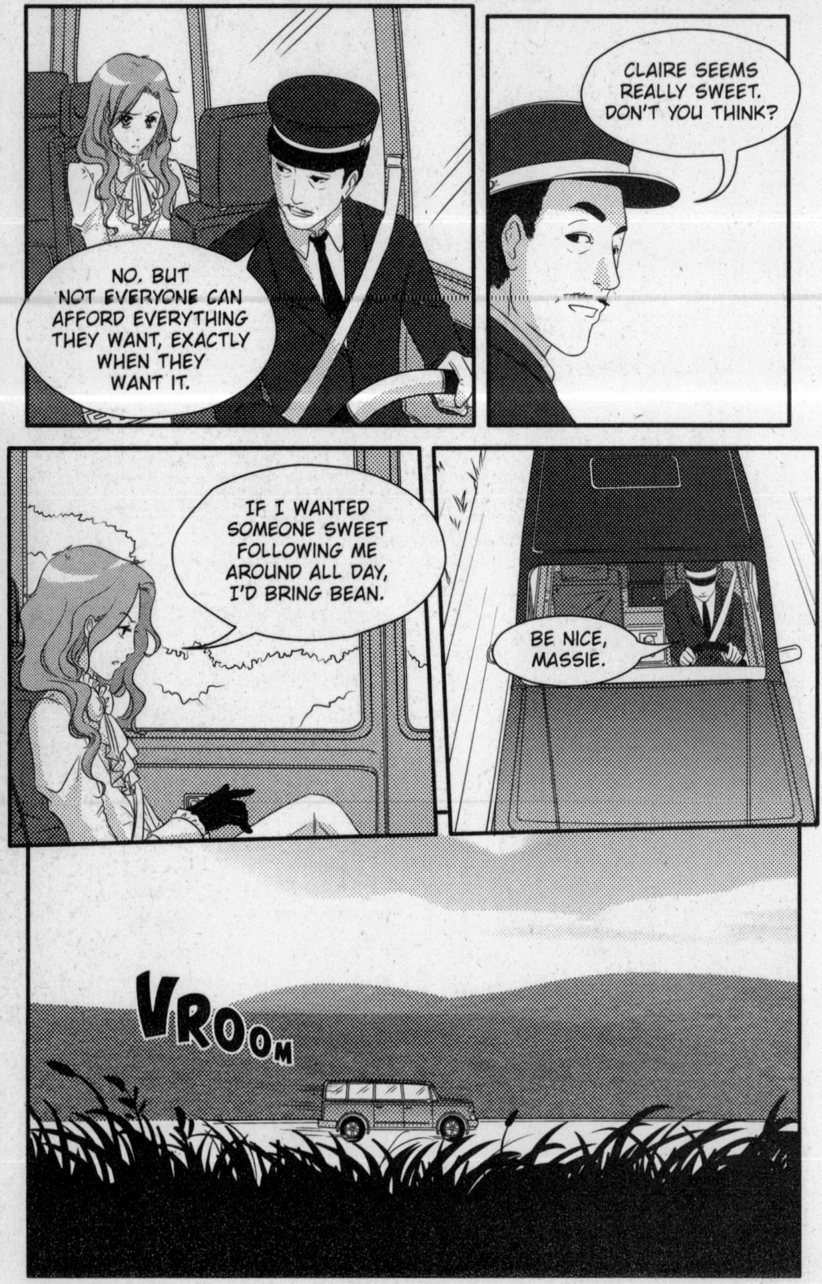
NO. BUT NOT EVERYONE CAN AFFORD EVERYTHING THEY WANT, EXACTLY WHEN THEY WANT IT.
CLAIRE SEEMS REALLY SWEET. DON'T YOU THINK?
IF I WANTED SOMEONE SWEET FOLLOWING ME AROUND ALL DAY, I'D BRING BEAN.
BE NICE, MASSIE.
VROOM

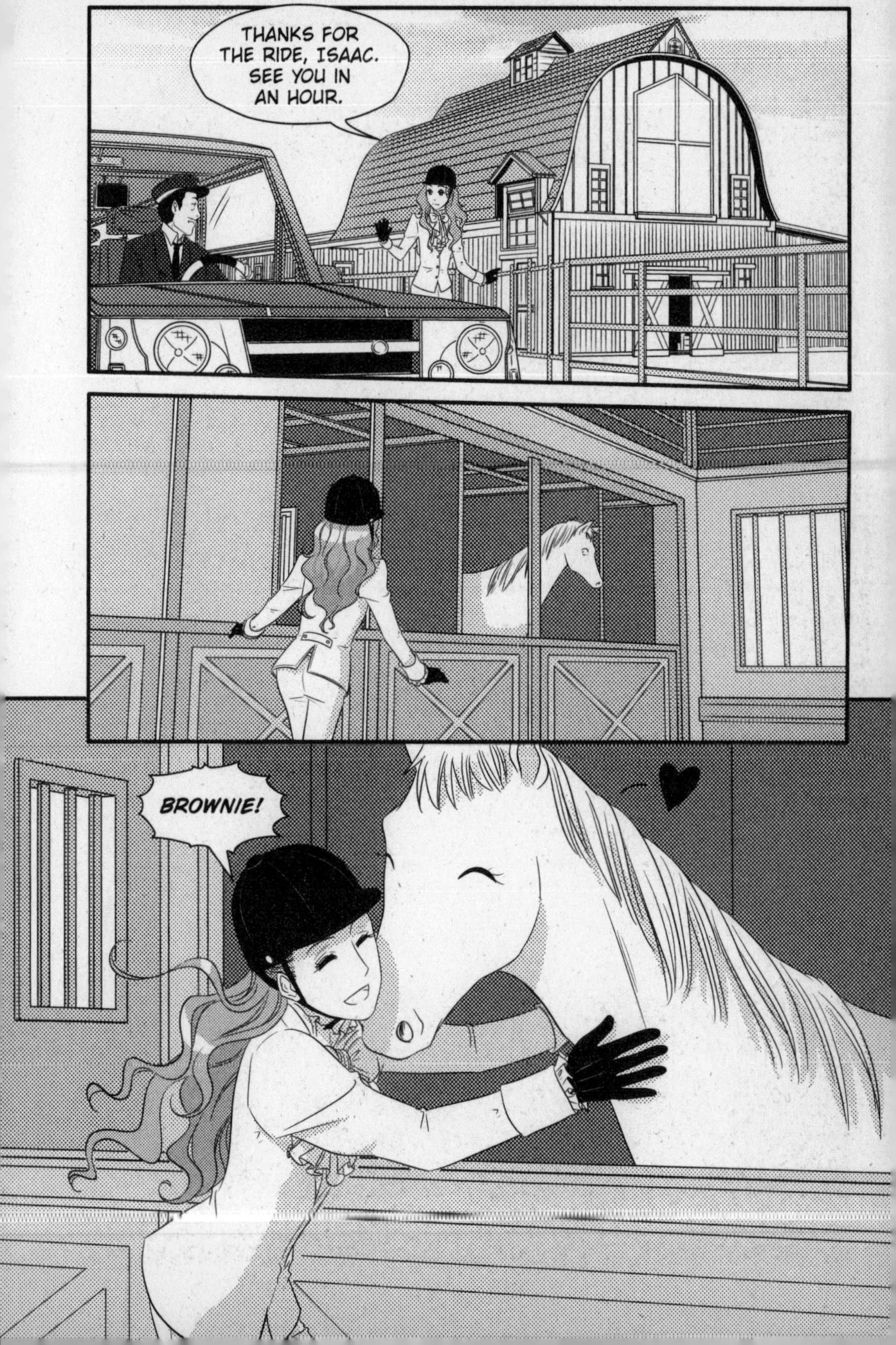
THANKS FOR THE RIDE, ISAAC. SEE YOU IN AN HOUR.
BROWNIE!

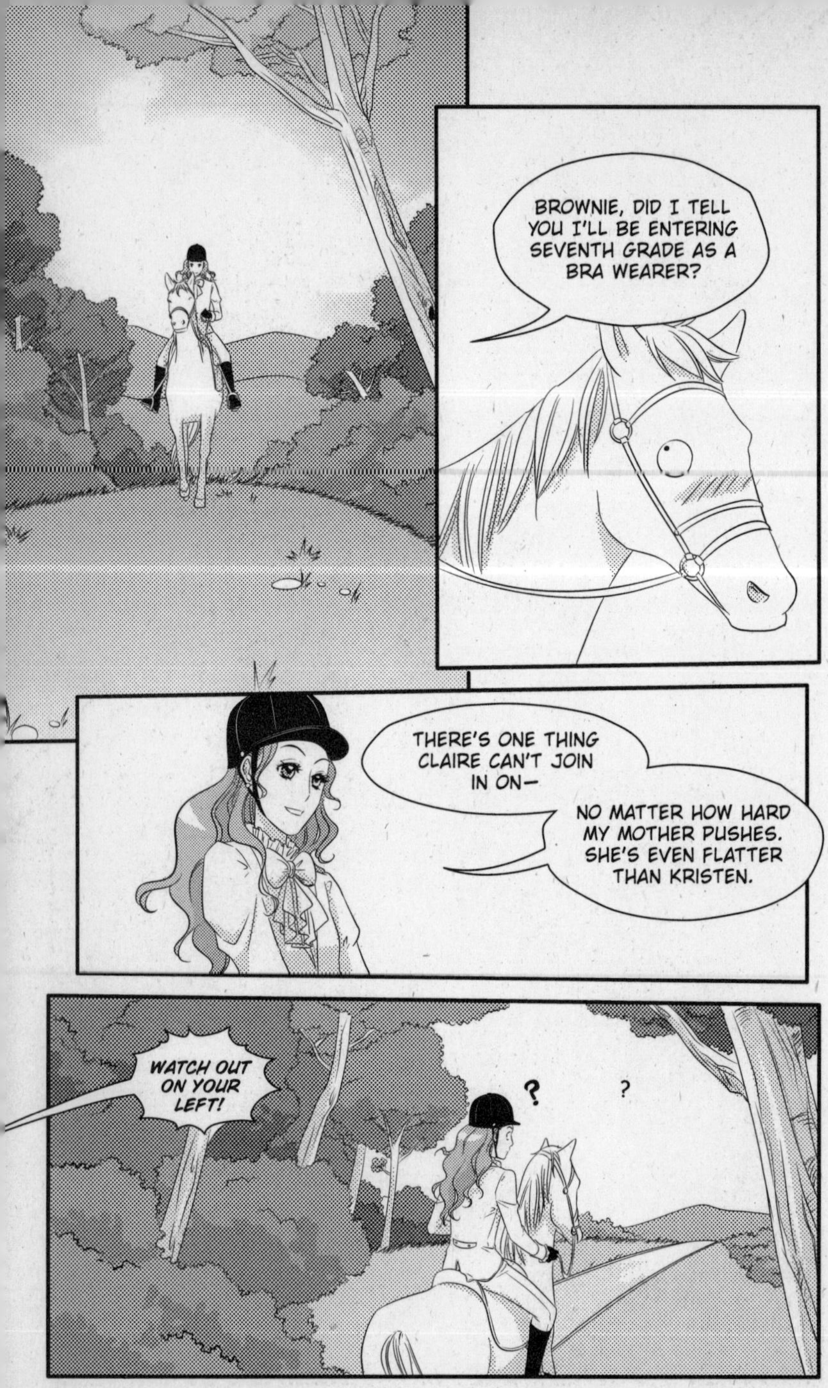
BROWNIE, DID I TELL YOU I'LL BE ENTERING SEVENTH GRADE AS A BRA WEARER?
THERE'S ONE THING CLAIRE CAN'T JOIN IN ON—
NO MATTER HOW HARD MY MOTHER PUSHES. SHE'S EVEN FLATTER THAN KRISTEN.
WATCH OUT ON YOUR LEFT!
?
?

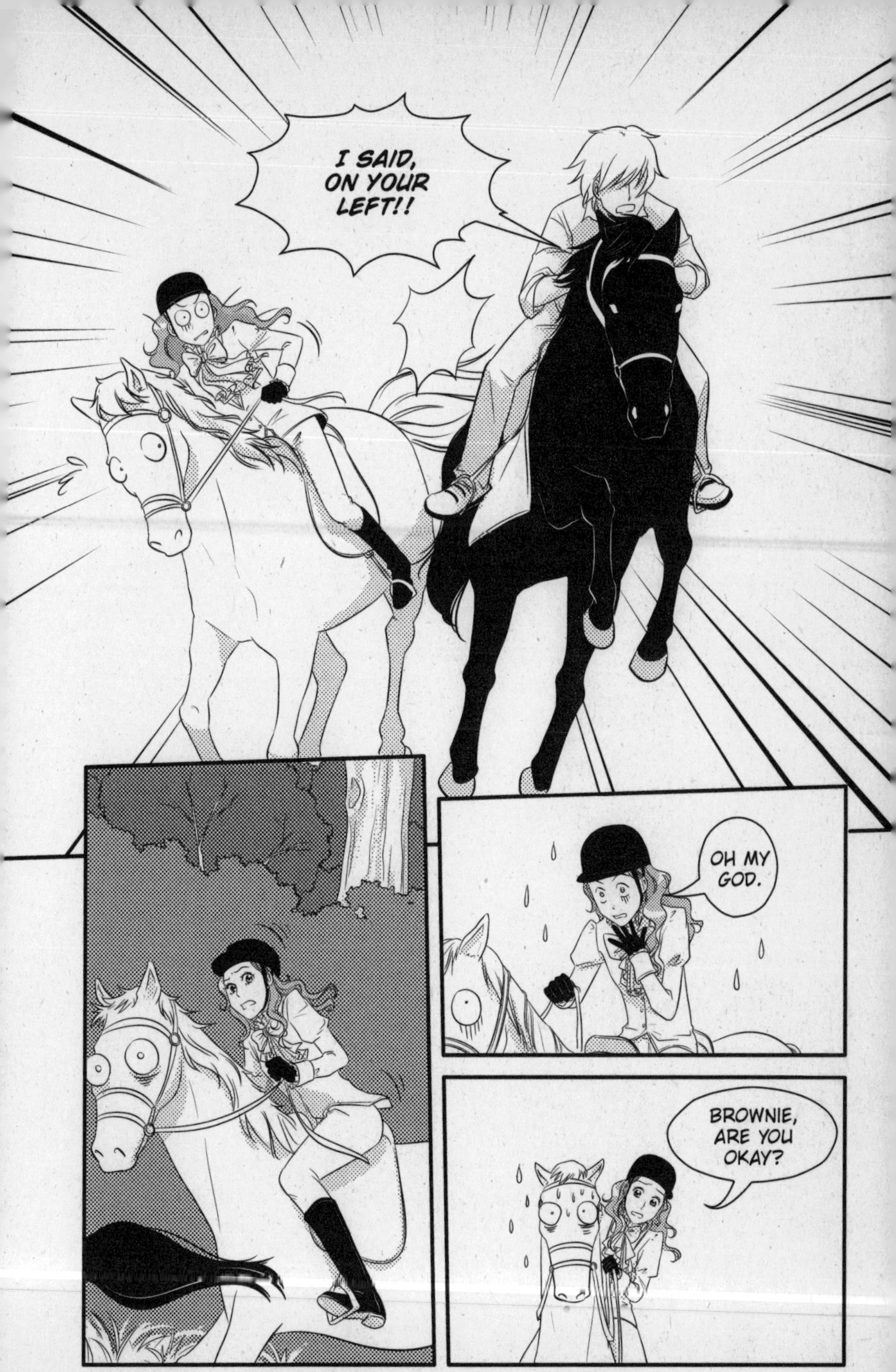
I SAID, ON YOUR LEFT!!
OH MY GOD.
BROWNIE, ARE YOU OKAY?

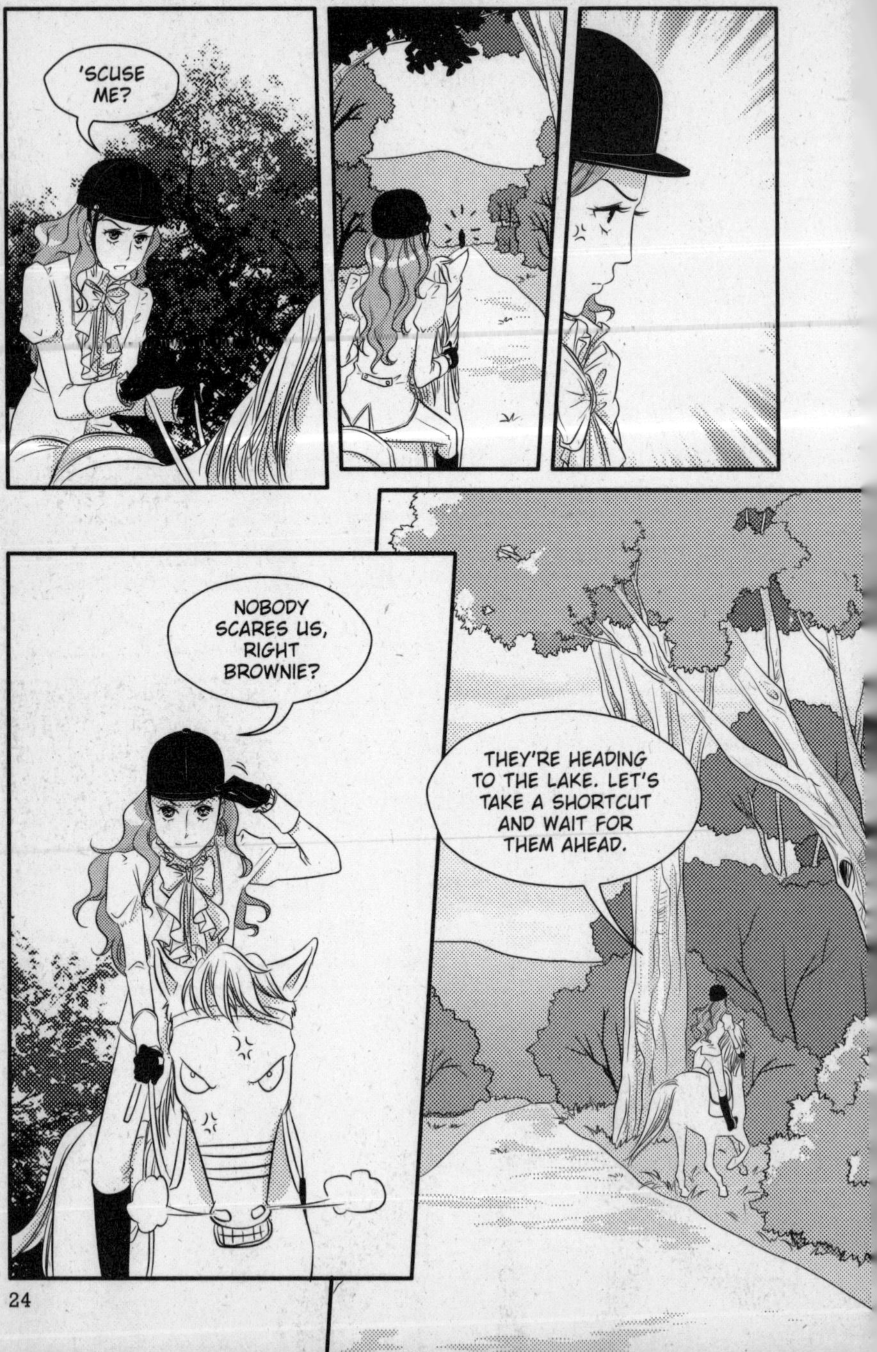
'SCUSE ME?
NOBODY SCARES US, RIGHT BROWNIE?
THEY'RE HEADING TO THE LAKE. LET'S TAKE A SHORTCUT AND WAIT FOR THEM AHEAD.

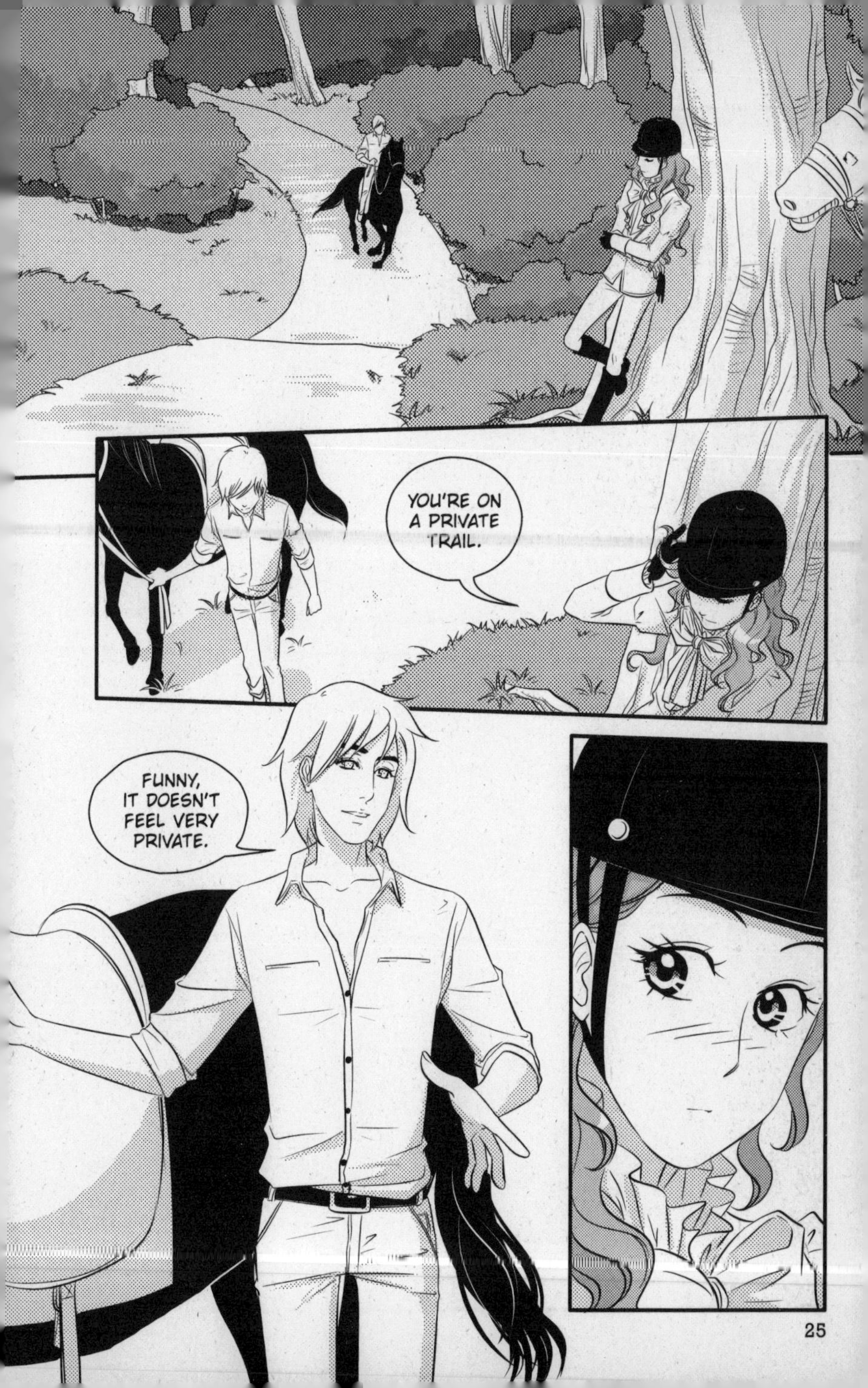
YOU'RE ON A PRIVATE TRAIL.
FUNNY, IT DOESN'T FEEL VERY PRIVATE.

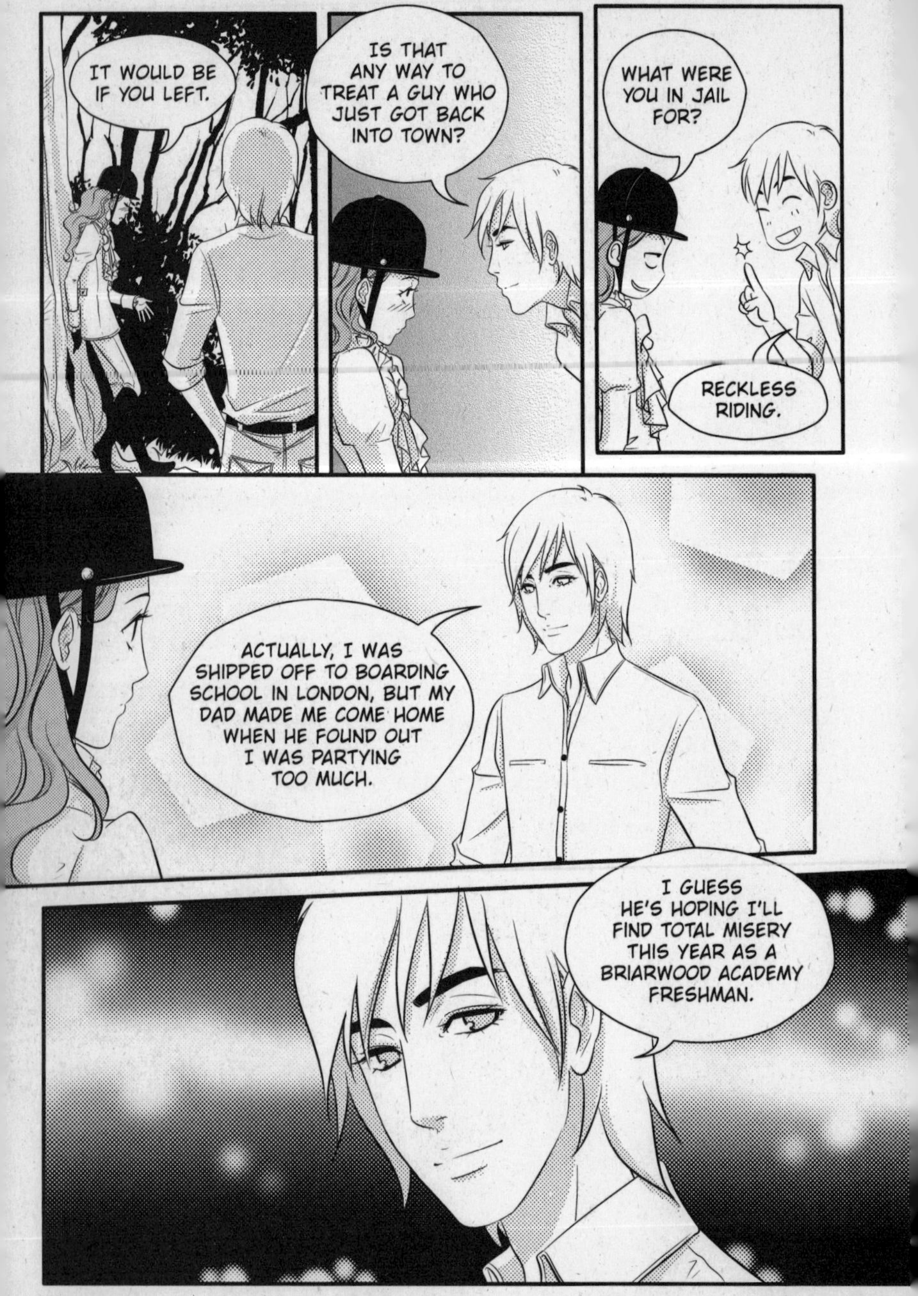
IT WOULD BE IF YOU LEFT.
IS THAT ANY WAY TO TREAT A GUY WHO JUST GOT BACK INTO TOWN?
WHAT WERE YOU IN JAIL FOR?
RECKLESS RIDING.
ACTUALLY, I WAS SHIPPED OFF TO BOARDING SCHOOL IN LONDON, BUT MY DAD MADE ME COME HOME WHEN HE FOUND OUT I WAS PARTYING TOO MUCH.
I GUESS HE'S HOPING I'LL FIND TOTAL MISERY THIS YEAR AS A BRIARWOOD ACADEMY FRESHMAN.

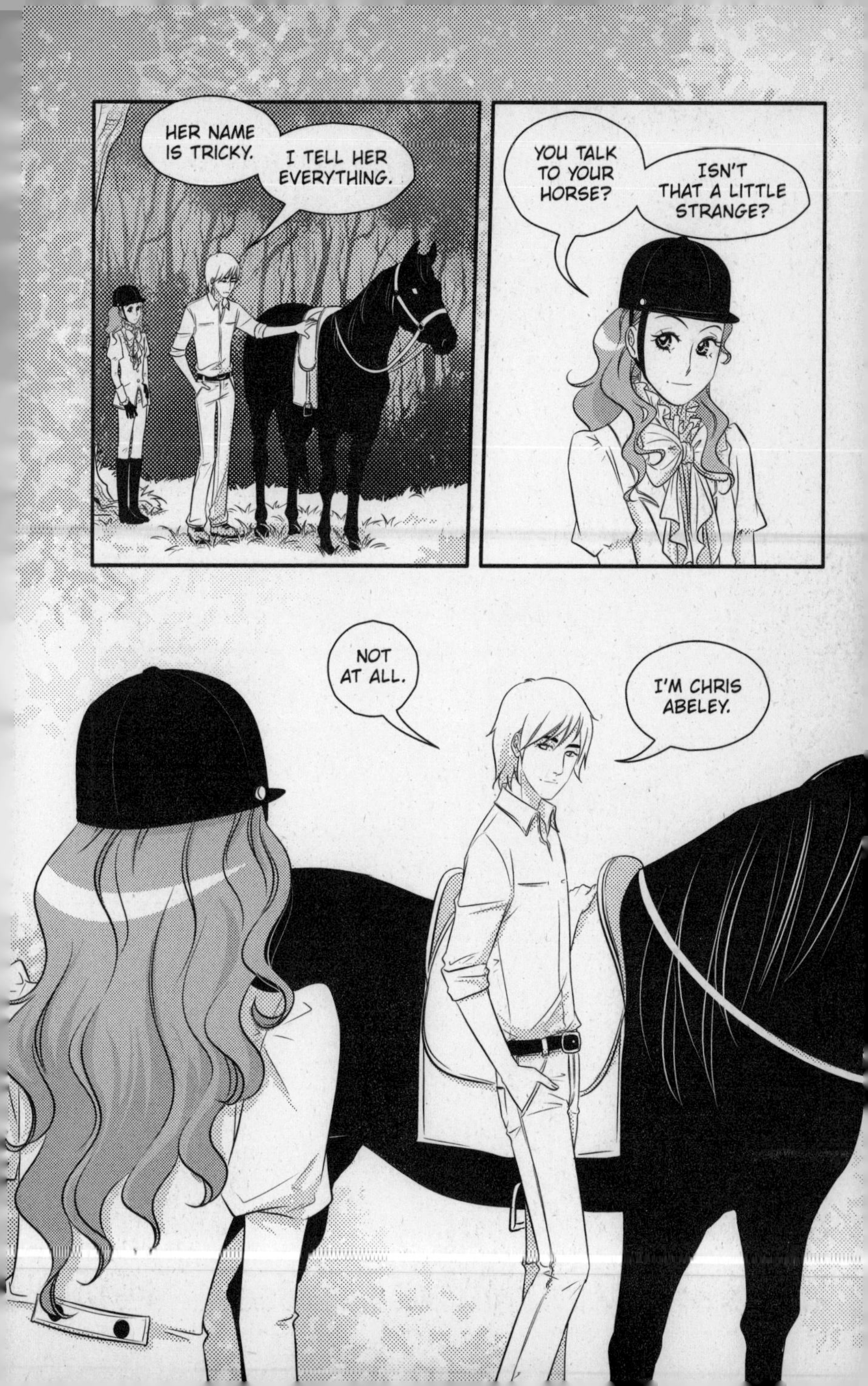
HER NAME IS TRICKY.
I TELL HER EVERYTHING.
YOU TALK TO YOUR HORSE?
ISN'T THAT A LITTLE STRANGE?
NOT AT ALL.
I'M CHRIS ABELEY.

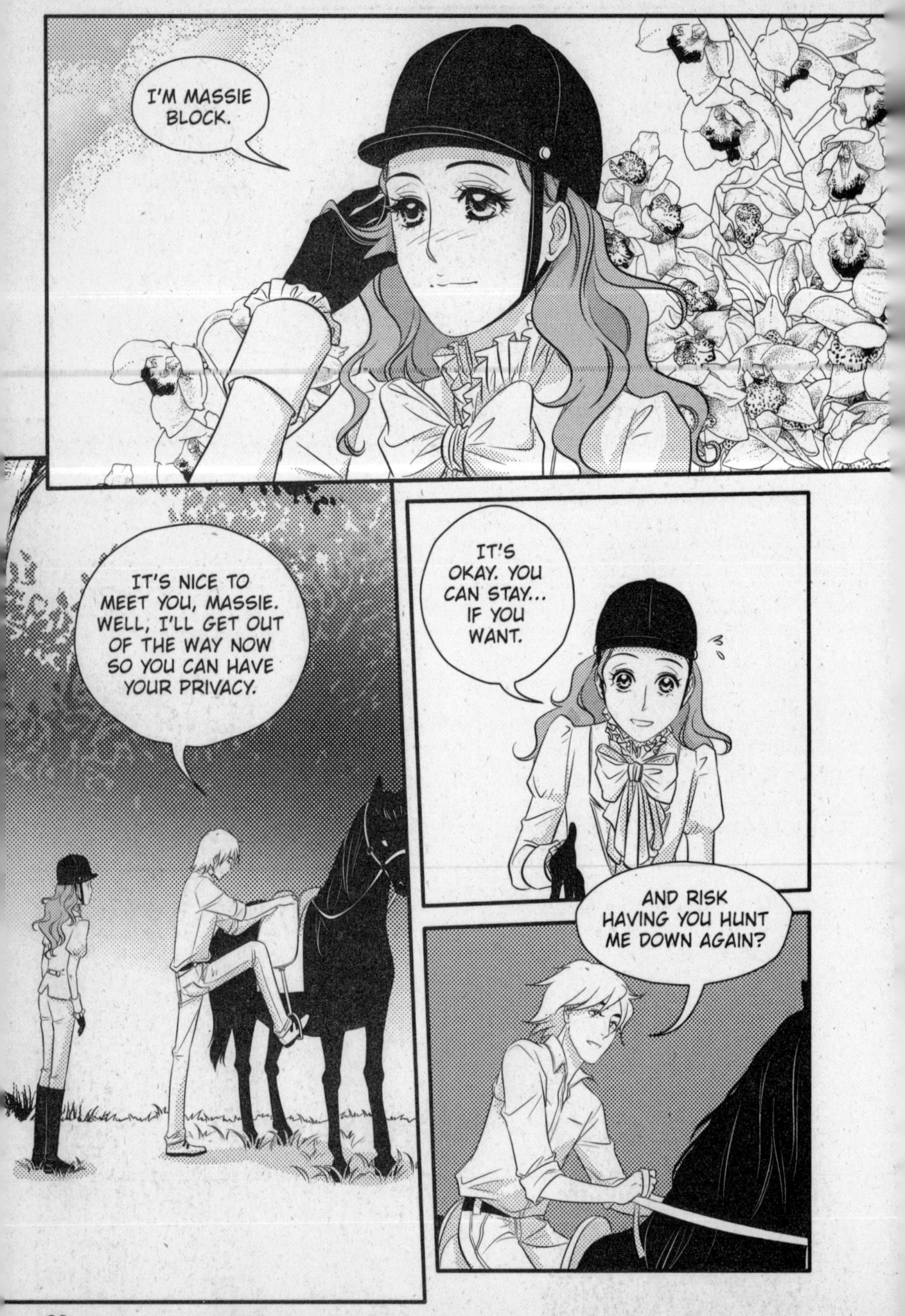
I'M MASSIE BLOCK.
IT'S NICE TO MEET YOU, MASSIE. WELL, I'LL GET OUT OF THE WAY NOW SO YOU CAN HAVE YOUR PRIVACY.
IT'S OKAY. YOU CAN STAY... IF YOU WANT.
AND RISK HAVING YOU HUNT ME DOWN AGAIN?

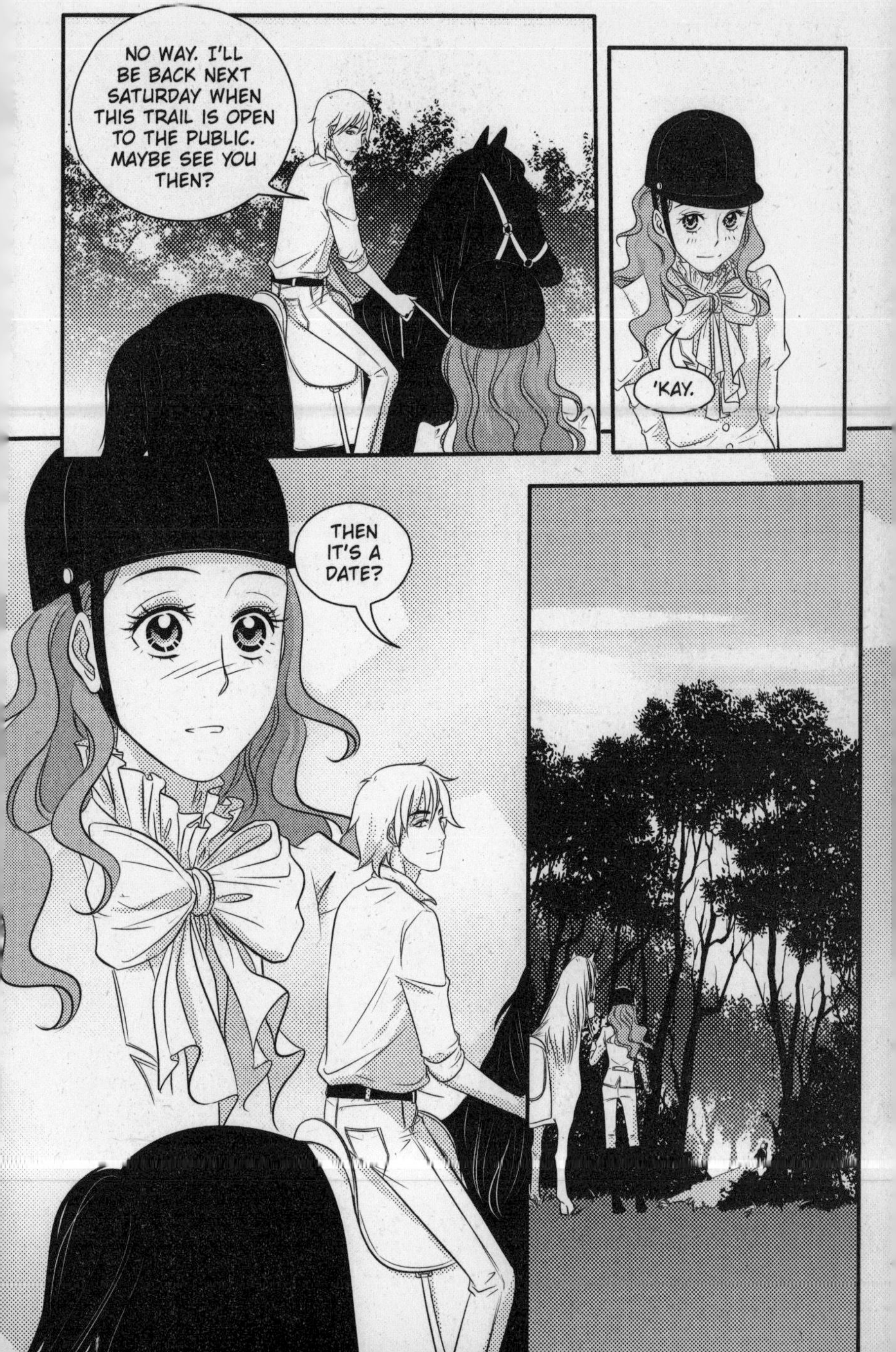
NO WAY. I'LL BE BACK NEXT SATURDAY WHEN THIS TRAIL IS OPEN TO THE PUBLIC. MAYBE SEE YOU THEN?
'KAY.
THEN IT'S A DATE?

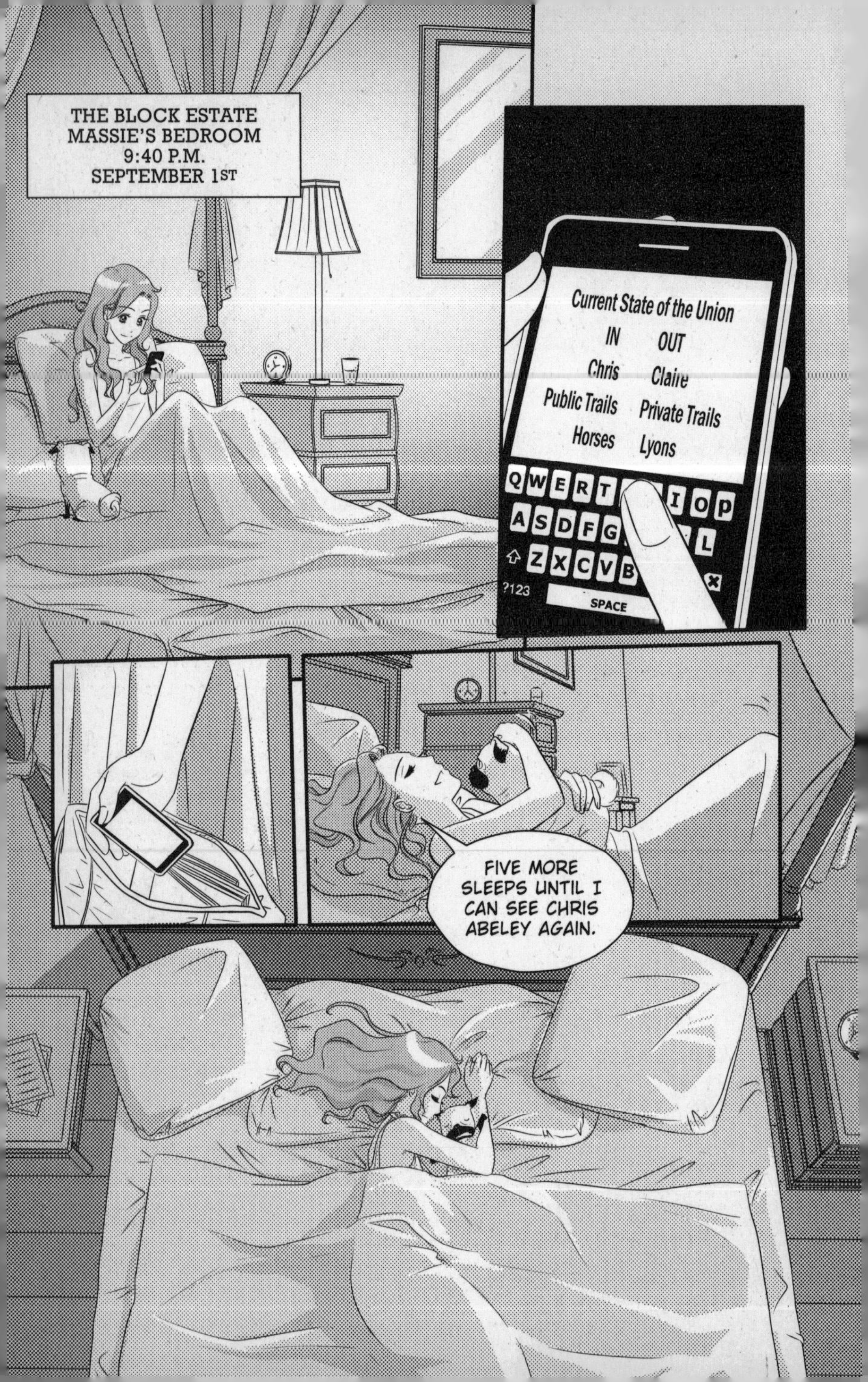
THE BLOCK ESTATE
MASSIE'S BEDROOM
9:40 P.M.
SEPTEMBER 1ST
Current State of the Union
IN OUT
Chris Claire
Public Trails Private Trails
Horses Lyons
SPACE
FIVE MORE SLEEPS UNTIL I CAN SEE CHRIS ABELEY AGAIN.

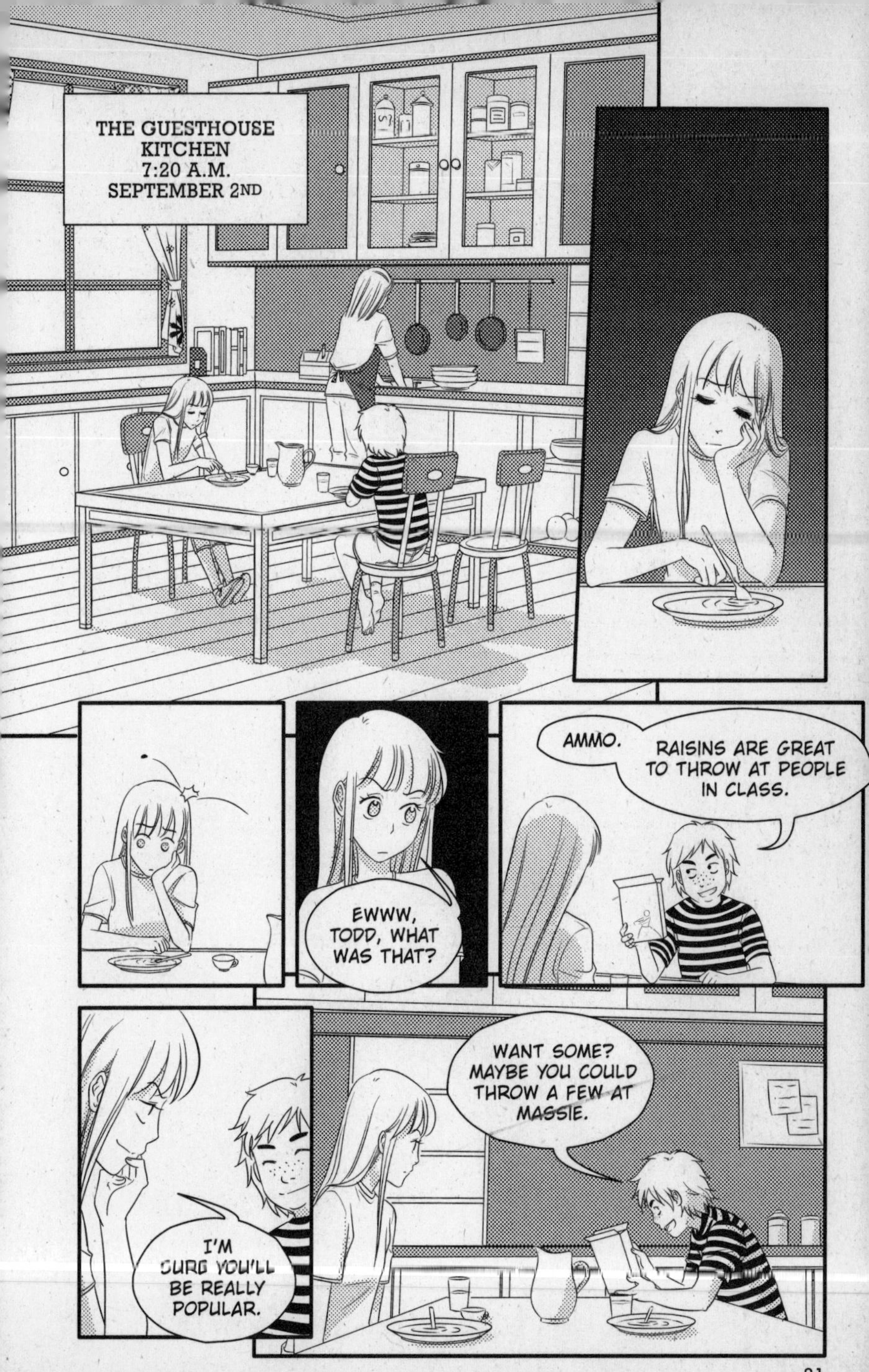
THE GUESTHOUSE KITCHEN 7:20 A.M. SEPTEMBER 2ND
EWWW, TODD, WHAT WAS THAT?
AMMO.
RAISINS ARE GREAT TO THROW AT PEOPLE IN CLASS.
I'M SURE YOU'LL BE REALLY POPULAR.
WANT SOME? MAYBE YOU COULD THROW A FEW AT MASSIE.

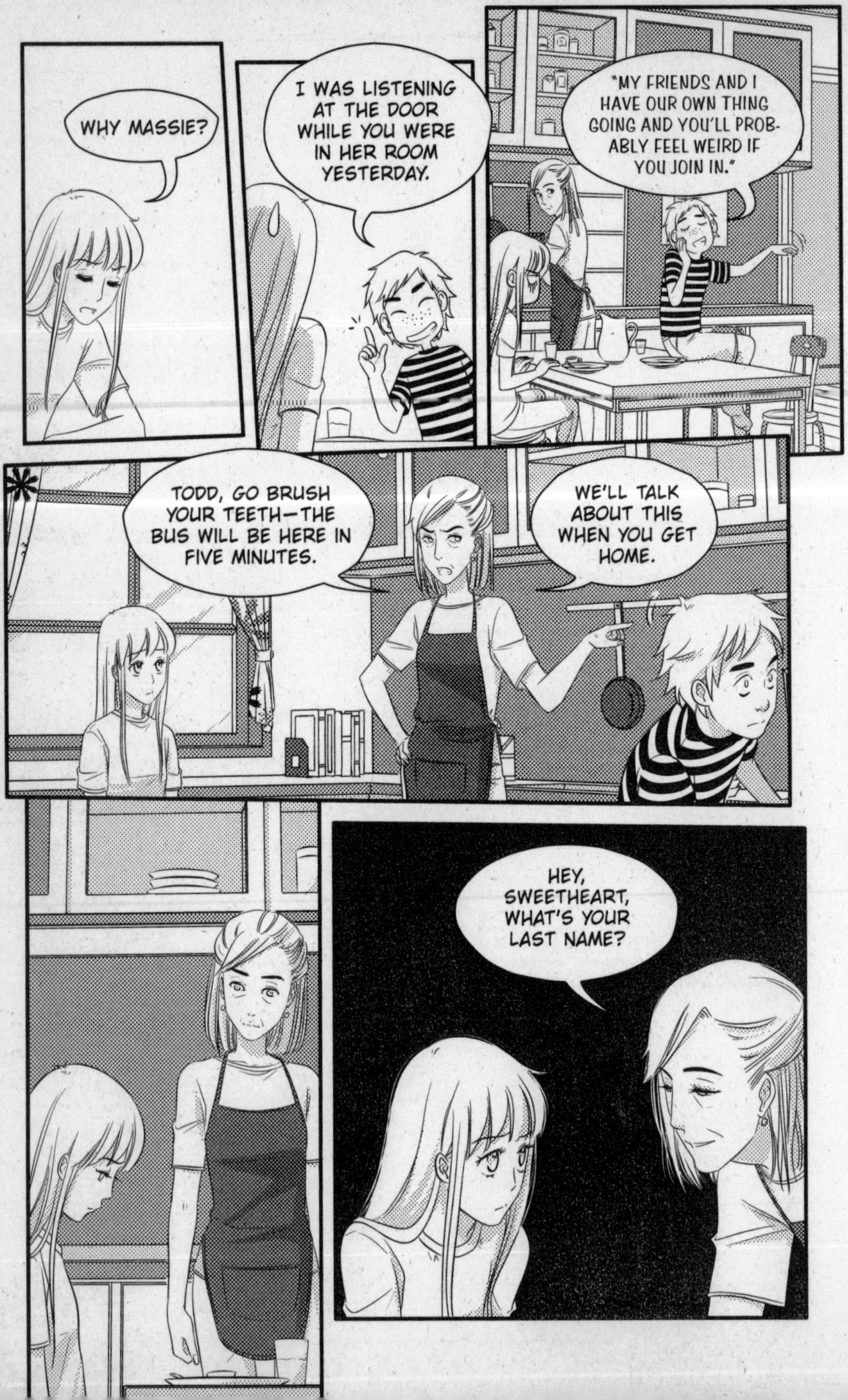

WHY MASSIE?
I WAS LISTENING AT THE DOOR WHILE YOU WERE IN HER ROOM YESTERDAY.
"MY FRIENDS AND I HAVE OUR OWN THING GOING AND YOU'LL PROB-ABLY FEEL WEIRD IF YOU JOIN IN."
TODD, GO BRUSH YOUR TEETH—THE BUS WILL BE HERE IN FIVE MINUTES.
WE'LL TALK ABOUT THIS WHEN YOU GET HOME.
HEY, SWEETHEART, WHAT'S YOUR LAST NAME?

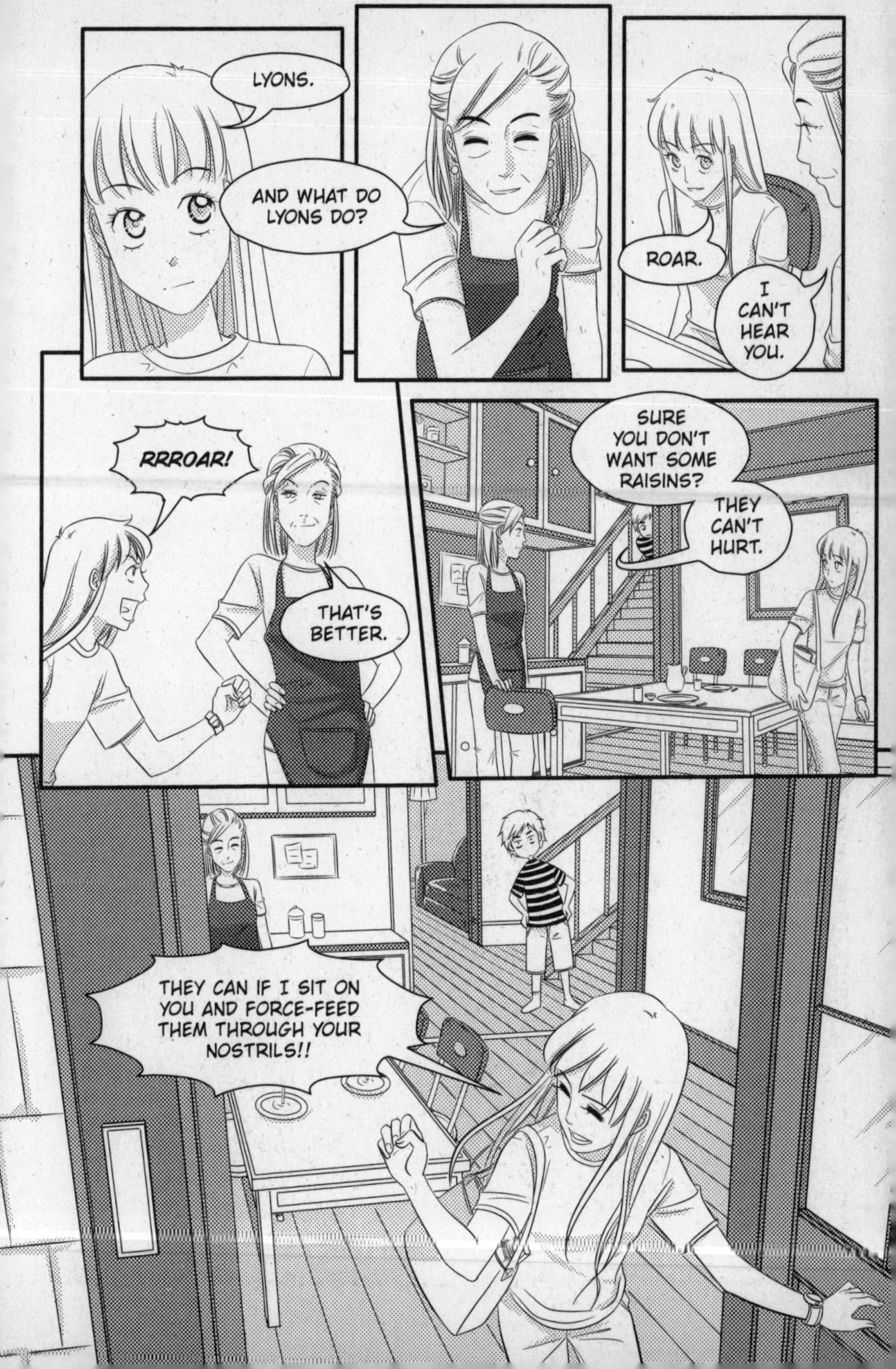
LYONS.
AND WHAT DO LYONS DO?
ROAR.
I CAN'T HEAR YOU.
RRROAR!
THAT'S BETTER.
SURE YOU DON'T WANT SOME RAISINS?
THEY CAN'T HURT.
THEY CAN IF I SIT ON YOU AND FORCE-FEED THEM THROUGH YOUR NOSTRILS!!

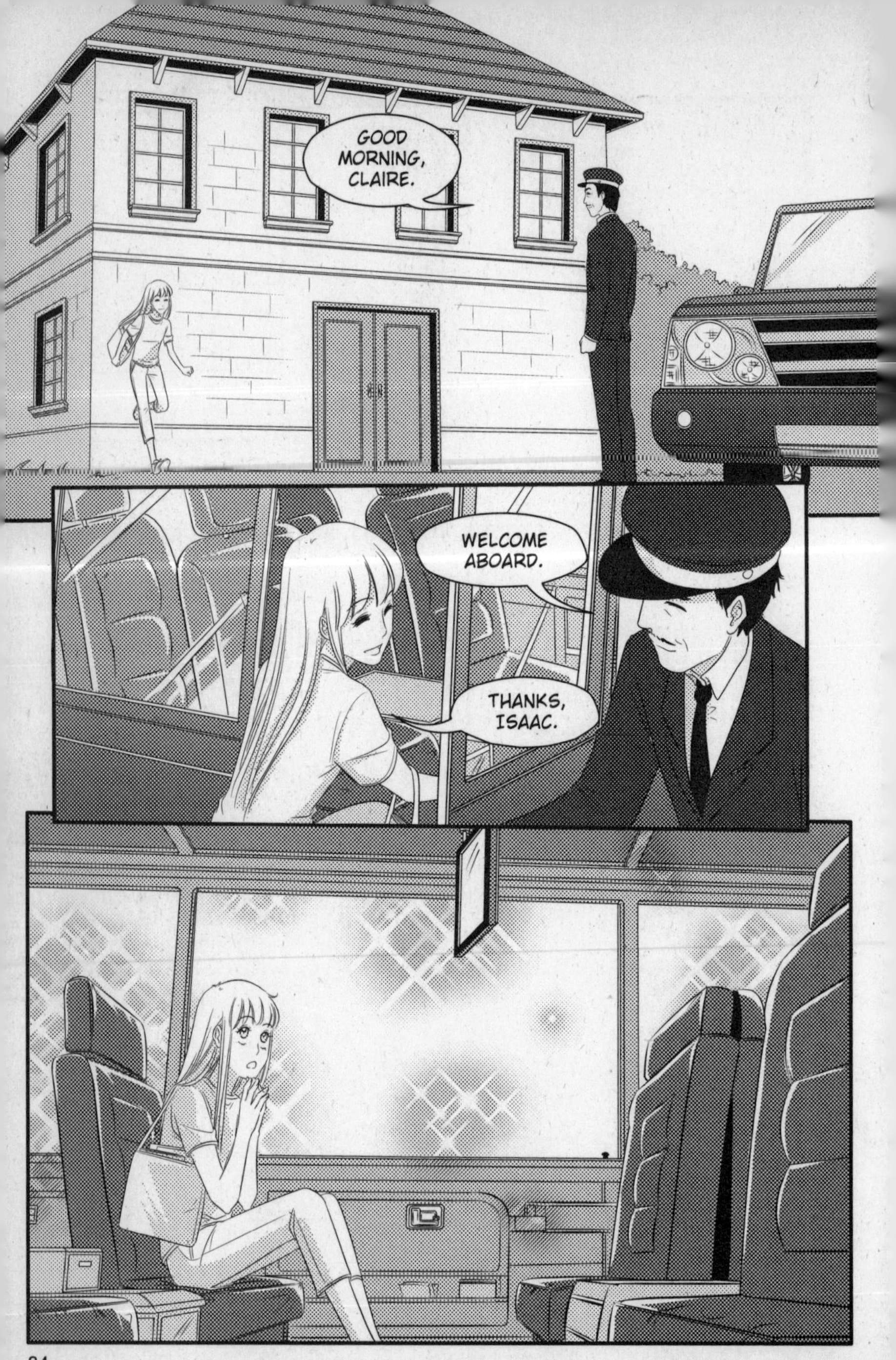
GOOD MORNING, CLAIRE.
WELCOME ABOARD.
THANKS, ISAAC.

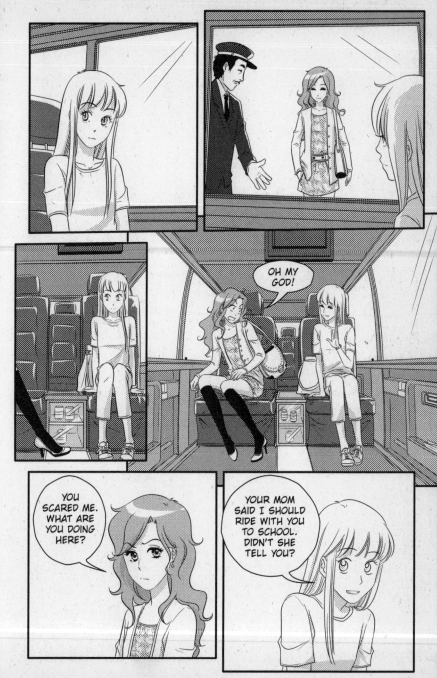

OH MY GOD!

YOU SCARED ME. WHAT ARE YOU DOING HERE?

YOUR MOM SAID I SHOULD RIDE WITH YOU TO SCHOOL. DIDN'T SHE TELL YOU?

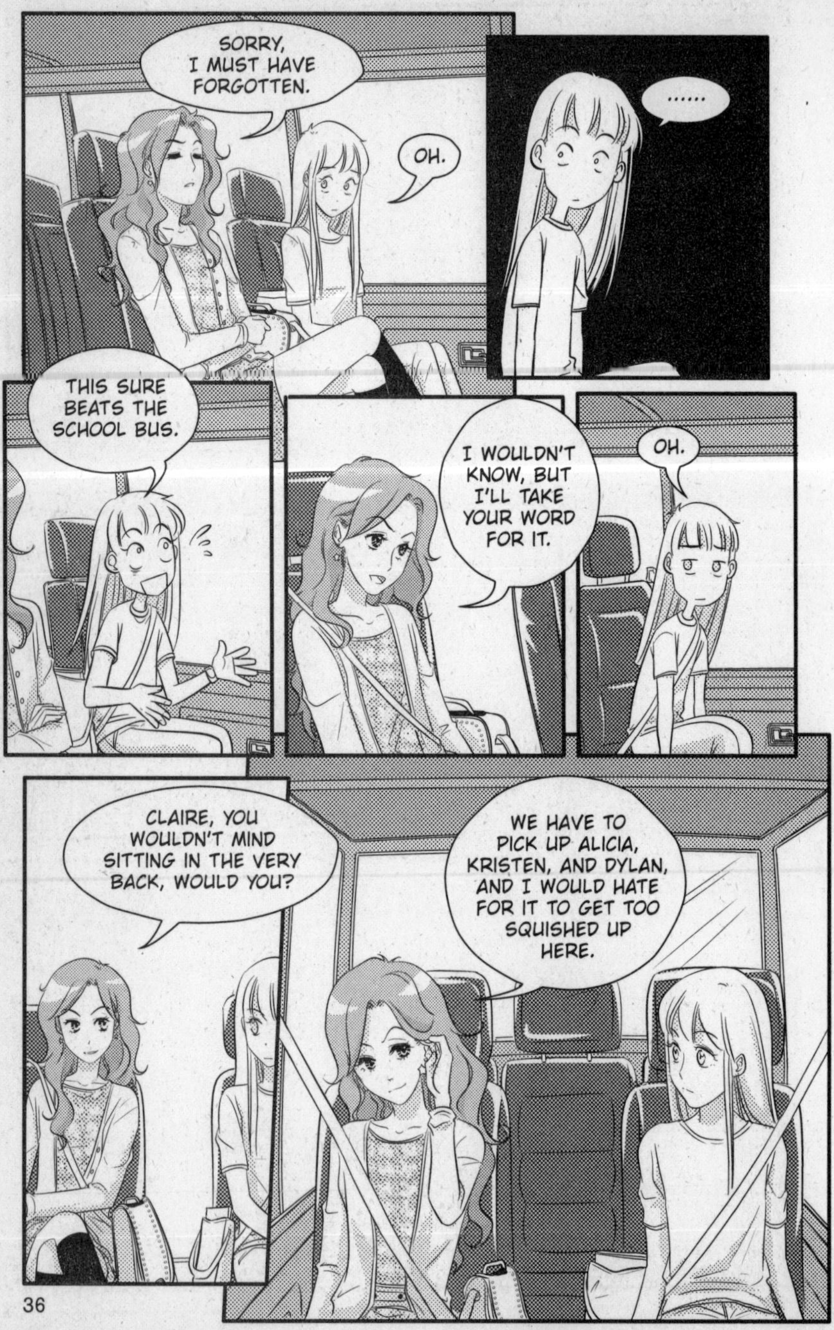
SORRY, I MUST HAVE FORGOTTEN.
OH.
......
THIS SURE BEATS THE SCHOOL BUS.
I WOULDN'T KNOW, BUT I'LL TAKE YOUR WORD FOR IT.
OH.
CLAIRE, YOU WOULDN'T MIND SITTING IN THE VERY BACK, WOULD YOU?
WE HAVE TO PICK UP ALICIA, KRISTEN, AND DYLAN, AND I WOULD HATE FOR IT TO GET TOO SQUISHED UP HERE.

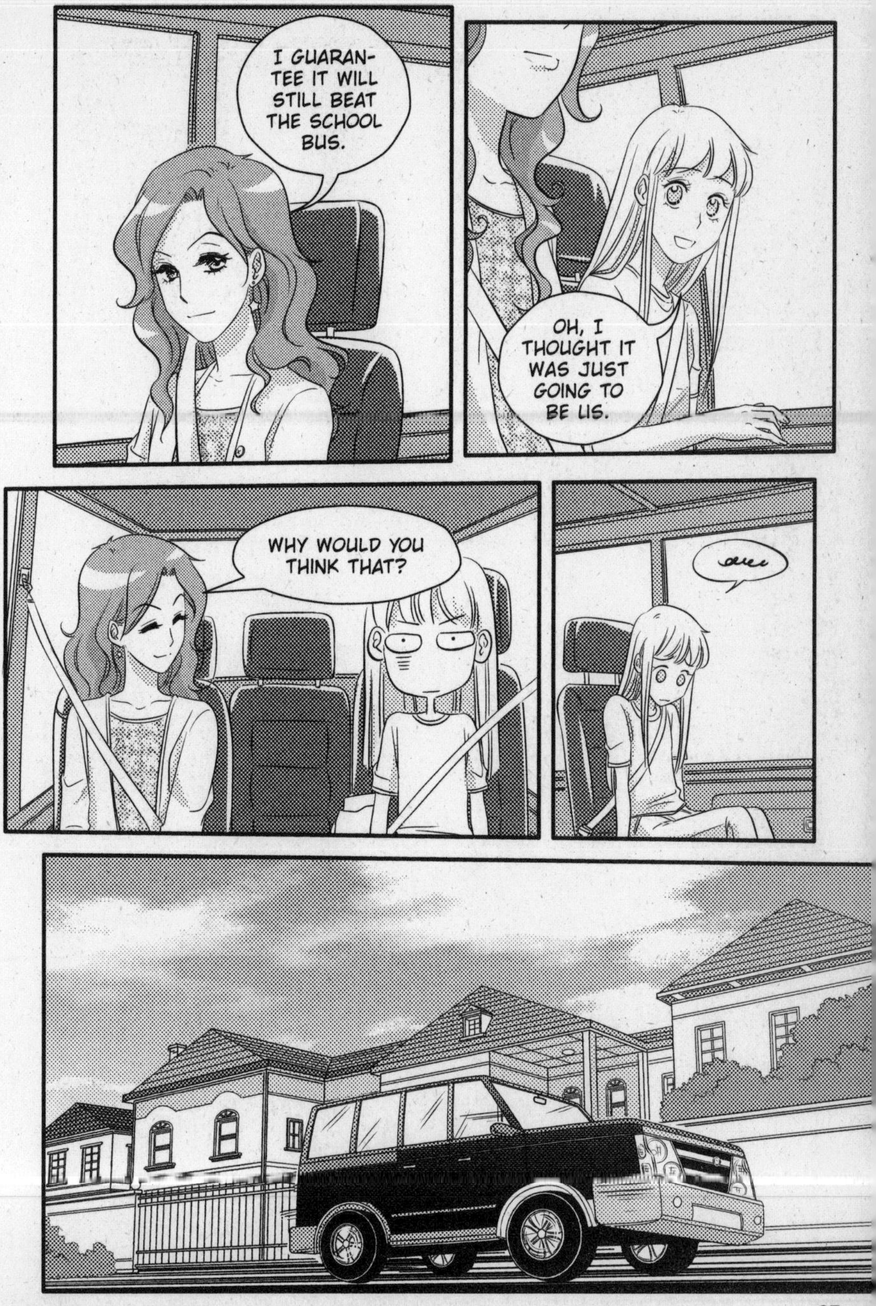
I GUARAN-TEE IT WILL STILL BEAT THE SCHOOL BUS.
OH, I THOUGHT IT WAS JUST GOING TO BE US.
WHY WOULD YOU THINK THAT?

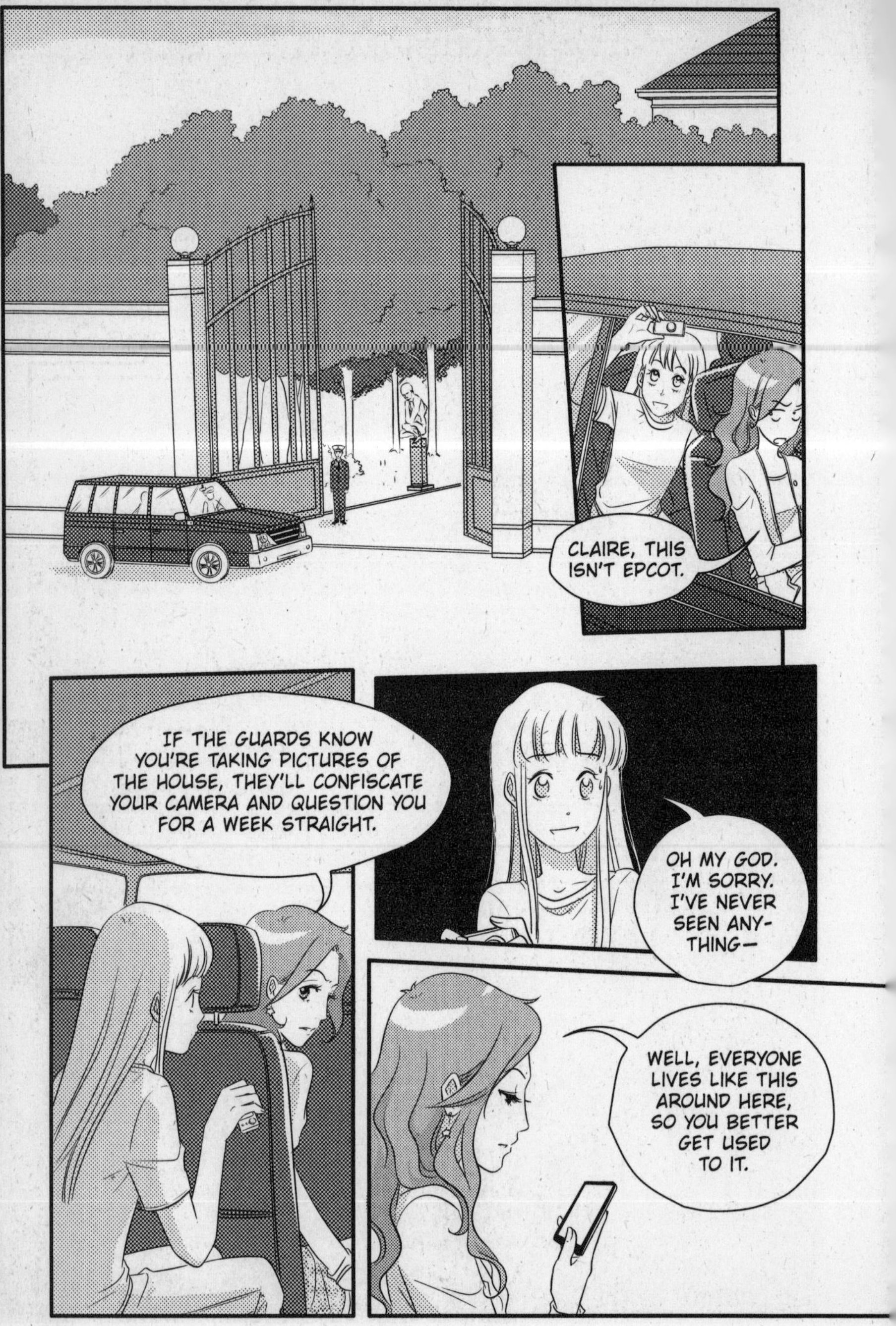
CLAIRE, THIS ISN'T EPCOT.
IF THE GUARDS KNOW YOU'RE TAKING PICTURES OF THE HOUSE, THEY'LL CONFISCATE YOUR CAMERA AND QUESTION YOU FOR A WEEK STRAIGHT.
OH MY GOD. I'M SORRY. I'VE NEVER SEEN ANY-THING—
WELL, EVERYONE LIVES LIKE THIS AROUND HERE, SO YOU BETTER GET USED TO IT.

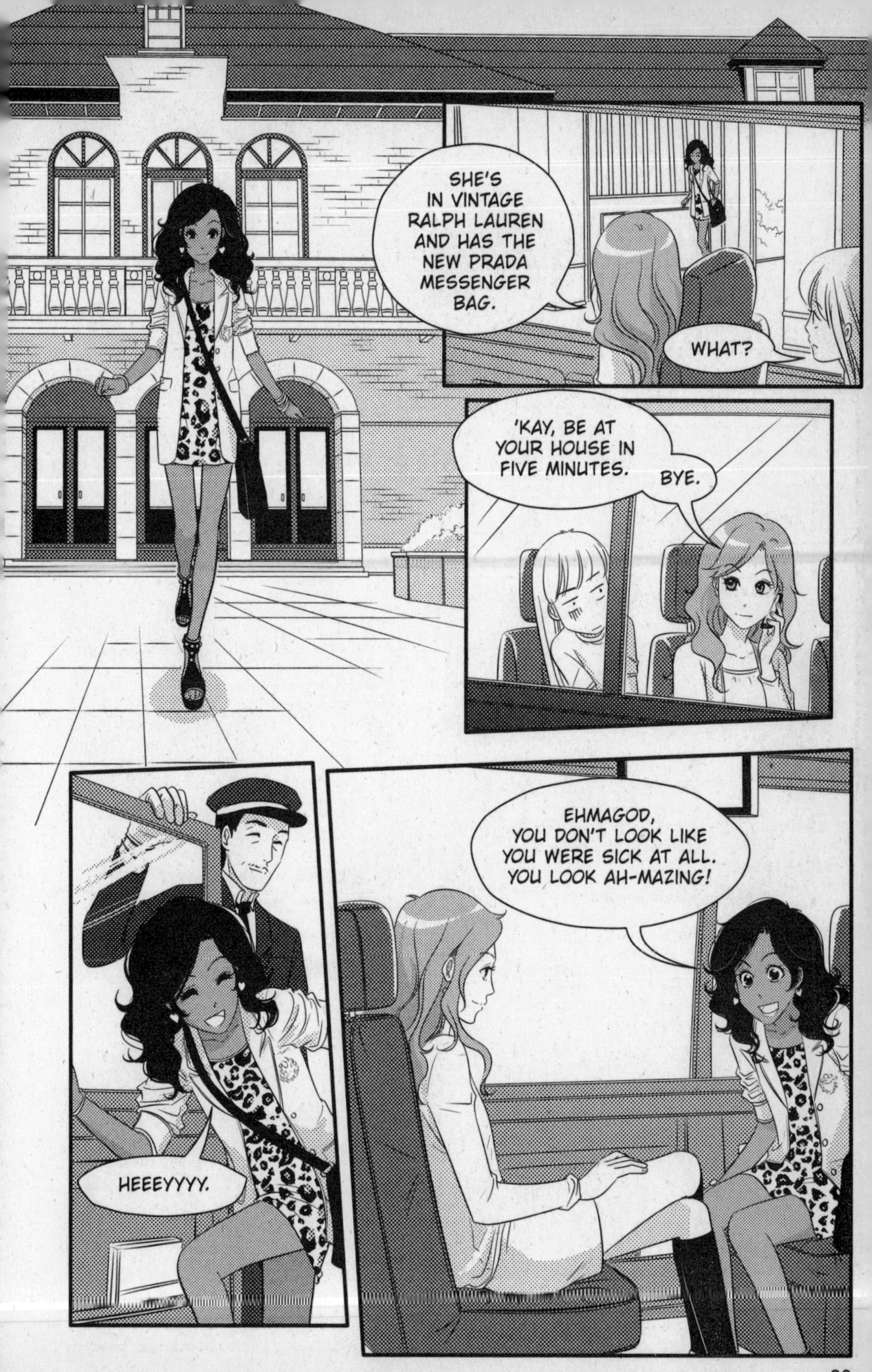
SHE'S IN VINTAGE RALPH LAUREN AND HAS THE NEW PRADA MESSENGER BAG.
WHAT?
'KAY, BE AT YOUR HOUSE IN FIVE MINUTES.
BYE.
HEEEYYYY.
EHMAGOD, YOU DON'T LOOK LIKE YOU WERE SICK AT ALL. YOU LOOK AH-MAZING!

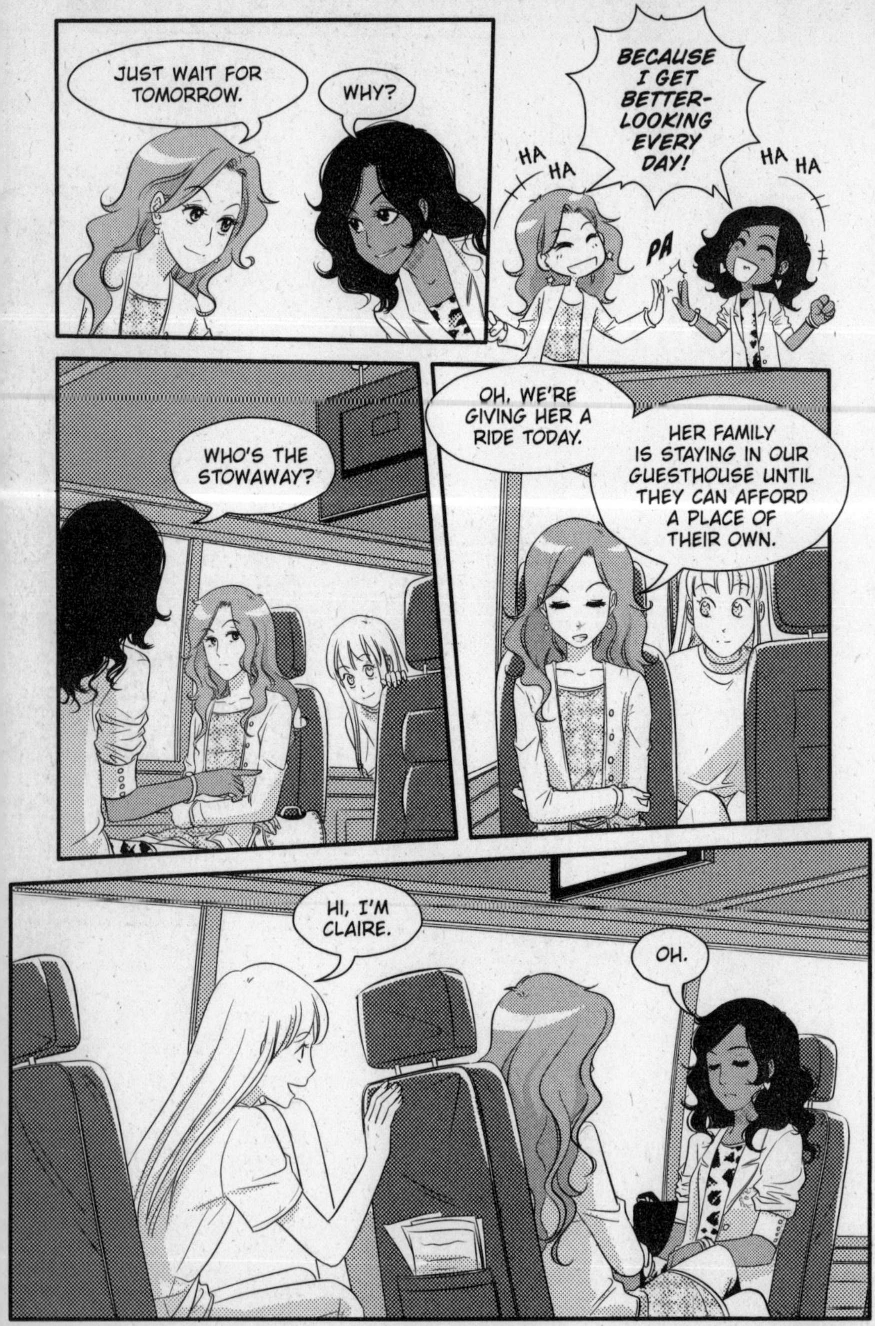
JUST WAIT FOR TOMORROW.
WHY?
BECAUSE I GET BETTER-LOOKING EVERY DAY!
HA HA
HA HA
PA
WHO'S THE STOWAWAY?
OH, WE'RE GIVING HER A RIDE TODAY.
HER FAMILY IS STAYING IN OUR GUESTHOUSE UNTIL THEY CAN AFFORD A PLACE OF THEIR OWN.
HI, I'M CLAIRE.
OH.

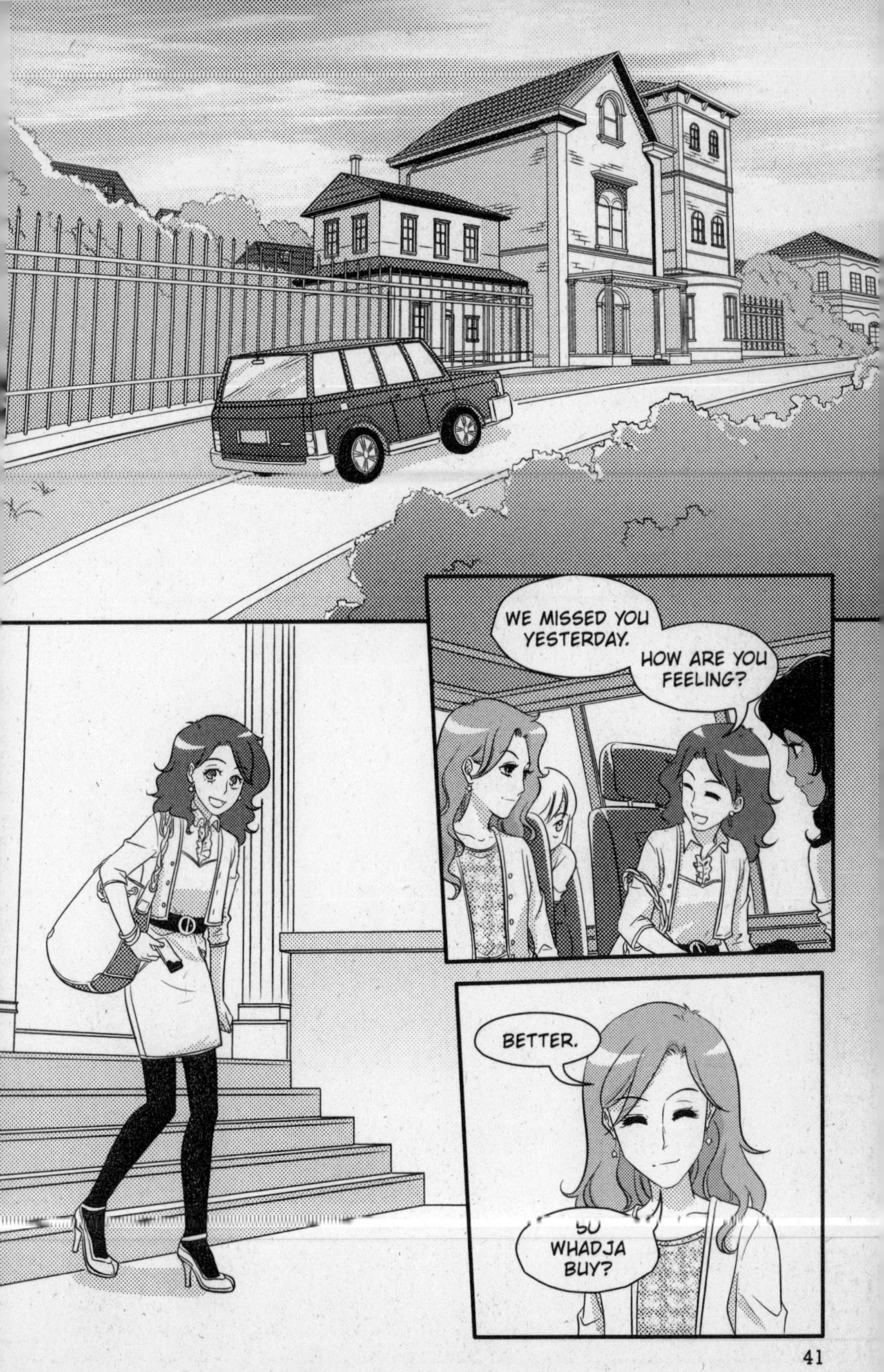
WE MISSED YOU YESTERDAY.
HOW ARE YOU FEELING?
BETTER.
SO WHADJA BUY?

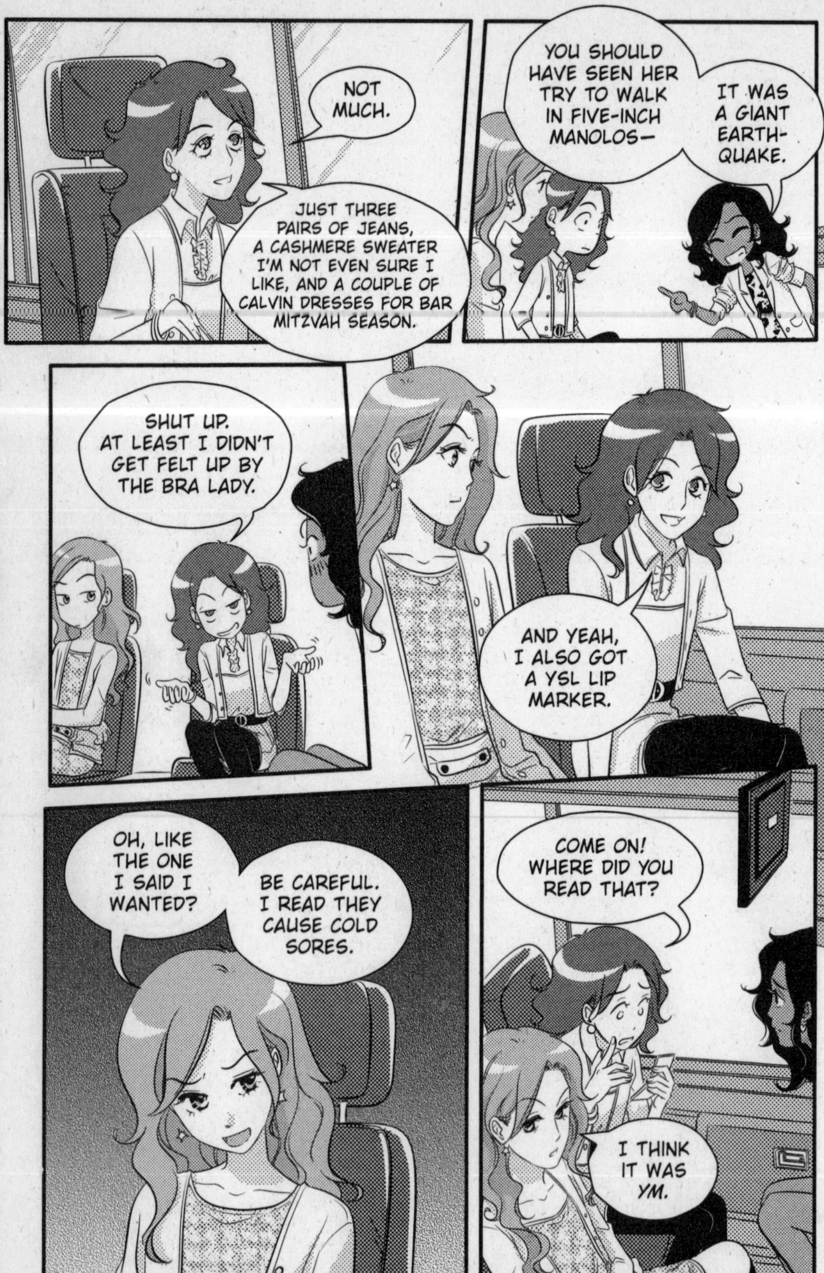
NOT MUCH.
JUST THREE PAIRS OF JEANS, A CASHMERE SWEATER I'M NOT EVEN SURE I LIKE, AND A COUPLE OF CALVIN DRESSES FOR BAR MITZVAH SEASON.
YOU SHOULD HAVE SEEN HER TRY TO WALK IN FIVE-INCH MANOLOS—
IT WAS A GIANT EARTH-QUAKE.
SHUT UP. AT LEAST I DIDN'T GET FELT UP BY THE BRA LADY.
AND YEAH, I ALSO GOT A YSL LIP MARKER.
OH, LIKE THE ONE I SAID I WANTED?
BE CAREFUL. I READ THEY CAUSE COLD SORES.
COME ON! WHERE DID YOU READ THAT?
I THINK IT WAS *YM*.

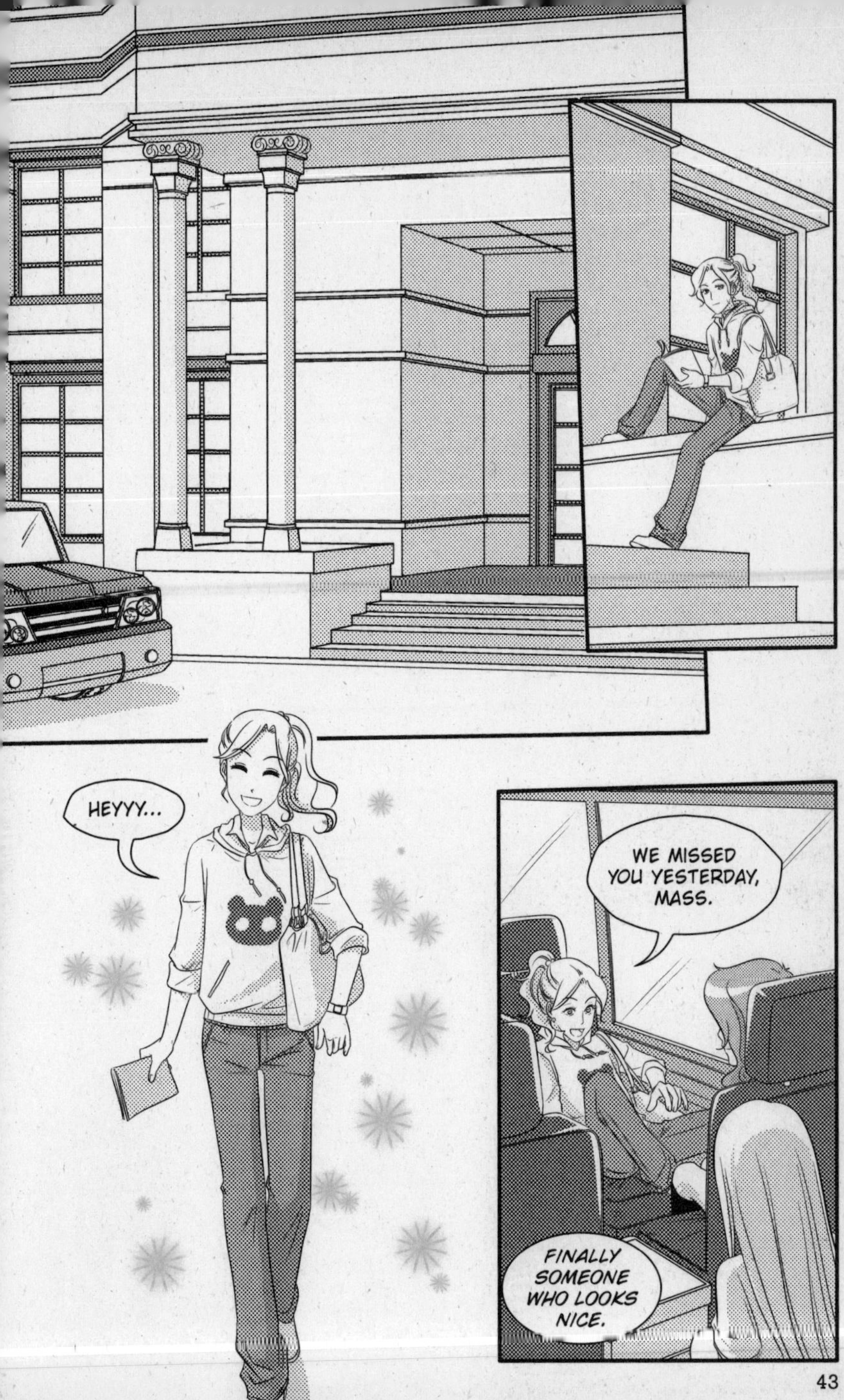
HEYYY...
WE MISSED YOU YESTERDAY, MASS.
FINALLY SOMEONE WHO LOOKS NICE.

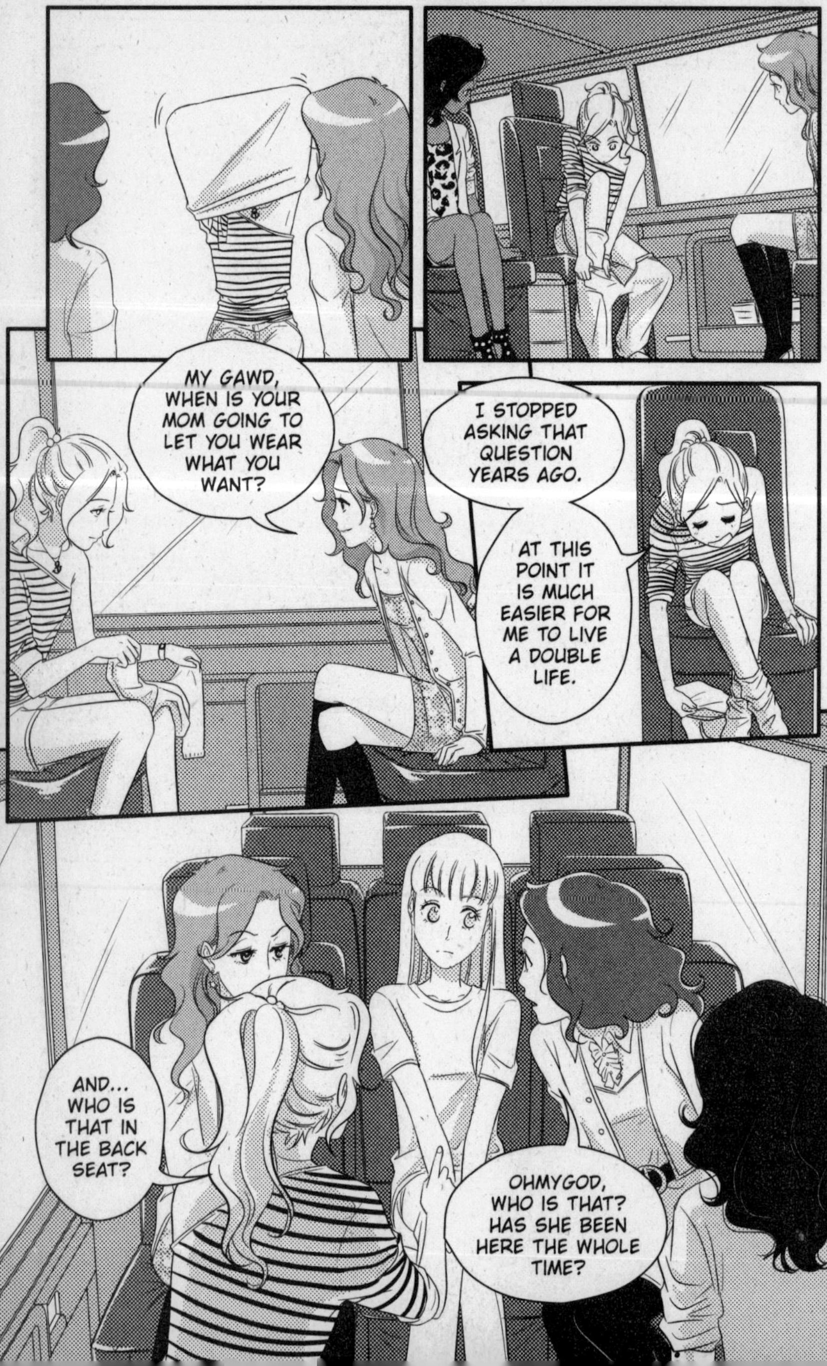
MY GAWD, WHEN IS YOUR MOM GOING TO LET YOU WEAR WHAT YOU WANT?
I STOPPED ASKING THAT QUESTION YEARS AGO.
AT THIS POINT IT IS MUCH EASIER FOR ME TO LIVE A DOUBLE LIFE.
AND... WHO IS THAT IN THE BACK SEAT?
OHMYGOD, WHO IS THAT? HAS SHE BEEN HERE THE WHOLE TIME?

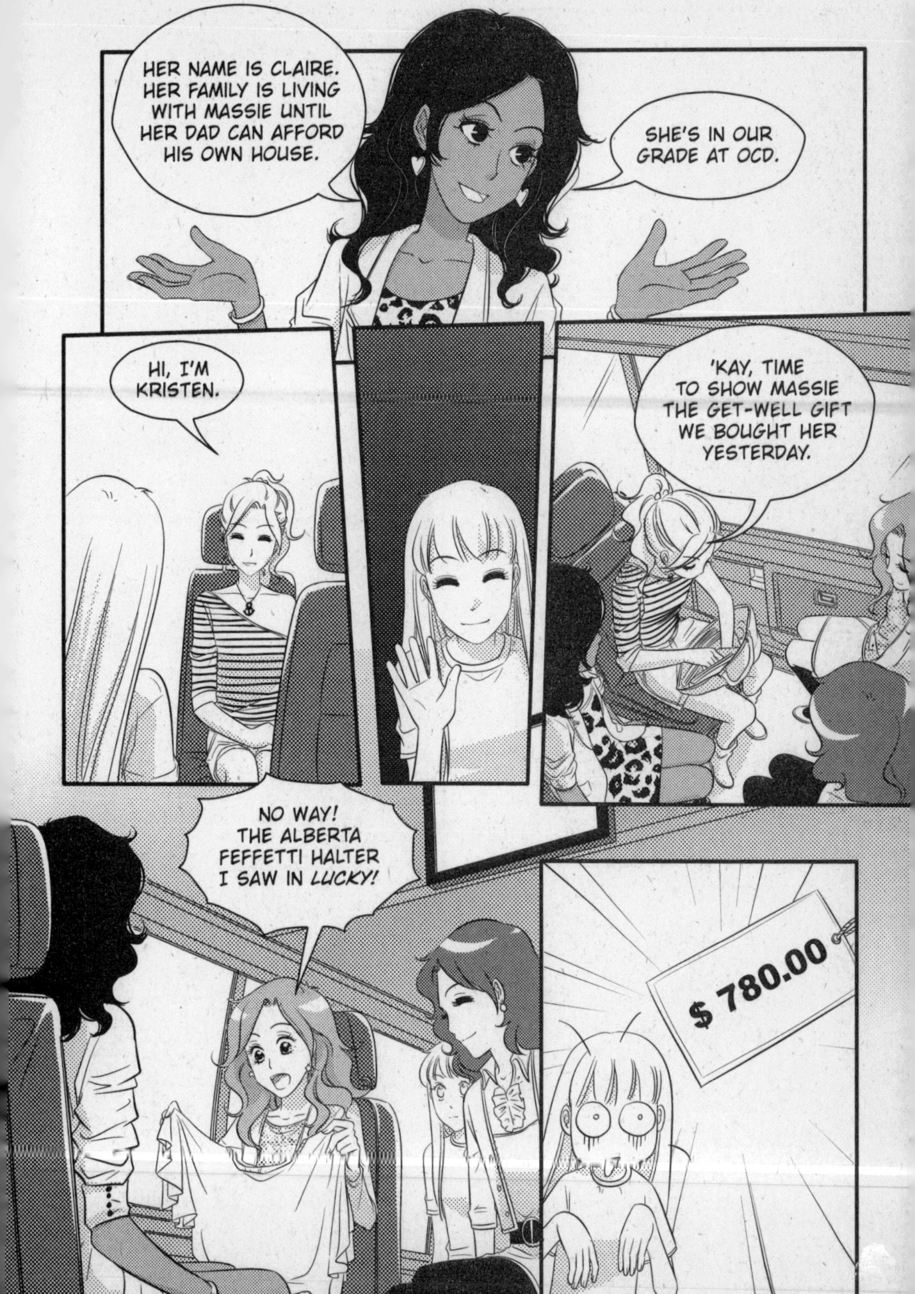
HER NAME IS CLAIRE. HER FAMILY IS LIVING WITH MASSIE UNTIL HER DAD CAN AFFORD HIS OWN HOUSE.
SHE'S IN OUR GRADE AT OCD.
HI, I'M KRISTEN.
'KAY, TIME TO SHOW MASSIE THE GET-WELL GIFT WE BOUGHT HER YESTERDAY.
NO WAY! THE ALBERTA FEFFETTI HALTER I SAW IN *LUCKY*!
$ 780.00

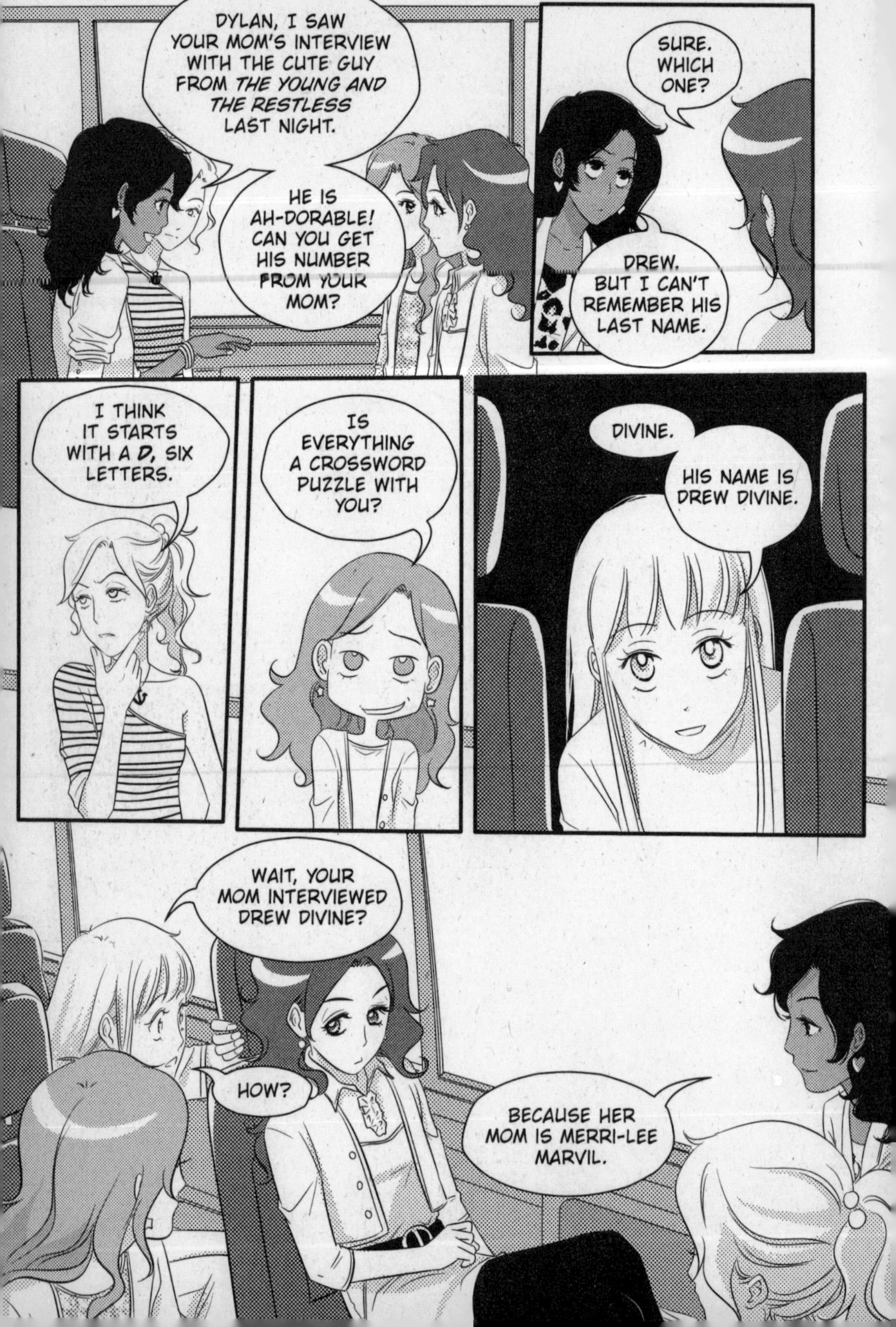
DYLAN, I SAW YOUR MOM'S INTERVIEW WITH THE CUTE GUY FROM *THE YOUNG AND THE RESTLESS* LAST NIGHT.
HE IS AH-DORABLE! CAN YOU GET HIS NUMBER FROM YOUR MOM?
SURE. WHICH ONE?
DREW. BUT I CAN'T REMEMBER HIS LAST NAME.
I THINK IT STARTS WITH A *D*, SIX LETTERS.
IS EVERYTHING A CROSSWORD PUZZLE WITH YOU?
DIVINE.
HIS NAME IS DREW DIVINE.
WAIT, YOUR MOM INTERVIEWED DREW DIVINE?
HOW?
BECAUSE HER MOM IS MERRI-LEE MARVIL.

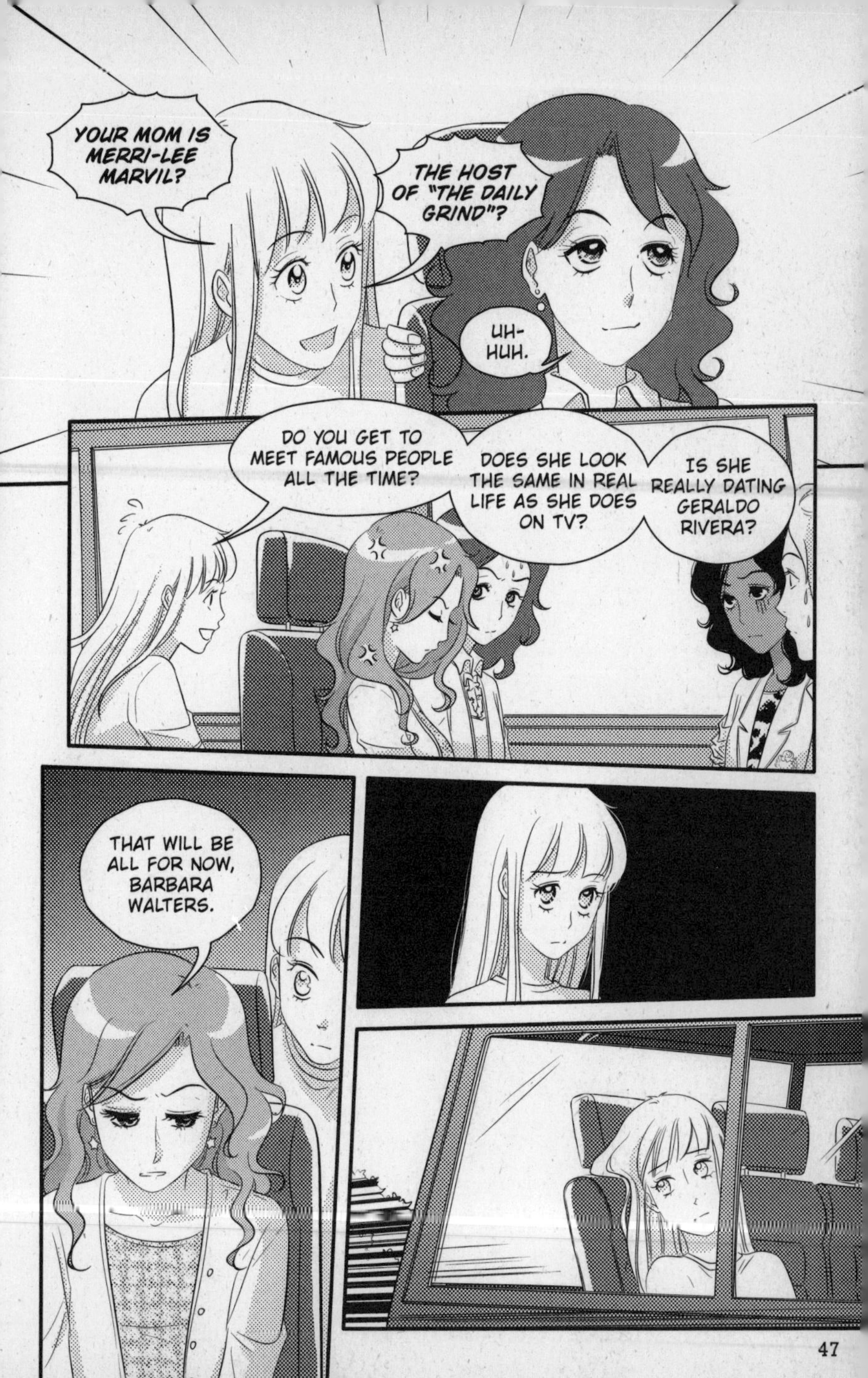

YOUR MOM IS MERRI-LEE MARVIL?
THE HOST OF "THE DAILY GRIND"?
UH-HUH.
DO YOU GET TO MEET FAMOUS PEOPLE ALL THE TIME?
DOES SHE LOOK THE SAME IN REAL LIFE AS SHE DOES ON TV?
IS SHE REALLY DATING GERALDO RIVERA?
THAT WILL BE ALL FOR NOW, BARBARA WALTERS.

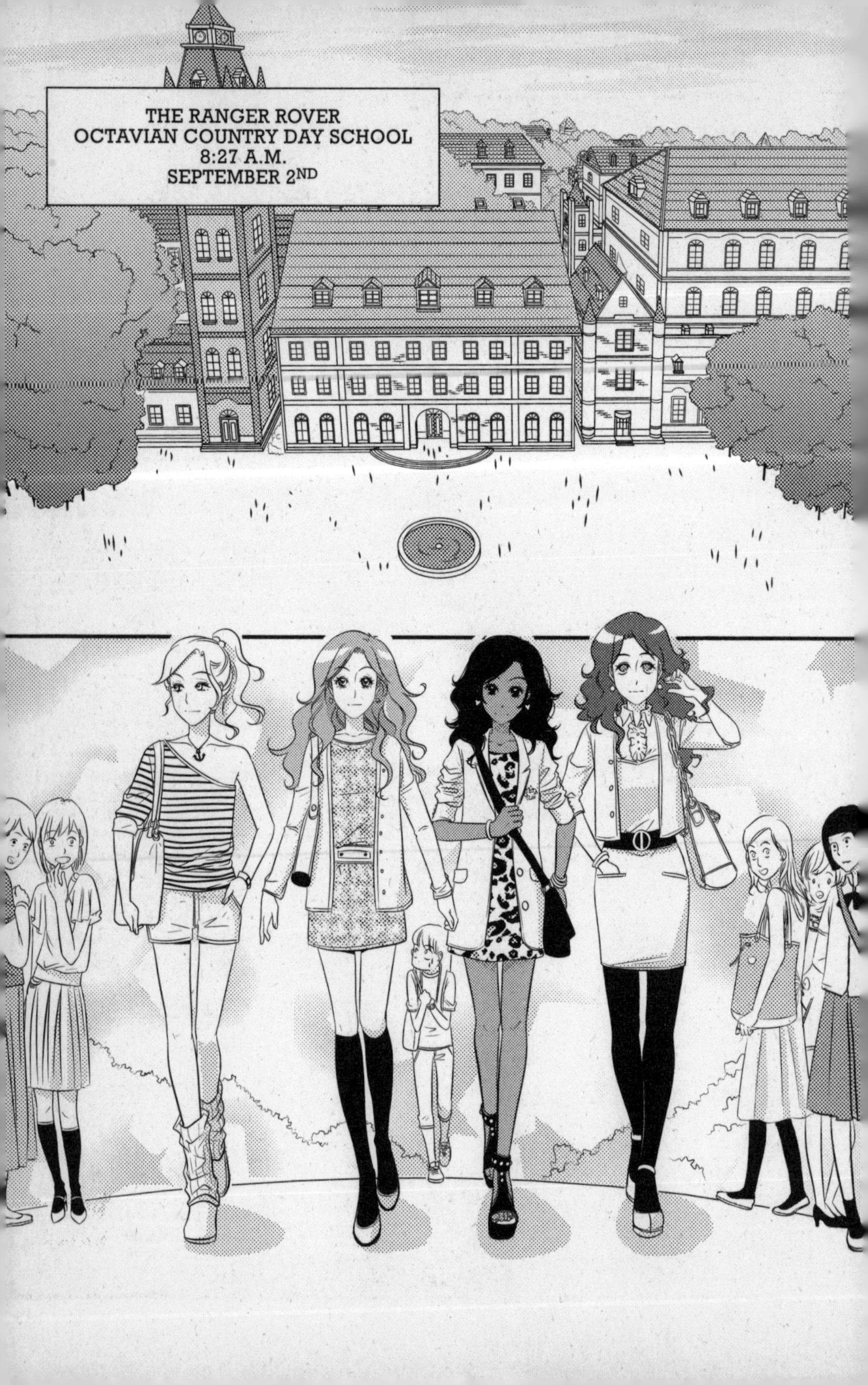
THE RANGER ROVER
OCTAVIAN COUNTRY DAY SCHOOL
8:27 A.M.
SEPTEMBER 2ND

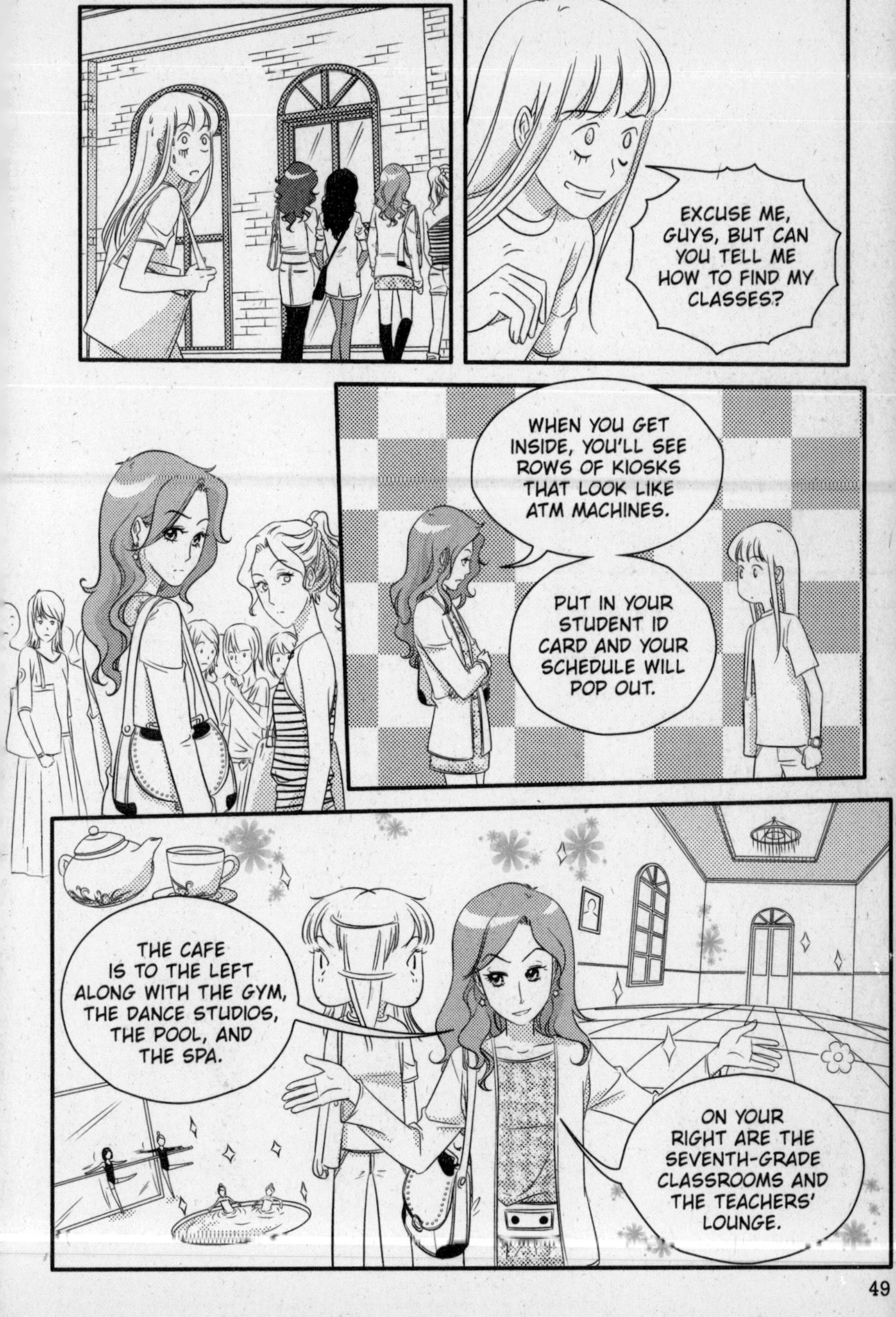
EXCUSE ME, GUYS, BUT CAN YOU TELL ME HOW TO FIND MY CLASSES?
WHEN YOU GET INSIDE, YOU'LL SEE ROWS OF KIOSKS THAT LOOK LIKE ATM MACHINES.
PUT IN YOUR STUDENT ID CARD AND YOUR SCHEDULE WILL POP OUT.
THE CAFE IS TO THE LEFT ALONG WITH THE GYM, THE DANCE STUDIOS, THE POOL, AND THE SPA.
ON YOUR RIGHT ARE THE SEVENTH-GRADE CLASSROOMS AND THE TEACHERS' LOUNGE.

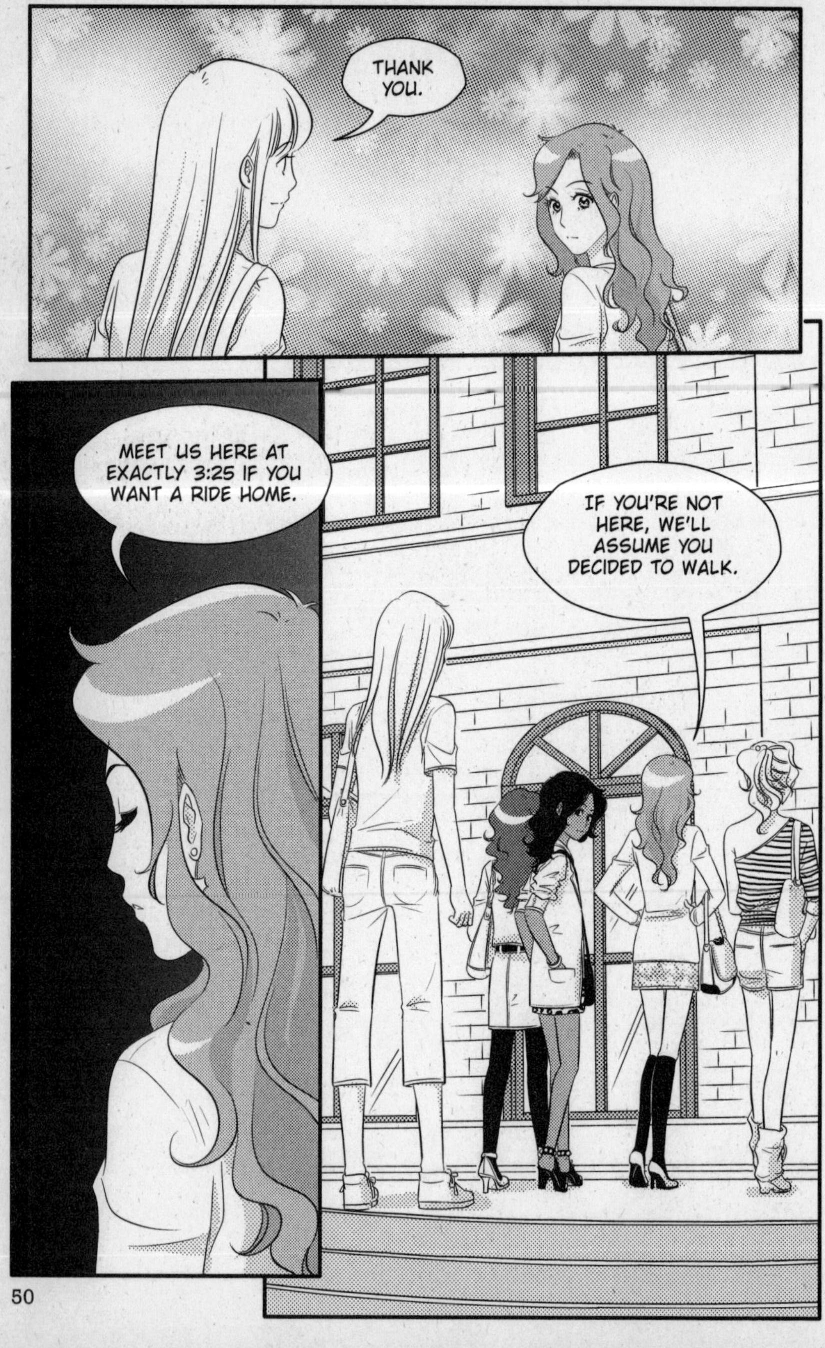
THANK YOU.
MEET US HERE AT EXACTLY 3:25 IF YOU WANT A RIDE HOME.
IF YOU'RE NOT HERE, WE'LL ASSUME YOU DECIDED TO WALK.

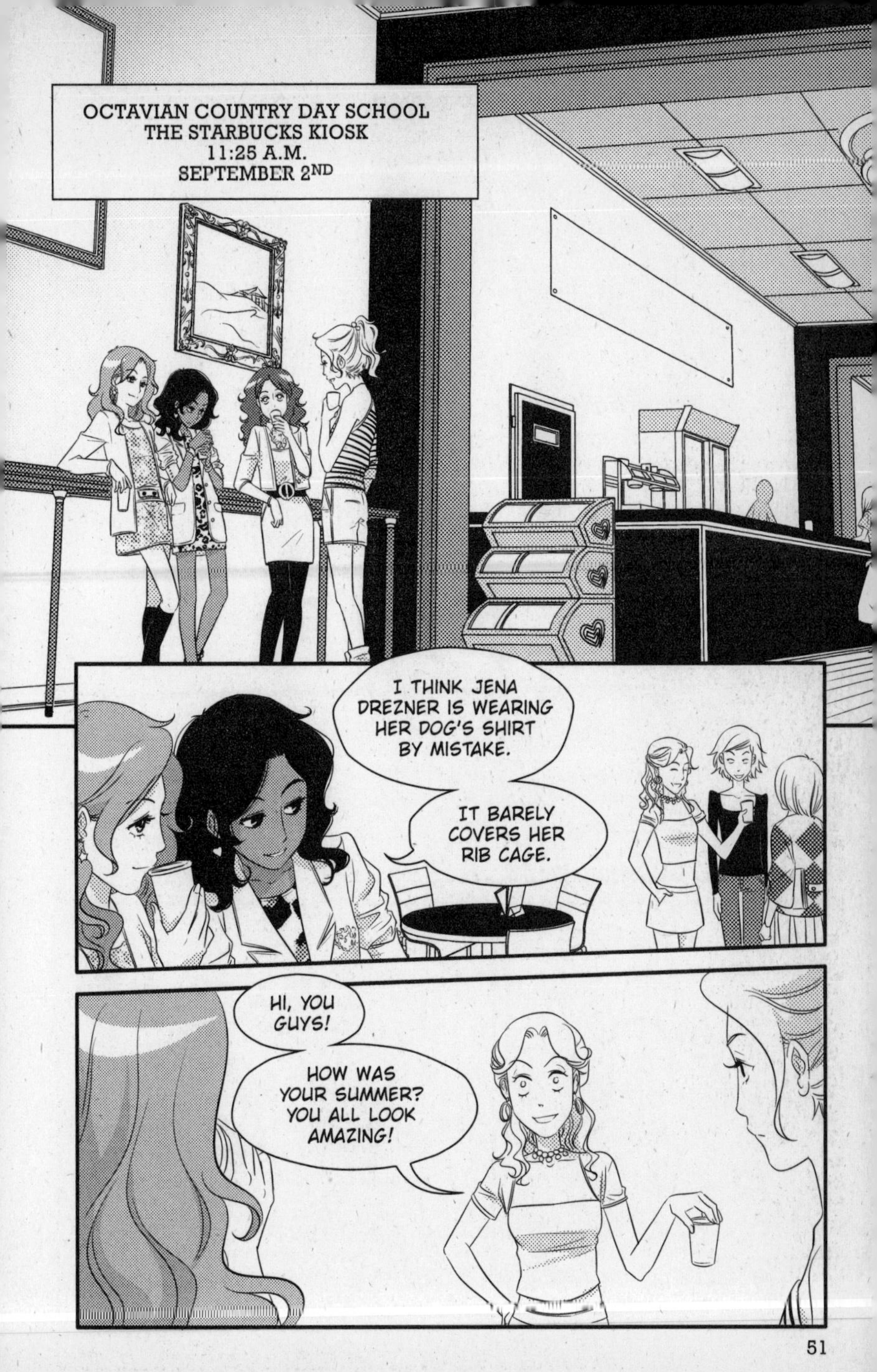
OCTAVIAN COUNTRY DAY SCHOOL
THE STARBUCKS KIOSK
11:25 A.M.
SEPTEMBER 2ND
I THINK JENA DREZNER IS WEARING HER DOG'S SHIRT BY MISTAKE.
IT BARELY COVERS HER RIB CAGE.
HI, YOU GUYS!
HOW WAS YOUR SUMMER? YOU ALL LOOK AMAZING!

HEY, MASSIE, I HEARD THAT YOU'RE TAKING THAT NEW GIRL UNDER YOUR WING.

WHAT?

YEAH, EVERYONE'S SAYING YOU HAVE A NEW BFF.

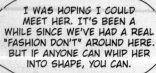

I WAS HOPING I COULD MEET HER. IT'S BEEN A WHILE SINCE WE'VE HAD A REAL "FASHION DON'T" AROUND HERE. BUT IF ANYONE CAN WHIP HER INTO SHAPE, YOU CAN.

CHECK YOUR SOURCE, JENA. OBVIOUSLY, IF I HAD A NEW BFF, SHE'D BE HERE RIGHT NOW.

I HEARD SHE PEED IN HER BED AT SLEEPOVER CAMP THIS SUMMER.

TWO GOSSIP POINTS.

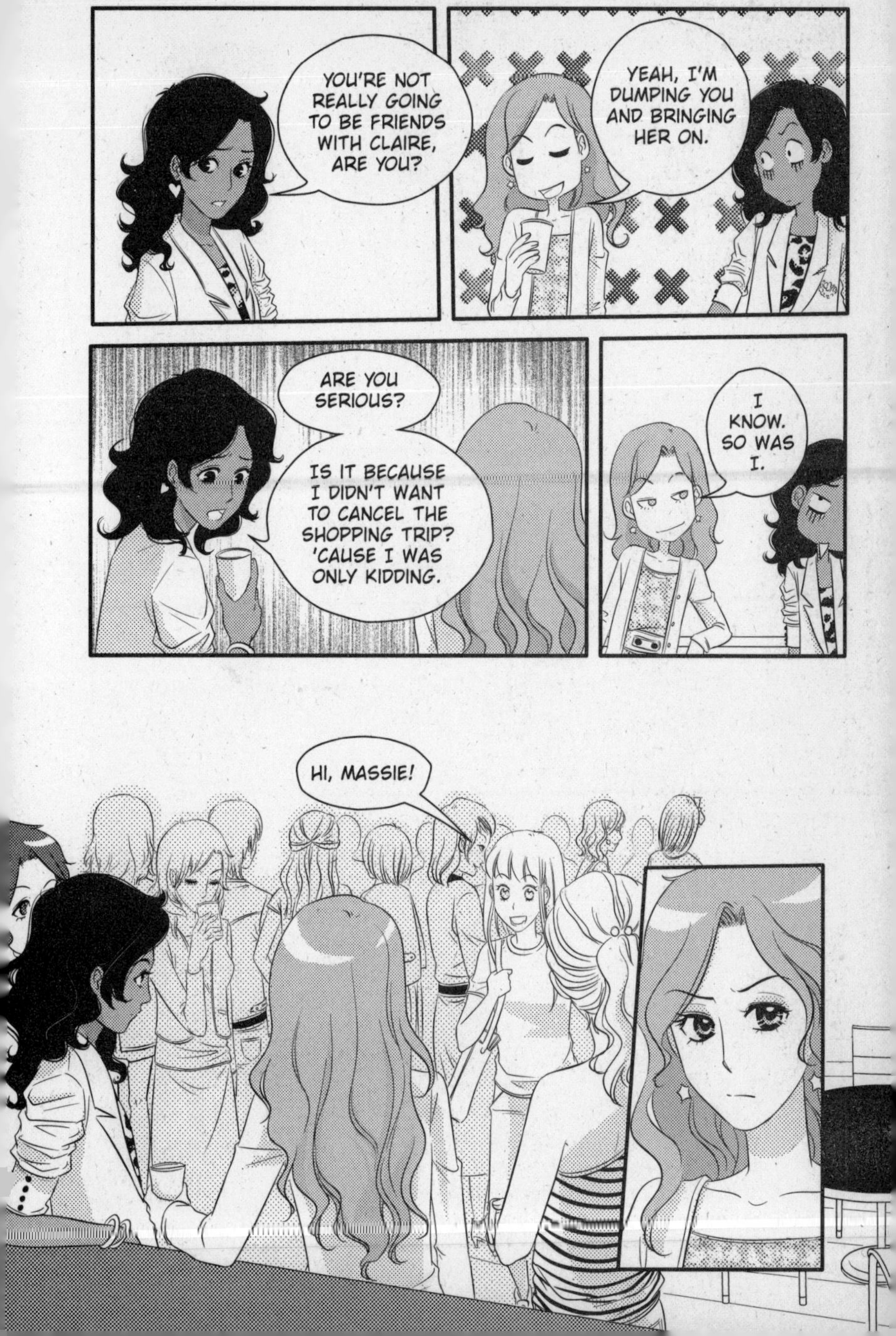
YOU'RE NOT REALLY GOING TO BE FRIENDS WITH CLAIRE, ARE YOU?
YEAH, I'M DUMPING YOU AND BRINGING HER ON.
ARE YOU SERIOUS?
IS IT BECAUSE I DIDN'T WANT TO CANCEL THE SHOPPING TRIP? 'CAUSE I WAS ONLY KIDDING.
I KNOW. SO WAS I.
HI, MASSIE!

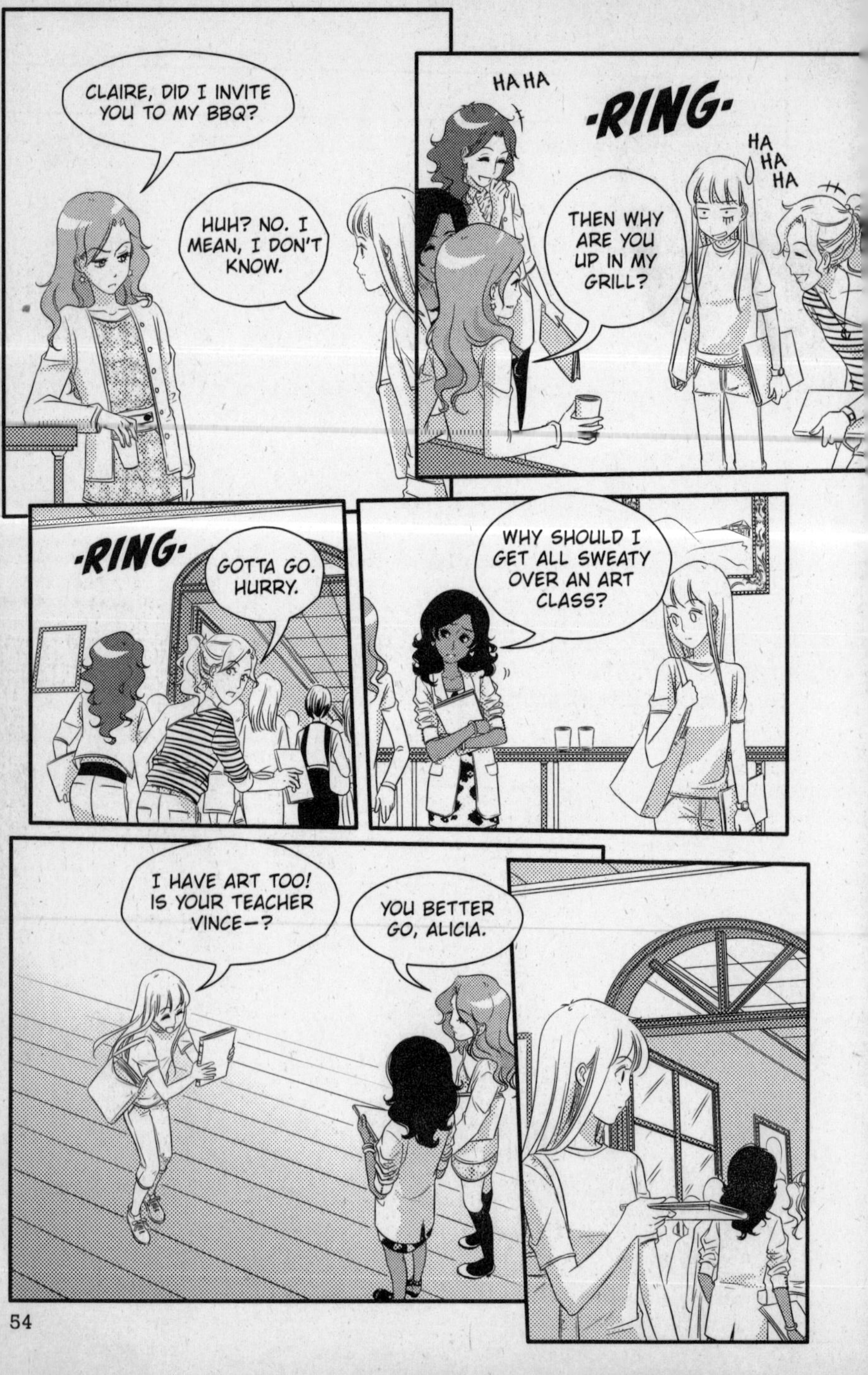

CLAIRE, DID I INVITE YOU TO MY BBQ?
HUH? NO. I MEAN, I DON'T KNOW.
HA HA
-RING-
THEN WHY ARE YOU UP IN MY GRILL?
HA HA HA
-RING-
GOTTA GO. HURRY.
WHY SHOULD I GET ALL SWEATY OVER AN ART CLASS?
I HAVE ART TOO! IS YOUR TEACHER VINCE—?
YOU BETTER GO, ALICIA.

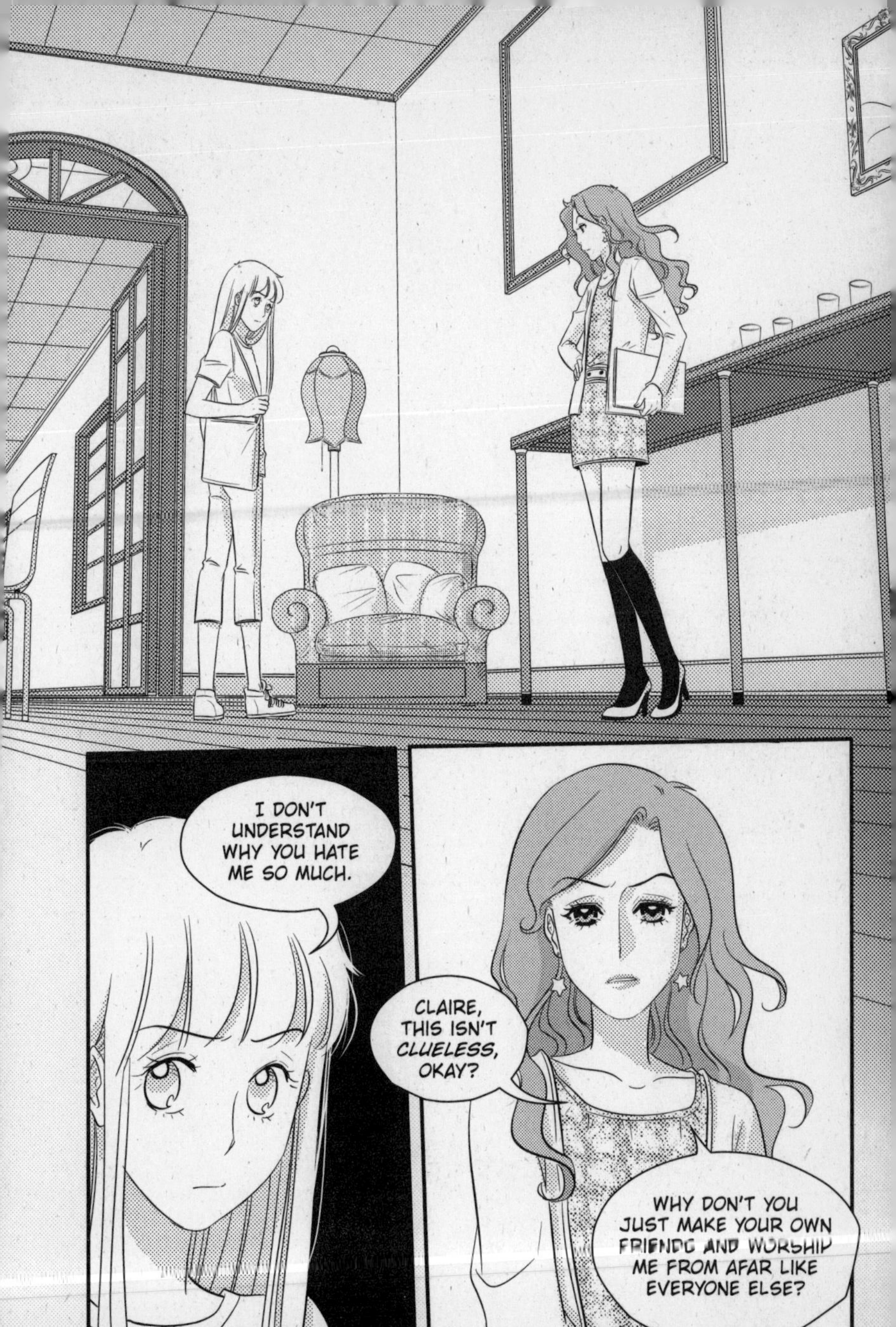
I DON'T UNDERSTAND WHY YOU HATE ME SO MUCH.
CLAIRE, THIS ISN'T *CLUELESS*, OKAY?
WHY DON'T YOU JUST MAKE YOUR OWN FRIENDS AND WORSHIP ME FROM AFAR LIKE EVERYONE ELSE?

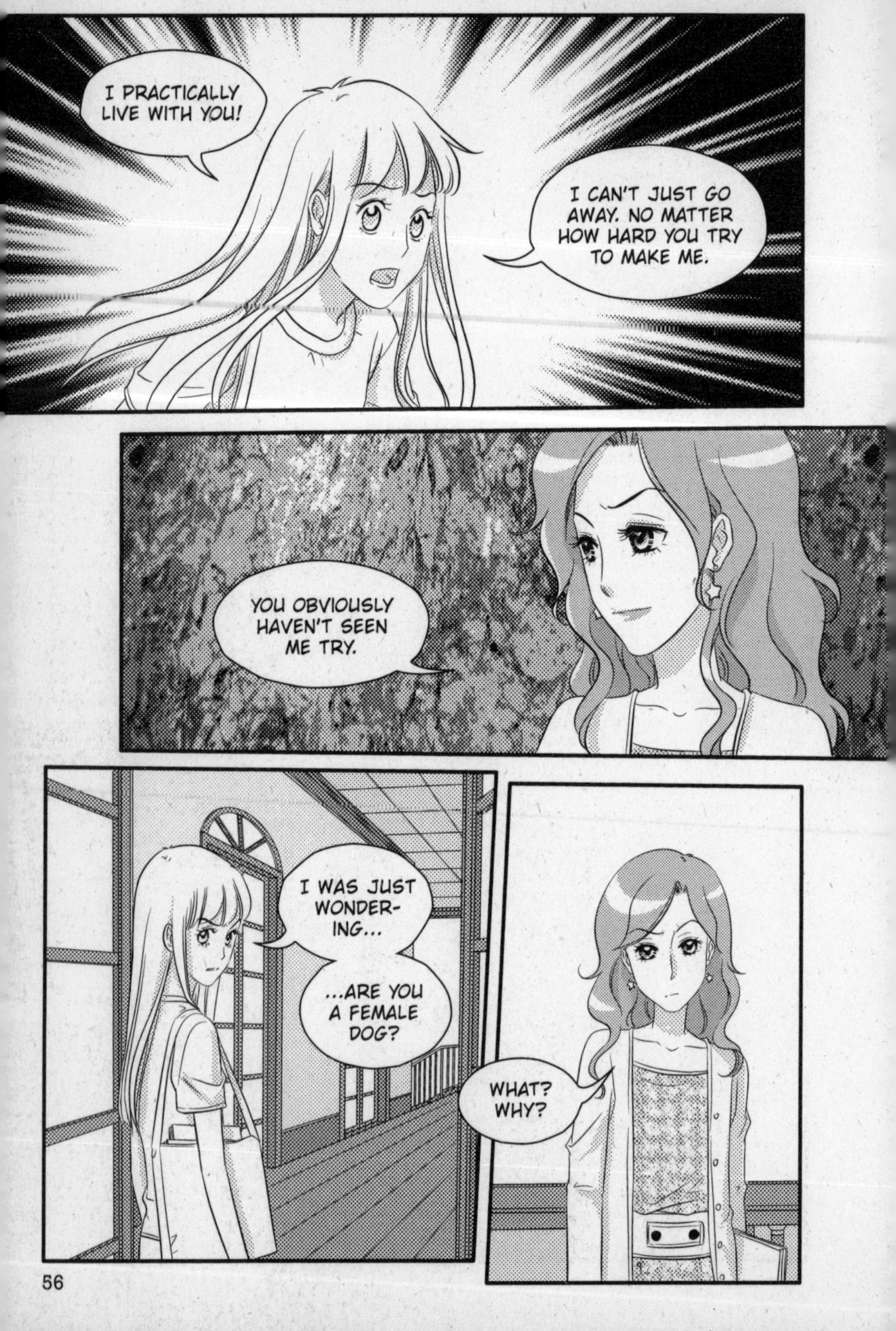
I PRACTICALLY LIVE WITH YOU!
I CAN'T JUST GO AWAY. NO MATTER HOW HARD YOU TRY TO MAKE ME.
YOU OBVIOUSLY HAVEN'T SEEN ME TRY.
I WAS JUST WONDER-ING...
...ARE YOU A FEMALE DOG?
WHAT? WHY?

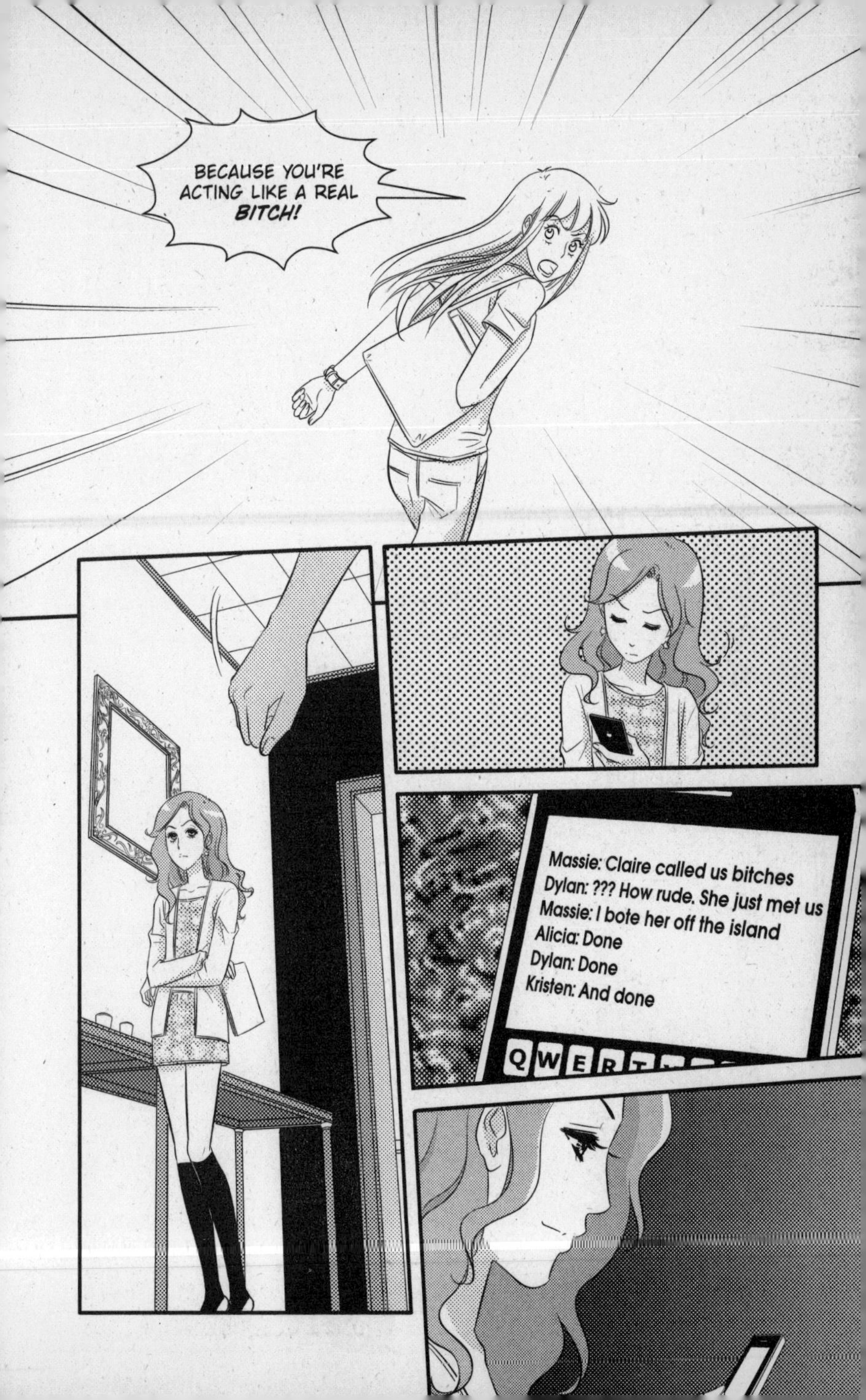
BECAUSE YOU'RE ACTING LIKE A REAL *BITCH!*
Massie: Claire called us bitches
Dylan: ??? How rude. She just met us
Massie: I bote her off the island
Alicia: Done
Dylan: Done
Kristen: And done
QWERT

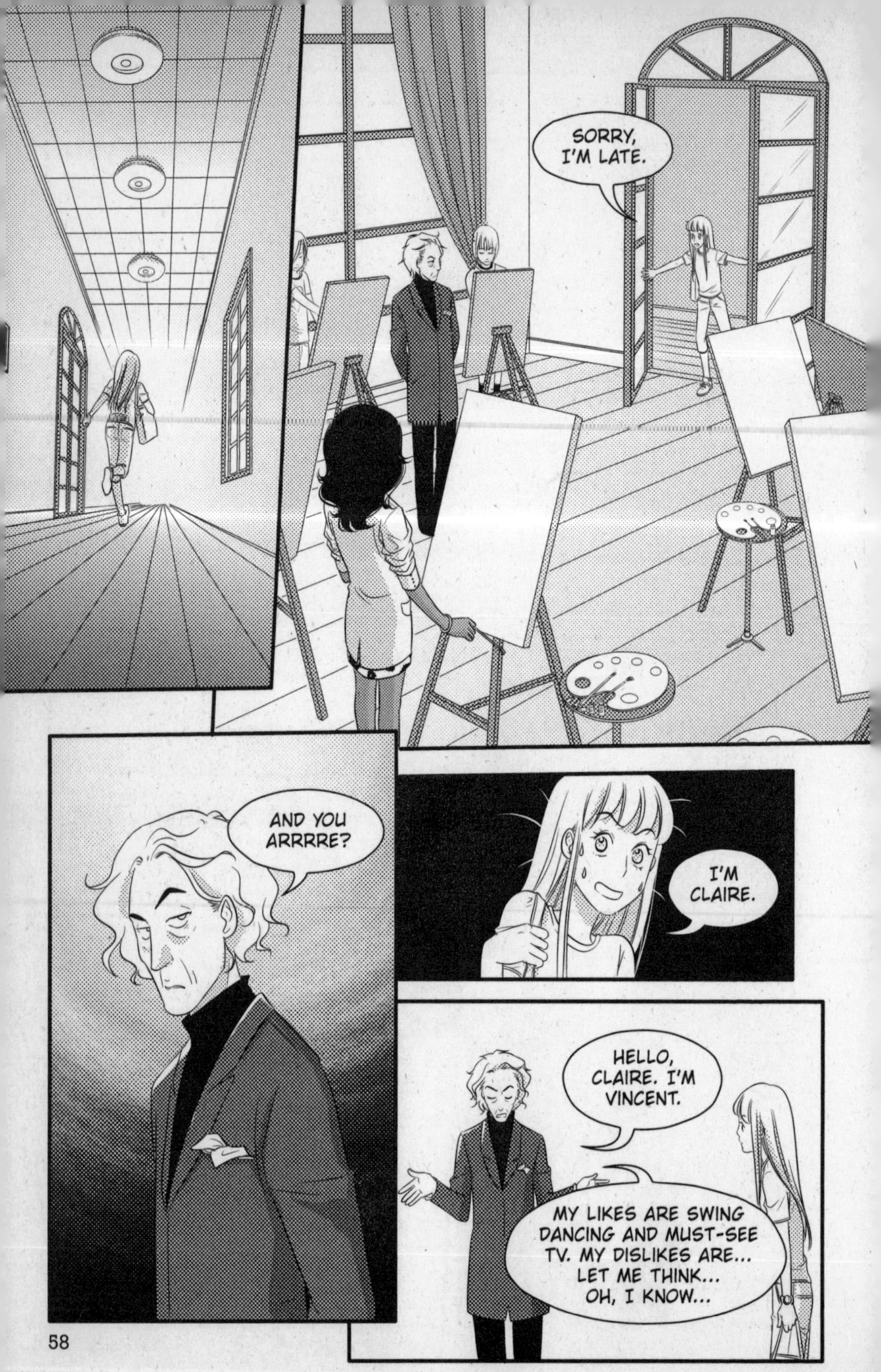
SORRY, I'M LATE.
AND YOU ARRRRE?
I'M CLAIRE.
HELLO, CLAIRE. I'M VINCENT.
MY LIKES ARE SWING DANCING AND MUST-SEE TV. MY DISLIKES ARE... LET ME THINK... OH, I KNOW...

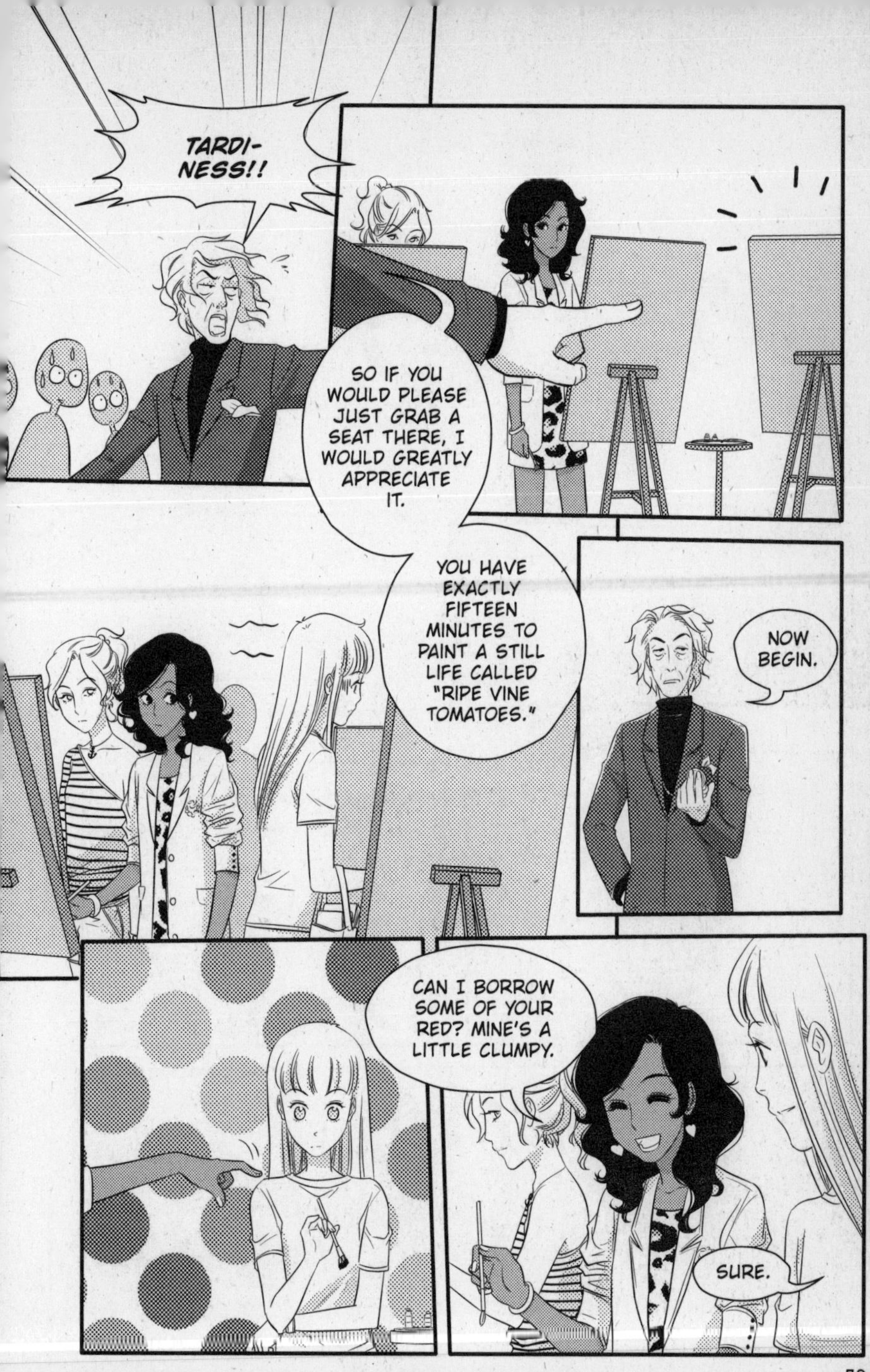

TARDI-NESS!!
SO IF YOU WOULD PLEASE JUST GRAB A SEAT THERE, I WOULD GREATLY APPRECIATE IT.
YOU HAVE EXACTLY FIFTEEN MINUTES TO PAINT A STILL LIFE CALLED "RIPE VINE TOMATOES."
NOW BEGIN.
CAN I BORROW SOME OF YOUR RED? MINE'S A LITTLE CLUMPY.
SURE.

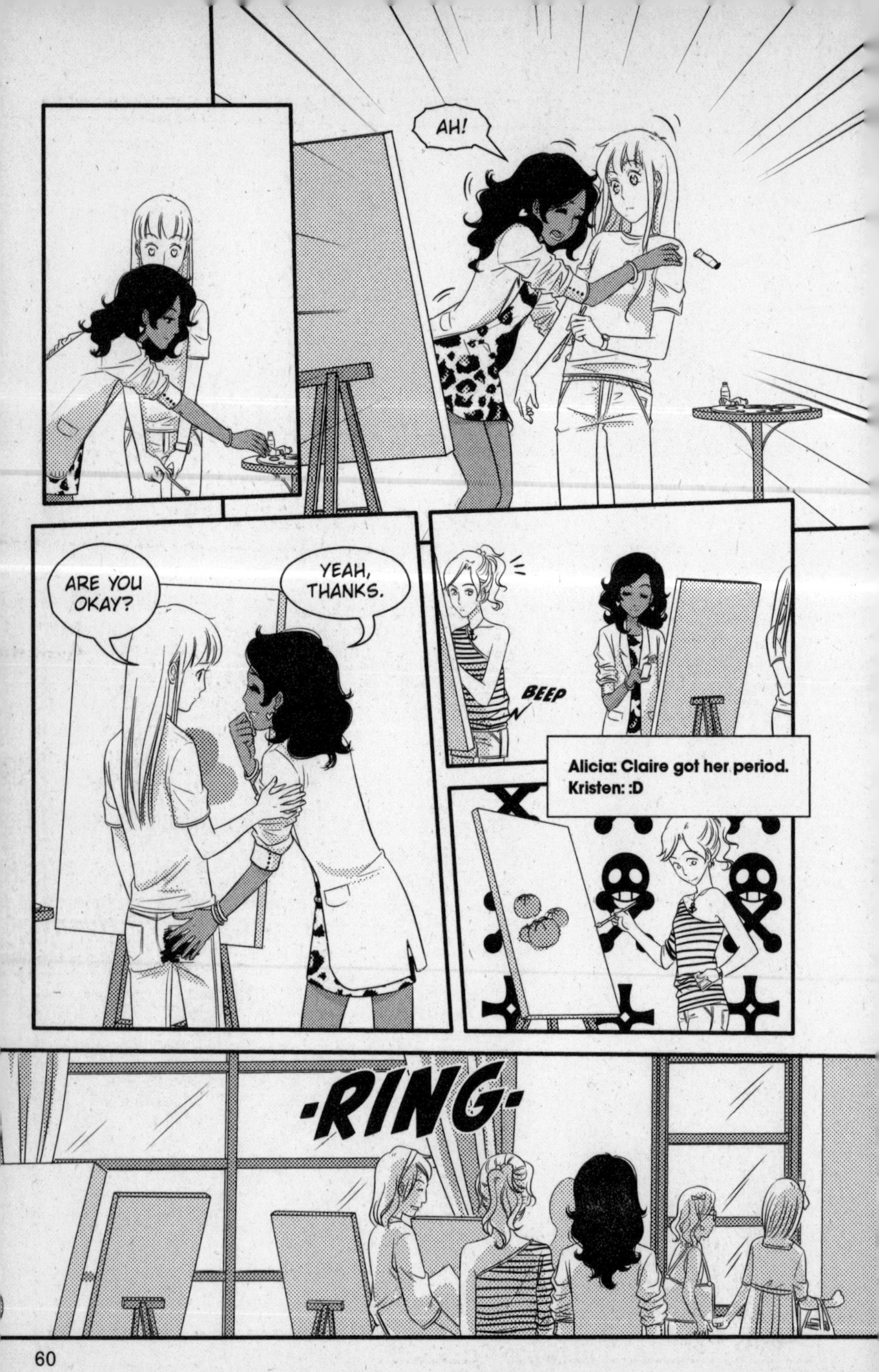
AH!
ARE YOU OKAY?
YEAH, THANKS.
BEEP
Alicia: Claire got her period.
Kristen: :D
-RING-

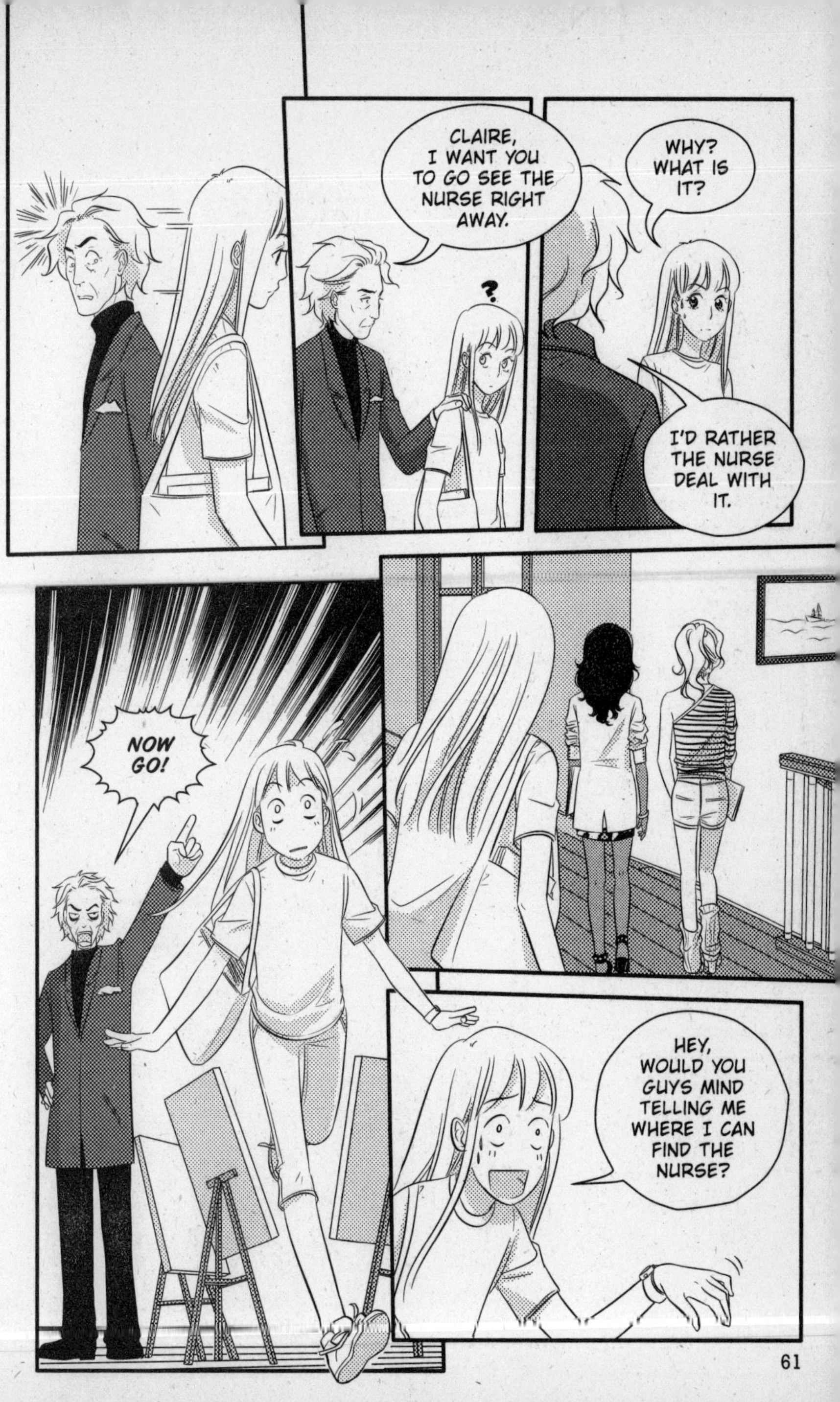
CLAIRE, I WANT YOU TO GO SEE THE NURSE RIGHT AWAY.
?
WHY? WHAT IS IT?
I'D RATHER THE NURSE DEAL WITH IT.
NOW GO!
HEY, WOULD YOU GUYS MIND TELLING ME WHERE I CAN FIND THE NURSE?

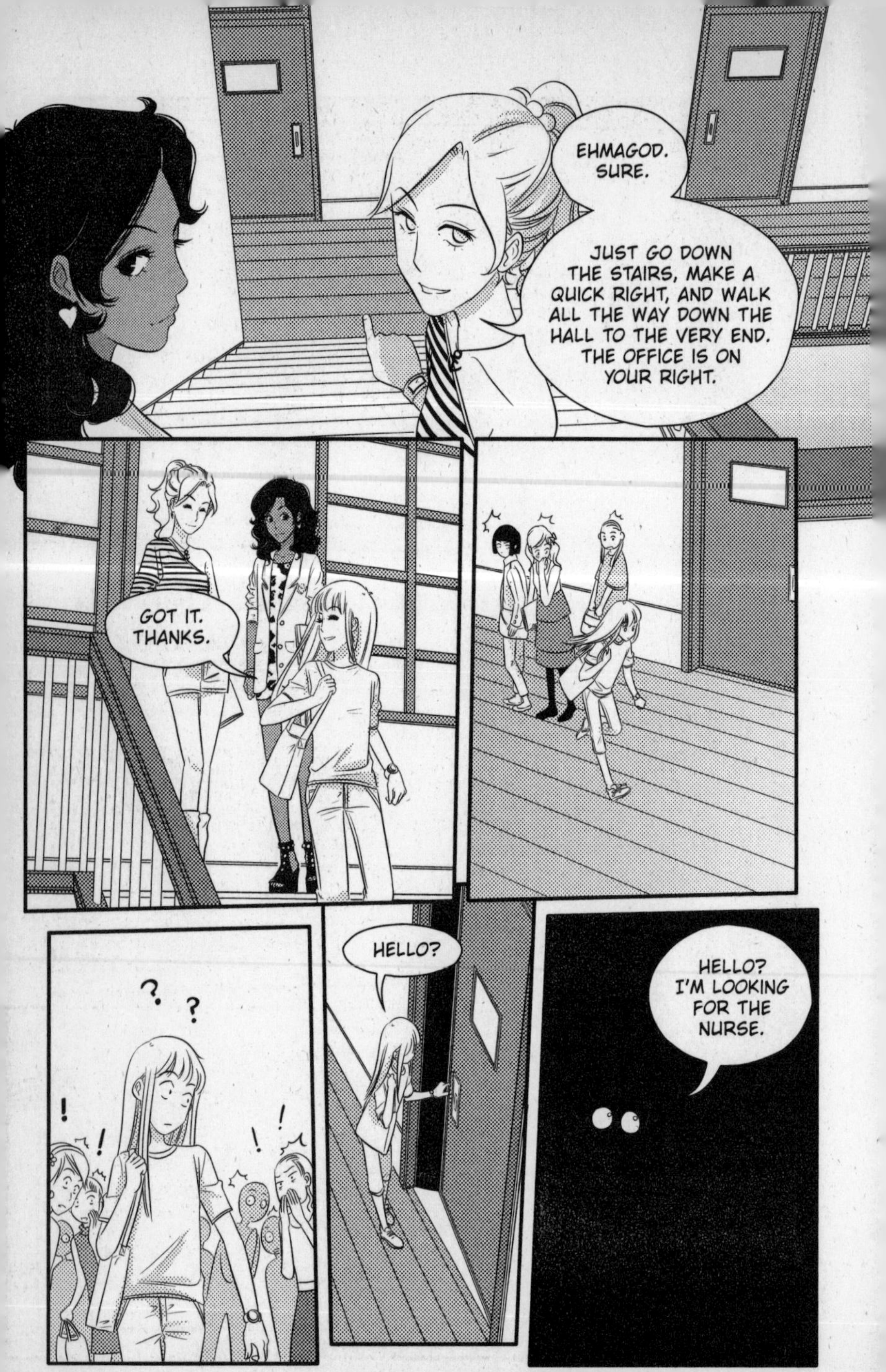
EHMAGOD. SURE.
JUST GO DOWN THE STAIRS, MAKE A QUICK RIGHT, AND WALK ALL THE WAY DOWN THE HALL TO THE VERY END. THE OFFICE IS ON YOUR RIGHT.
GOT IT. THANKS.
HELLO?
HELLO? I'M LOOKING FOR THE NURSE.

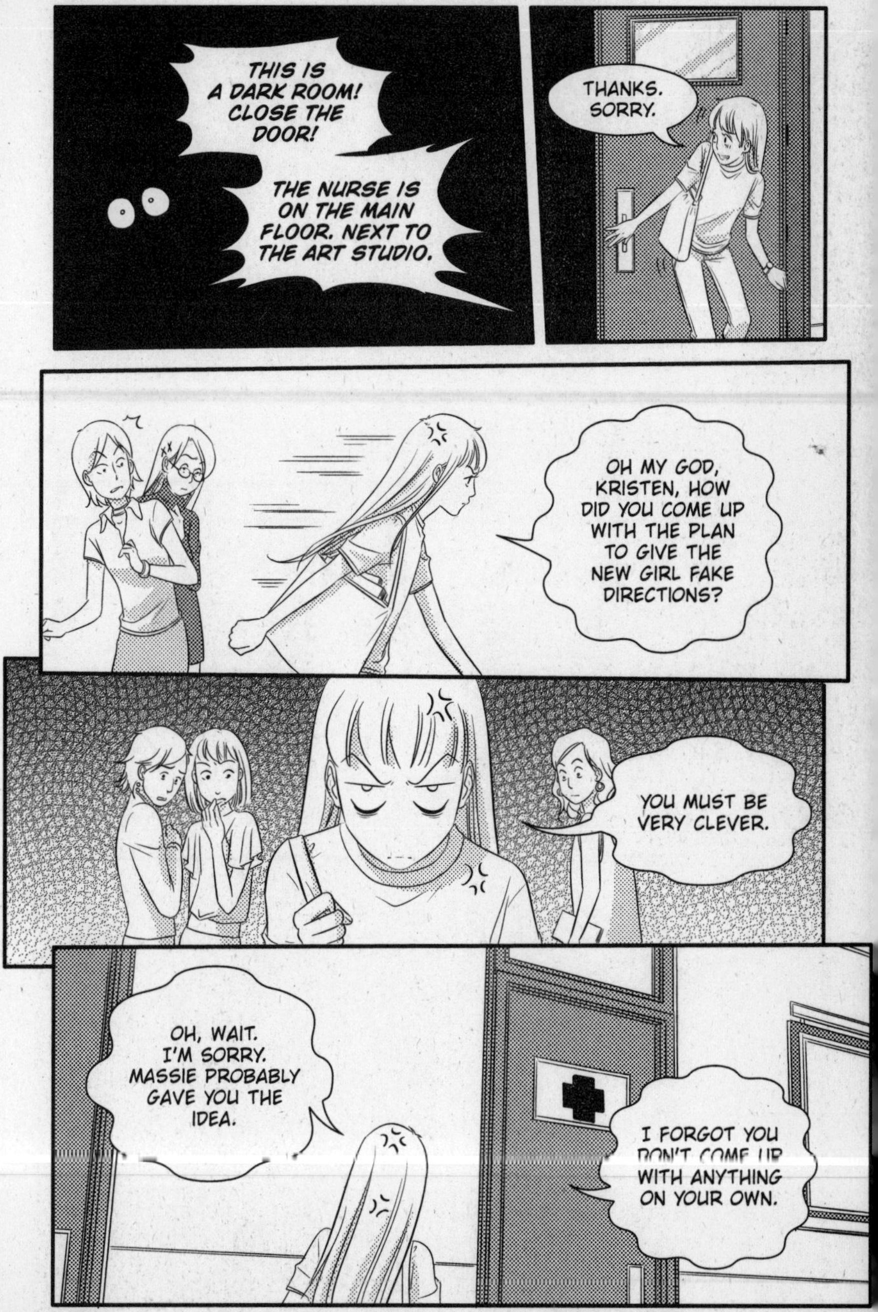
THIS IS A DARK ROOM! CLOSE THE DOOR!
THE NURSE IS ON THE MAIN FLOOR. NEXT TO THE ART STUDIO.
THANKS. SORRY.
OH MY GOD, KRISTEN, HOW DID YOU COME UP WITH THE PLAN TO GIVE THE NEW GIRL FAKE DIRECTIONS?
YOU MUST BE VERY CLEVER.
OH, WAIT. I'M SORRY. MASSIE PROBABLY GAVE YOU THE IDEA.
I FORGOT YOU DON'T COME UP WITH ANYTHING ON YOUR OWN.

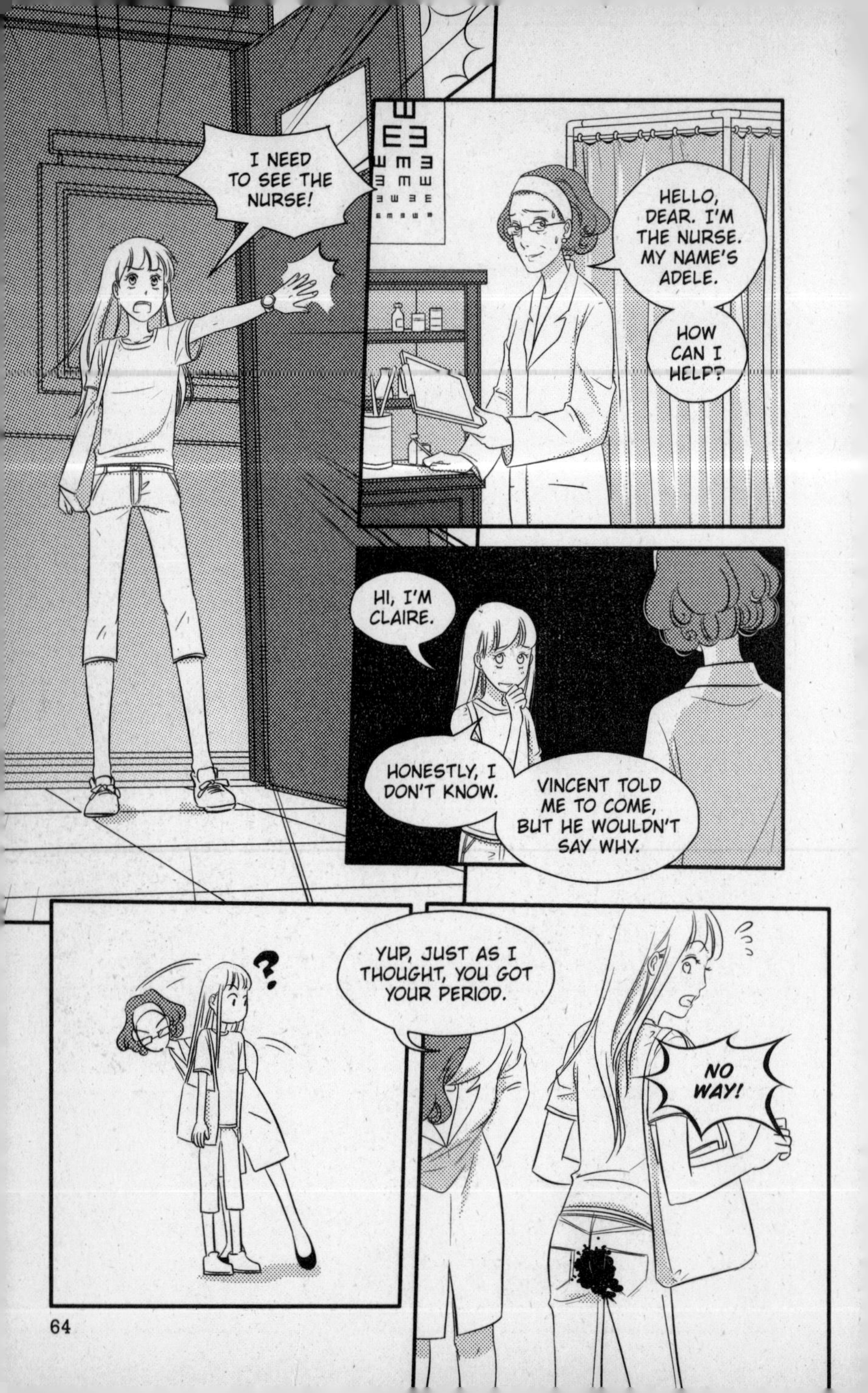
I NEED TO SEE THE NURSE!
HELLO, DEAR. I'M THE NURSE. MY NAME'S ADELE.
HOW CAN I HELP?
HI, I'M CLAIRE.
HONESTLY, I DON'T KNOW.
VINCENT TOLD ME TO COME, BUT HE WOULDN'T SAY WHY.
?
YUP, JUST AS I THOUGHT, YOU GOT YOUR PERIOD.
NO WAY!

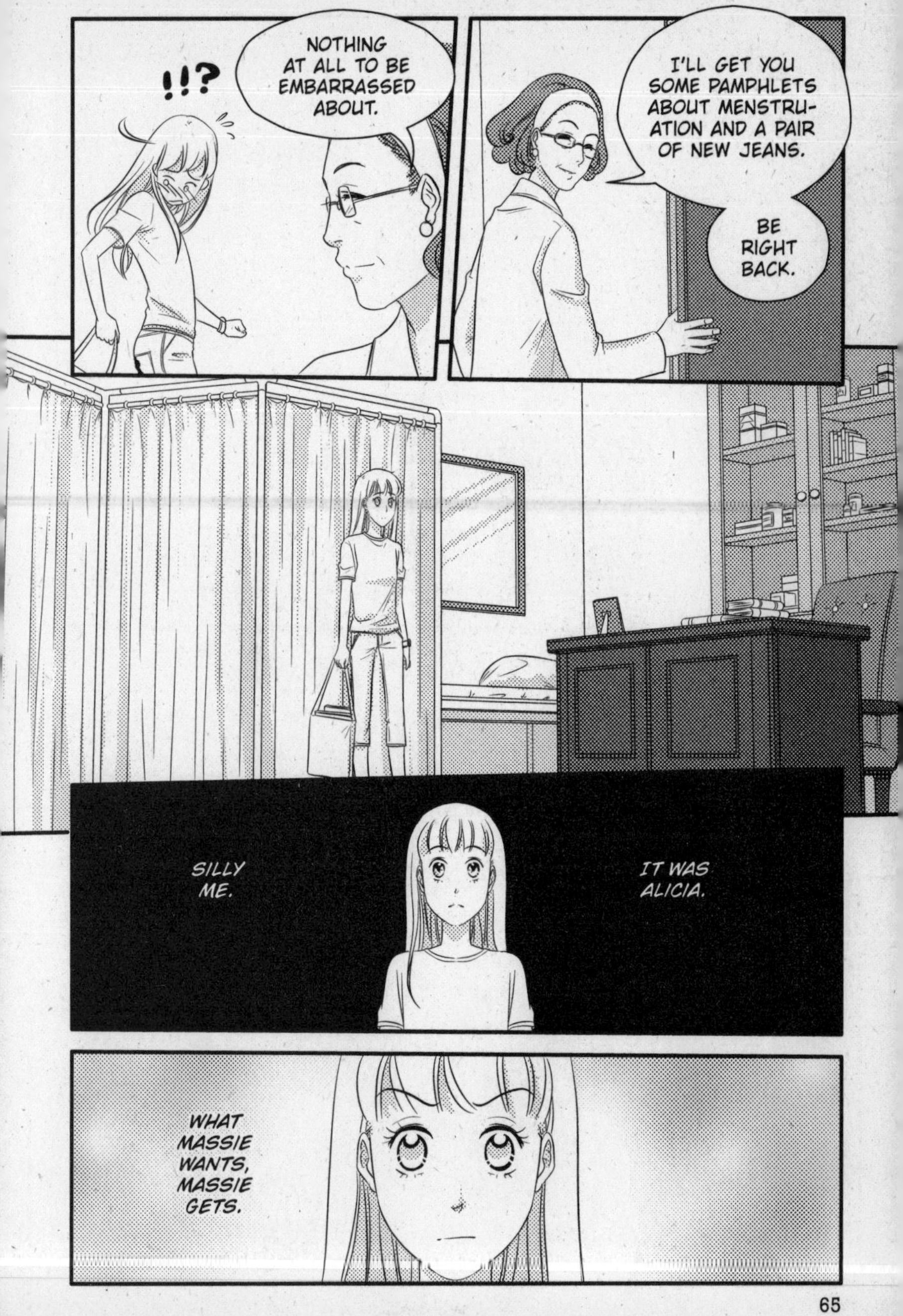
!!?
NOTHING AT ALL TO BE EMBARRASSED ABOUT.
I'LL GET YOU SOME PAMPHLETS ABOUT MENSTRU- ATION AND A PAIR OF NEW JEANS.
BE RIGHT BACK.
SILLY ME.
IT WAS ALICIA.
WHAT MASSIE WANTS, MASSIE GETS.

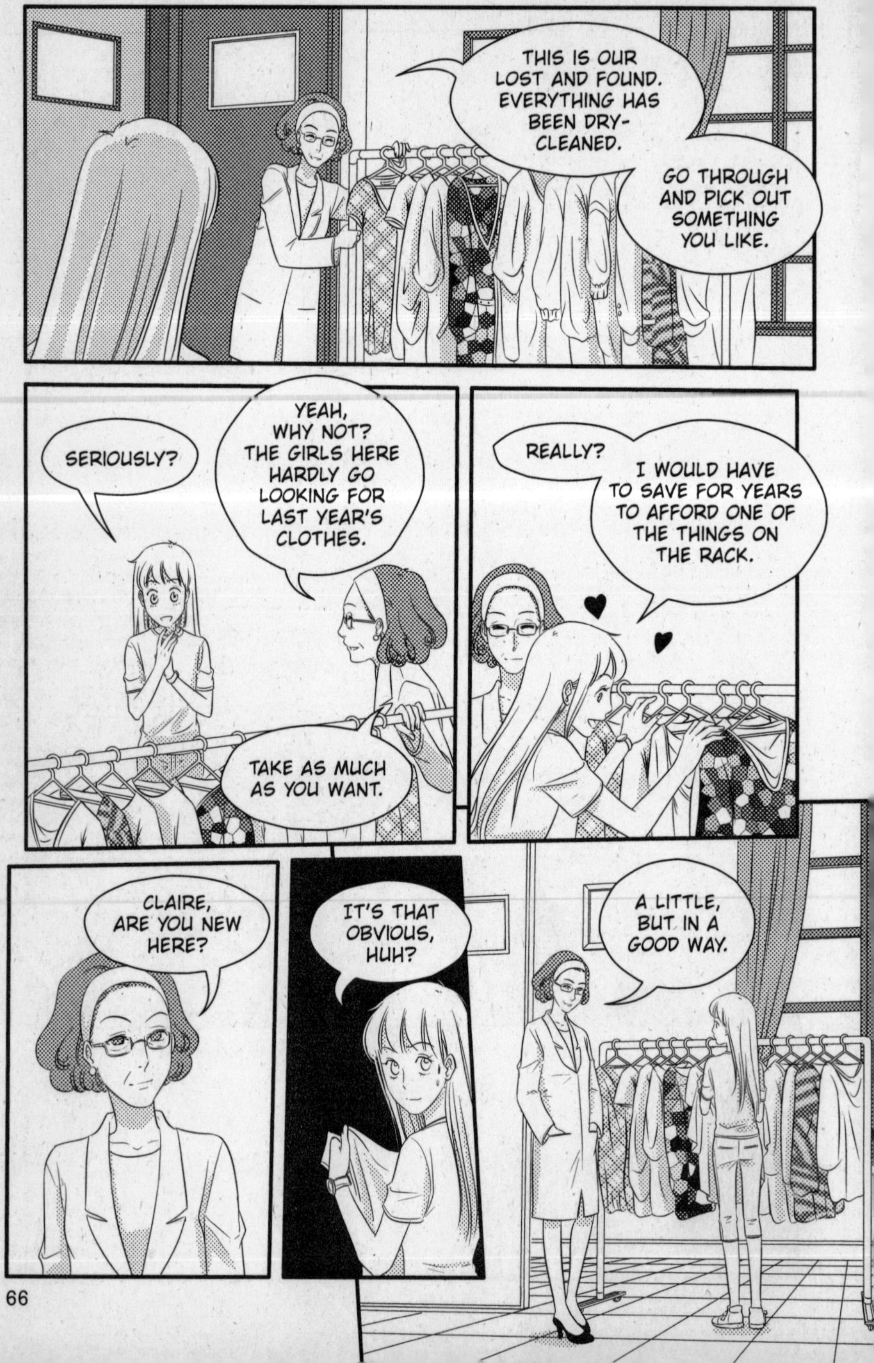
THIS IS OUR LOST AND FOUND. EVERYTHING HAS BEEN DRY-CLEANED.
GO THROUGH AND PICK OUT SOMETHING YOU LIKE.
SERIOUSLY?
YEAH, WHY NOT? THE GIRLS HERE HARDLY GO LOOKING FOR LAST YEAR'S CLOTHES.
TAKE AS MUCH AS YOU WANT.
REALLY?
I WOULD HAVE TO SAVE FOR YEARS TO AFFORD ONE OF THE THINGS ON THE RACK.
CLAIRE, ARE YOU NEW HERE?
IT'S THAT OBVIOUS, HUH?
A LITTLE, BUT IN A GOOD WAY.

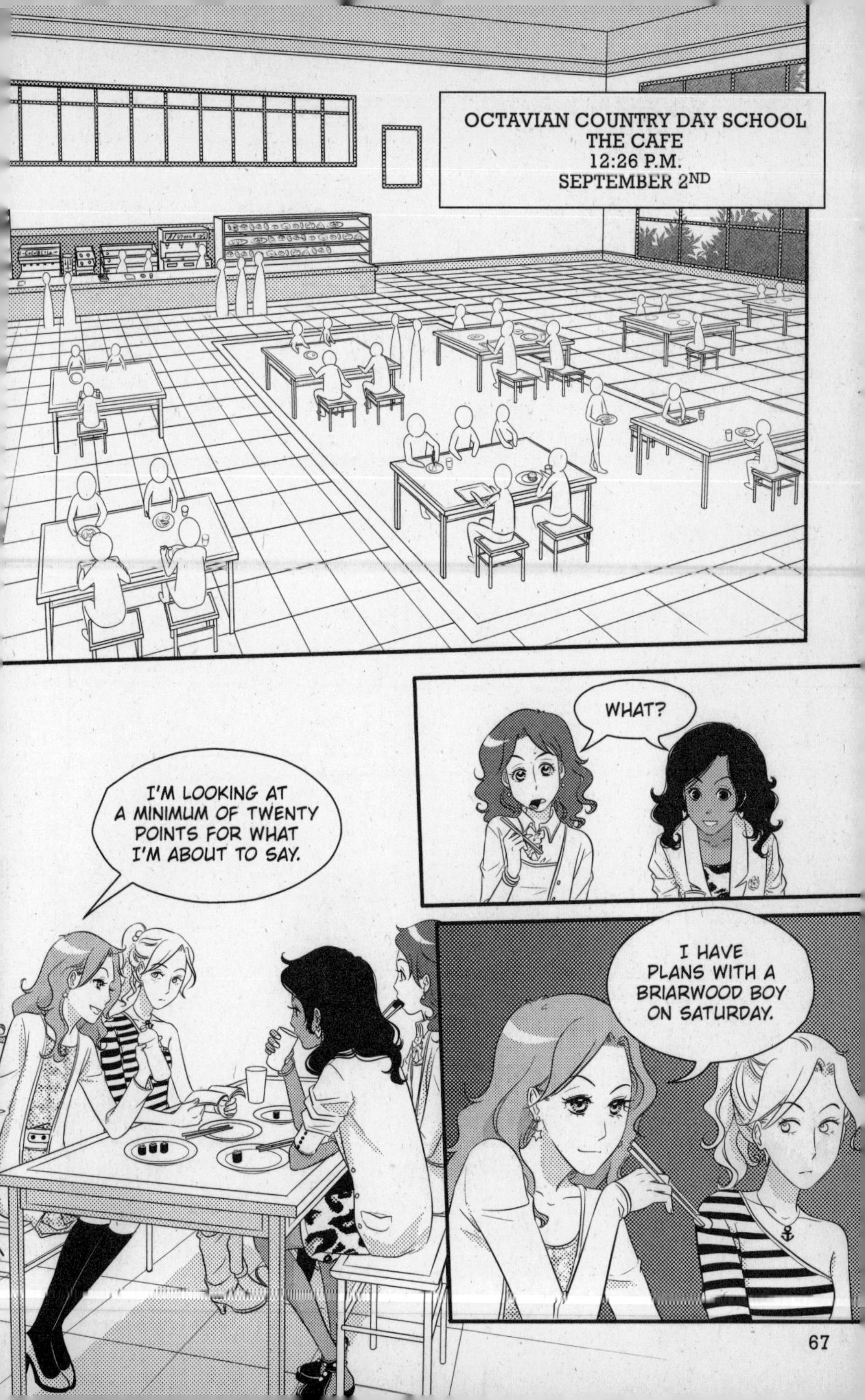
OCTAVIAN COUNTRY DAY SCHOOL
THE CAFE
12:26 P.M.
SEPTEMBER 2ND
I'M LOOKING AT A MINIMUM OF TWENTY POINTS FOR WHAT I'M ABOUT TO SAY.
WHAT?
I HAVE PLANS WITH A BRIARWOOD BOY ON SATURDAY.

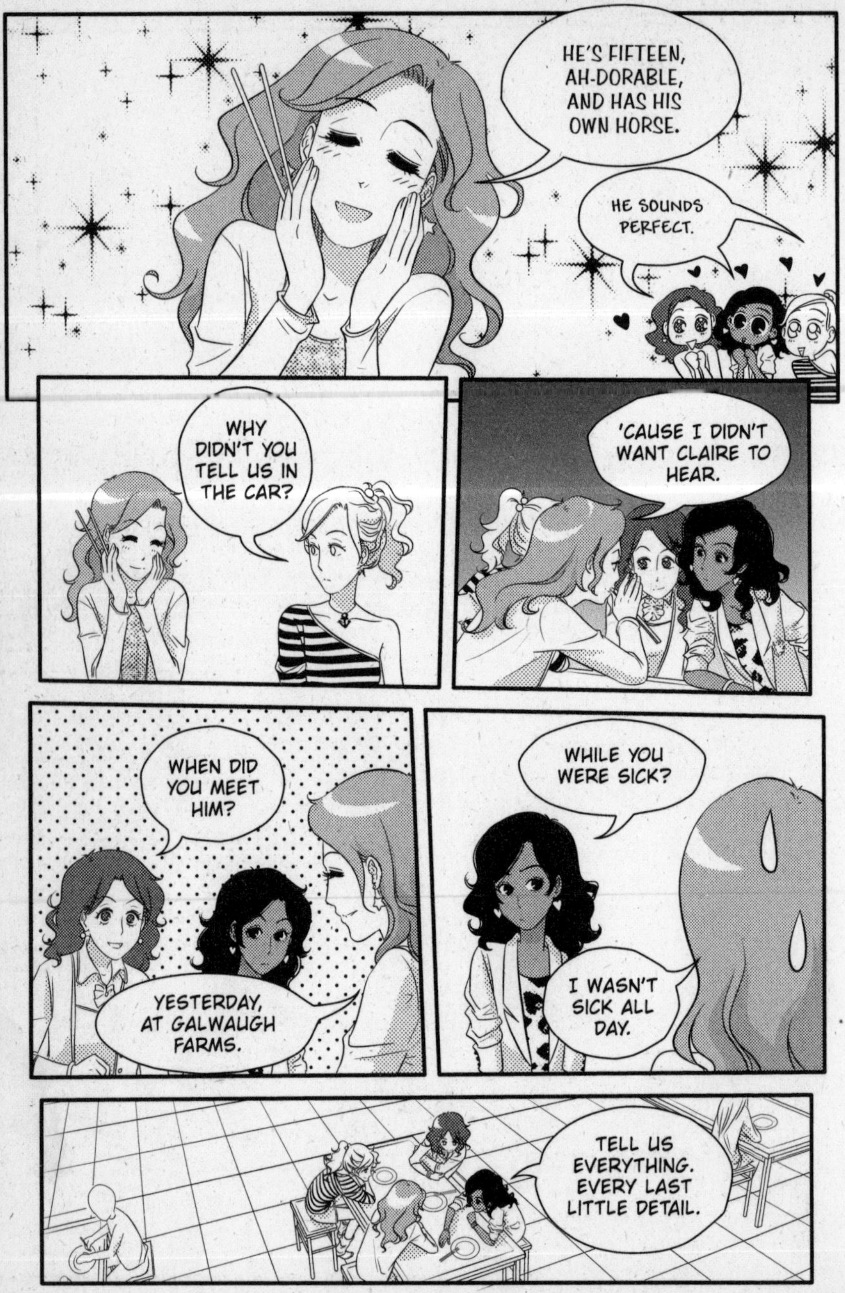
HE'S FIFTEEN, AH-DORABLE, AND HAS HIS OWN HORSE.
HE SOUNDS PERFECT.
WHY DIDN'T YOU TELL US IN THE CAR?
'CAUSE I DIDN'T WANT CLAIRE TO HEAR.
WHEN DID YOU MEET HIM?
YESTERDAY, AT GALWAUGH FARMS.
WHILE YOU WERE SICK?
I WASN'T SICK ALL DAY.
TELL US EVERYTHING. EVERY LAST LITTLE DETAIL.

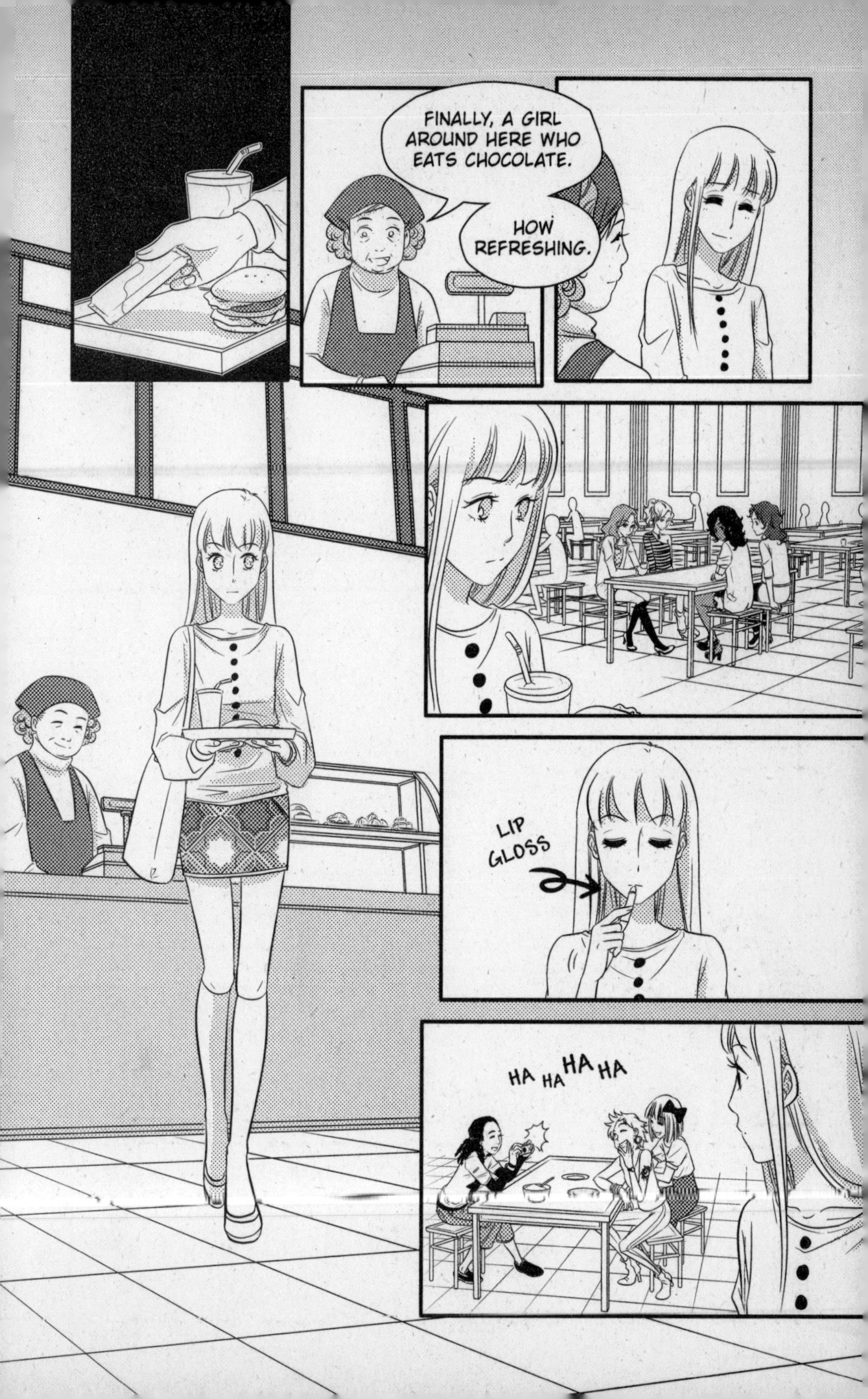
FINALLY, A GIRL AROUND HERE WHO EATS CHOCOLATE.
HOW REFRESHING.
LIP GLOSS
HA HA HA HA

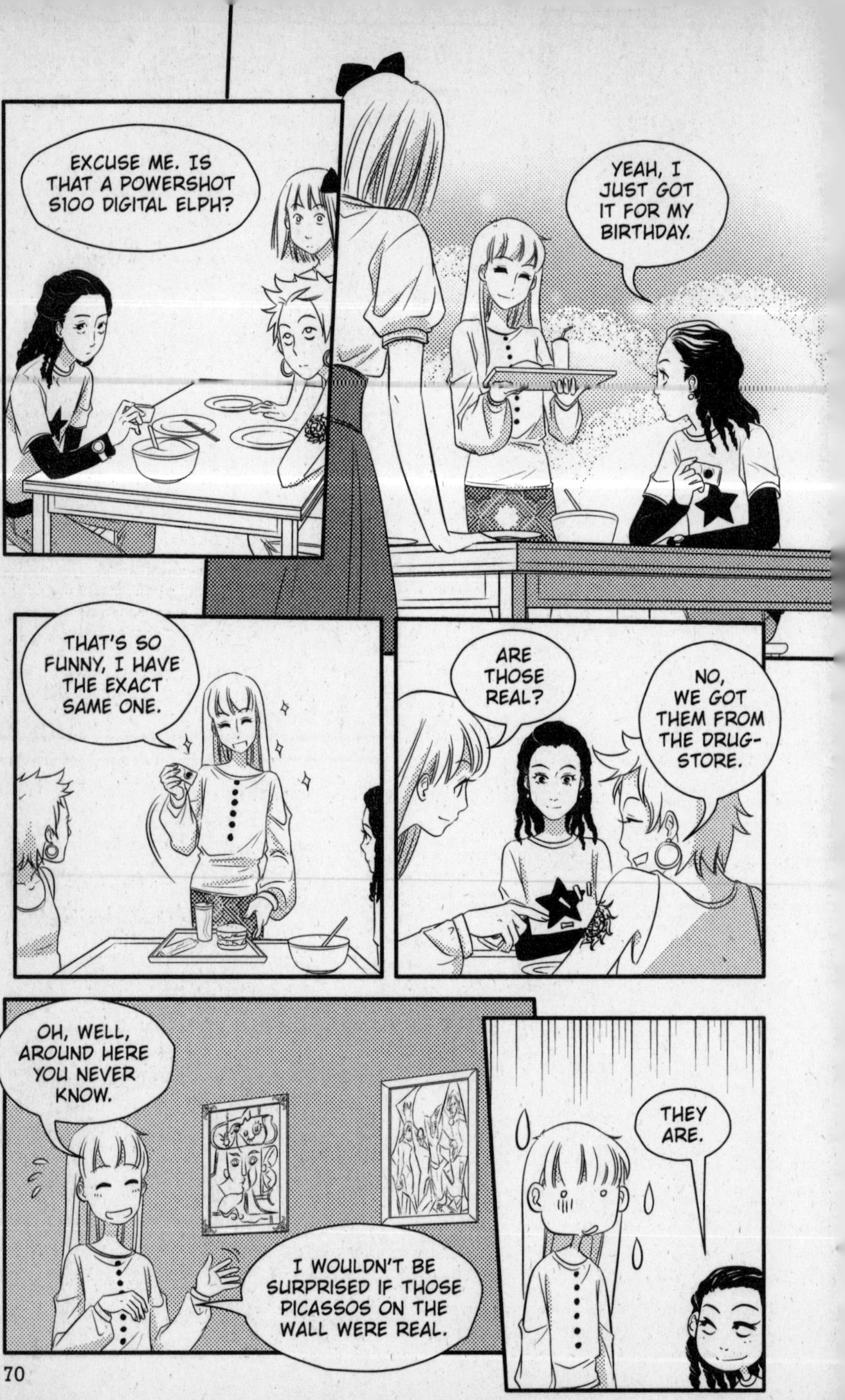
EXCUSE ME. IS THAT A POWERSHOT S100 DIGITAL ELPH?
YEAH, I JUST GOT IT FOR MY BIRTHDAY.
THAT'S SO FUNNY, I HAVE THE EXACT SAME ONE.
ARE THOSE REAL?
NO, WE GOT THEM FROM THE DRUG-STORE.
OH, WELL, AROUND HERE YOU NEVER KNOW.
I WOULDN'T BE SURPRISED IF THOSE PICASSOS ON THE WALL WERE REAL.
THEY ARE.

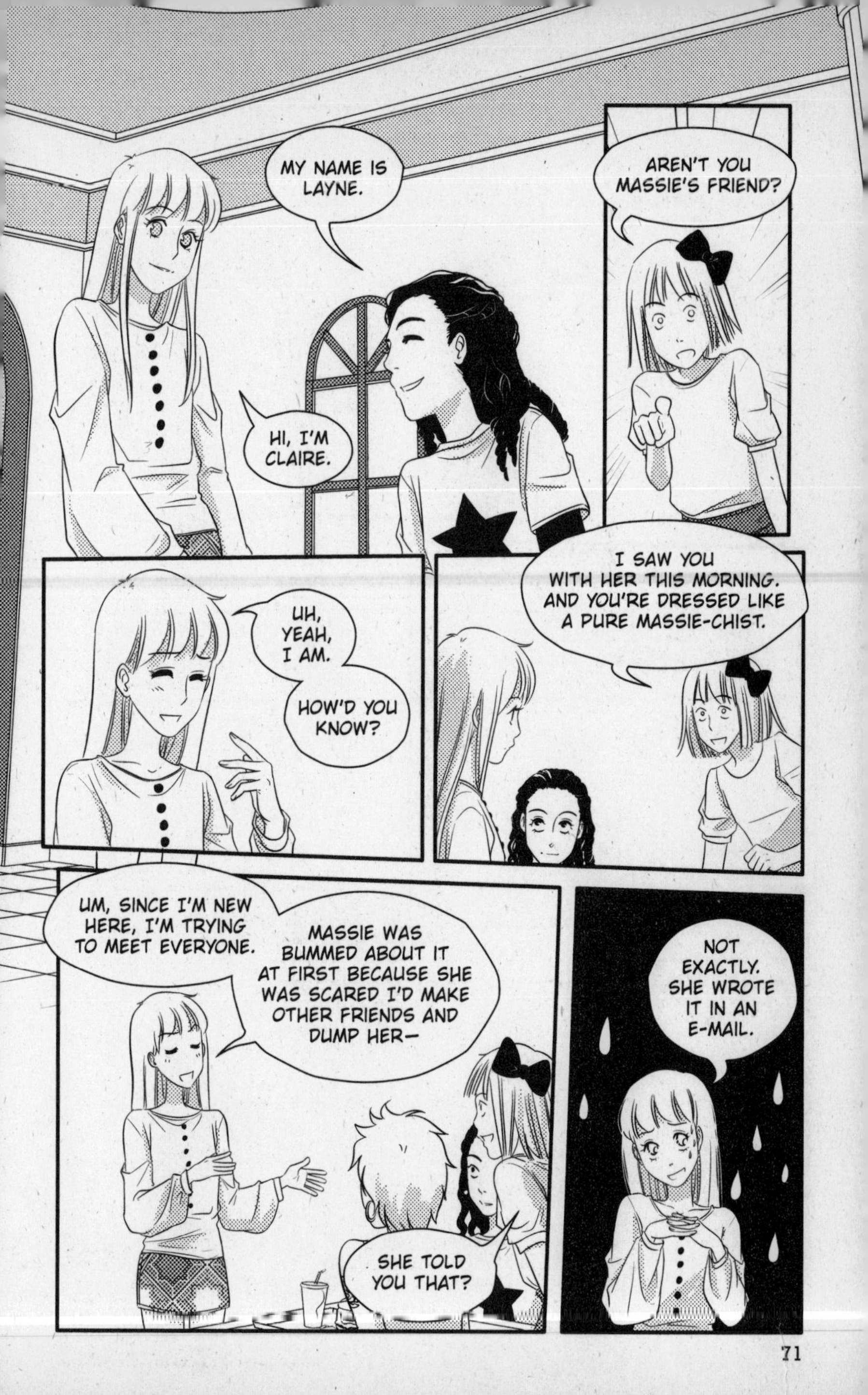
MY NAME IS LAYNE.
HI, I'M CLAIRE.
AREN'T YOU MASSIE'S FRIEND?
UH, YEAH, I AM.
HOW'D YOU KNOW?
I SAW YOU WITH HER THIS MORNING. AND YOU'RE DRESSED LIKE A PURE MASSIE-CHIST.
UM, SINCE I'M NEW HERE, I'M TRYING TO MEET EVERYONE.
MASSIE WAS BUMMED ABOUT IT AT FIRST BECAUSE SHE WAS SCARED I'D MAKE OTHER FRIENDS AND DUMP HER—
SHE TOLD YOU THAT?
NOT EXACTLY. SHE WROTE IT IN AN E-MAIL.

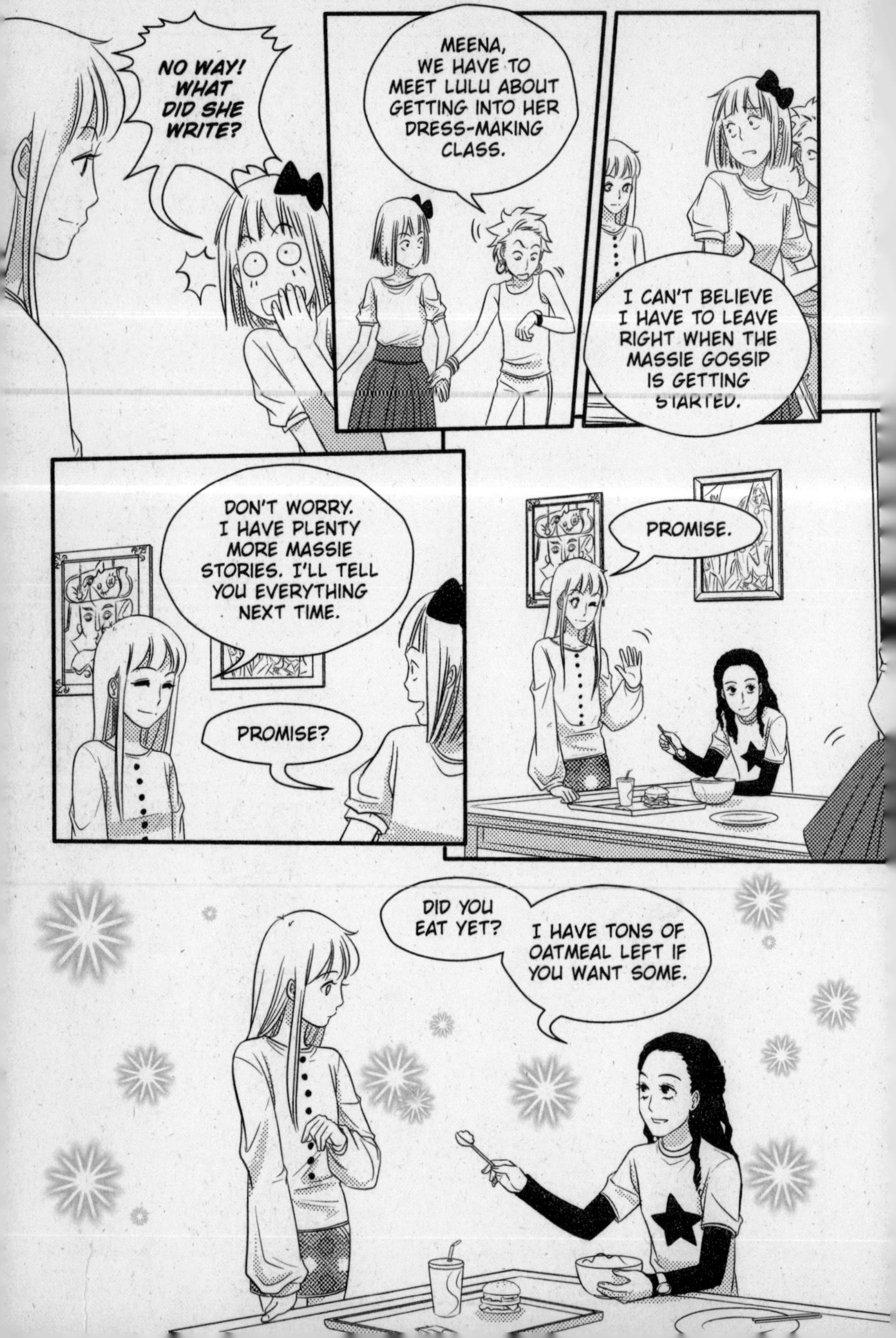
NO WAY! WHAT DID SHE WRITE?
MEENA, WE HAVE TO MEET LULU ABOUT GETTING INTO HER DRESS-MAKING CLASS.
I CAN'T BELIEVE I HAVE TO LEAVE RIGHT WHEN THE MASSIE GOSSIP IS GETTING STARTED.
DON'T WORRY. I HAVE PLENTY MORE MASSIE STORIES. I'LL TELL YOU EVERYTHING NEXT TIME.
PROMISE?
PROMISE.
DID YOU EAT YET?
I HAVE TONS OF OATMEAL LEFT IF YOU WANT SOME.

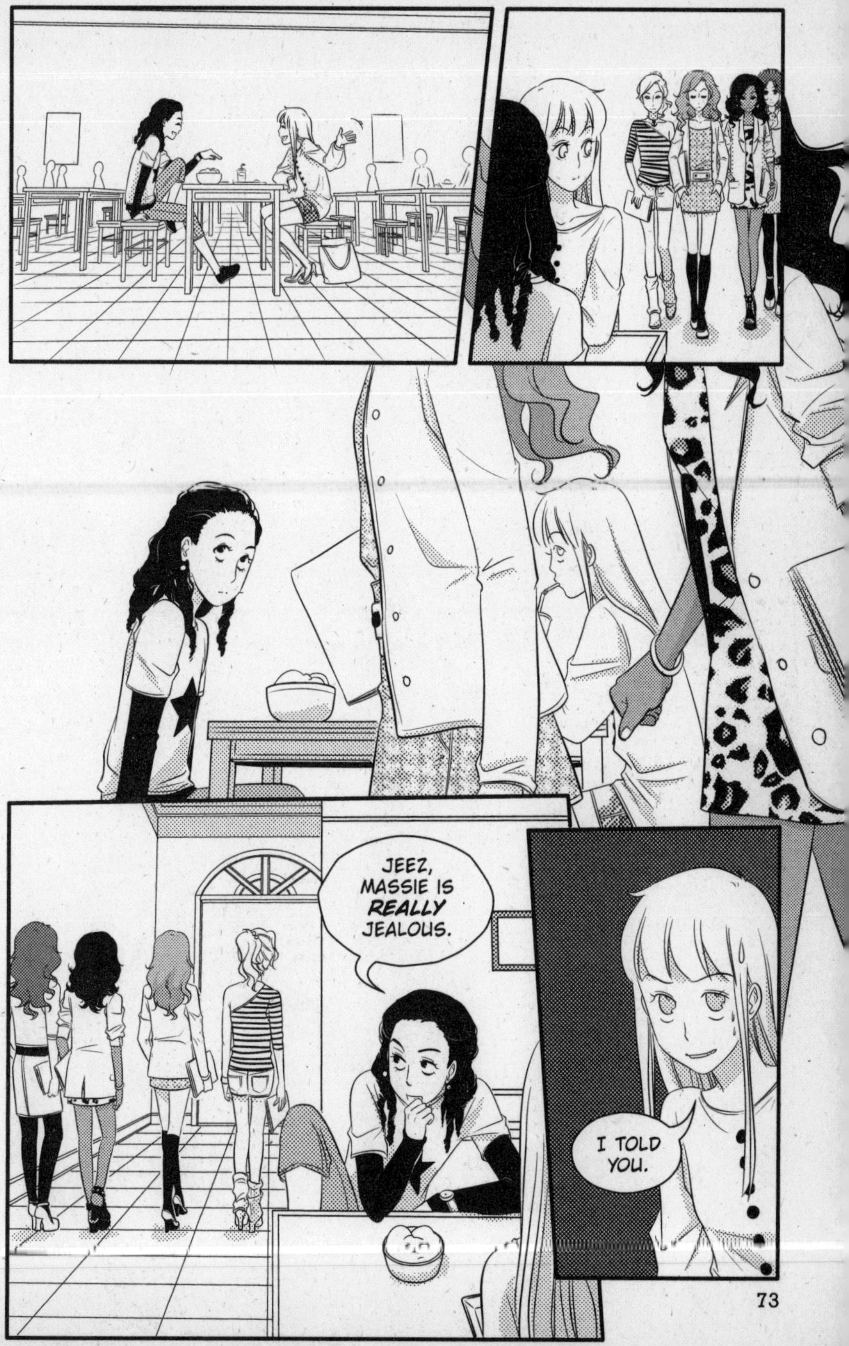
JEEZ, MASSIE IS *REALLY* JEALOUS.
I TOLD YOU.

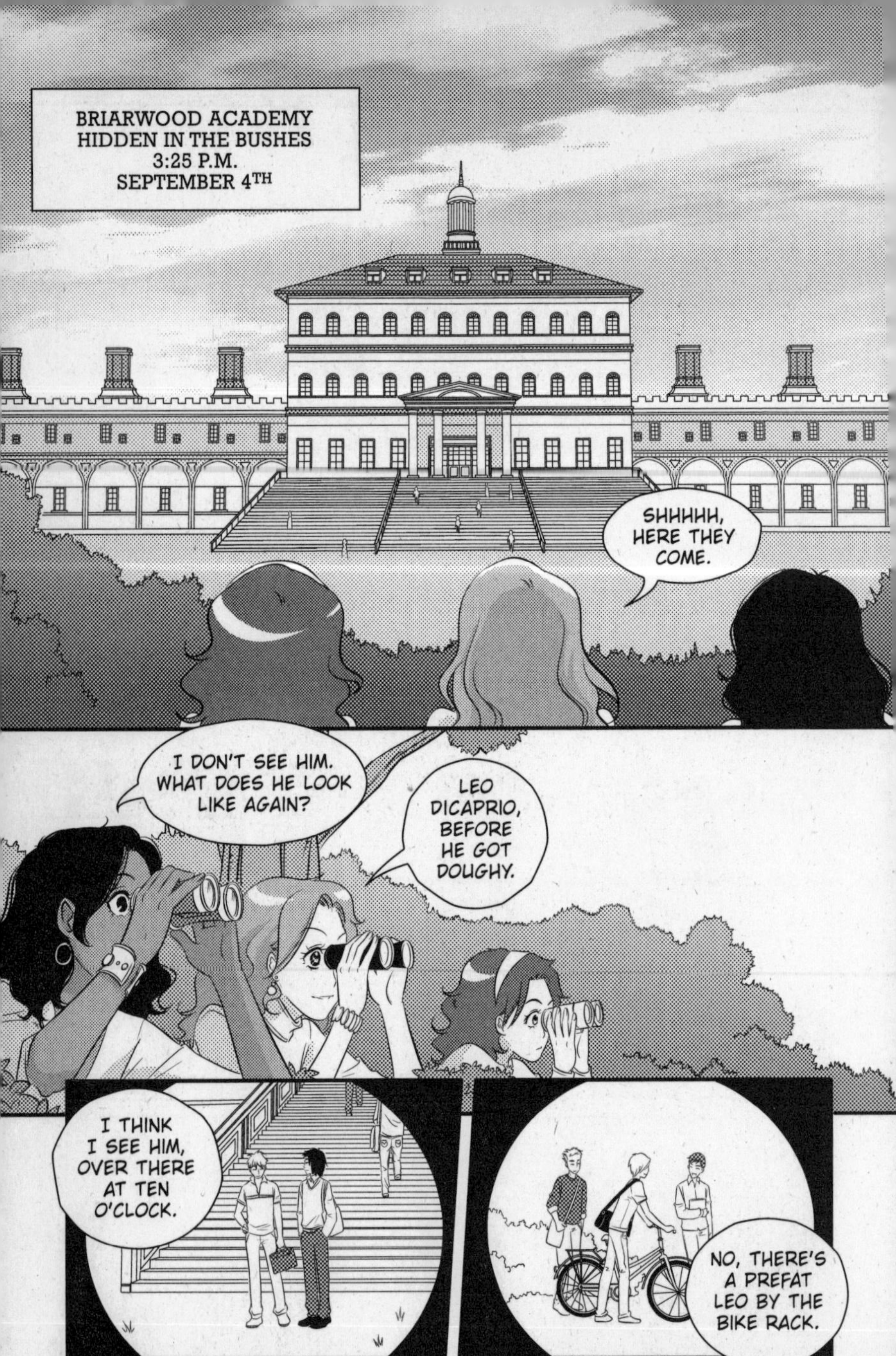
BRIARWOOD ACADEMY
HIDDEN IN THE BUSHES
3:25 P.M.
SEPTEMBER 4TH
SHHHHH, HERE THEY COME.
I DON'T SEE HIM. WHAT DOES HE LOOK LIKE AGAIN?
LEO DICAPRIO, BEFORE HE GOT DOUGHY.
I THINK I SEE HIM, OVER THERE AT TEN O'CLOCK.
NO, THERE'S A PREFAT LEO BY THE BIKE RACK.

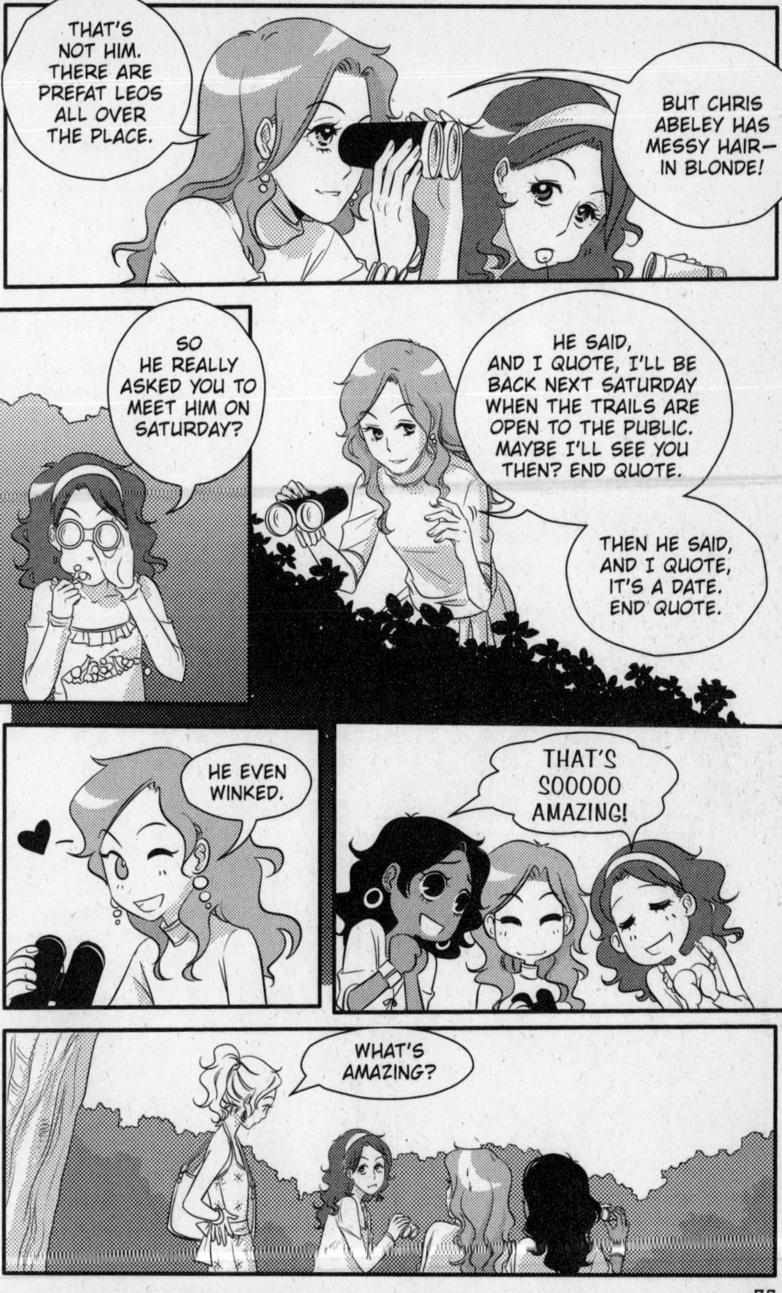
THAT'S NOT HIM. THERE ARE PREFAT LEOS ALL OVER THE PLACE.
BUT CHRIS ABELEY HAS MESSY HAIR—IN BLONDE!
SO HE REALLY ASKED YOU TO MEET HIM ON SATURDAY?
HE SAID, AND I QUOTE, I'LL BE BACK NEXT SATURDAY WHEN THE TRAILS ARE OPEN TO THE PUBLIC. MAYBE I'LL SEE YOU THEN? END QUOTE.
THEN HE SAID, AND I QUOTE, IT'S A DATE. END QUOTE.
HE EVEN WINKED.
THAT'S SOOOOO AMAZING!
WHAT'S AMAZING?

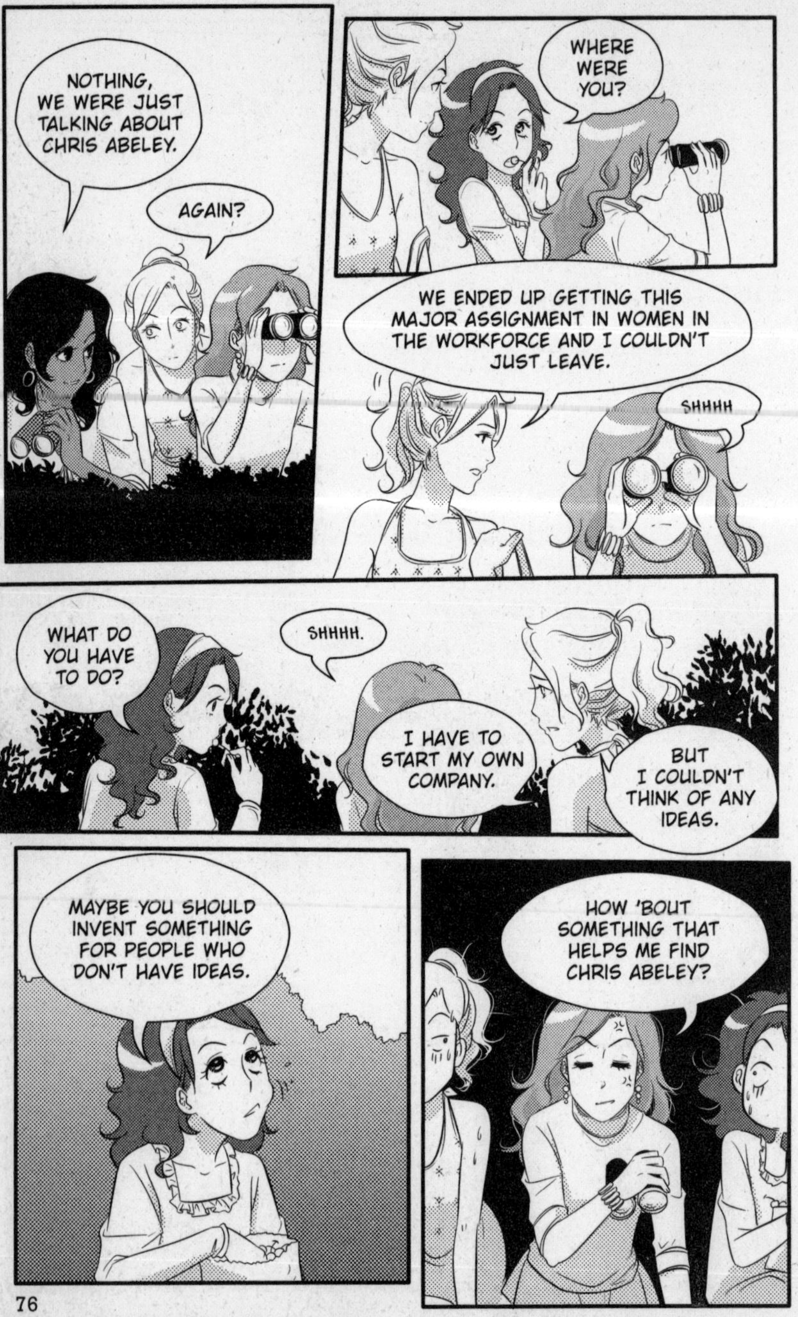
NOTHING, WE WERE JUST TALKING ABOUT CHRIS ABELEY.
AGAIN?
WHERE WERE YOU?
WE ENDED UP GETTING THIS MAJOR ASSIGNMENT IN WOMEN IN THE WORKFORCE AND I COULDN'T JUST LEAVE.
SHHHH
WHAT DO YOU HAVE TO DO?
SHHHH.
I HAVE TO START MY OWN COMPANY.
BUT I COULDN'T THINK OF ANY IDEAS.
MAYBE YOU SHOULD INVENT SOMETHING FOR PEOPLE WHO DON'T HAVE IDEAS.
HOW 'BOUT SOMETHING THAT HELPS ME FIND CHRIS ABELEY?

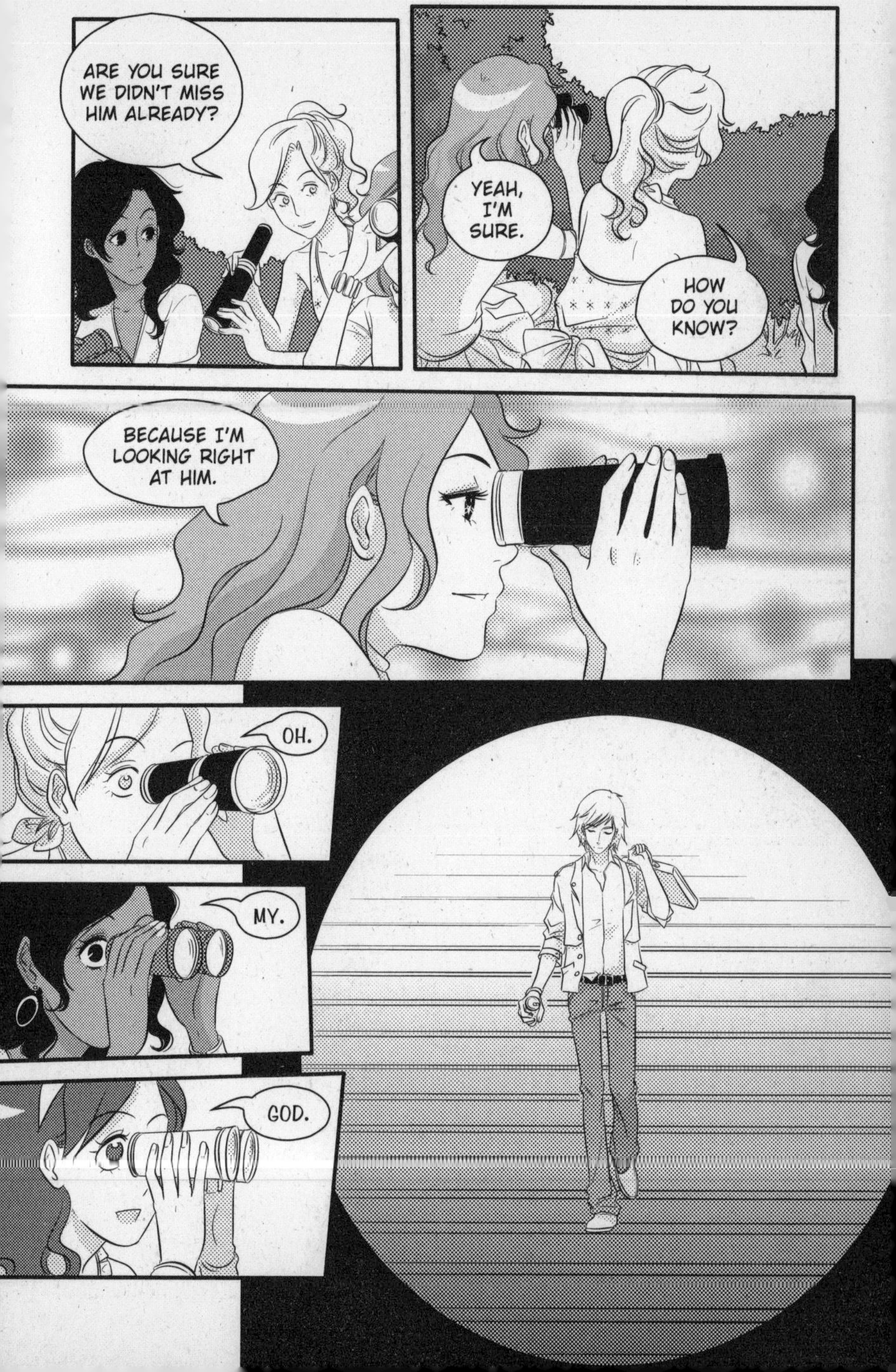
ARE YOU SURE WE DIDN'T MISS HIM ALREADY?
YEAH, I'M SURE.
HOW DO YOU KNOW?
BECAUSE I'M LOOKING RIGHT AT HIM.
OH.
MY.
GOD.

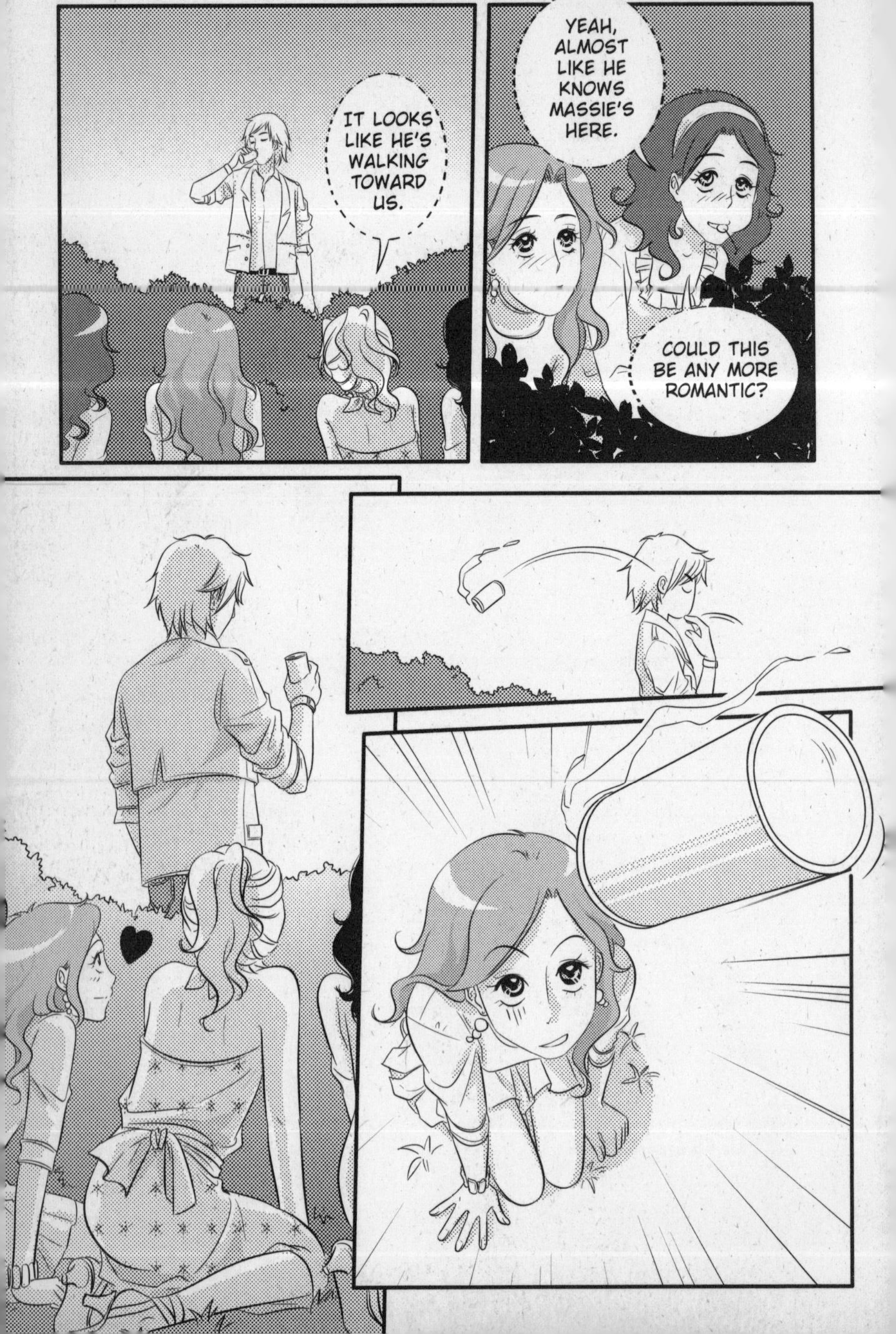
IT LOOKS LIKE HE'S WALKING TOWARD US.
YEAH, ALMOST LIKE HE KNOWS MASSIE'S HERE.
COULD THIS BE ANY MORE ROMANTIC?

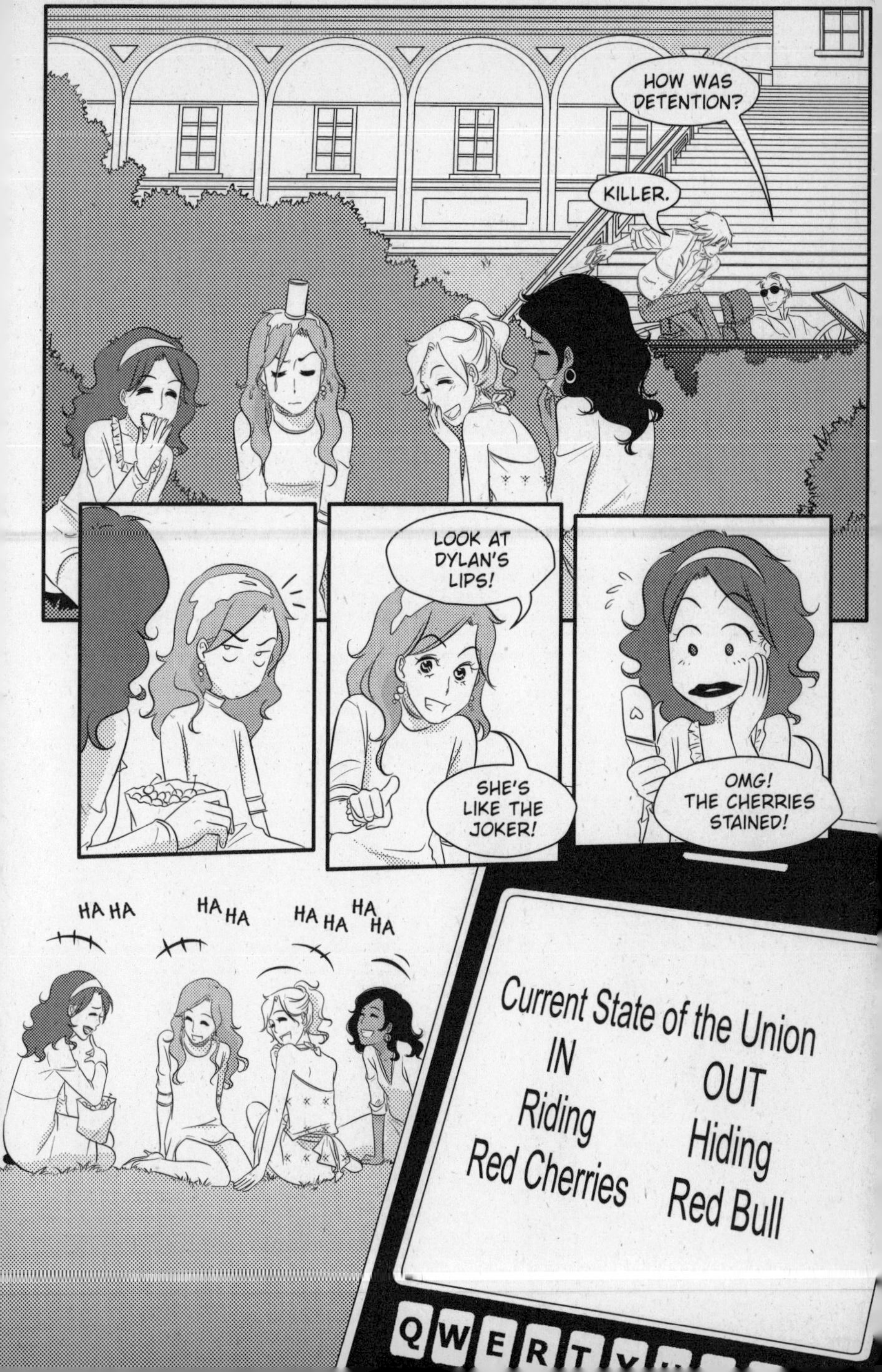
HOW WAS DETENTION?
KILLER.
LOOK AT DYLAN'S LIPS!
SHE'S LIKE THE JOKER!
OMG! THE CHERRIES STAINED!
HA HA
HA HA
HA HA
HA HA
Current State of the Union
IN
OUT
Riding
Hiding
Red Cherries
Red Bull
QWERTY

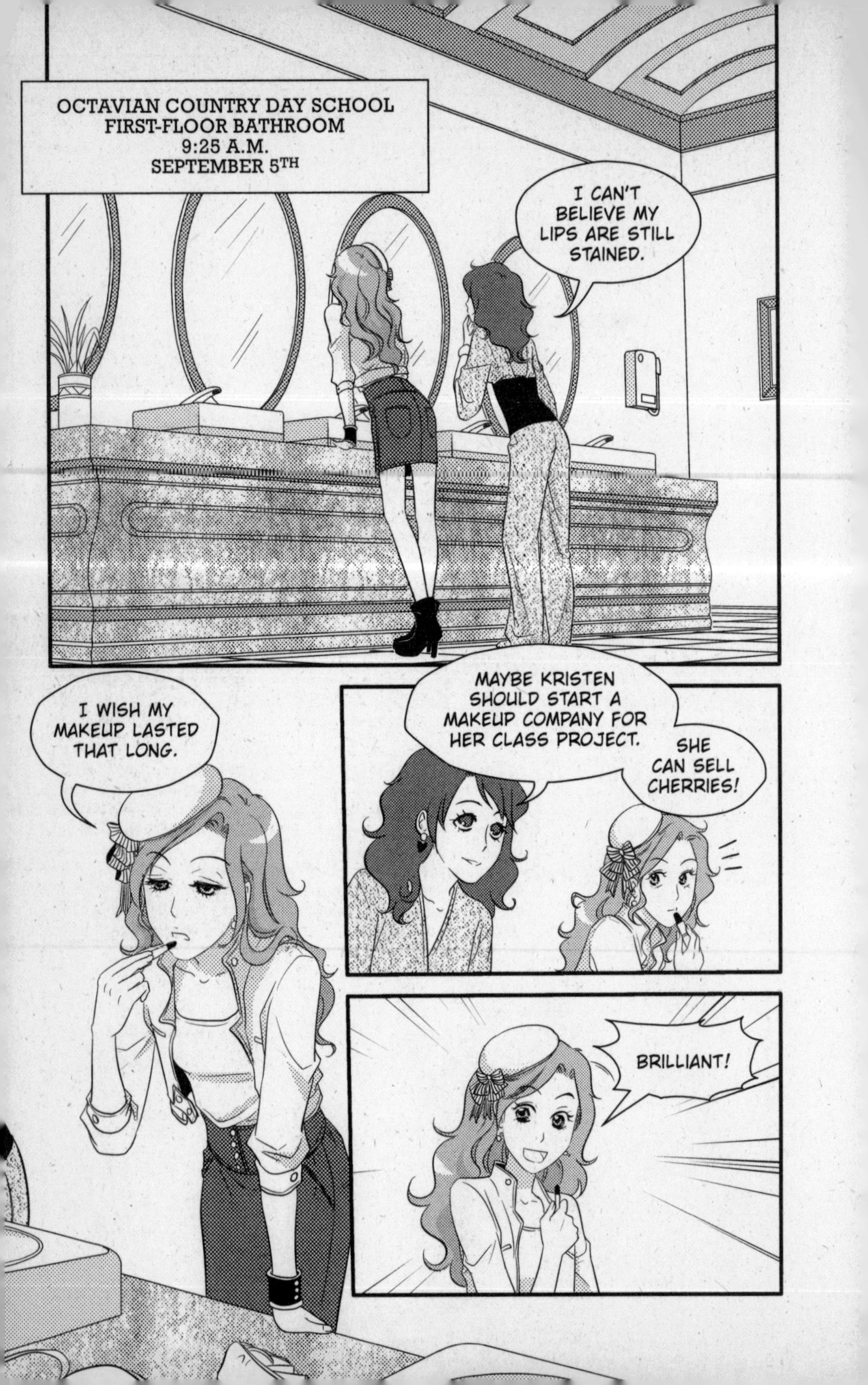
OCTAVIAN COUNTRY DAY SCHOOL
FIRST-FLOOR BATHROOM
9:25 A.M.
SEPTEMBER 5TH
I CAN'T BELIEVE MY LIPS ARE STILL STAINED.
I WISH MY MAKEUP LASTED THAT LONG.
MAYBE KRISTEN SHOULD START A MAKEUP COMPANY FOR HER CLASS PROJECT.
SHE CAN SELL CHERRIES!
BRILLIANT!

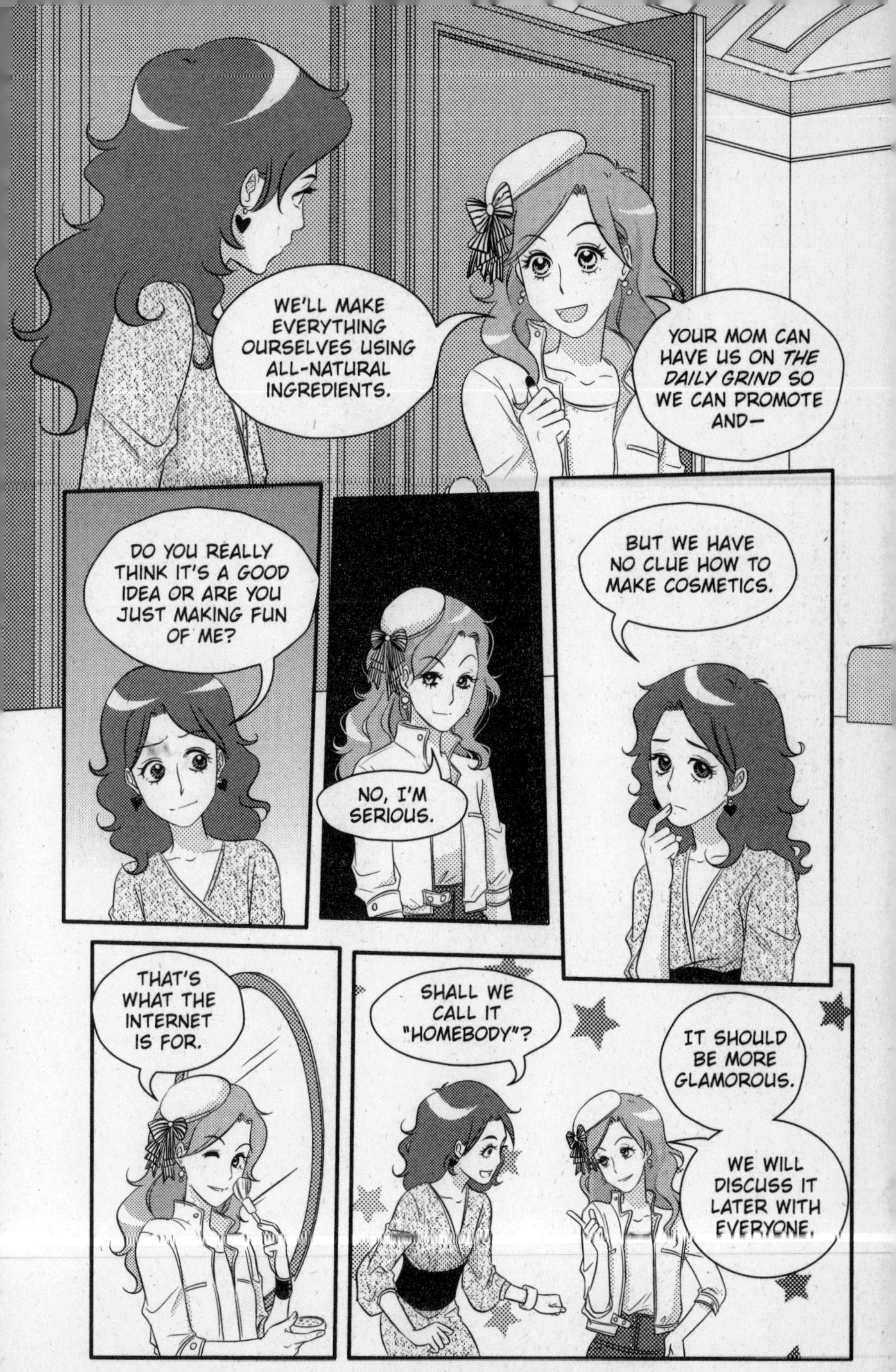
WE'LL MAKE EVERYTHING OURSELVES USING ALL-NATURAL INGREDIENTS.
YOUR MOM CAN HAVE US ON *THE DAILY GRIND* SO WE CAN PROMOTE AND—
DO YOU REALLY THINK IT'S A GOOD IDEA OR ARE YOU JUST MAKING FUN OF ME?
NO, I'M SERIOUS.
BUT WE HAVE NO CLUE HOW TO MAKE COSMETICS.
THAT'S WHAT THE INTERNET IS FOR.
SHALL WE CALL IT "HOMEBODY"?
IT SHOULD BE MORE GLAMOROUS.
WE WILL DISCUSS IT LATER WITH EVERYONE.

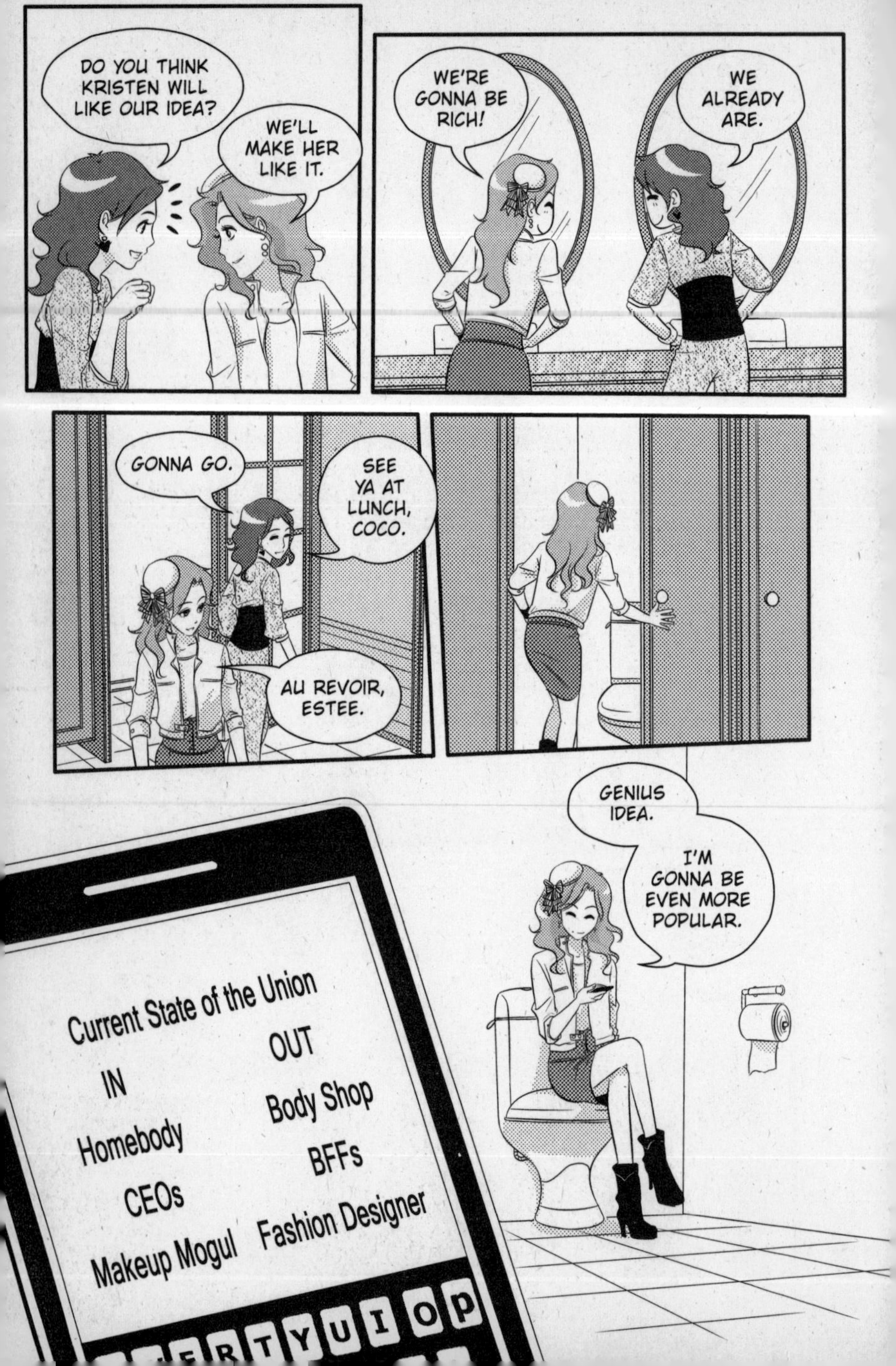
DO YOU THINK KRISTEN WILL LIKE OUR IDEA?
WE'LL MAKE HER LIKE IT.
WE'RE GONNA BE RICH!
WE ALREADY ARE.
GONNA GO.
SEE YA AT LUNCH, COCO.
AU REVOIR, ESTEE.
GENIUS IDEA.
I'M GONNA BE EVEN MORE POPULAR.
Current State of the Union
IN
OUT
Homebody
Body Shop
CEOs
BFFs
Makeup Mogul
Fashion Designer
R T Y U I O P

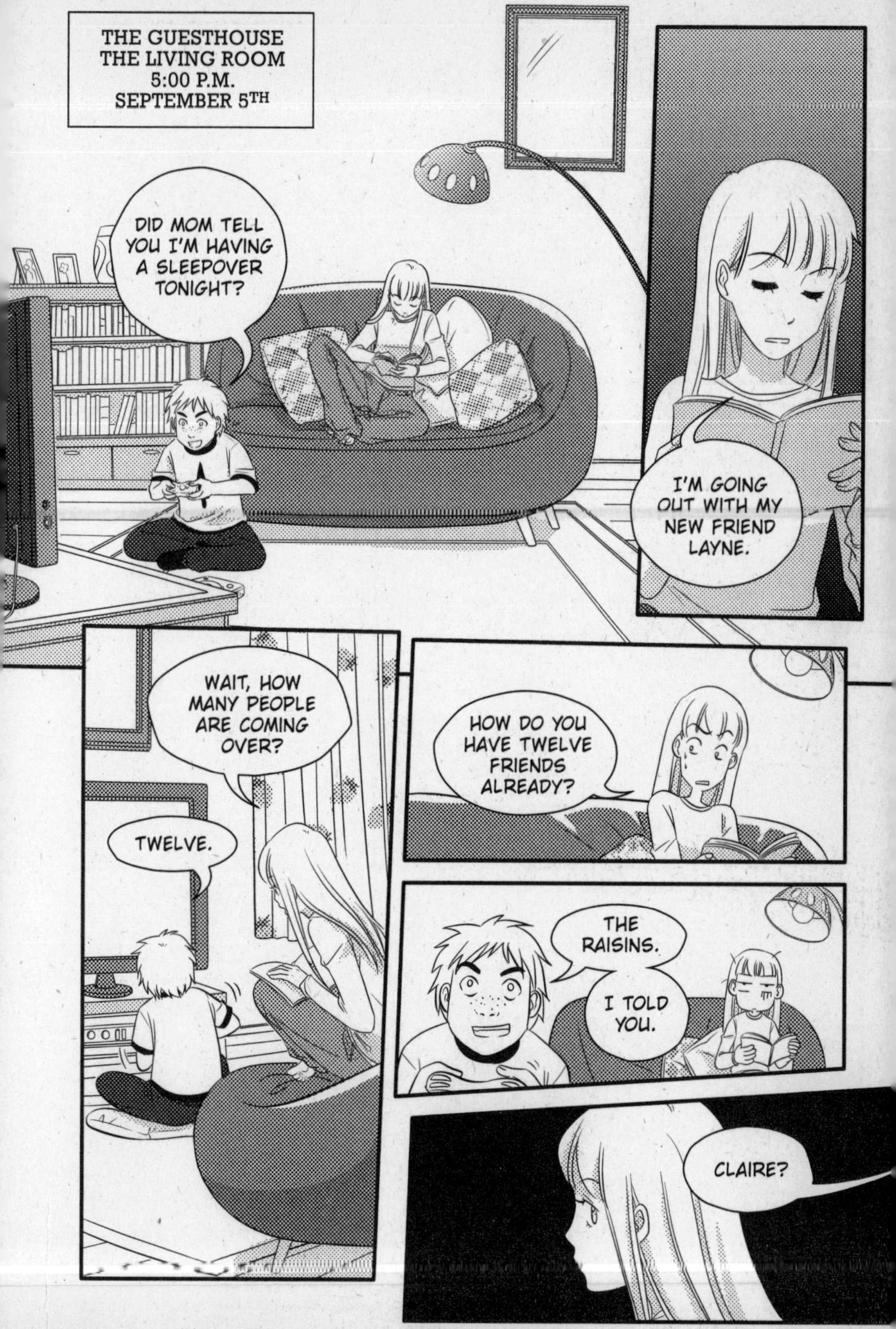
THE GUESTHOUSE
THE LIVING ROOM
5:00 P.M.
SEPTEMBER 5TH
DID MOM TELL YOU I'M HAVING A SLEEPOVER TONIGHT?
I'M GOING OUT WITH MY NEW FRIEND LAYNE.
WAIT, HOW MANY PEOPLE ARE COMING OVER?
TWELVE.
HOW DO YOU HAVE TWELVE FRIENDS ALREADY?
THE RAISINS.
I TOLD YOU.
CLAIRE?

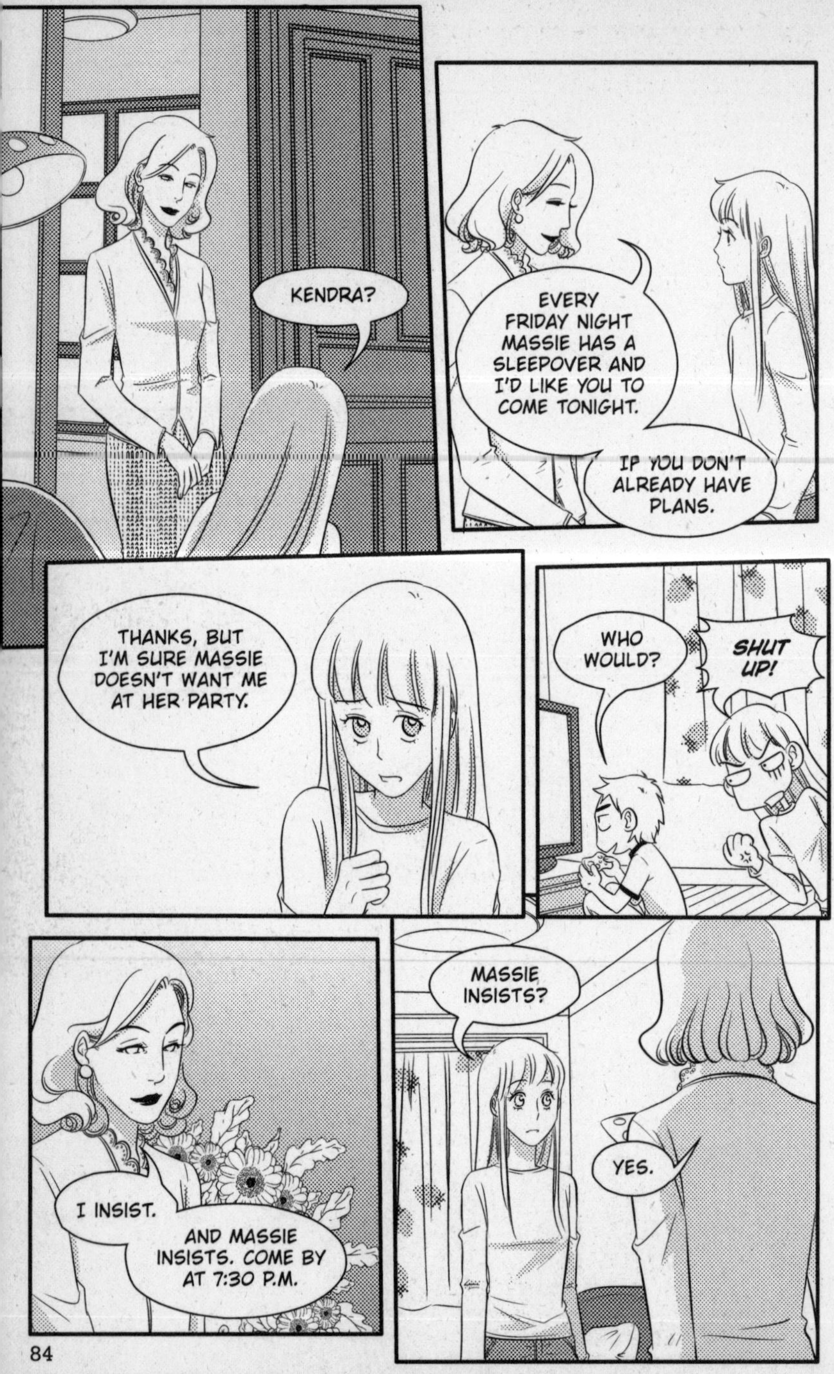
KENDRA?
EVERY FRIDAY NIGHT MASSIE HAS A SLEEPOVER AND I'D LIKE YOU TO COME TONIGHT.
IF YOU DON'T ALREADY HAVE PLANS.
THANKS, BUT I'M SURE MASSIE DOESN'T WANT ME AT HER PARTY.
WHO WOULD?
SHUT UP!
I INSIST.
AND MASSIE INSISTS. COME BY AT 7:30 P.M.
MASSIE INSISTS?
YES.

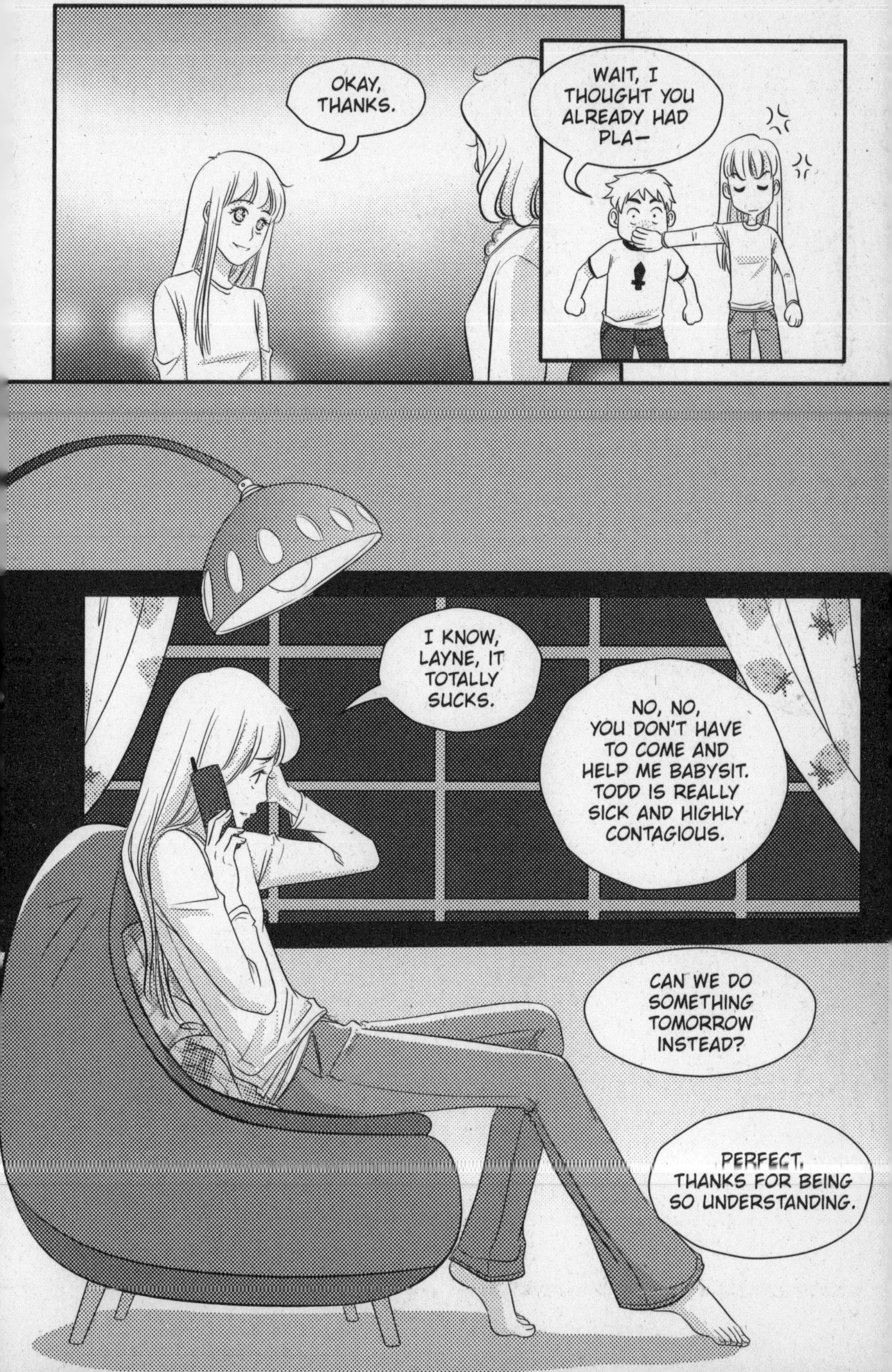
OKAY, THANKS.
WAIT, I THOUGHT YOU ALREADY HAD PLA—
I KNOW, LAYNE, IT TOTALLY SUCKS.
NO, NO, YOU DON'T HAVE TO COME AND HELP ME BABYSIT. TODD IS REALLY SICK AND HIGHLY CONTAGIOUS.
CAN WE DO SOMETHING TOMORROW INSTEAD?
PERFECT. THANKS FOR BEING SO UNDERSTANDING.

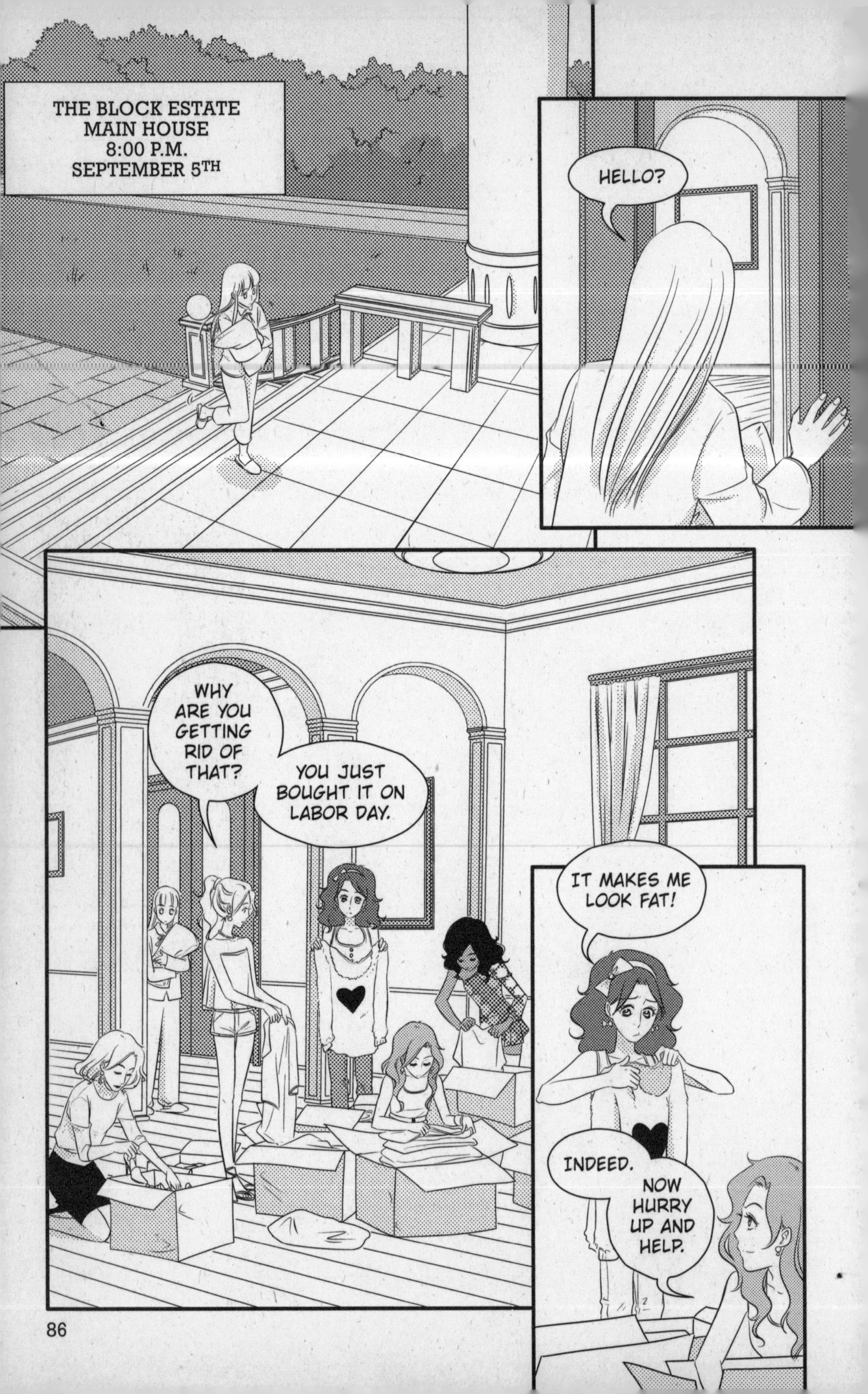

THE BLOCK ESTATE MAIN HOUSE 8:00 P.M. SEPTEMBER 5TH
HELLO?
WHY ARE YOU GETTING RID OF THAT?
YOU JUST BOUGHT IT ON LABOR DAY.
IT MAKES ME LOOK FAT!
INDEED.
NOW HURRY UP AND HELP.

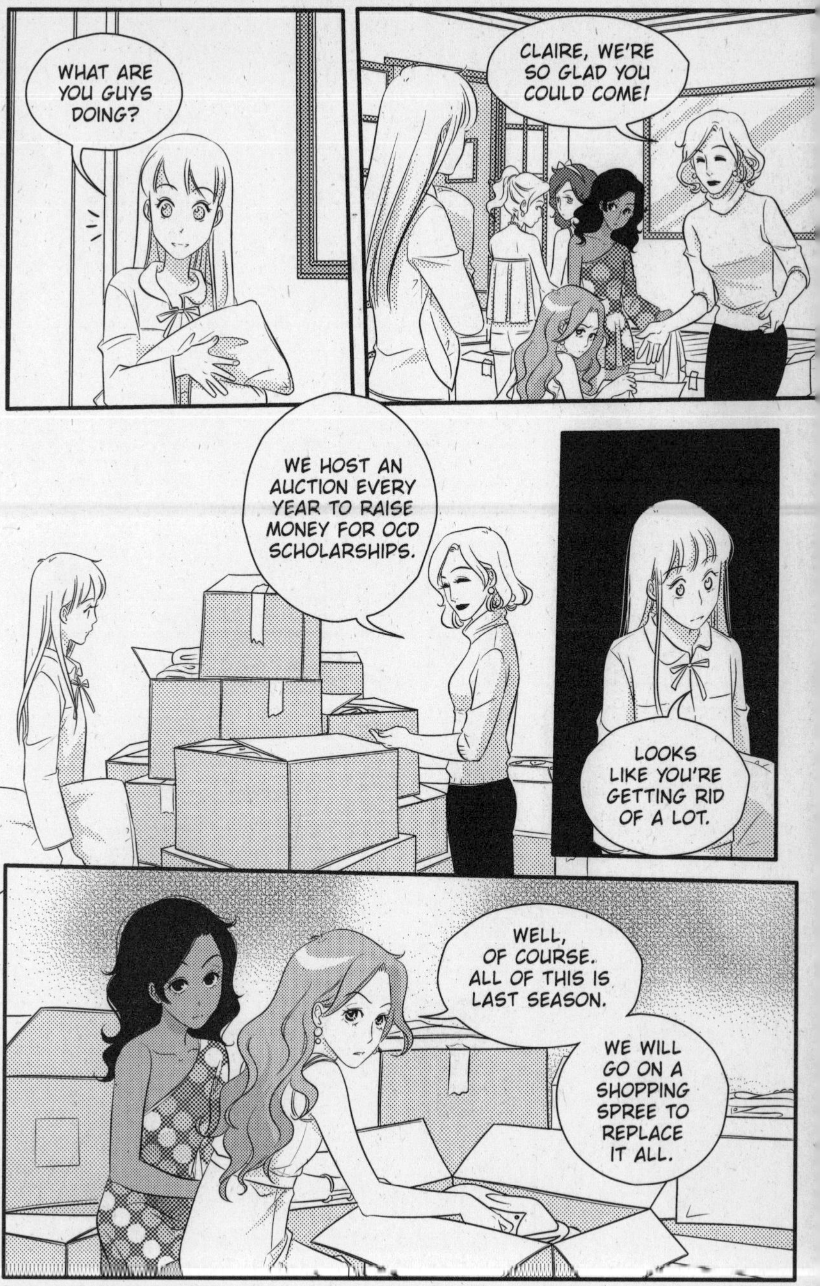
WHAT ARE YOU GUYS DOING?
CLAIRE, WE'RE SO GLAD YOU COULD COME!
WE HOST AN AUCTION EVERY YEAR TO RAISE MONEY FOR OCD SCHOLARSHIPS.
LOOKS LIKE YOU'RE GETTING RID OF A LOT.
WELL, OF COURSE. ALL OF THIS IS LAST SEASON.
WE WILL GO ON A SHOPPING SPREE TO REPLACE IT ALL.

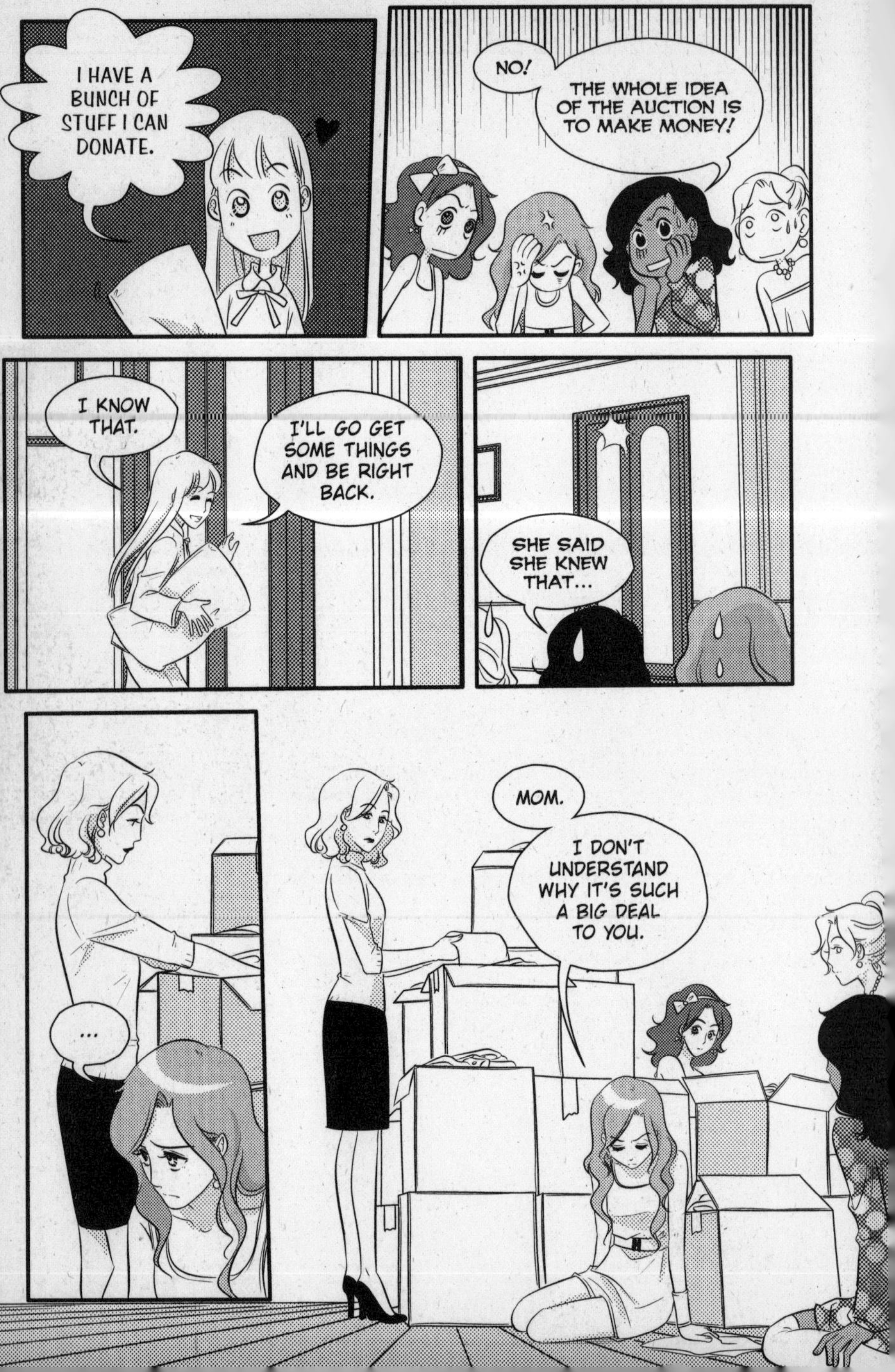
I HAVE A BUNCH OF STUFF I CAN DONATE.
NO!
THE WHOLE IDEA OF THE AUCTION IS TO MAKE MONEY!
I KNOW THAT.
I'LL GO GET SOME THINGS AND BE RIGHT BACK.
SHE SAID SHE KNEW THAT...
...
MOM.
I DON'T UNDERSTAND WHY IT'S SUCH A BIG DEAL TO YOU.

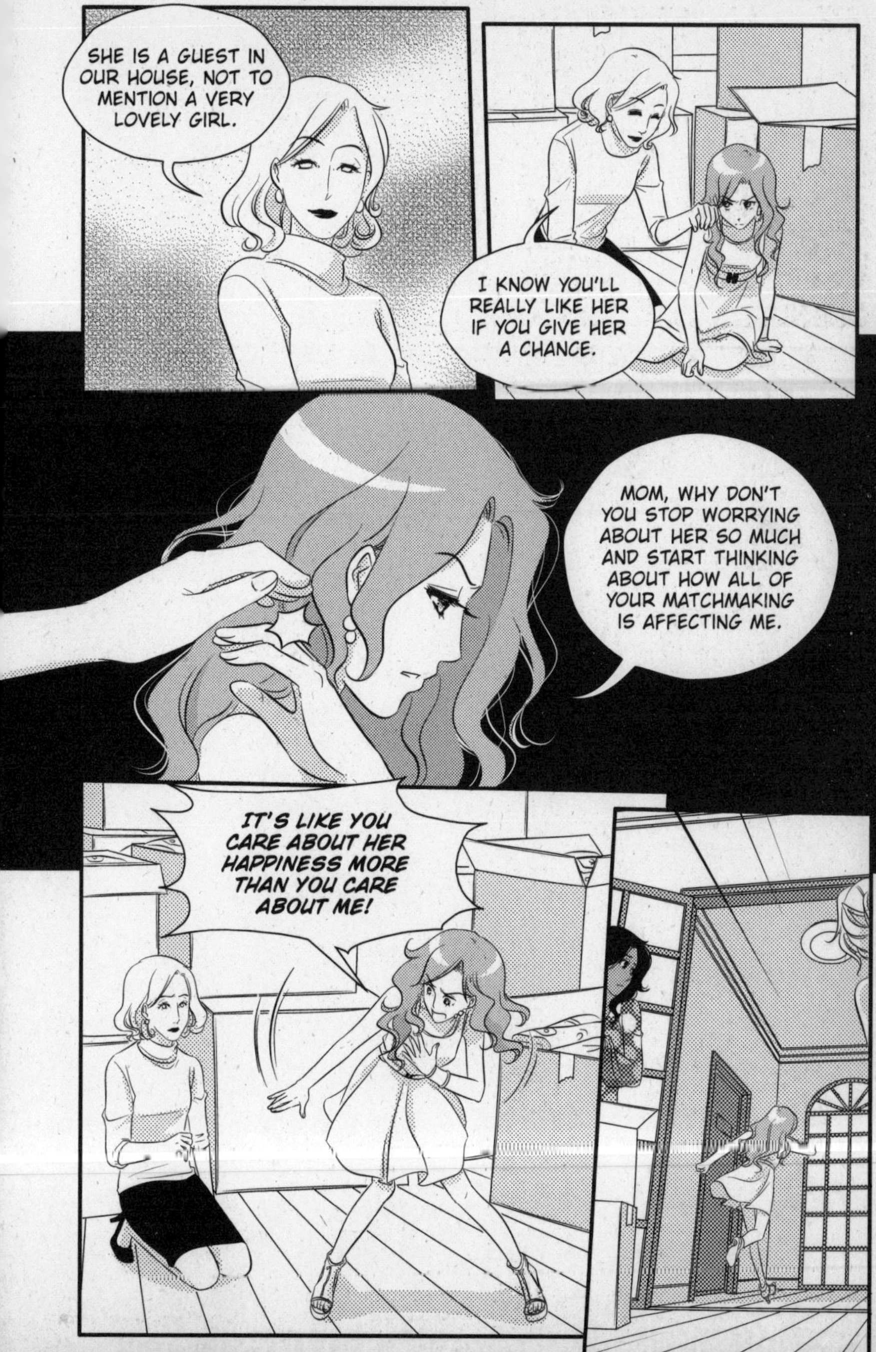
SHE IS A GUEST IN OUR HOUSE, NOT TO MENTION A VERY LOVELY GIRL.
I KNOW YOU'LL REALLY LIKE HER IF YOU GIVE HER A CHANCE.
MOM, WHY DON'T YOU STOP WORRYING ABOUT HER SO MUCH AND START THINKING ABOUT HOW ALL OF YOUR MATCHMAKING IS AFFECTING ME.
IT'S LIKE YOU CARE ABOUT HER HAPPINESS MORE THAN YOU CARE ABOUT ME!

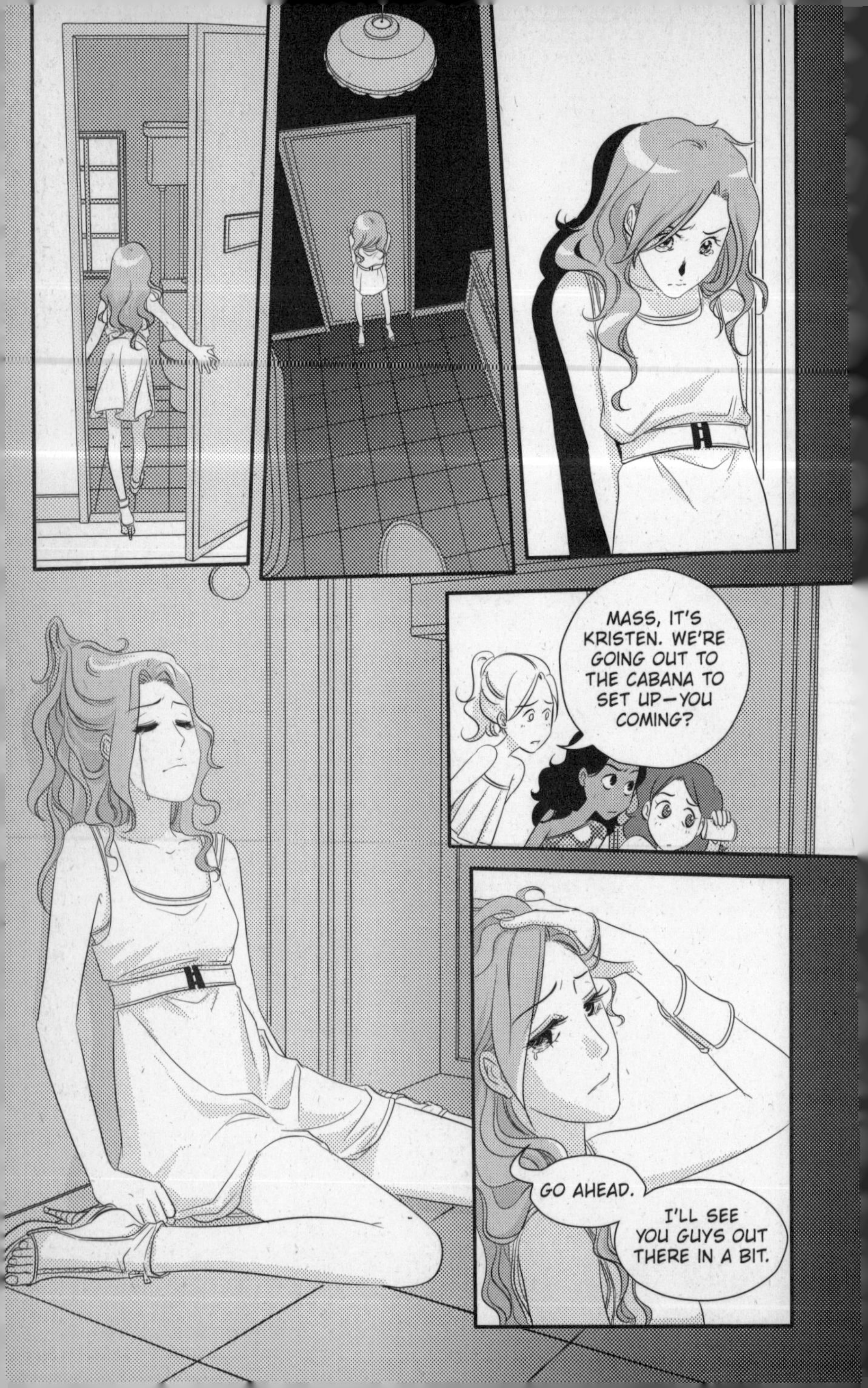
MASS, IT'S KRISTEN. WE'RE GOING OUT TO THE CABANA TO SET UP—YOU COMING?
GO AHEAD.
I'LL SEE YOU GUYS OUT THERE IN A BIT.

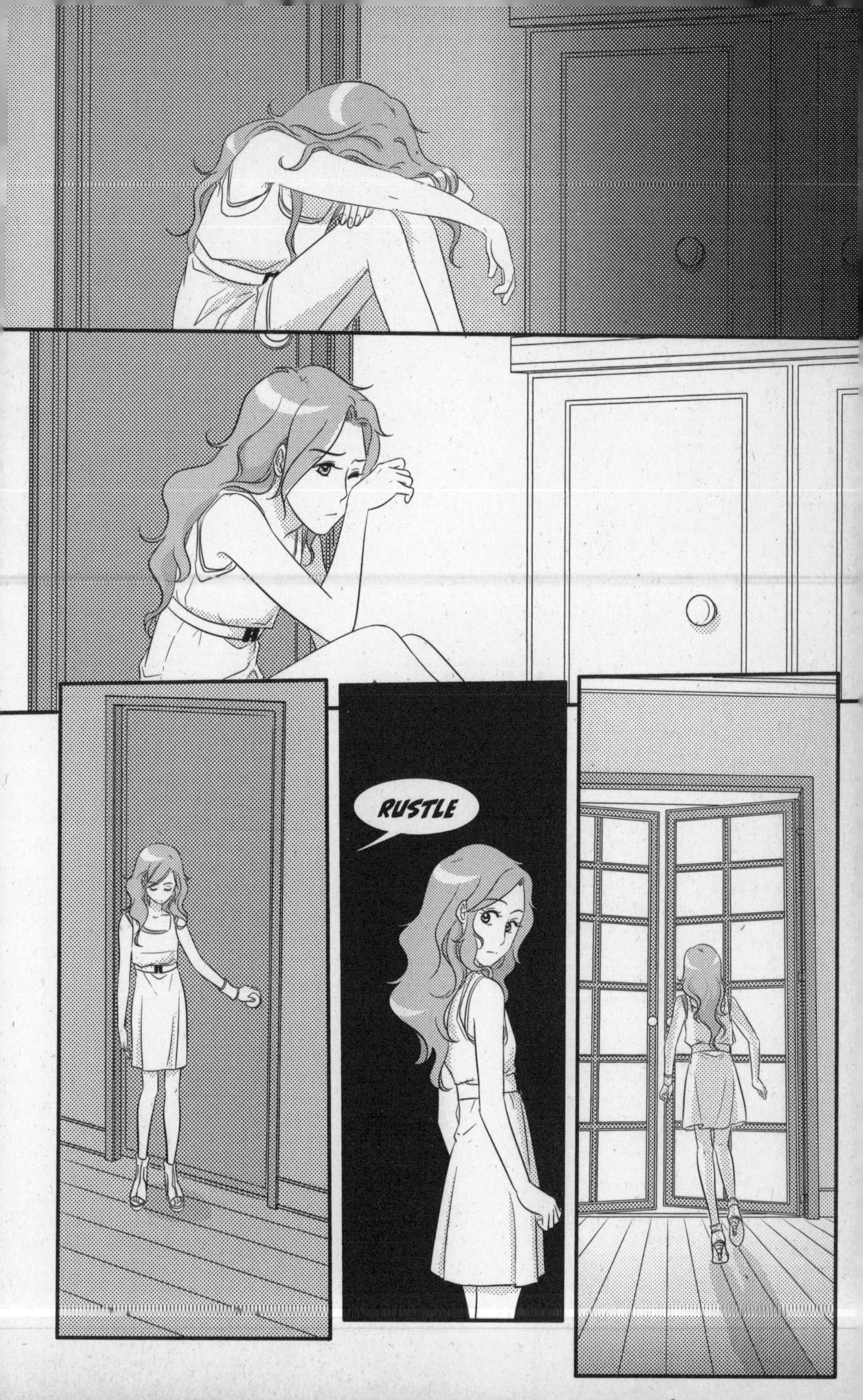
RUSTLE

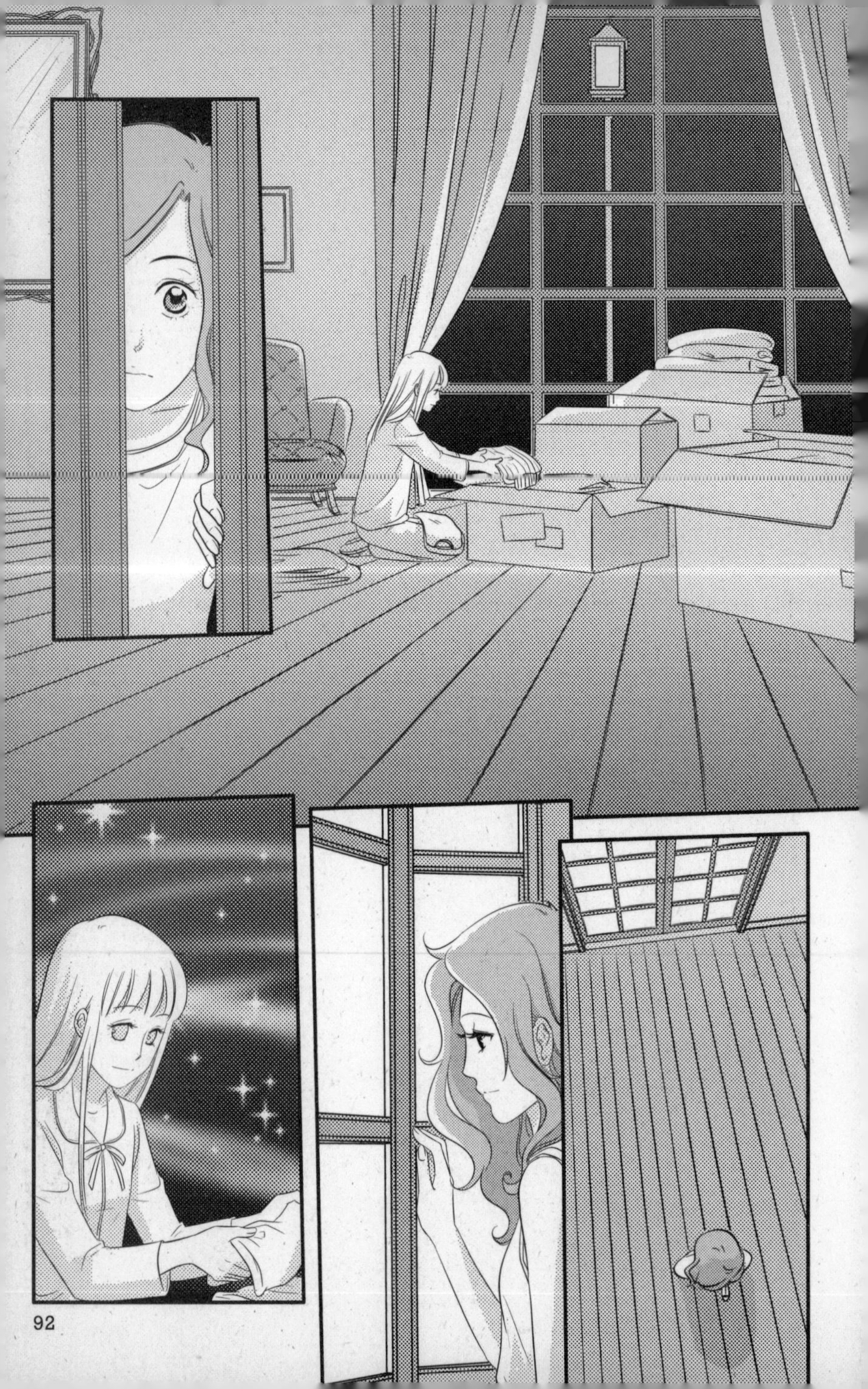

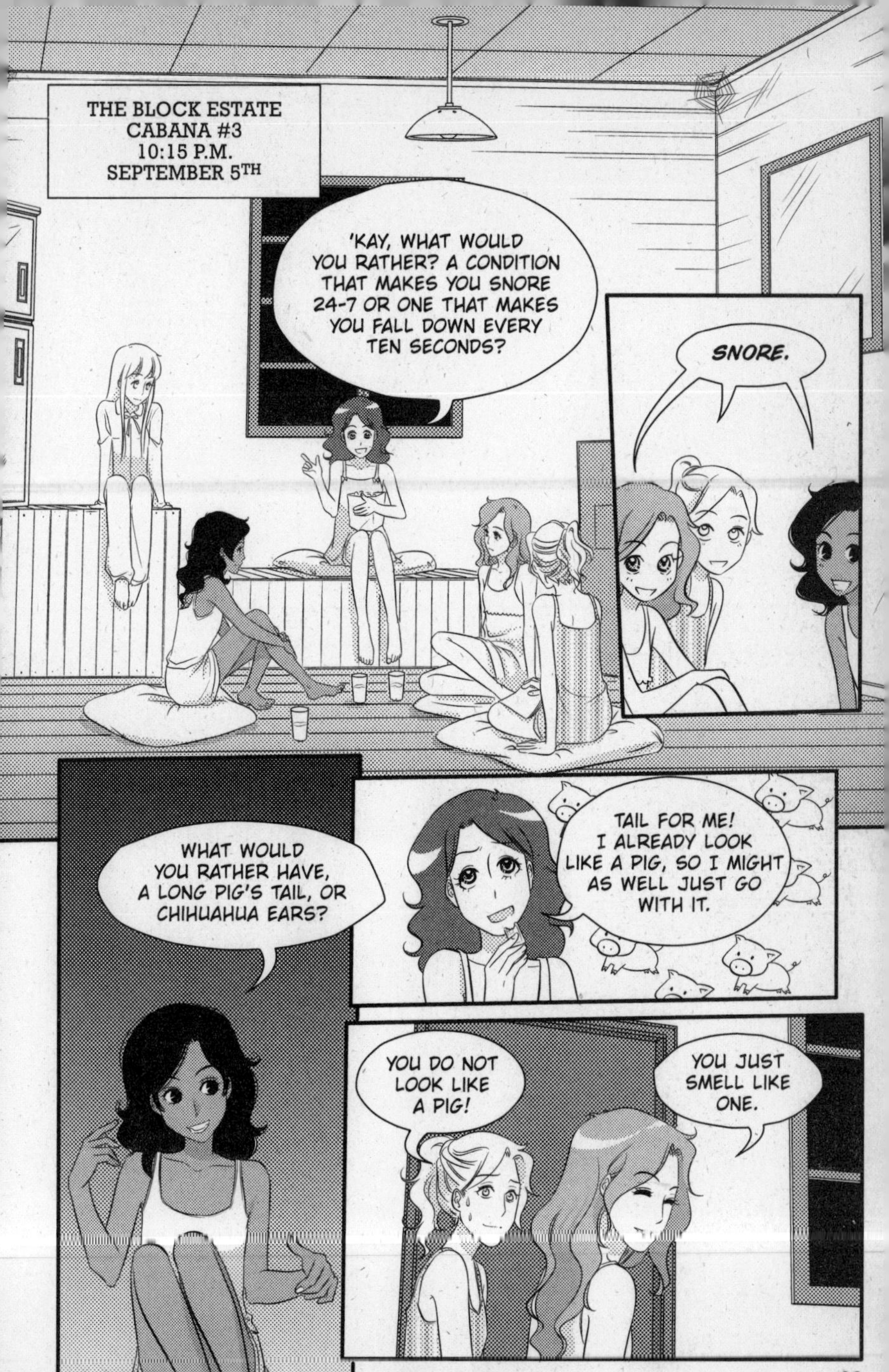
THE BLOCK ESTATE CABANA #3 10:15 P.M. SEPTEMBER 5TH
'KAY, WHAT WOULD YOU RATHER? A CONDITION THAT MAKES YOU SNORE 24-7 OR ONE THAT MAKES YOU FALL DOWN EVERY TEN SECONDS?
SNORE.
WHAT WOULD YOU RATHER HAVE, A LONG PIG'S TAIL, OR CHIHUAHUA EARS?
TAIL FOR ME! I ALREADY LOOK LIKE A PIG, SO I MIGHT AS WELL JUST GO WITH IT.
YOU DO NOT LOOK LIKE A PIG!
YOU JUST SMELL LIKE ONE.

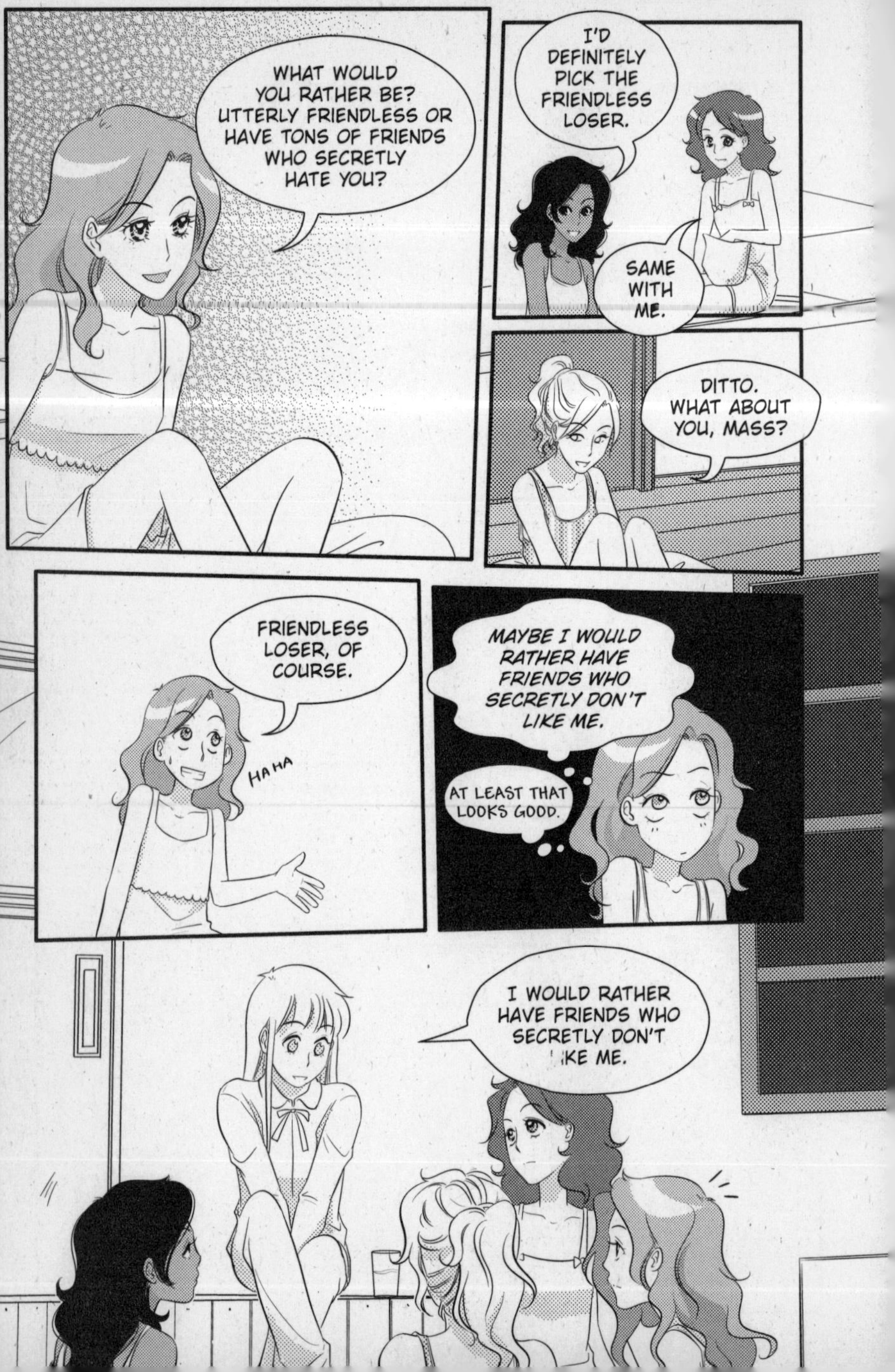
WHAT WOULD YOU RATHER BE? UTTERLY FRIENDLESS OR HAVE TONS OF FRIENDS WHO SECRETLY HATE YOU?
I'D DEFINITELY PICK THE FRIENDLESS LOSER.
SAME WITH ME.
DITTO. WHAT ABOUT YOU, MASS?
FRIENDLESS LOSER, OF COURSE.
HAHA
MAYBE I WOULD RATHER HAVE FRIENDS WHO SECRETLY DON'T LIKE ME.
AT LEAST THAT LOOKS GOOD.
I WOULD RATHER HAVE FRIENDS WHO SECRETLY DON'T KE ME.

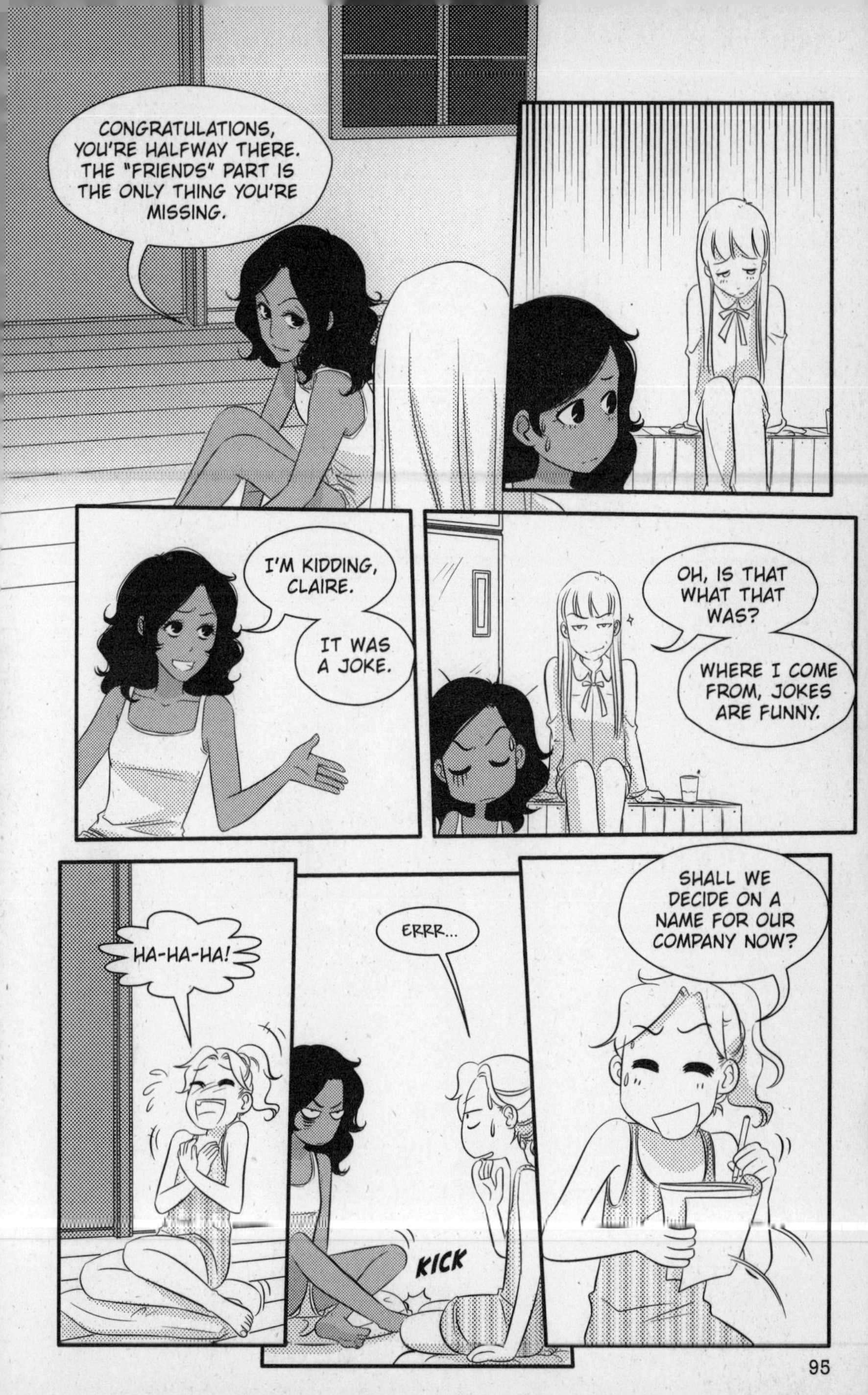

CONGRATULATIONS, YOU'RE HALFWAY THERE. THE "FRIENDS" PART IS THE ONLY THING YOU'RE MISSING.
I'M KIDDING, CLAIRE.
IT WAS A JOKE.
OH, IS THAT WHAT THAT WAS?
WHERE I COME FROM, JOKES ARE FUNNY.
HA-HA-HA!
ERRR...
KICK
SHALL WE DECIDE ON A NAME FOR OUR COMPANY NOW?

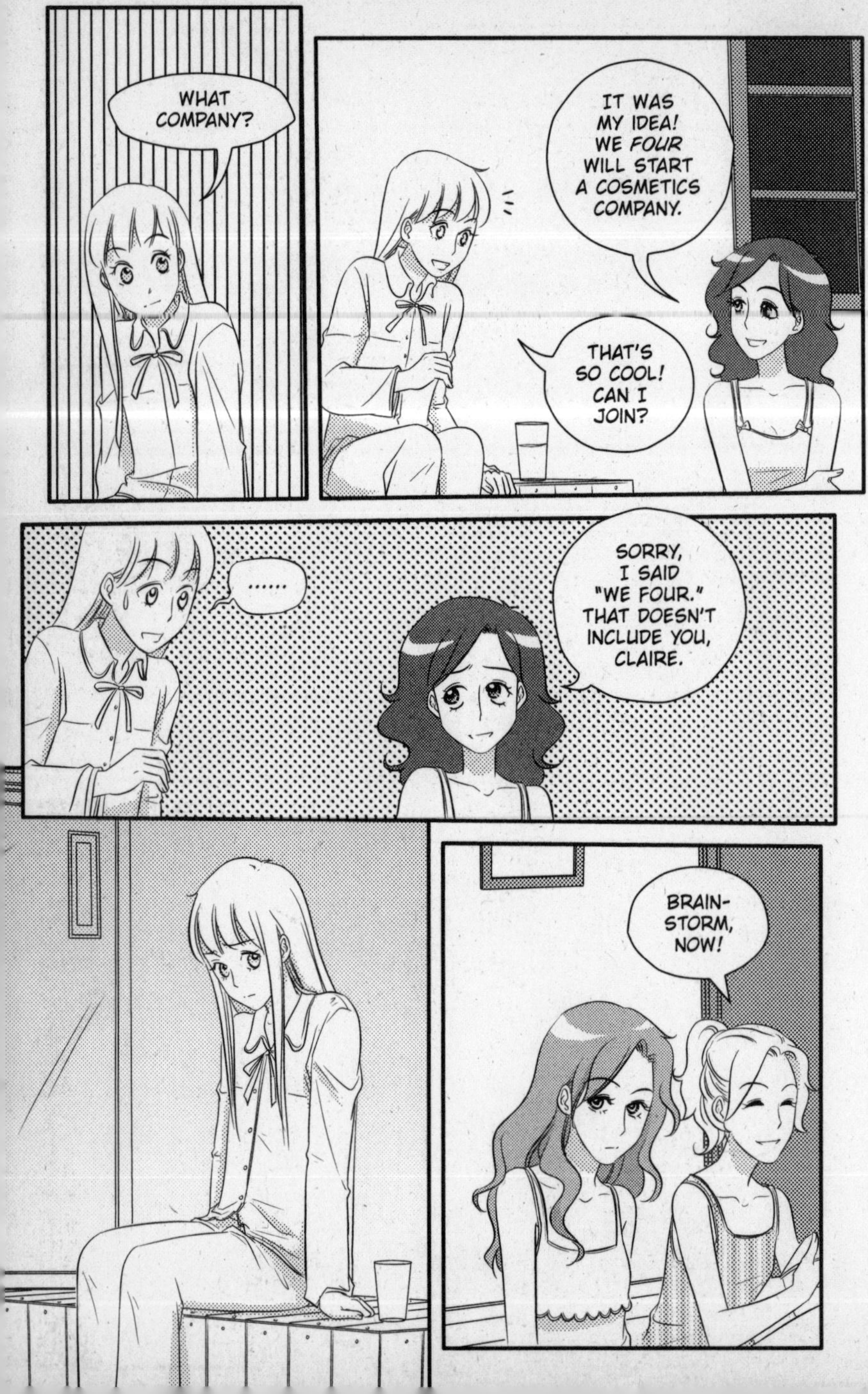
WHAT COMPANY?
IT WAS MY IDEA! WE *FOUR* WILL START A COSMETICS COMPANY.
THAT'S SO COOL! CAN I JOIN?
......
SORRY, I SAID "WE FOUR." THAT DOESN'T INCLUDE YOU, CLAIRE.
BRAIN-STORM, NOW!

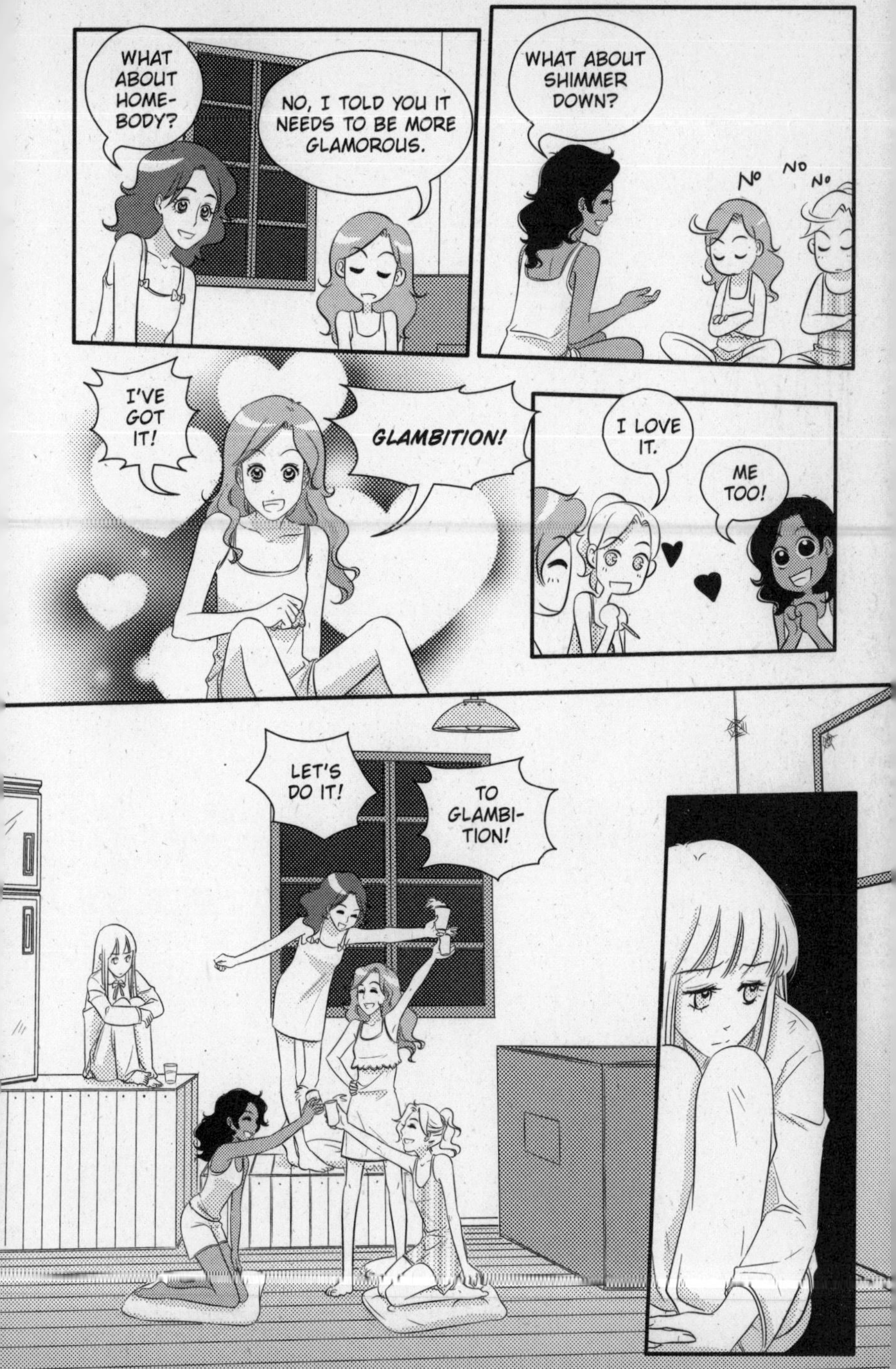
WHAT ABOUT HOME-BODY?
NO, I TOLD YOU IT NEEDS TO BE MORE GLAMOROUS.
WHAT ABOUT SHIMMER DOWN?
NO NO NO
I'VE GOT IT!
GLAMBITION!
I LOVE IT.
ME TOO!
LET'S DO IT!
TO GLAMBI-TION!

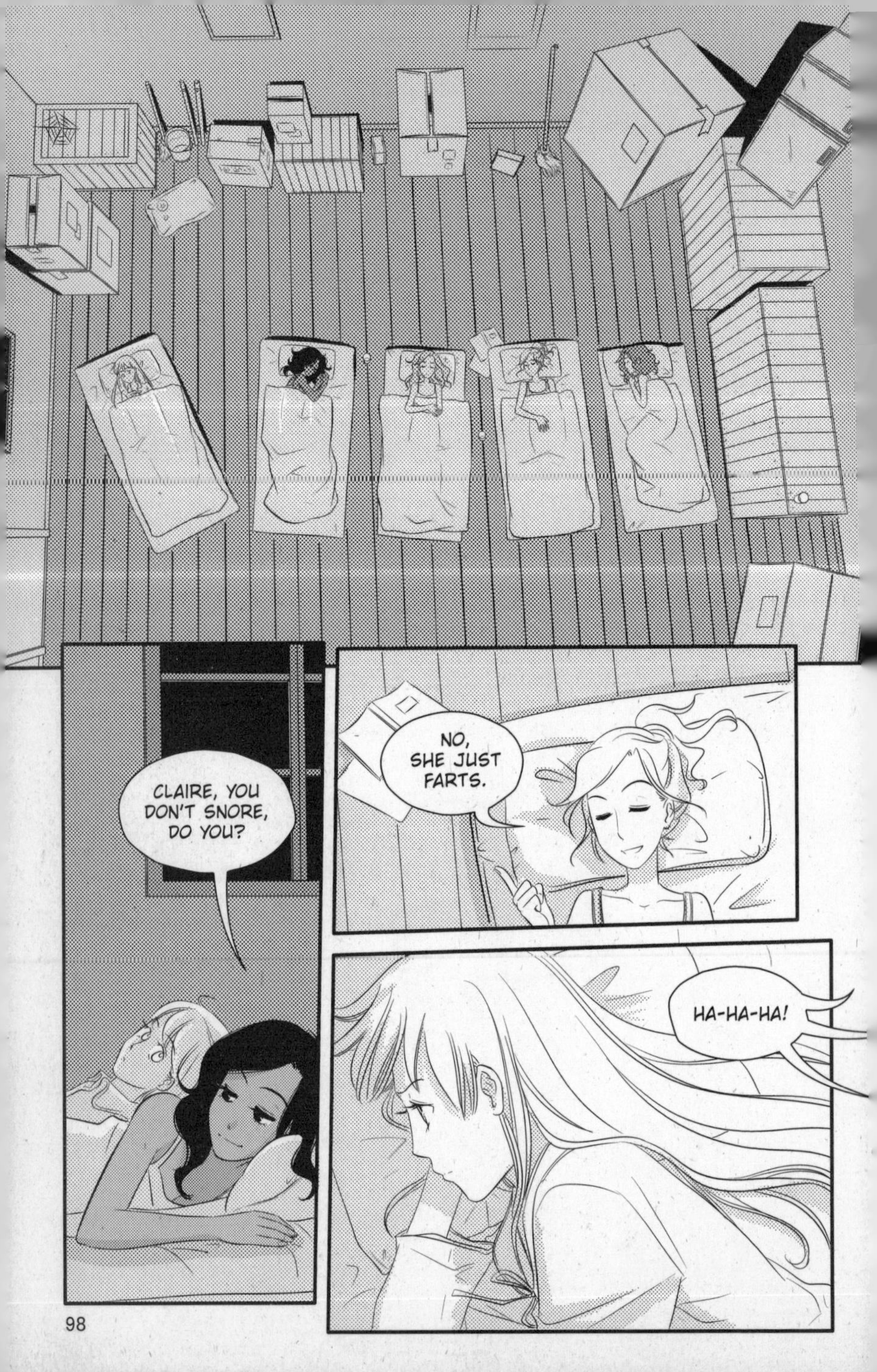
CLAIRE, YOU DON'T SNORE, DO YOU?
NO, SHE JUST FARTS.
HA-HA-HA!

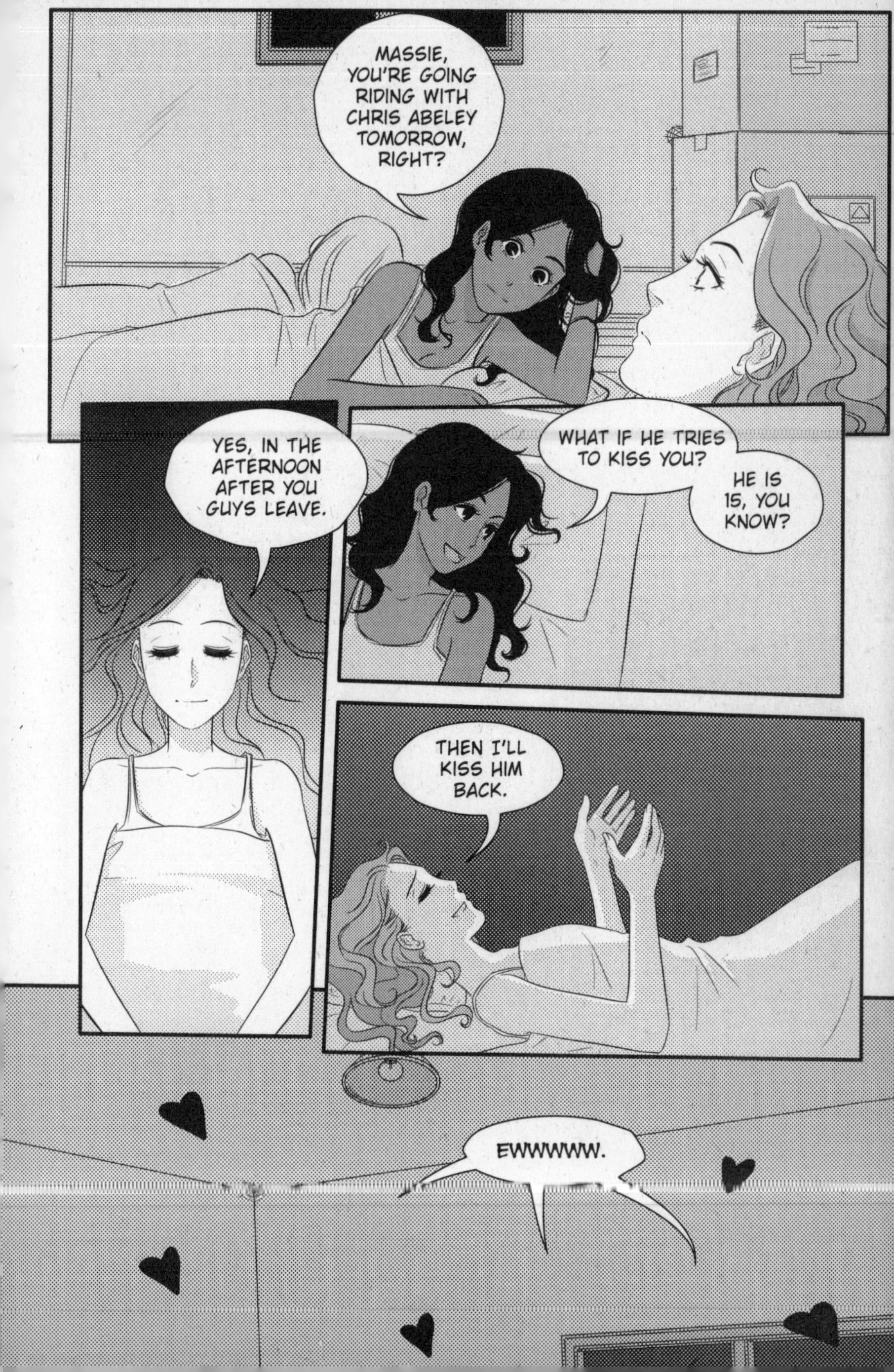
MASSIE, YOU'RE GOING RIDING WITH CHRIS ABELEY TOMORROW, RIGHT?
YES, IN THE AFTERNOON AFTER YOU GUYS LEAVE.
WHAT IF HE TRIES TO KISS YOU?
HE IS 15, YOU KNOW?
THEN I'LL KISS HIM BACK.
EWWWWW.

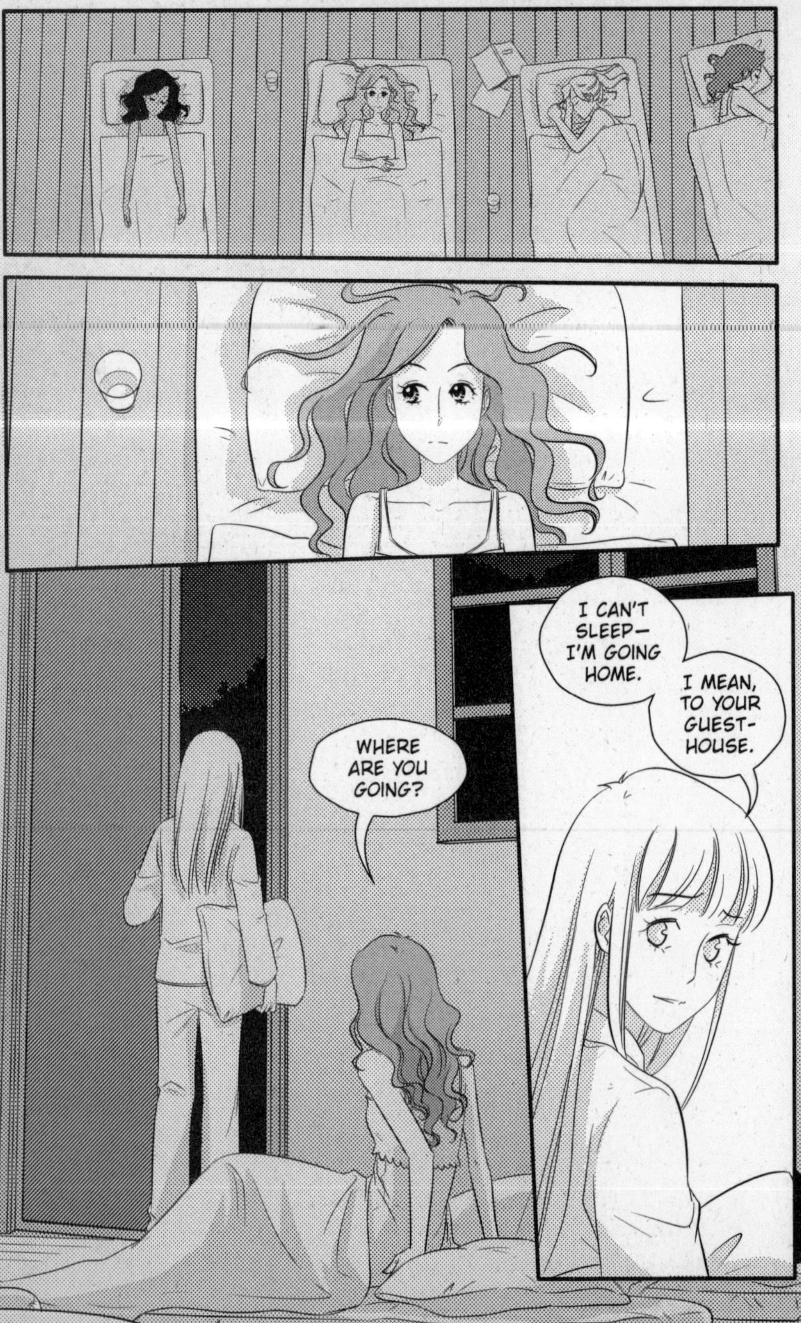
WHERE ARE YOU GOING?
I CAN'T SLEEP— I'M GOING HOME.
I MEAN, TO YOUR GUEST-HOUSE.

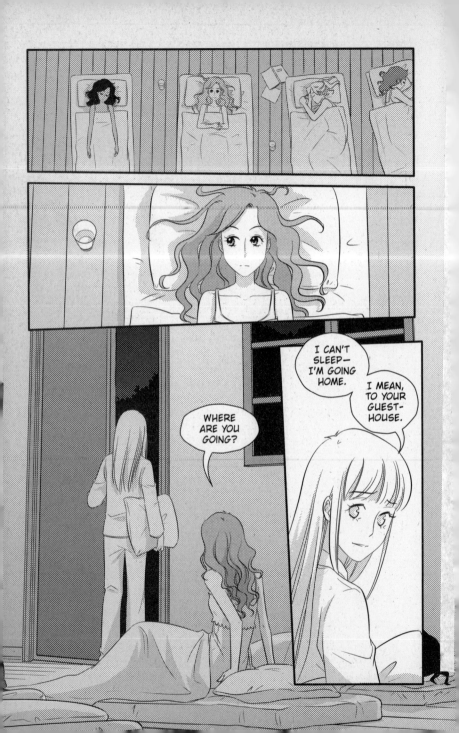

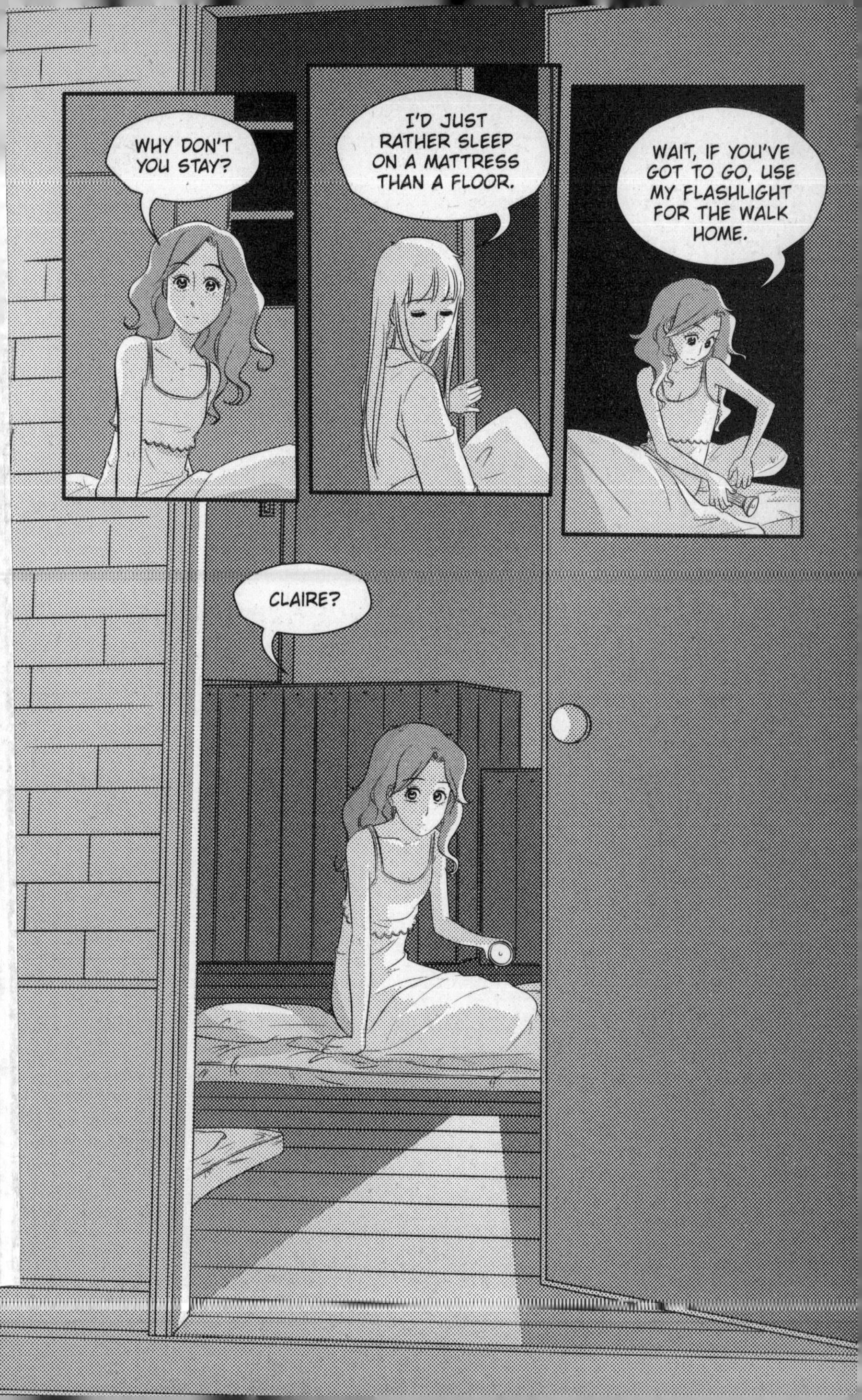
WHY DON'T YOU STAY?
I'D JUST RATHER SLEEP ON A MATTRESS THAN A FLOOR.
WAIT, IF YOU'VE GOT TO GO, USE MY FLASHLIGHT FOR THE WALK HOME.
CLAIRE?

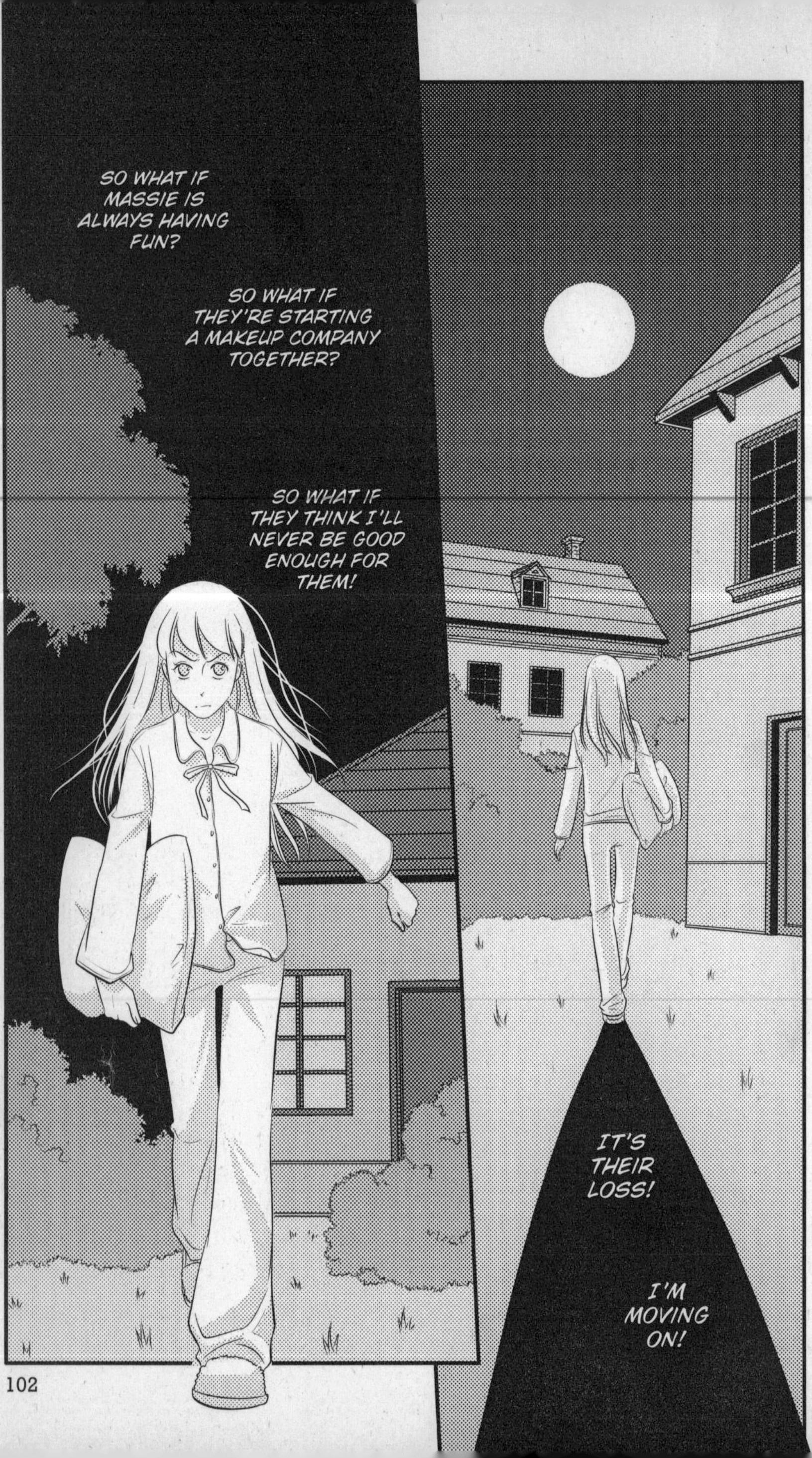
SO WHAT IF MASSIE IS ALWAYS HAVING FUN?
SO WHAT IF THEY'RE STARTING A MAKEUP COMPANY TOGETHER?
SO WHAT IF THEY THINK I'LL NEVER BE GOOD ENOUGH FOR THEM!
IT'S THEIR LOSS!
I'M MOVING ON!

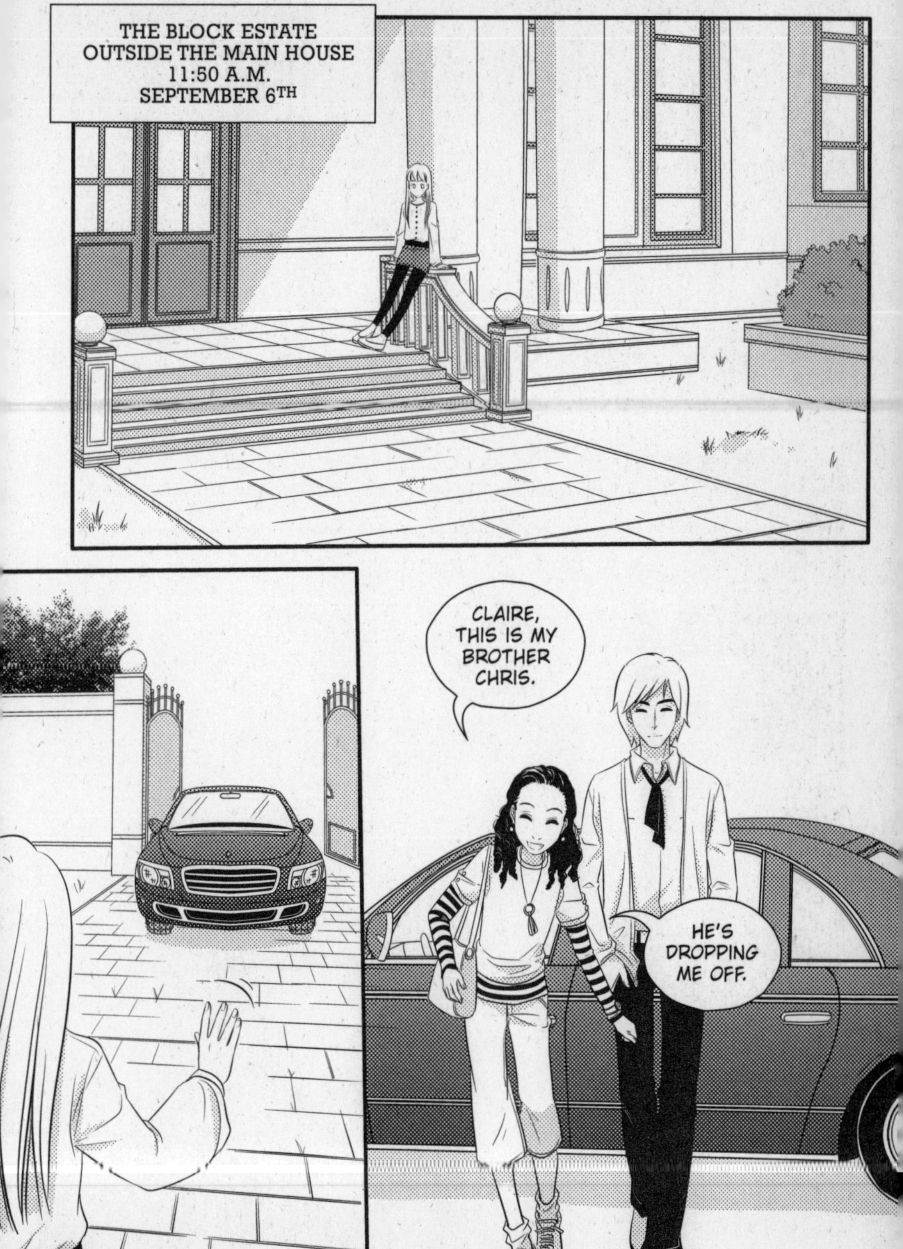
THE BLOCK ESTATE
OUTSIDE THE MAIN HOUSE
11:50 A.M.
SEPTEMBER 6TH
CLAIRE, THIS IS MY BROTHER CHRIS.
HE'S DROPPING ME OFF.

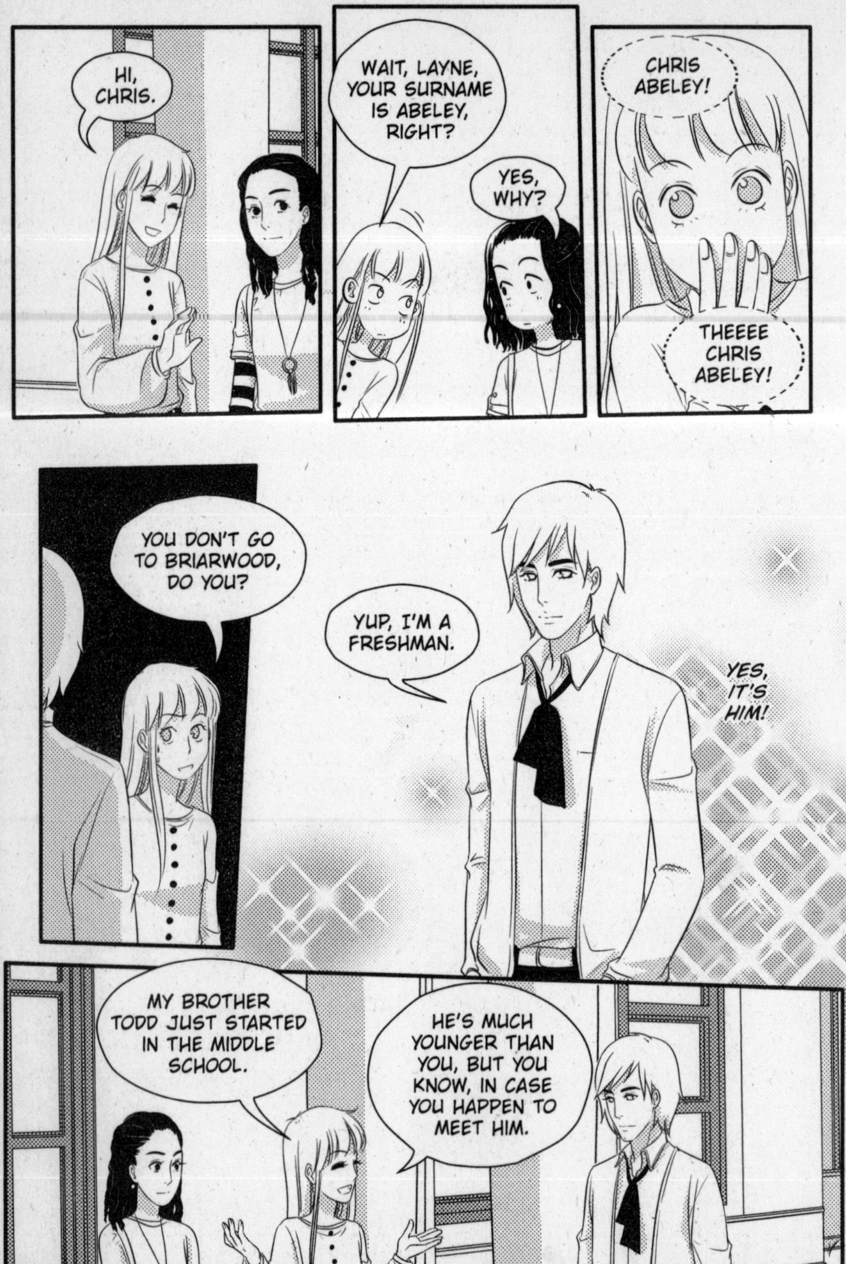
HI, CHRIS.
WAIT, LAYNE, YOUR SURNAME IS ABELEY, RIGHT?
YES, WHY?
CHRIS ABELEY!
THEEEE CHRIS ABELEY!
YOU DON'T GO TO BRIARWOOD, DO YOU?
YUP, I'M A FRESHMAN.
YES, IT'S HIM!
MY BROTHER TODD JUST STARTED IN THE MIDDLE SCHOOL.
HE'S MUCH YOUNGER THAN YOU, BUT YOU KNOW, IN CASE YOU HAPPEN TO MEET HIM.

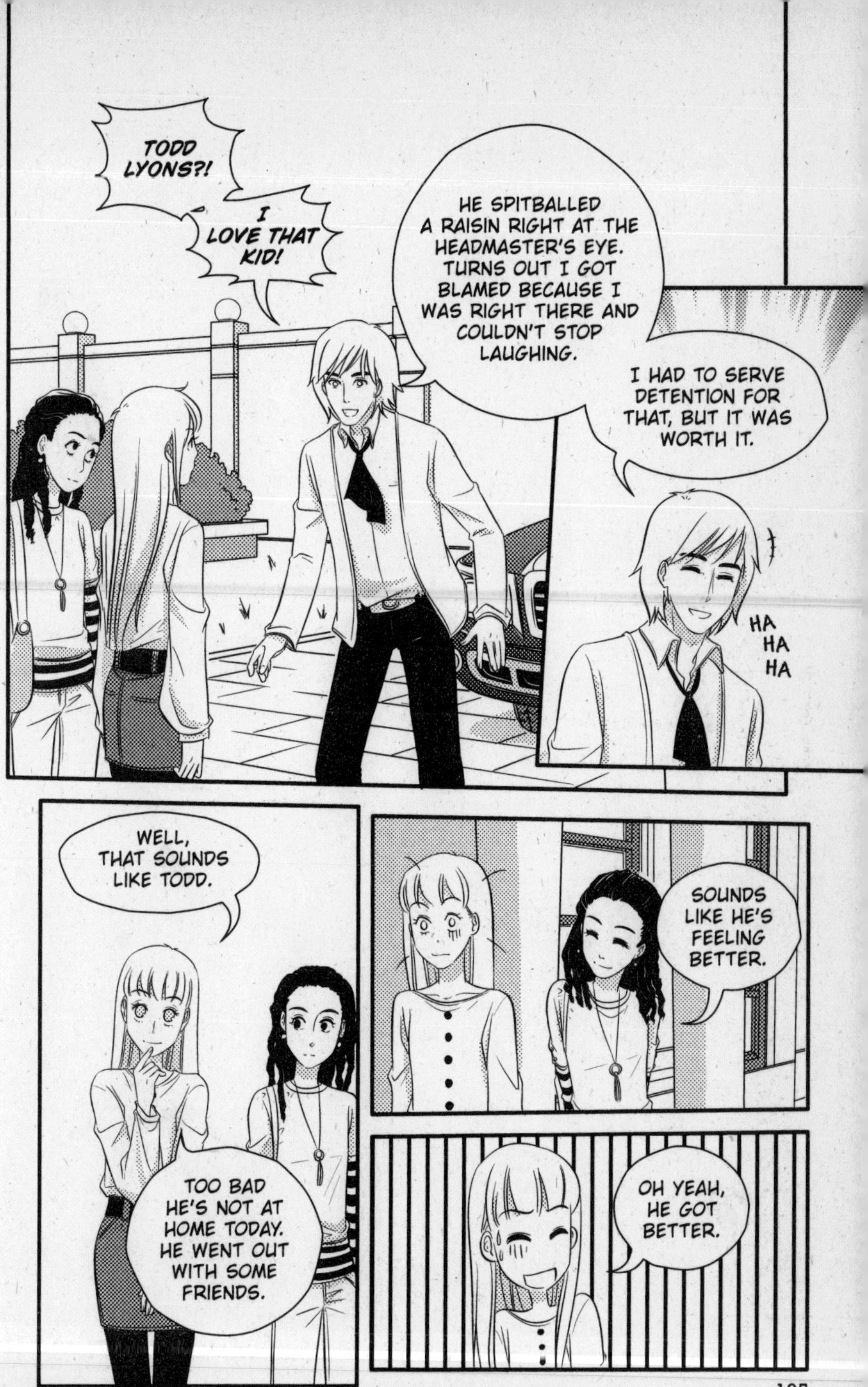
TODD LYONS?!
I LOVE THAT KID!
HE SPITBALLED A RAISIN RIGHT AT THE HEADMASTER'S EYE. TURNS OUT I GOT BLAMED BECAUSE I WAS RIGHT THERE AND COULDN'T STOP LAUGHING.
I HAD TO SERVE DETENTION FOR THAT, BUT IT WAS WORTH IT.
HA HA HA
WELL, THAT SOUNDS LIKE TODD.
TOO BAD HE'S NOT AT HOME TODAY. HE WENT OUT WITH SOME FRIENDS.
SOUNDS LIKE HE'S FEELING BETTER.
OH YEAH, HE GOT BETTER.

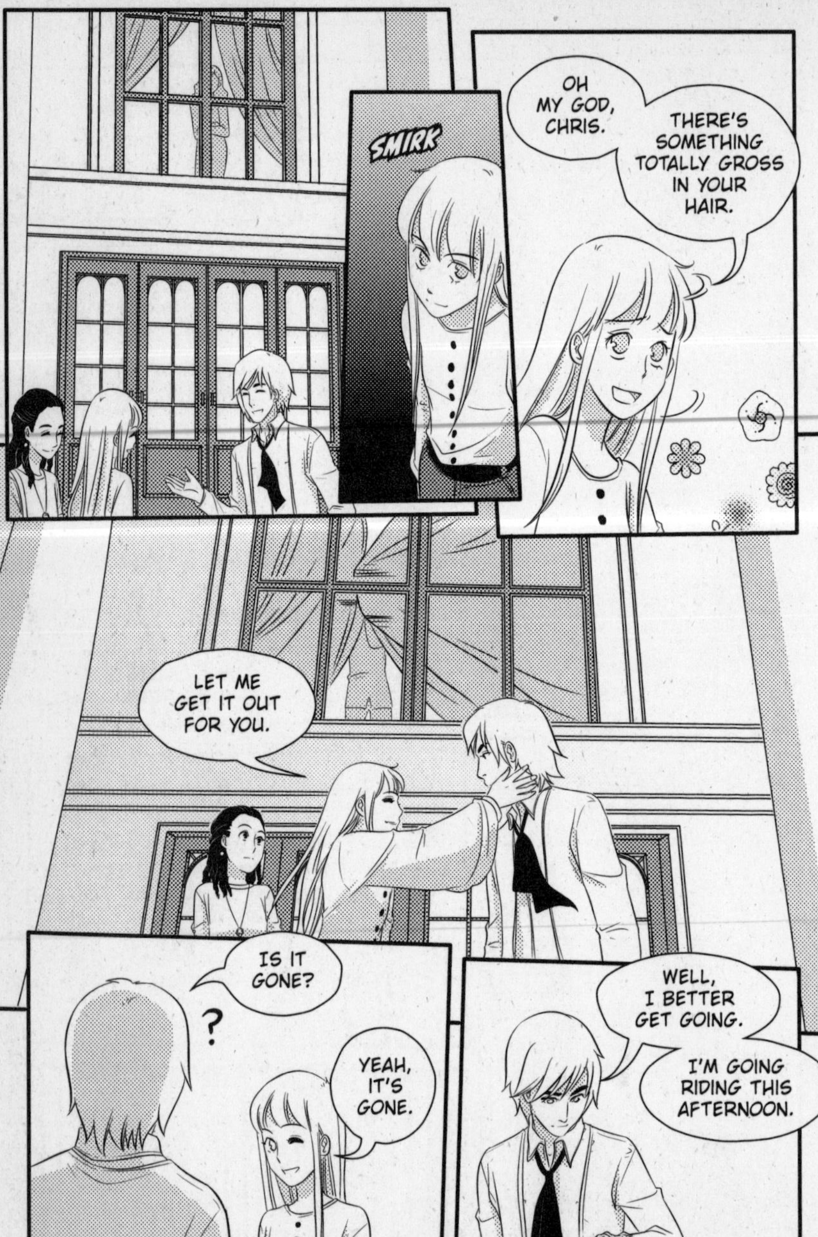
SMIRK
OH MY GOD, CHRIS.
THERE'S SOMETHING TOTALLY GROSS IN YOUR HAIR.
LET ME GET IT OUT FOR YOU.
IS IT GONE?
?
YEAH, IT'S GONE.
WELL, I BETTER GET GOING.
I'M GOING RIDING THIS AFTERNOON.

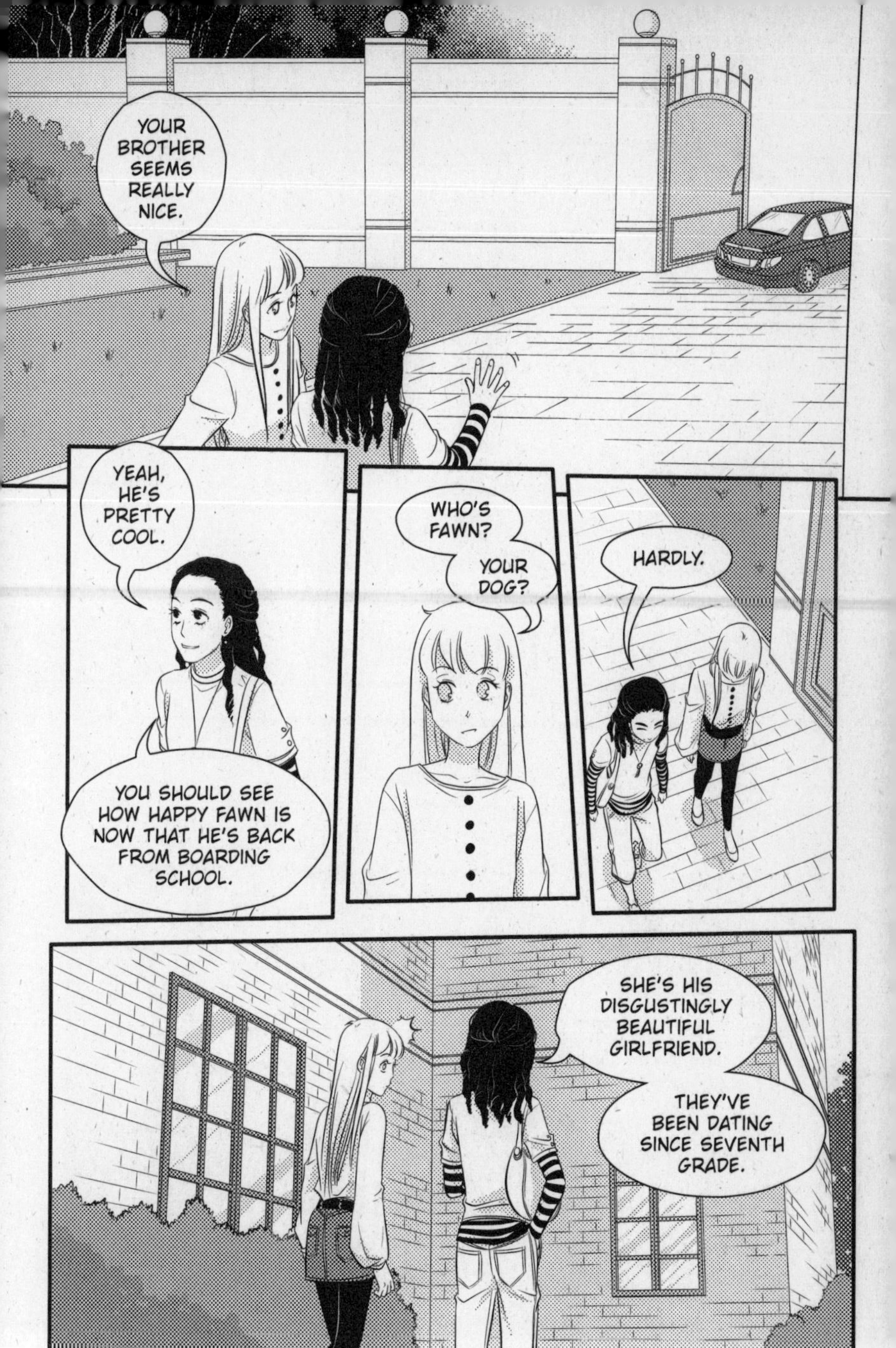
YOUR BROTHER SEEMS REALLY NICE.
YEAH, HE'S PRETTY COOL.
YOU SHOULD SEE HOW HAPPY FAWN IS NOW THAT HE'S BACK FROM BOARDING SCHOOL.
WHO'S FAWN?
YOUR DOG?
HARDLY.
SHE'S HIS DISGUSTINGLY BEAUTIFUL GIRLFRIEND.
THEY'VE BEEN DATING SINCE SEVENTH GRADE.

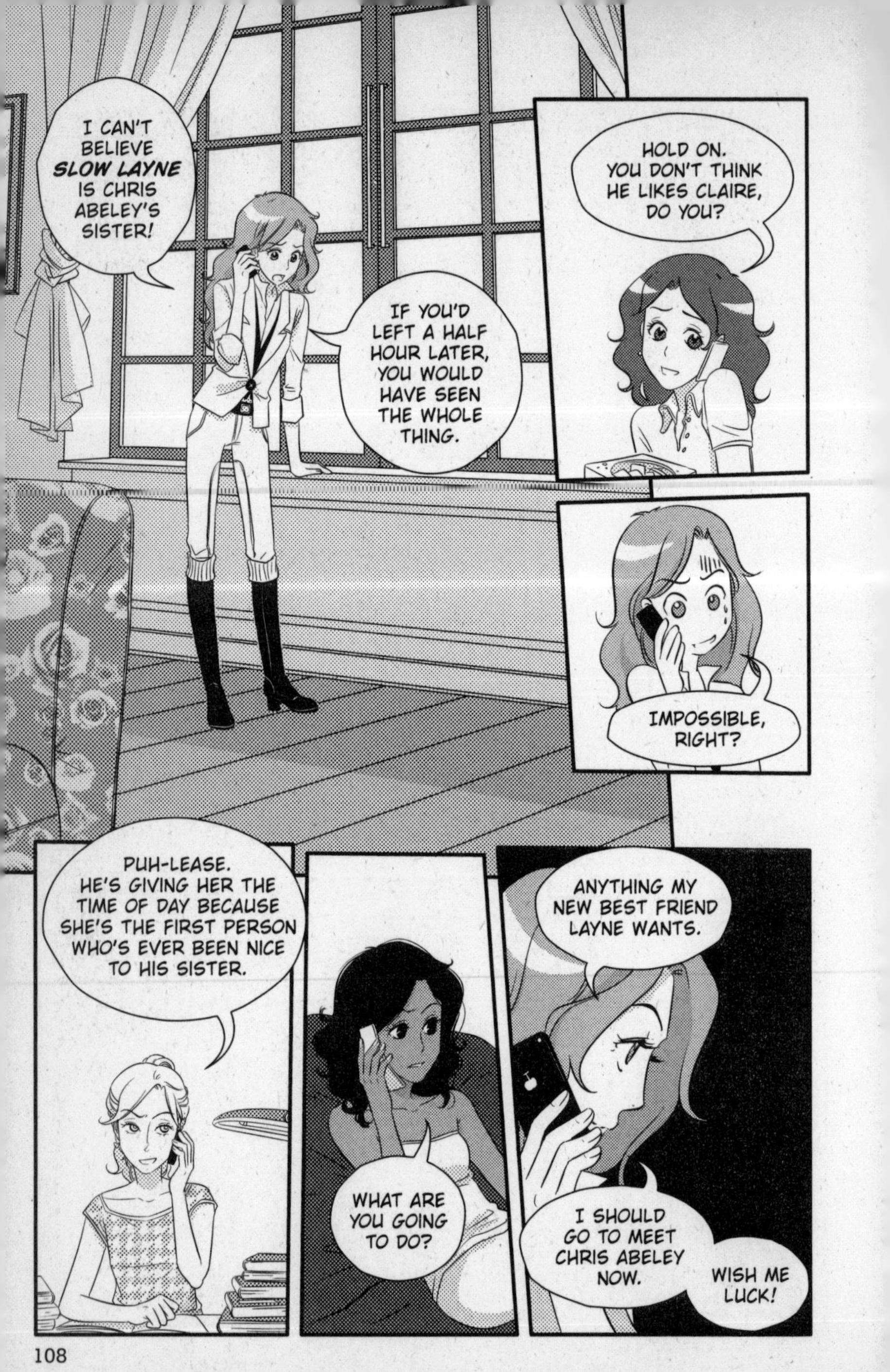
I CAN'T BELIEVE ***SLOW LAYNE*** IS CHRIS ABELEY'S SISTER!
IF YOU'D LEFT A HALF HOUR LATER, YOU WOULD HAVE SEEN THE WHOLE THING.
HOLD ON. YOU DON'T THINK HE LIKES CLAIRE, DO YOU?
IMPOSSIBLE, RIGHT?
PUH-LEASE. HE'S GIVING HER THE TIME OF DAY BECAUSE SHE'S THE FIRST PERSON WHO'S EVER BEEN NICE TO HIS SISTER.
WHAT ARE YOU GOING TO DO?
ANYTHING MY NEW BEST FRIEND LAYNE WANTS.
I SHOULD GO TO MEET CHRIS ABELEY NOW.
WISH ME LUCK!

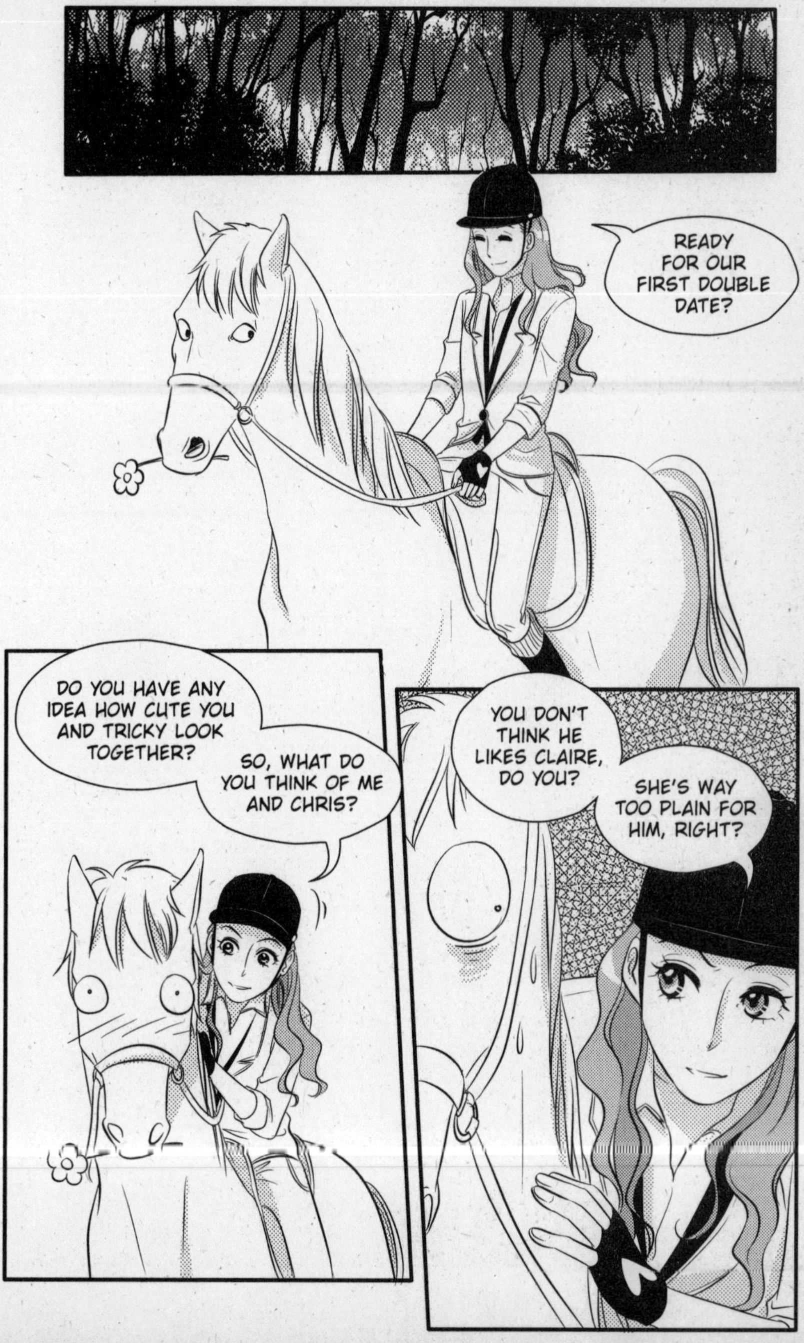
READY FOR OUR FIRST DOUBLE DATE?
DO YOU HAVE ANY IDEA HOW CUTE YOU AND TRICKY LOOK TOGETHER?
SO, WHAT DO YOU THINK OF ME AND CHRIS?
YOU DON'T THINK HE LIKES CLAIRE, DO YOU?
SHE'S WAY TOO PLAIN FOR HIM, RIGHT?

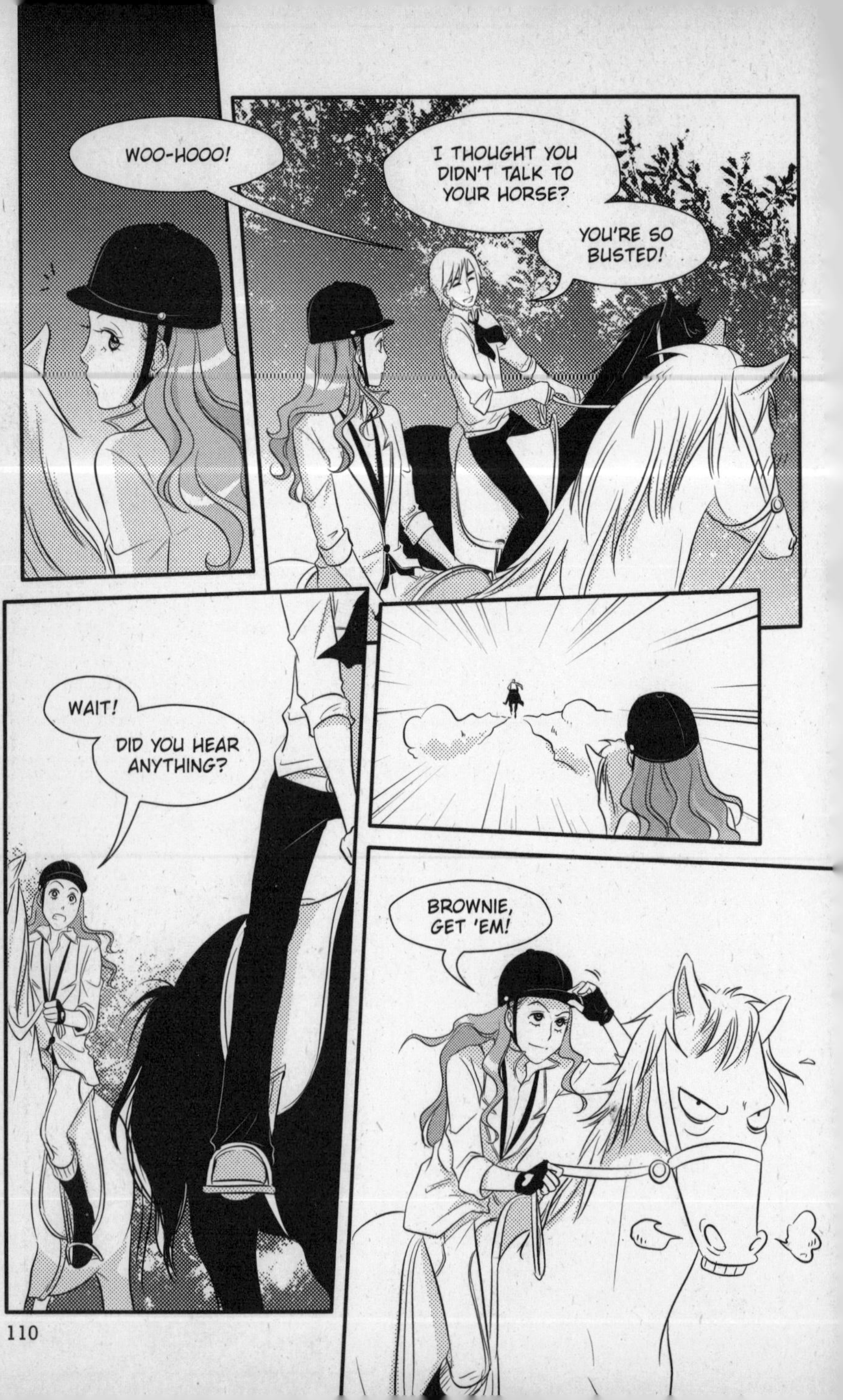
WOO-HOOO!
I THOUGHT YOU DIDN'T TALK TO YOUR HORSE?
YOU'RE SO BUSTED!
WAIT!
DID YOU HEAR ANYTHING?
BROWNIE, GET 'EM!

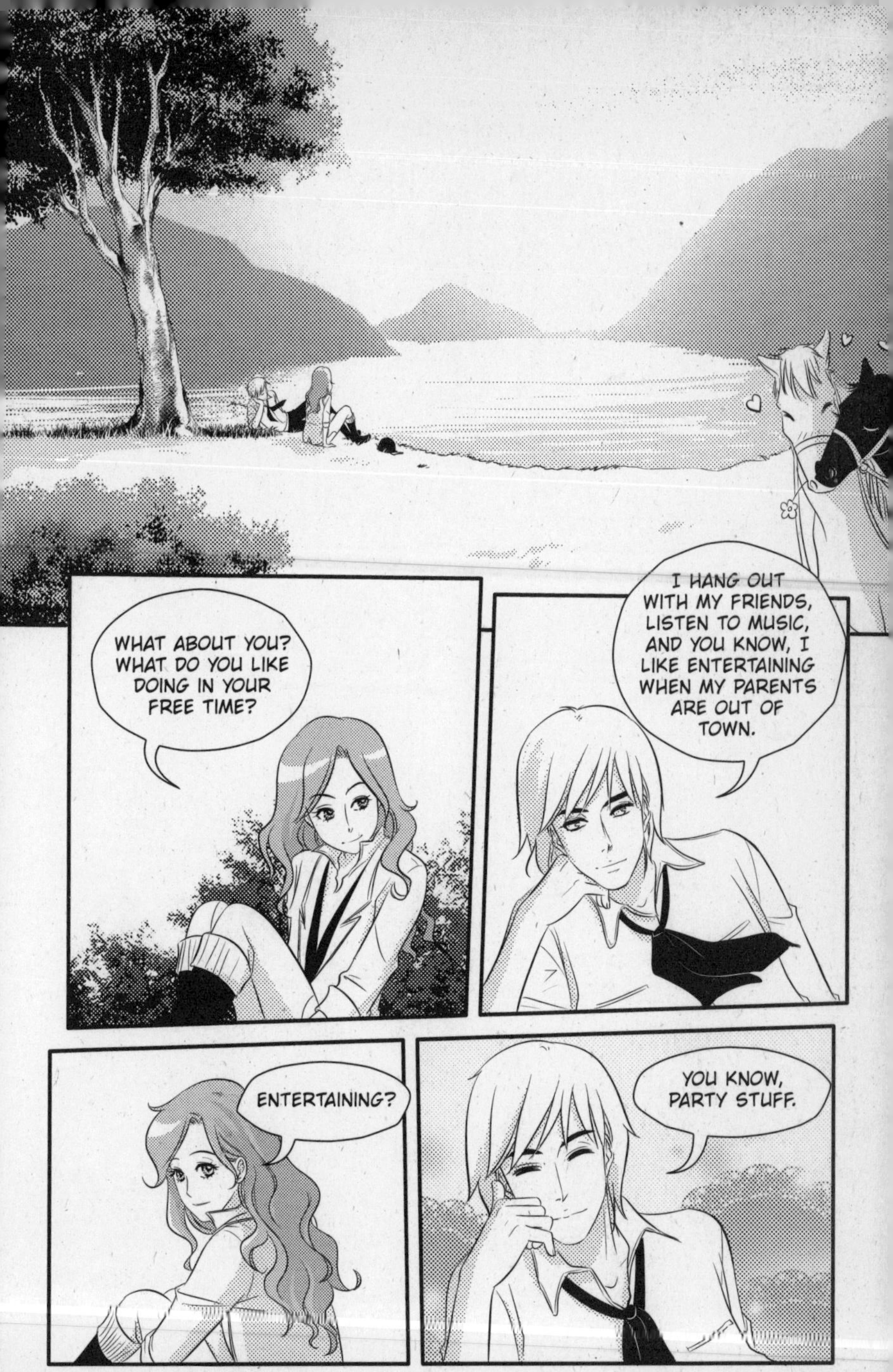
WHAT ABOUT YOU? WHAT DO YOU LIKE DOING IN YOUR FREE TIME?
I HANG OUT WITH MY FRIENDS, LISTEN TO MUSIC, AND YOU KNOW, I LIKE ENTERTAINING WHEN MY PARENTS ARE OUT OF TOWN.
ENTERTAINING?
YOU KNOW, PARTY STUFF.

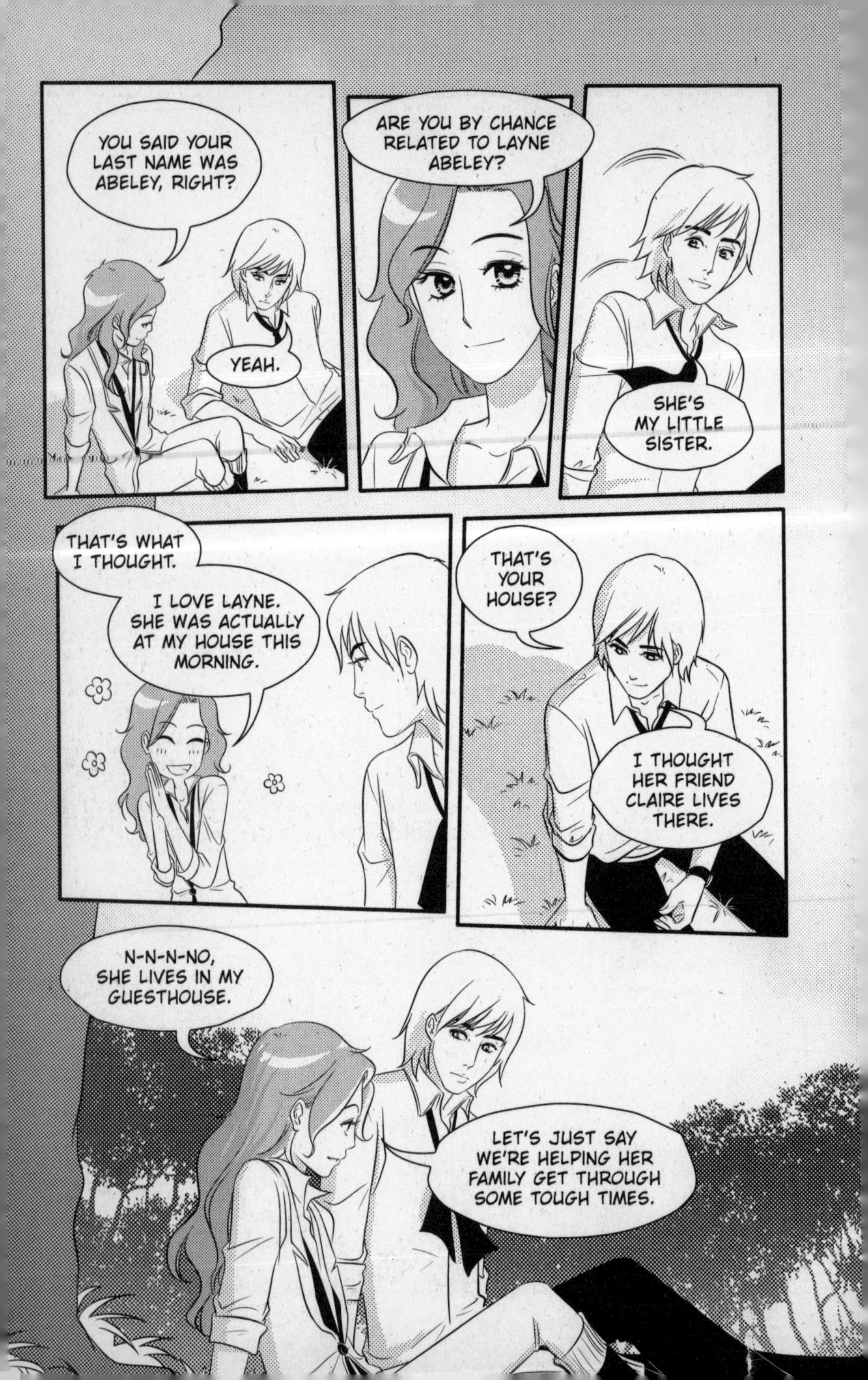
YOU SAID YOUR LAST NAME WAS ABELEY, RIGHT?
YEAH.
ARE YOU BY CHANCE RELATED TO LAYNE ABELEY?
SHE'S MY LITTLE SISTER.
THAT'S WHAT I THOUGHT.
I LOVE LAYNE. SHE WAS ACTUALLY AT MY HOUSE THIS MORNING.
THAT'S YOUR HOUSE?
I THOUGHT HER FRIEND CLAIRE LIVES THERE.
N-N-N-NO, SHE LIVES IN MY GUESTHOUSE.
LET'S JUST SAY WE'RE HELPING HER FAMILY GET THROUGH SOME TOUGH TIMES.

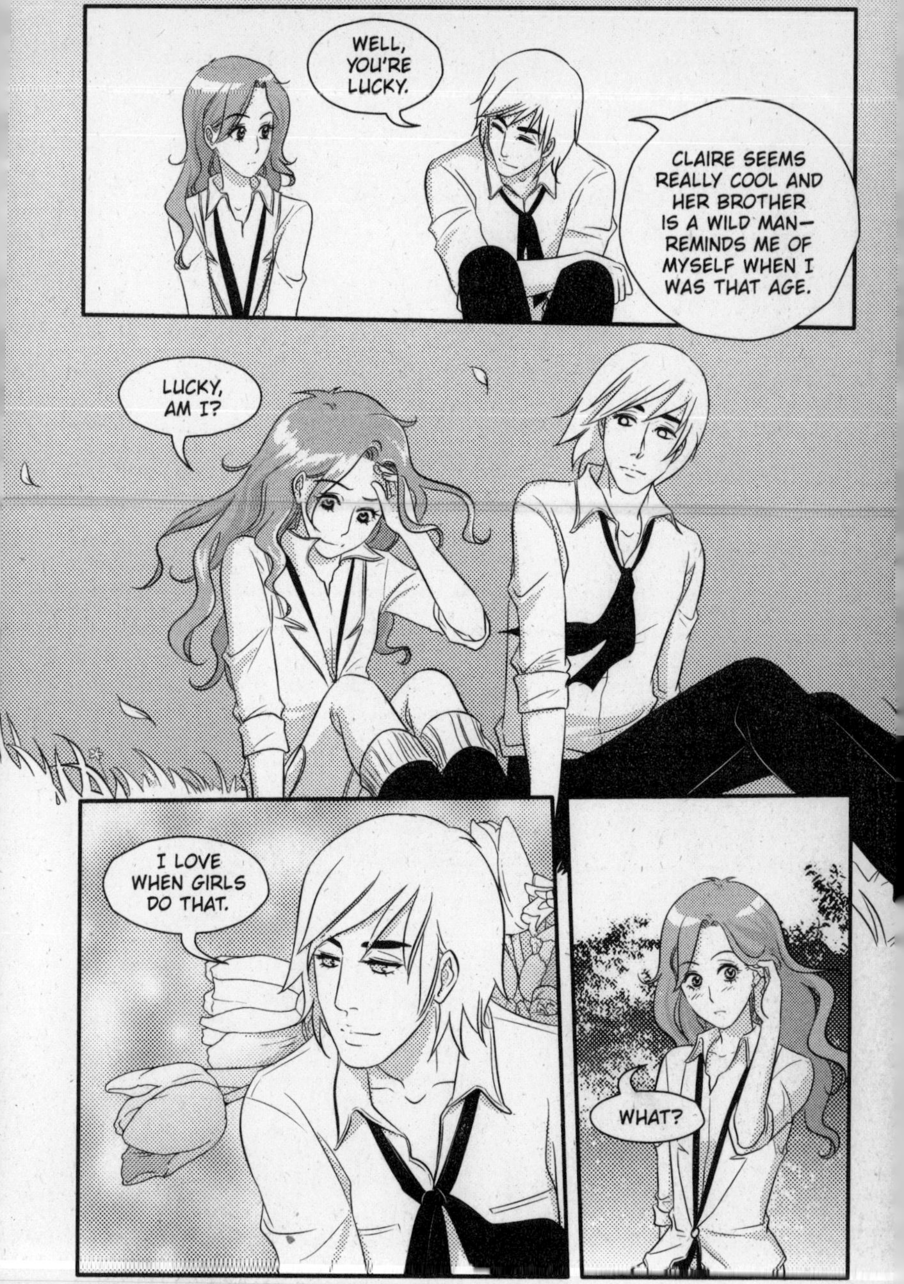
WELL, YOU'RE LUCKY.
CLAIRE SEEMS REALLY COOL AND HER BROTHER IS A WILD MAN—REMINDS ME OF MYSELF WHEN I WAS THAT AGE.
LUCKY, AM I?
I LOVE WHEN GIRLS DO THAT.
WHAT?

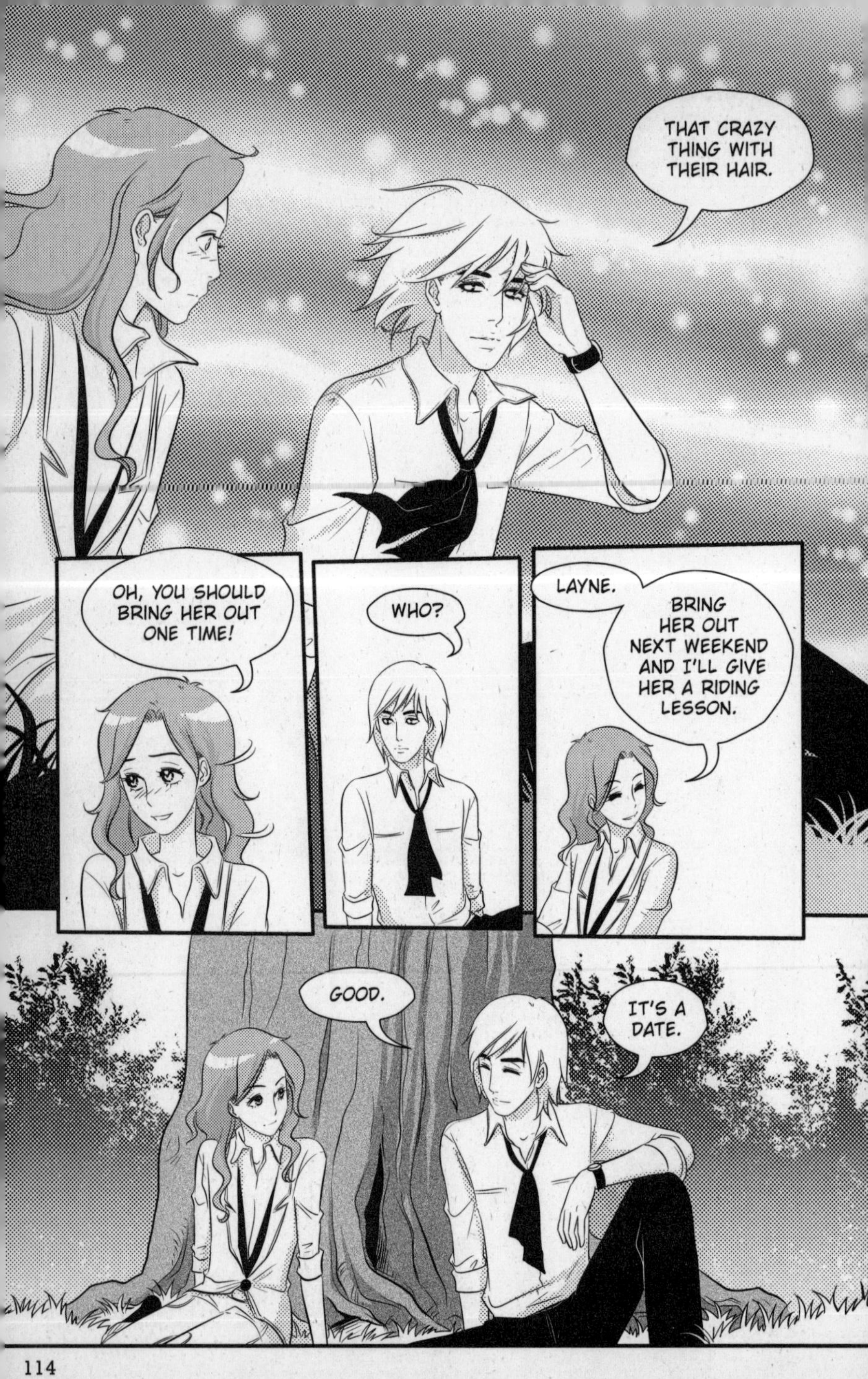
THAT CRAZY THING WITH THEIR HAIR.
OH, YOU SHOULD BRING HER OUT ONE TIME!
WHO?
LAYNE.
BRING HER OUT NEXT WEEKEND AND I'LL GIVE HER A RIDING LESSON.
GOOD.
IT'S A DATE.

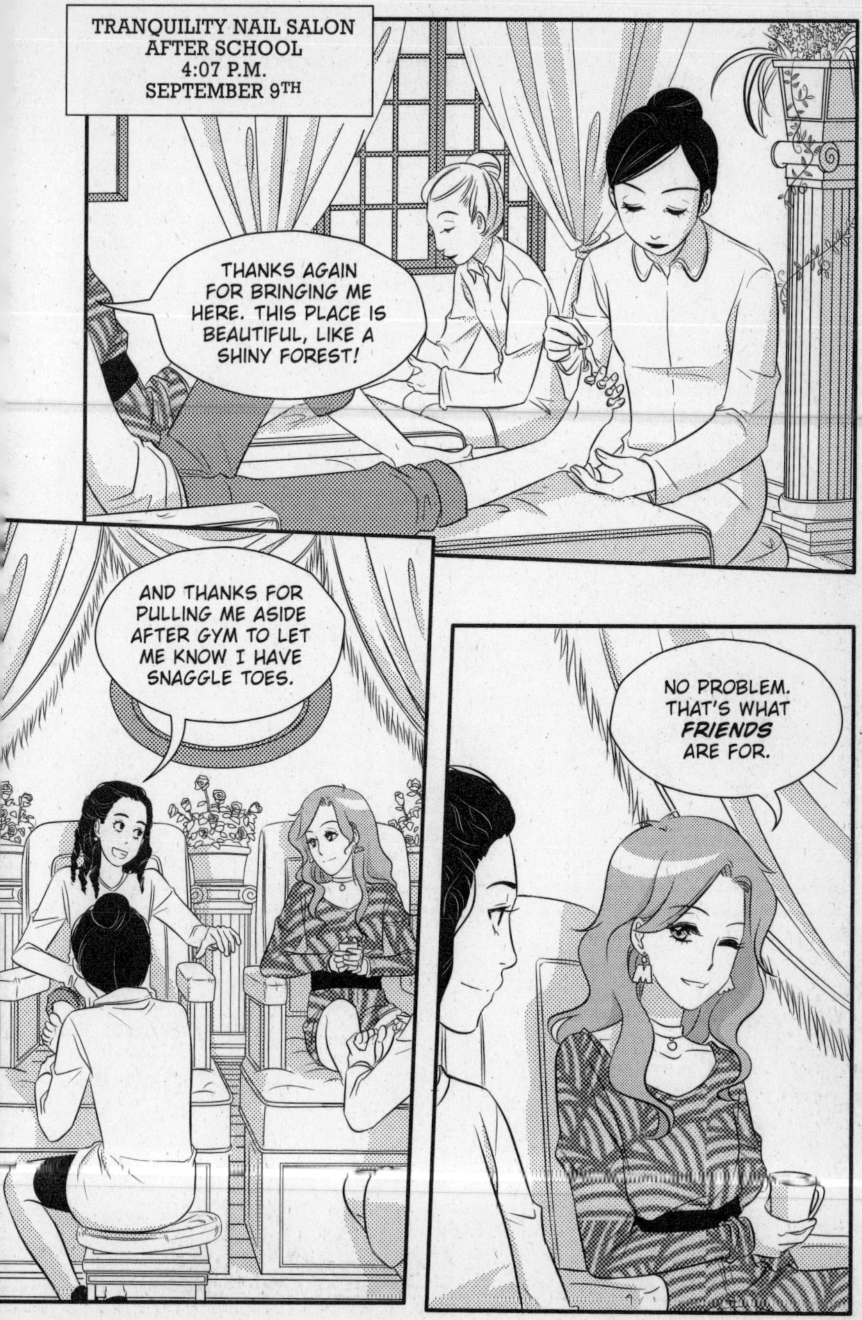
TRANQUILITY NAIL SALON AFTER SCHOOL 4:07 P.M. SEPTEMBER 9TH
THANKS AGAIN FOR BRINGING ME HERE. THIS PLACE IS BEAUTIFUL, LIKE A SHINY FOREST!
AND THANKS FOR PULLING ME ASIDE AFTER GYM TO LET ME KNOW I HAVE SNAGGLE TOES.
NO PROBLEM. THAT'S WHAT *FRIENDS* ARE FOR.

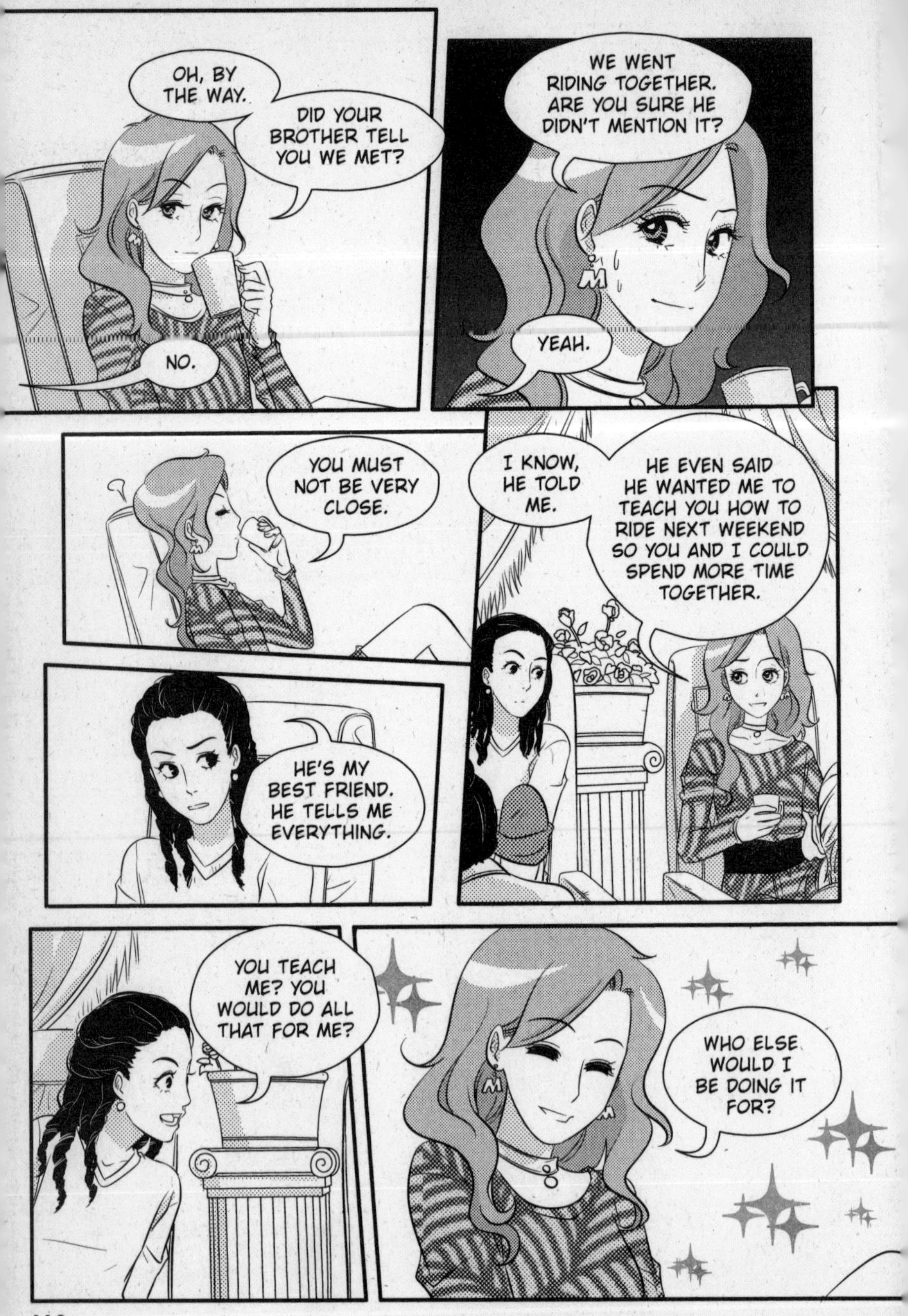
OH, BY THE WAY.
DID YOUR BROTHER TELL YOU WE MET?
NO.
WE WENT RIDING TOGETHER. ARE YOU SURE HE DIDN'T MENTION IT?
YEAH.
YOU MUST NOT BE VERY CLOSE.
HE'S MY BEST FRIEND. HE TELLS ME EVERYTHING.
I KNOW, HE TOLD ME.
HE EVEN SAID HE WANTED ME TO TEACH YOU HOW TO RIDE NEXT WEEKEND SO YOU AND I COULD SPEND MORE TIME TOGETHER.
YOU TEACH ME? YOU WOULD DO ALL THAT FOR ME?
WHO ELSE WOULD I BE DOING IT FOR?

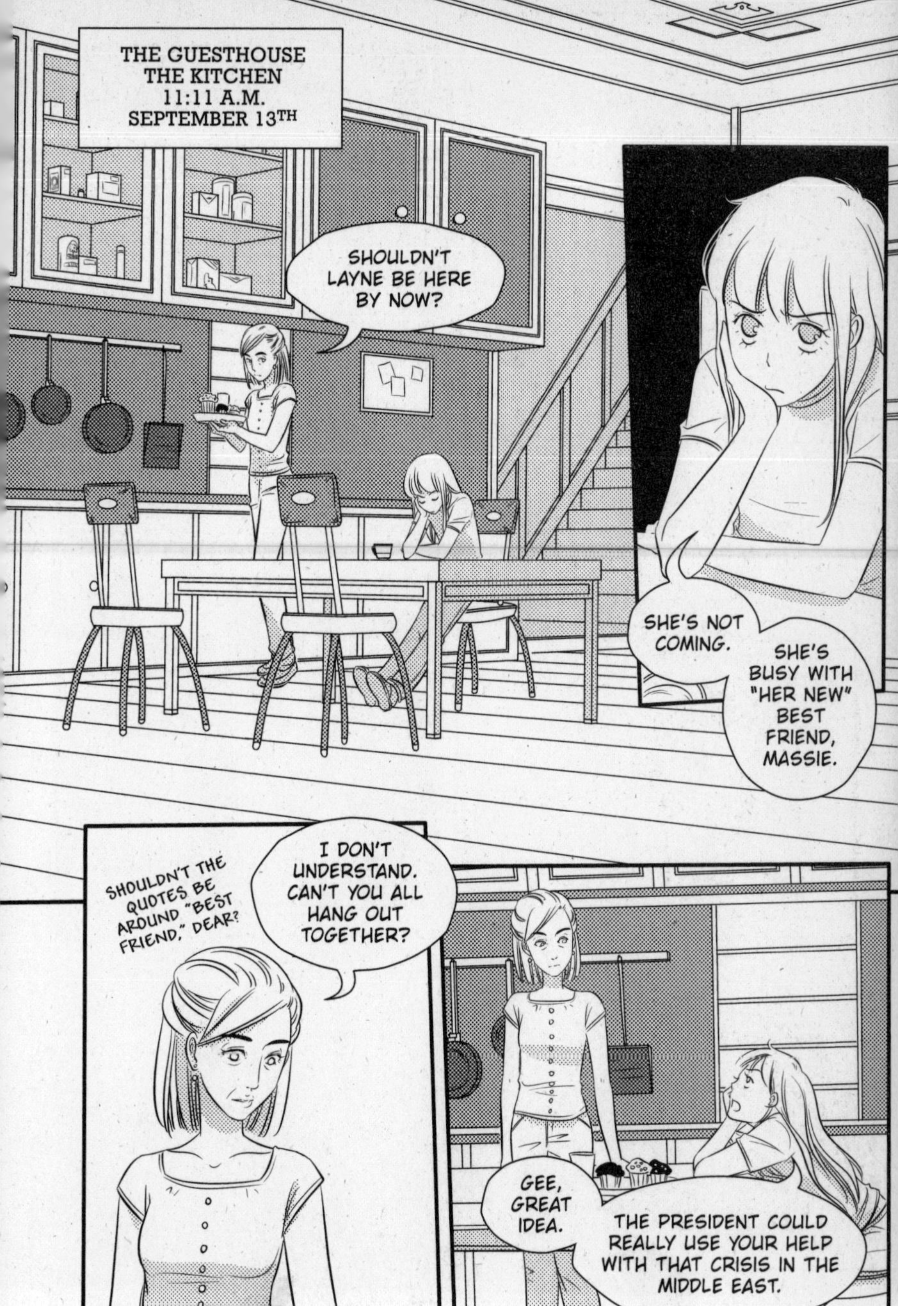
THE GUESTHOUSE
THE KITCHEN
11:11 A.M.
SEPTEMBER 13TH
SHOULDN'T LAYNE BE HERE BY NOW?
SHE'S NOT COMING.
SHE'S BUSY WITH "HER NEW" BEST FRIEND, MASSIE.
SHOULDN'T THE QUOTES BE AROUND "BEST FRIEND," DEAR?
I DON'T UNDERSTAND. CAN'T YOU ALL HANG OUT TOGETHER?
GEE, GREAT IDEA.
THE PRESIDENT COULD REALLY USE YOUR HELP WITH THAT CRISIS IN THE MIDDLE EAST.

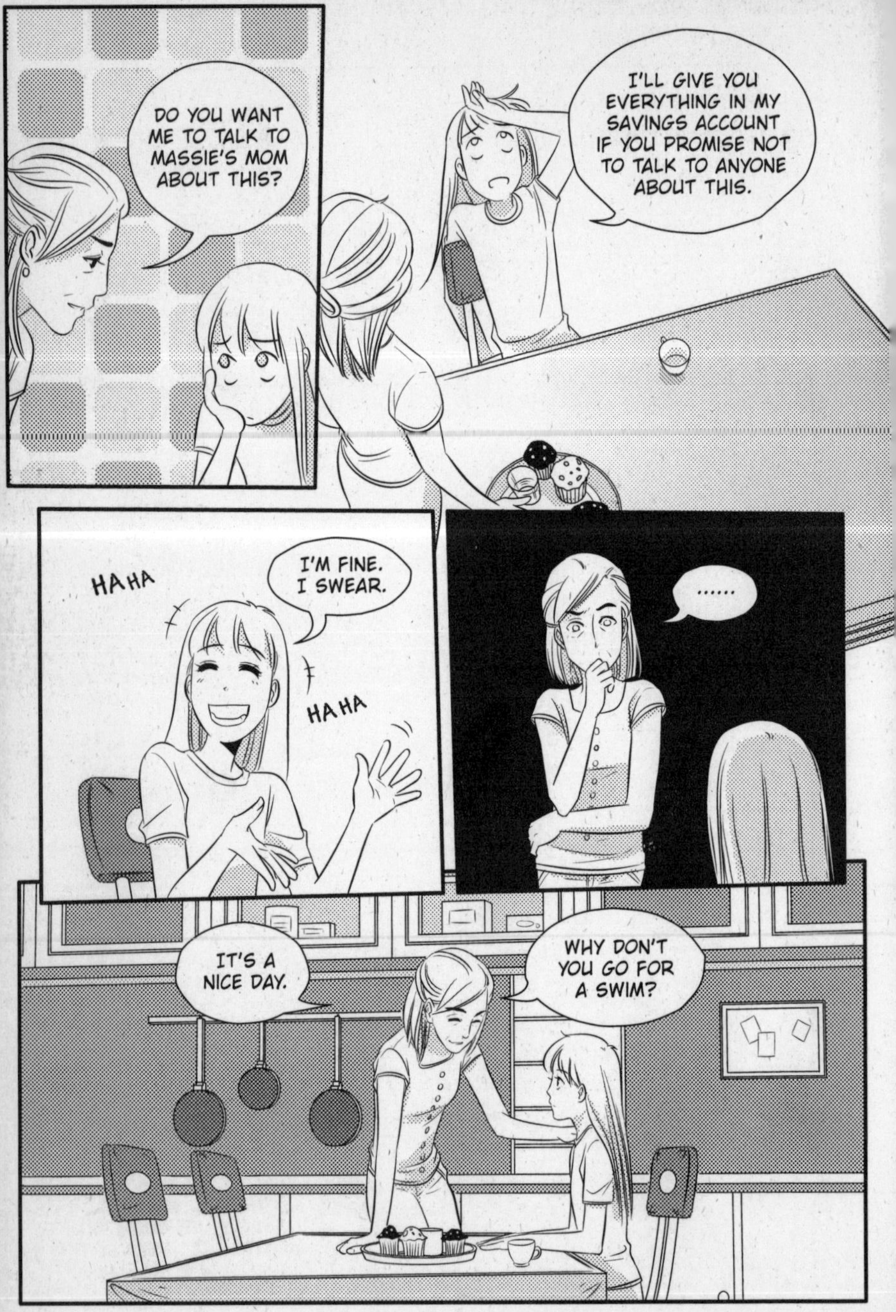
DO YOU WANT ME TO TALK TO MASSIE'S MOM ABOUT THIS?
I'LL GIVE YOU EVERYTHING IN MY SAVINGS ACCOUNT IF YOU PROMISE NOT TO TALK TO ANYONE ABOUT THIS.
HAHA
I'M FINE. I SWEAR.
HAHA
......
IT'S A NICE DAY.
WHY DON'T YOU GO FOR A SWIM?

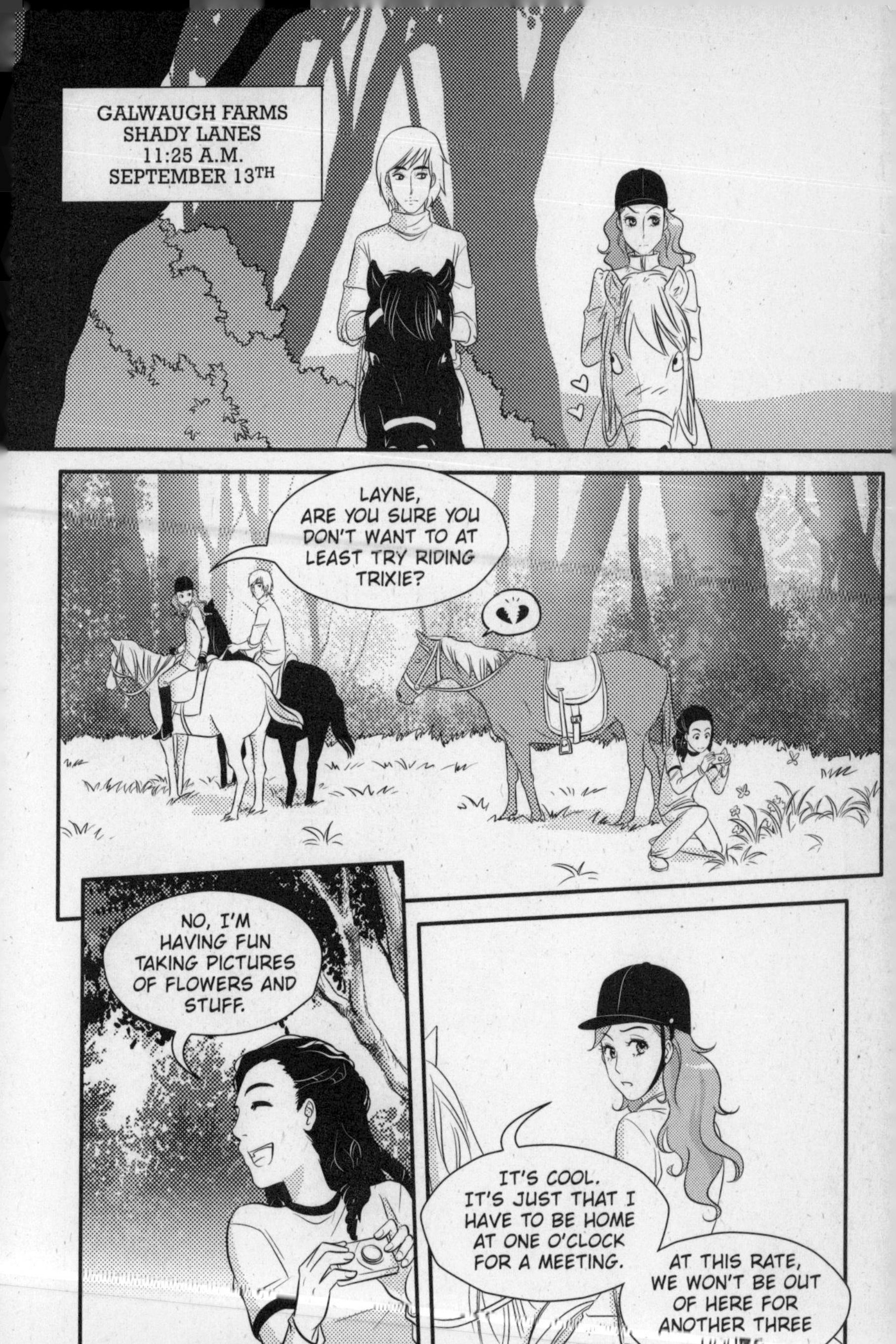
GALWAUGH FARMS SHADY LANES 11:25 A.M. SEPTEMBER 13TH
LAYNE, ARE YOU SURE YOU DON'T WANT TO AT LEAST TRY RIDING TRIXIE?
NO, I'M HAVING FUN TAKING PICTURES OF FLOWERS AND STUFF.
IT'S COOL. IT'S JUST THAT I HAVE TO BE HOME AT ONE O'CLOCK FOR A MEETING.
AT THIS RATE, WE WON'T BE OUT OF HERE FOR ANOTHER THREE HOURS.

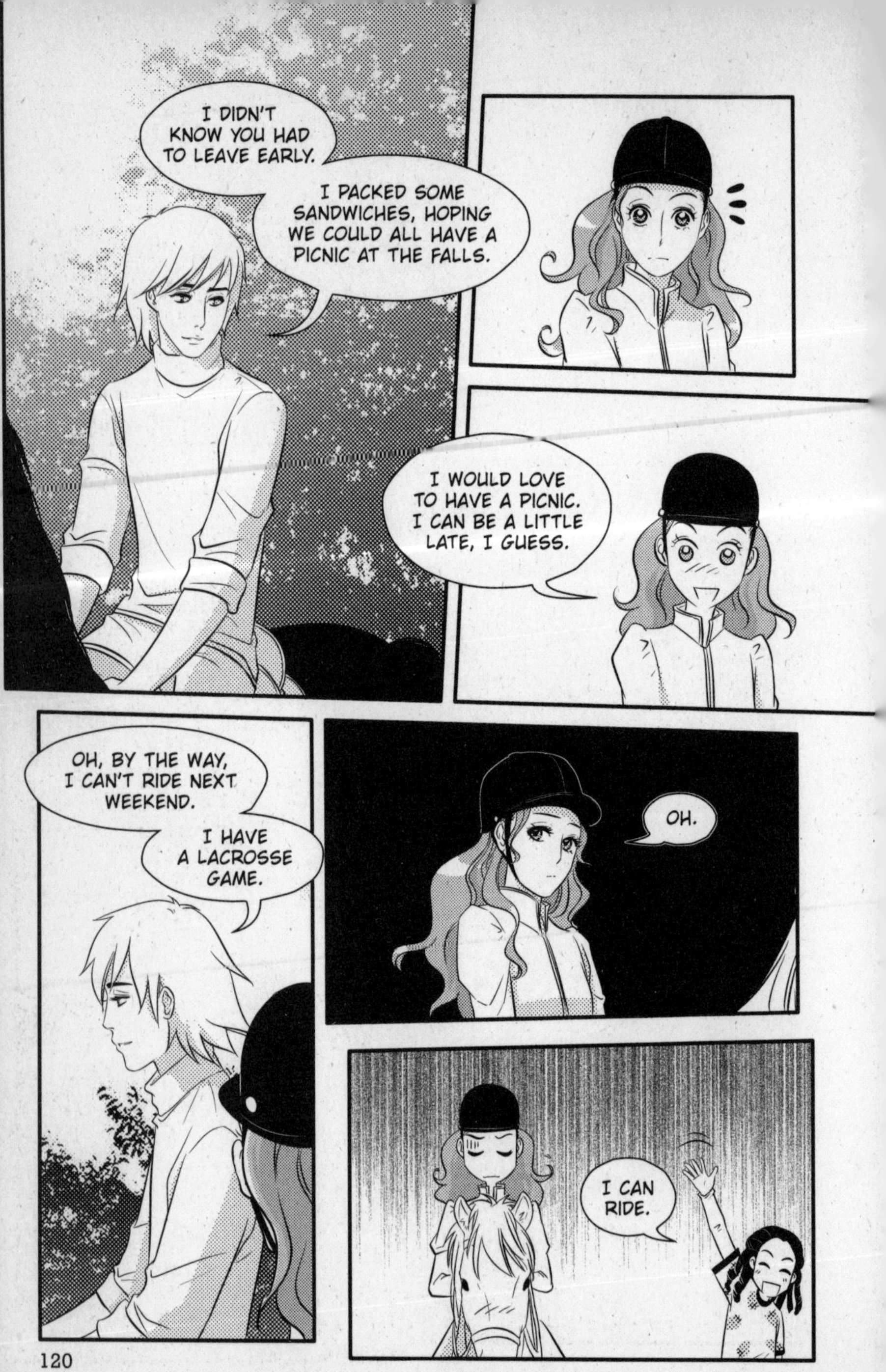
I DIDN'T KNOW YOU HAD TO LEAVE EARLY.
I PACKED SOME SANDWICHES, HOPING WE COULD ALL HAVE A PICNIC AT THE FALLS.
I WOULD LOVE TO HAVE A PICNIC. I CAN BE A LITTLE LATE, I GUESS.
OH, BY THE WAY, I CAN'T RIDE NEXT WEEKEND.
I HAVE A LACROSSE GAME.
OH.
I CAN RIDE.

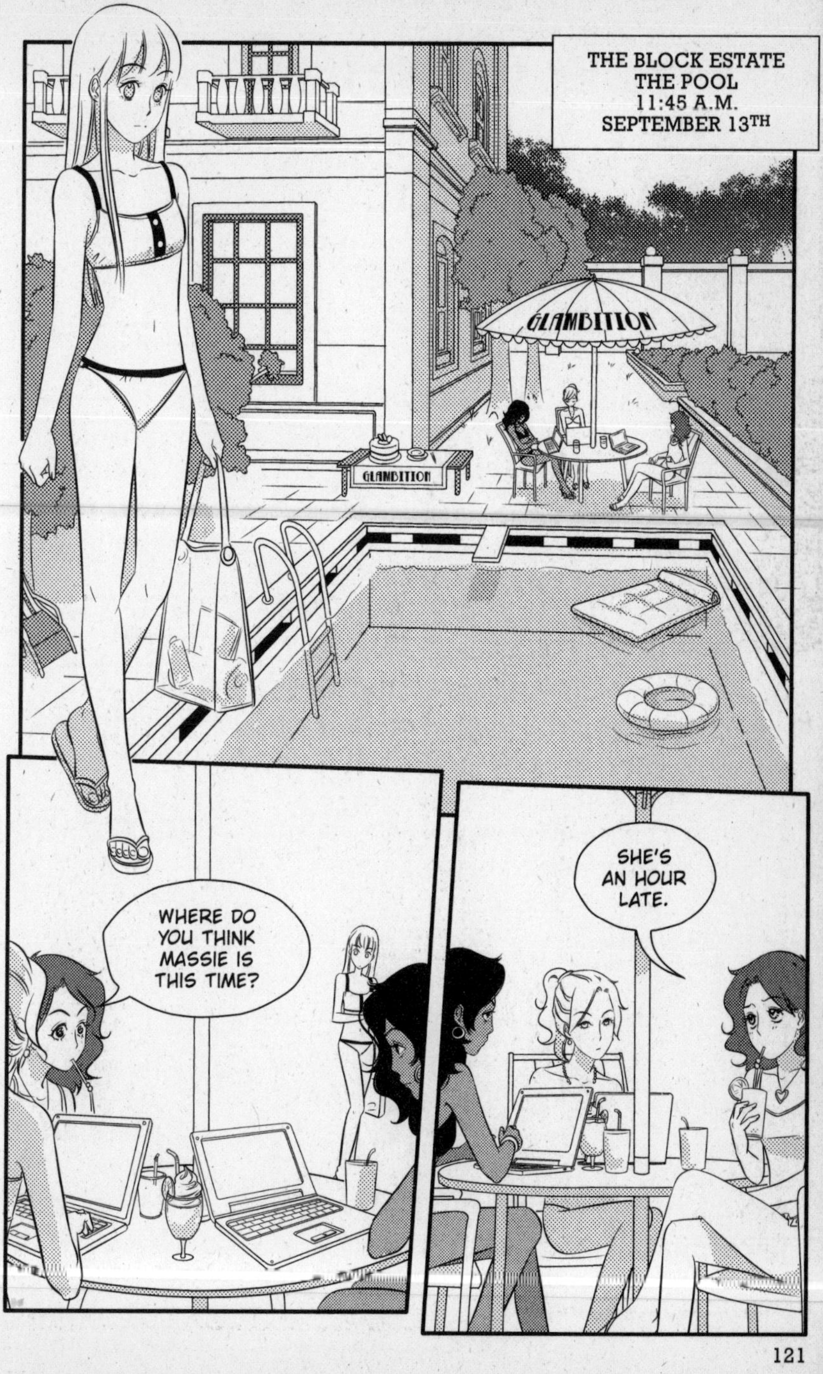
THE BLOCK ESTATE
THE POOL
11:45 A.M.
SEPTEMBER 13TH
GLAMBITION
GLAMBITION
WHERE DO YOU THINK MASSIE IS THIS TIME?
SHE'S AN HOUR LATE.

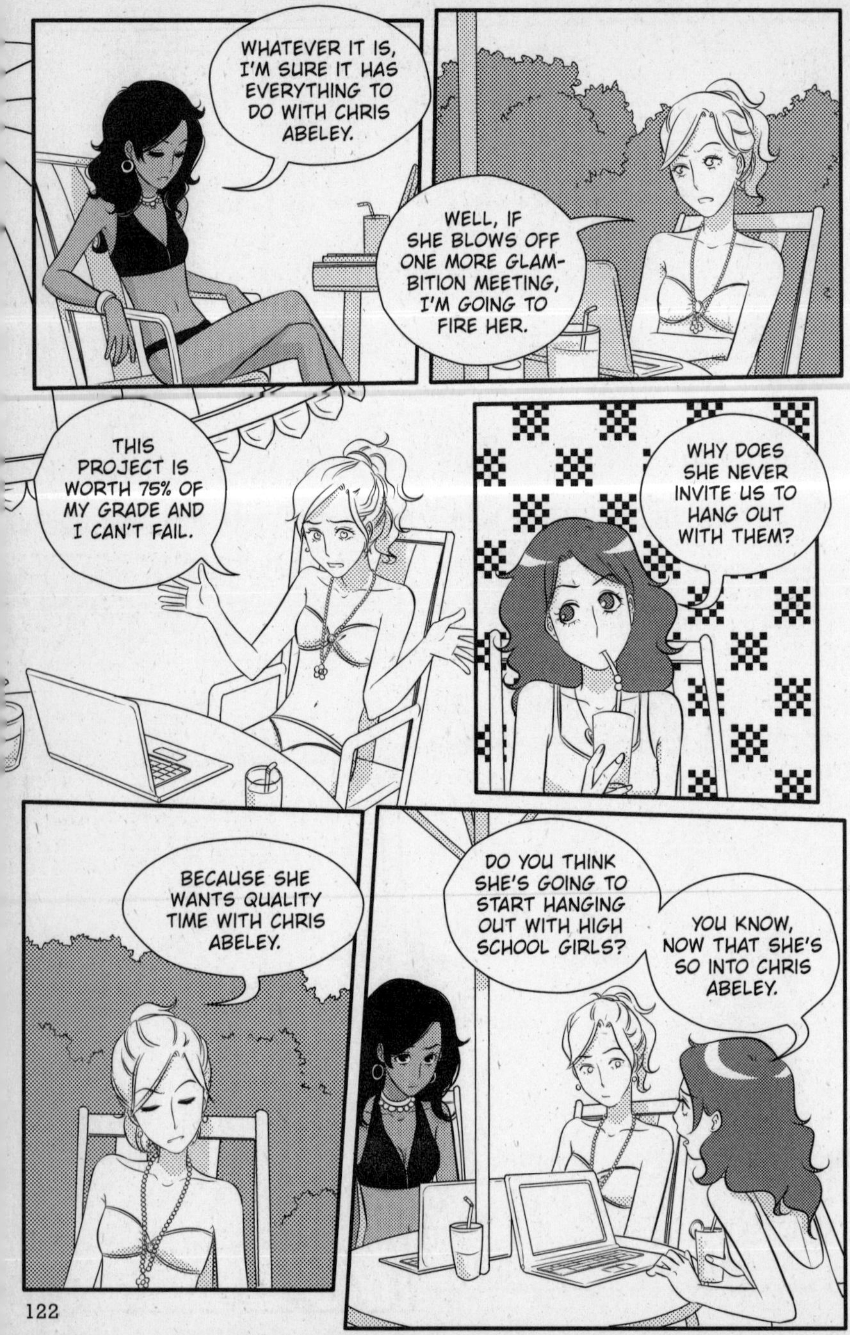
WHATEVER IT IS, I'M SURE IT HAS EVERYTHING TO DO WITH CHRIS ABELEY.
WELL, IF SHE BLOWS OFF ONE MORE GLAM-BITION MEETING, I'M GOING TO FIRE HER.
THIS PROJECT IS WORTH 75% OF MY GRADE AND I CAN'T FAIL.
WHY DOES SHE NEVER INVITE US TO HANG OUT WITH THEM?
BECAUSE SHE WANTS QUALITY TIME WITH CHRIS ABELEY.
DO YOU THINK SHE'S GOING TO START HANGING OUT WITH HIGH SCHOOL GIRLS?
YOU KNOW, NOW THAT SHE'S SO INTO CHRIS ABELEY.

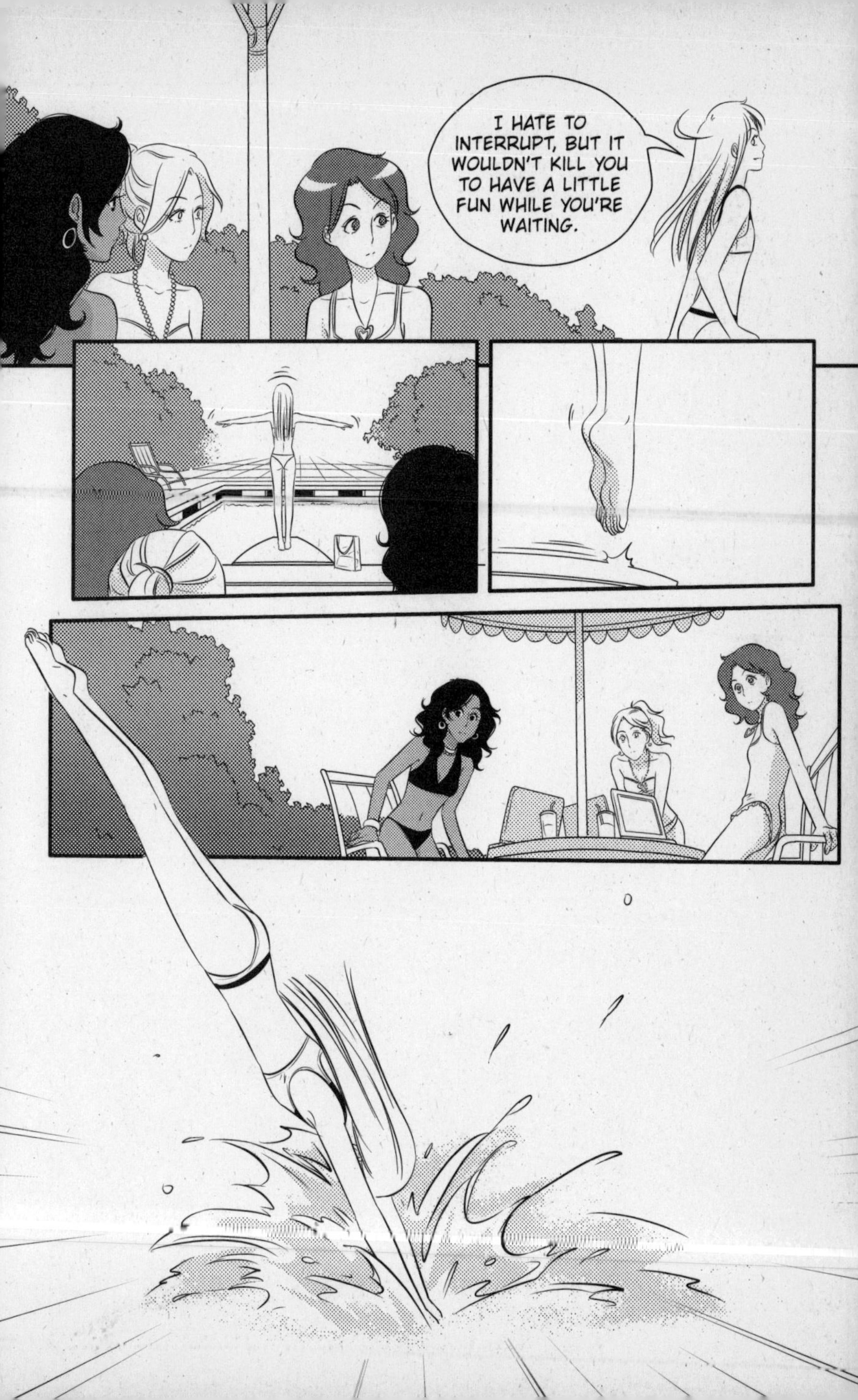
I HATE TO INTERRUPT, BUT IT WOULDN'T KILL YOU TO HAVE A LITTLE FUN WHILE YOU'RE WAITING.

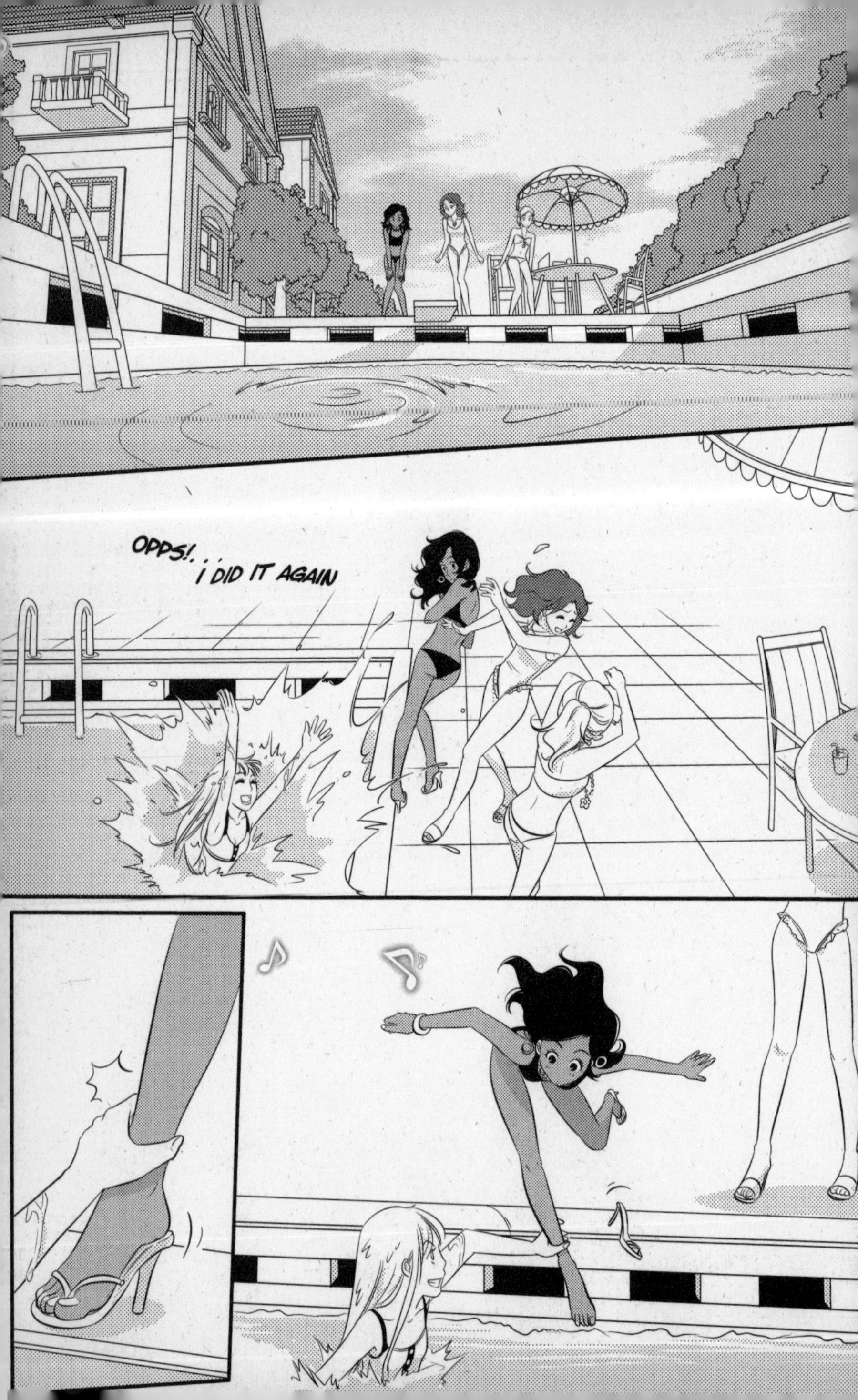
OPPS!. . I DID IT AGAIN

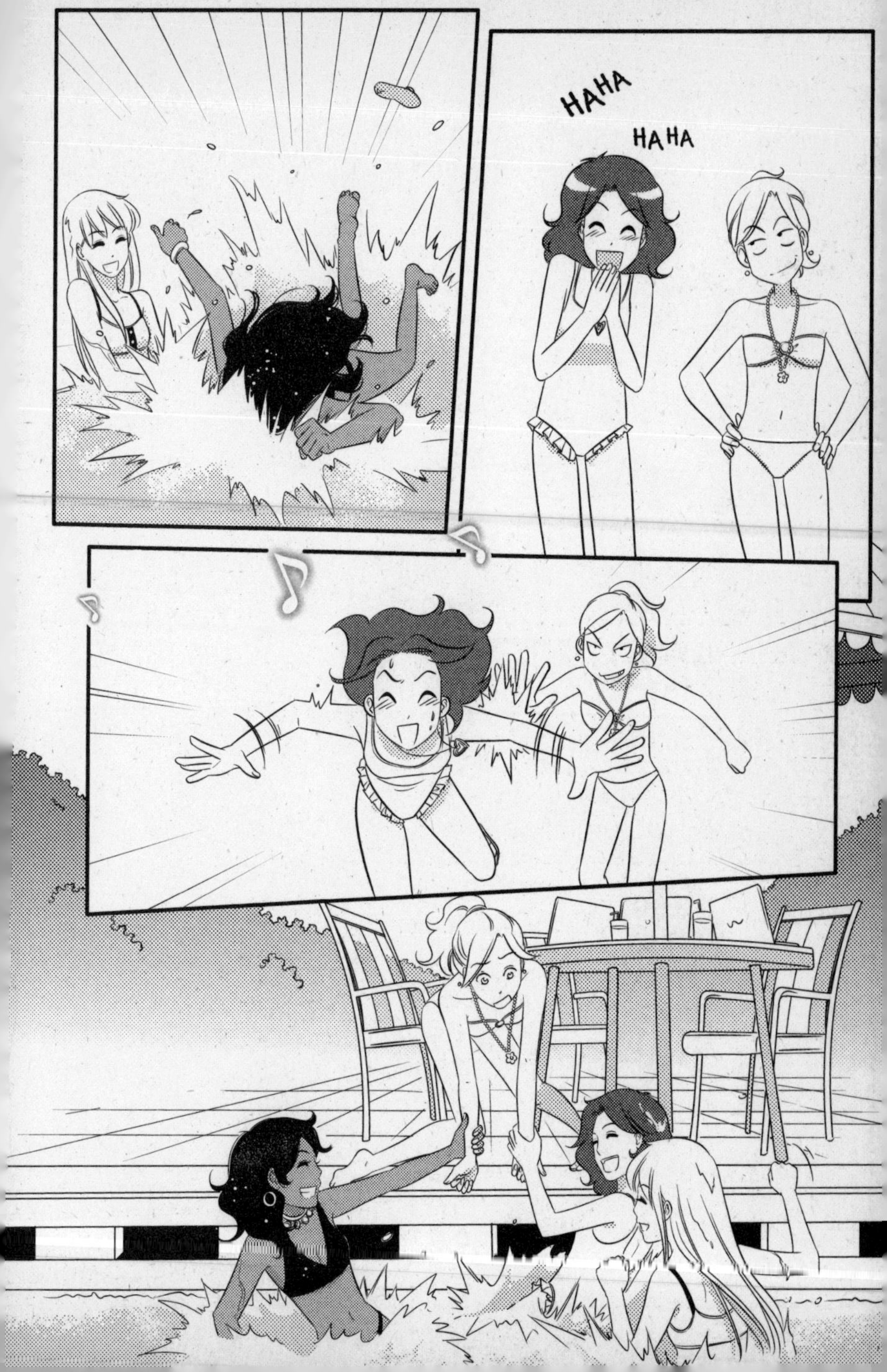
HAHA
HAHA

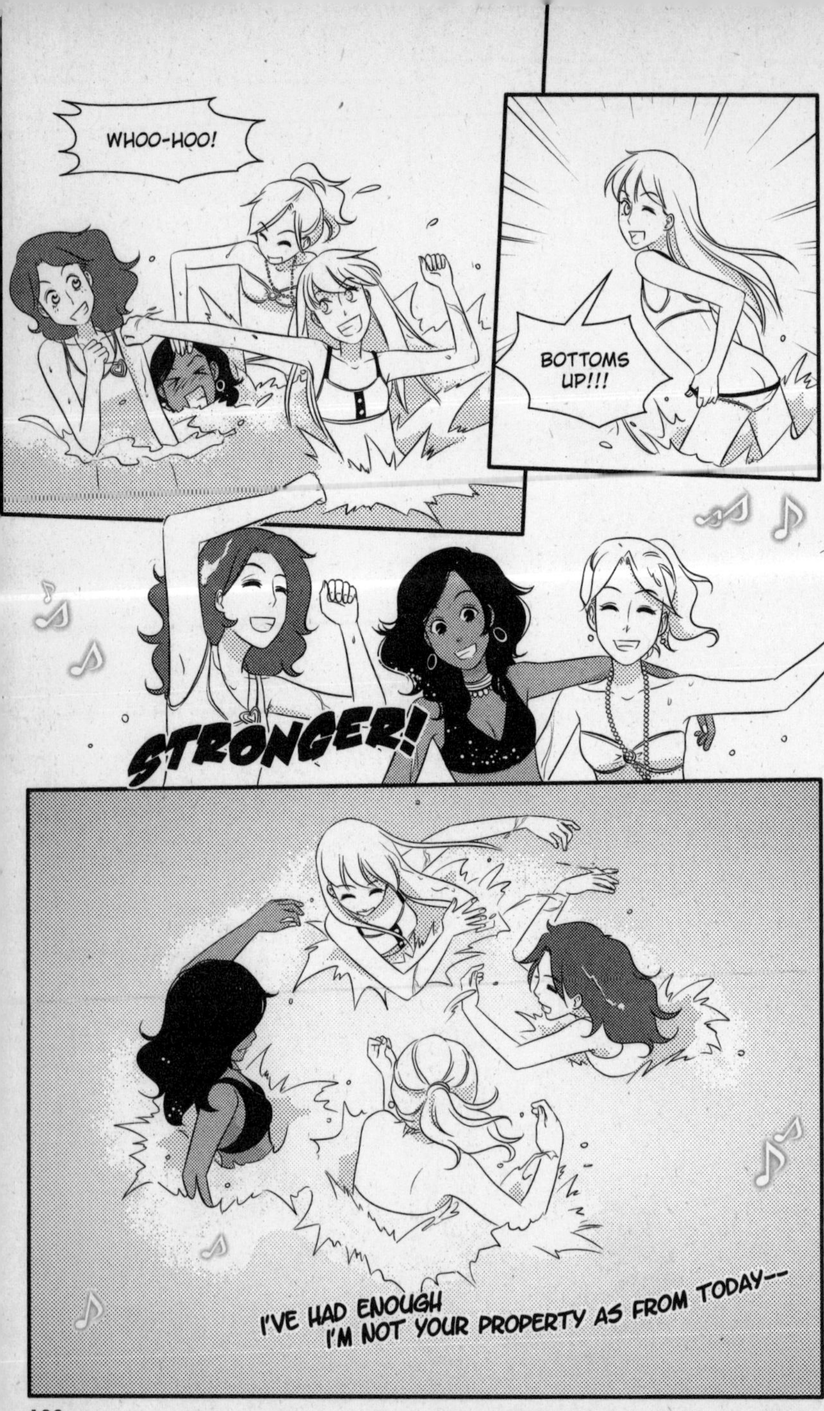
WHOO-HOO!
BOTTOMS UP!!!
STRONGER!
I'VE HAD ENOUGH
I'M NOT YOUR PROPERTY AS FROM TODAY--

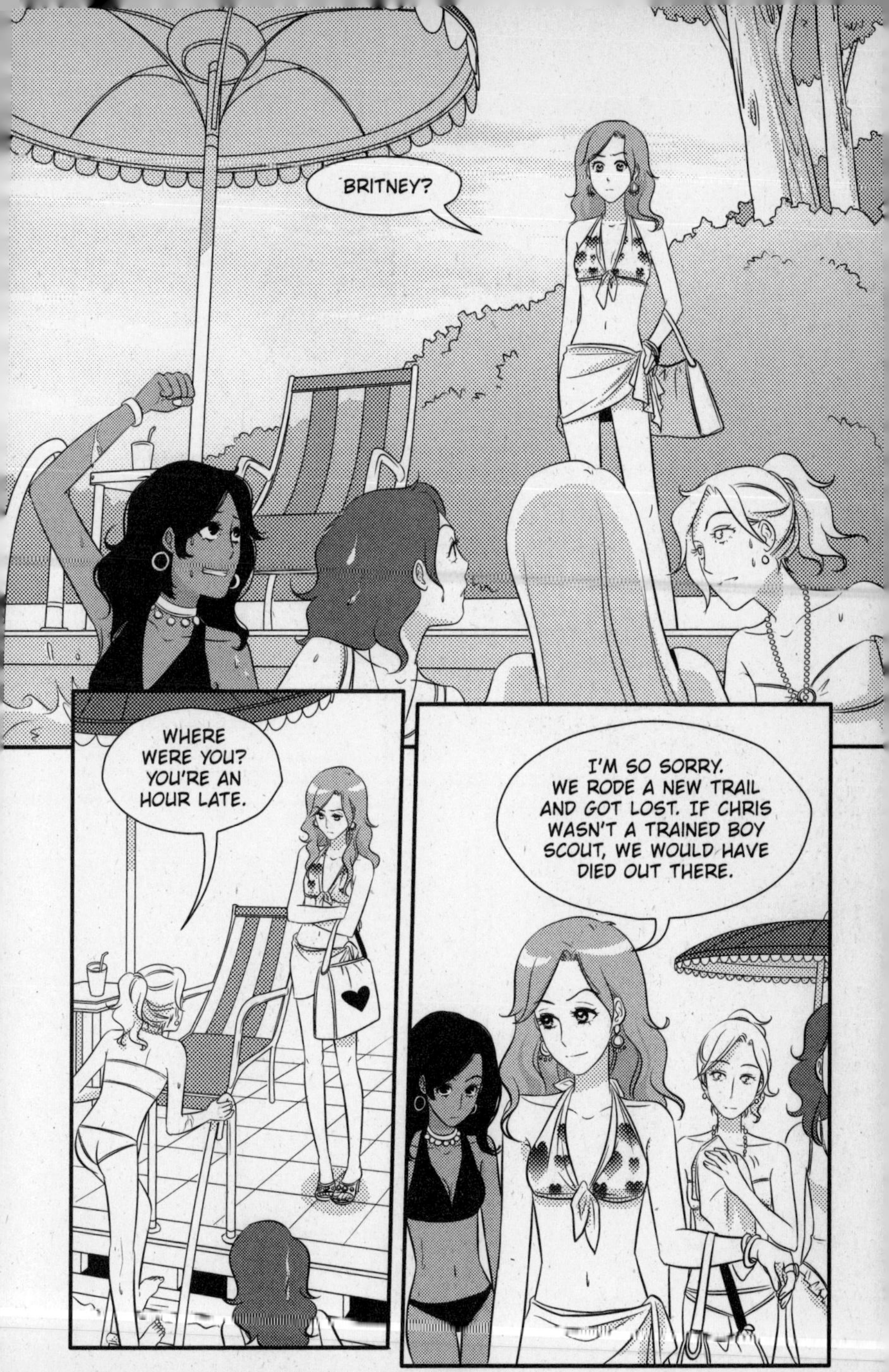
BRITNEY?
WHERE WERE YOU? YOU'RE AN HOUR LATE.
I'M SO SORRY. WE RODE A NEW TRAIL AND GOT LOST. IF CHRIS WASN'T A TRAINED BOY SCOUT, WE WOULD HAVE DIED OUT THERE.

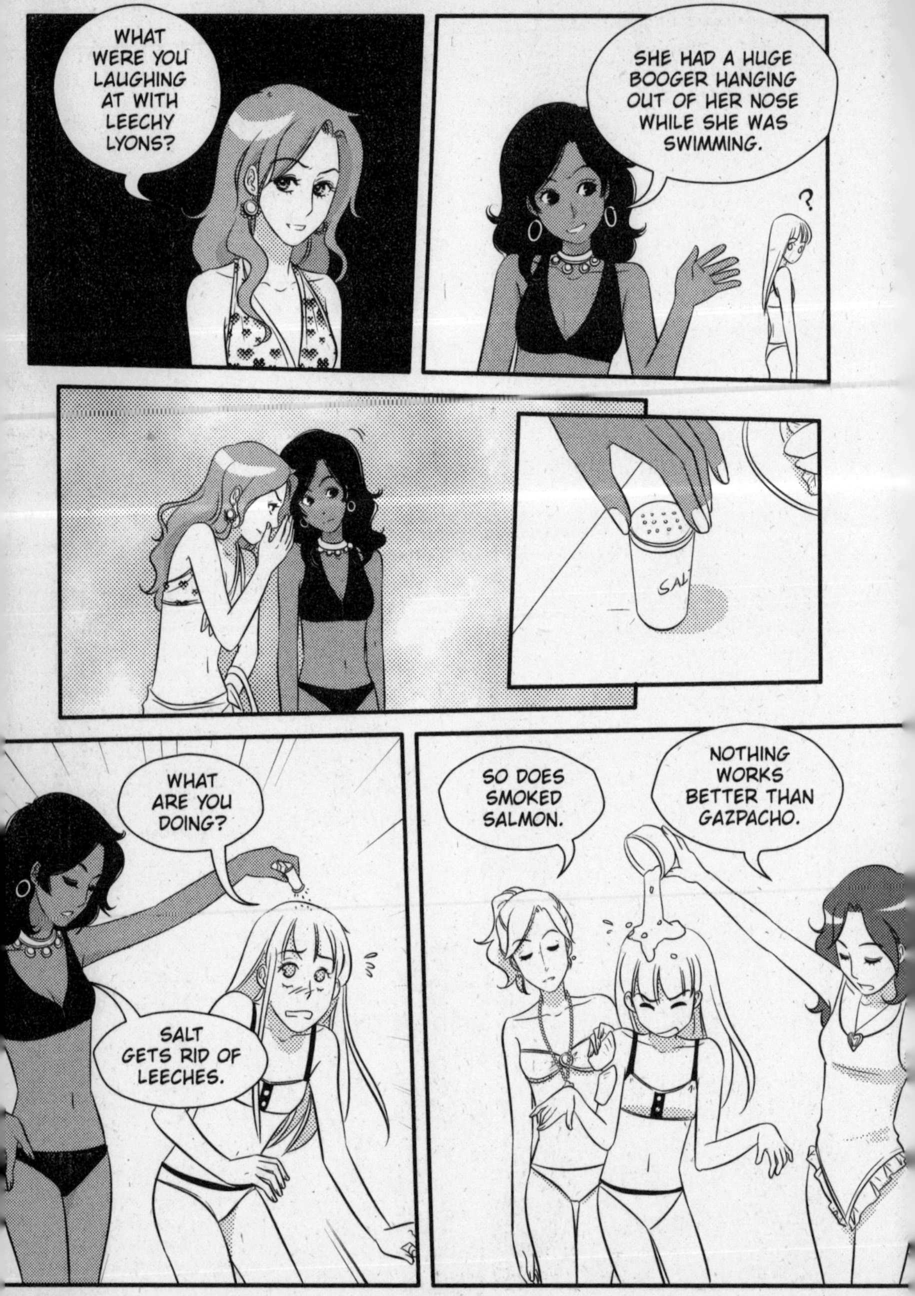
WHAT WERE YOU LAUGHING AT WITH LEECHY LYONS?
SHE HAD A HUGE BOOGER HANGING OUT OF HER NOSE WHILE SHE WAS SWIMMING.
?
SALT
WHAT ARE YOU DOING?
SALT GETS RID OF LEECHES.
SO DOES SMOKED SALMON.
NOTHING WORKS BETTER THAN GAZPACHO.

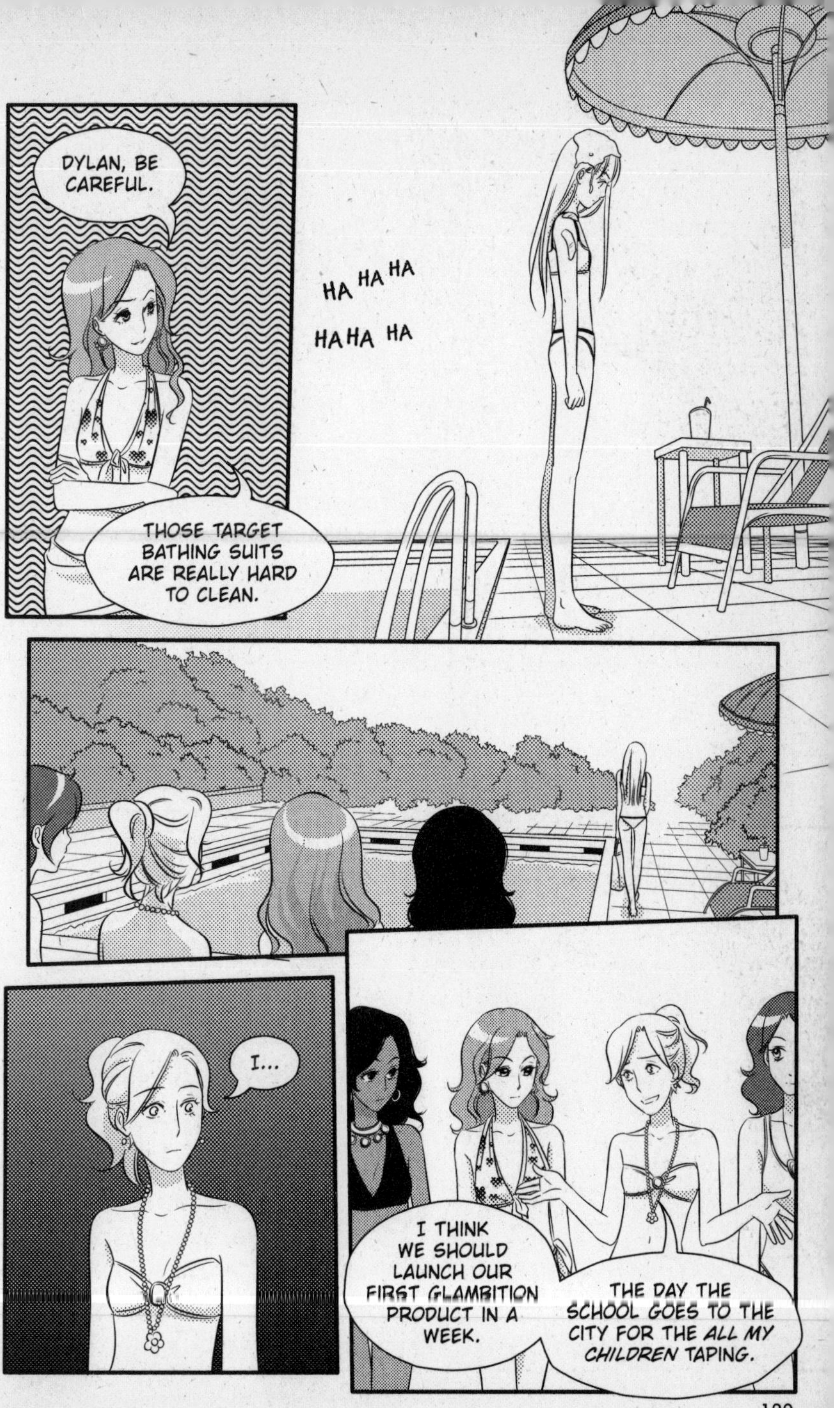
DYLAN, BE CAREFUL.
THOSE TARGET BATHING SUITS ARE REALLY HARD TO CLEAN.
HA HA HA
HA HA HA
I...
I THINK WE SHOULD LAUNCH OUR FIRST GLAMBITION PRODUCT IN A WEEK.
THE DAY THE SCHOOL GOES TO THE CITY FOR THE *ALL MY CHILDREN* TAPING.

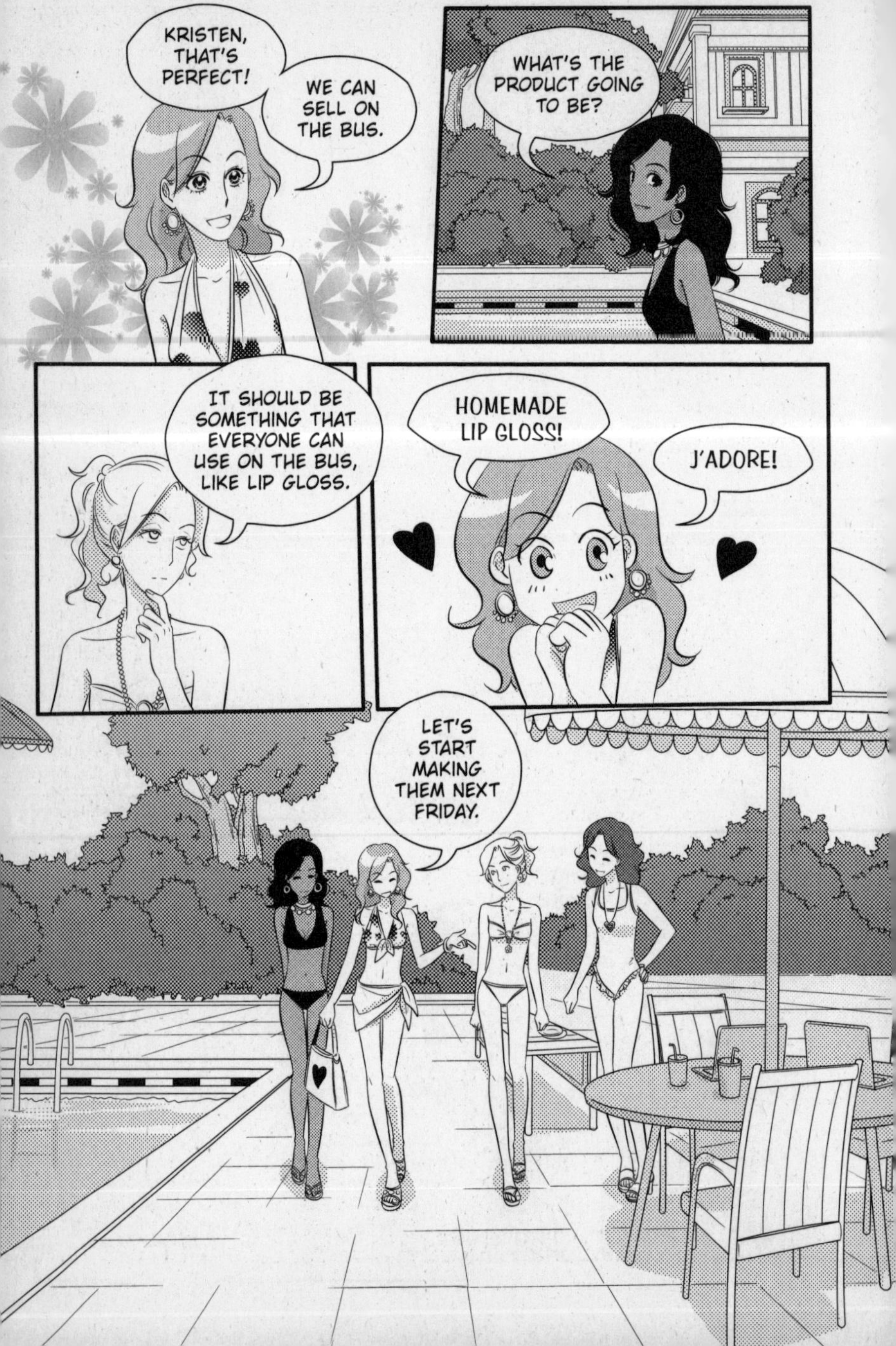
KRISTEN, THAT'S PERFECT!
WE CAN SELL ON THE BUS.
WHAT'S THE PRODUCT GOING TO BE?
IT SHOULD BE SOMETHING THAT EVERYONE CAN USE ON THE BUS, LIKE LIP GLOSS.
HOMEMADE LIP GLOSS!
J'ADORE!
LET'S START MAKING THEM NEXT FRIDAY.

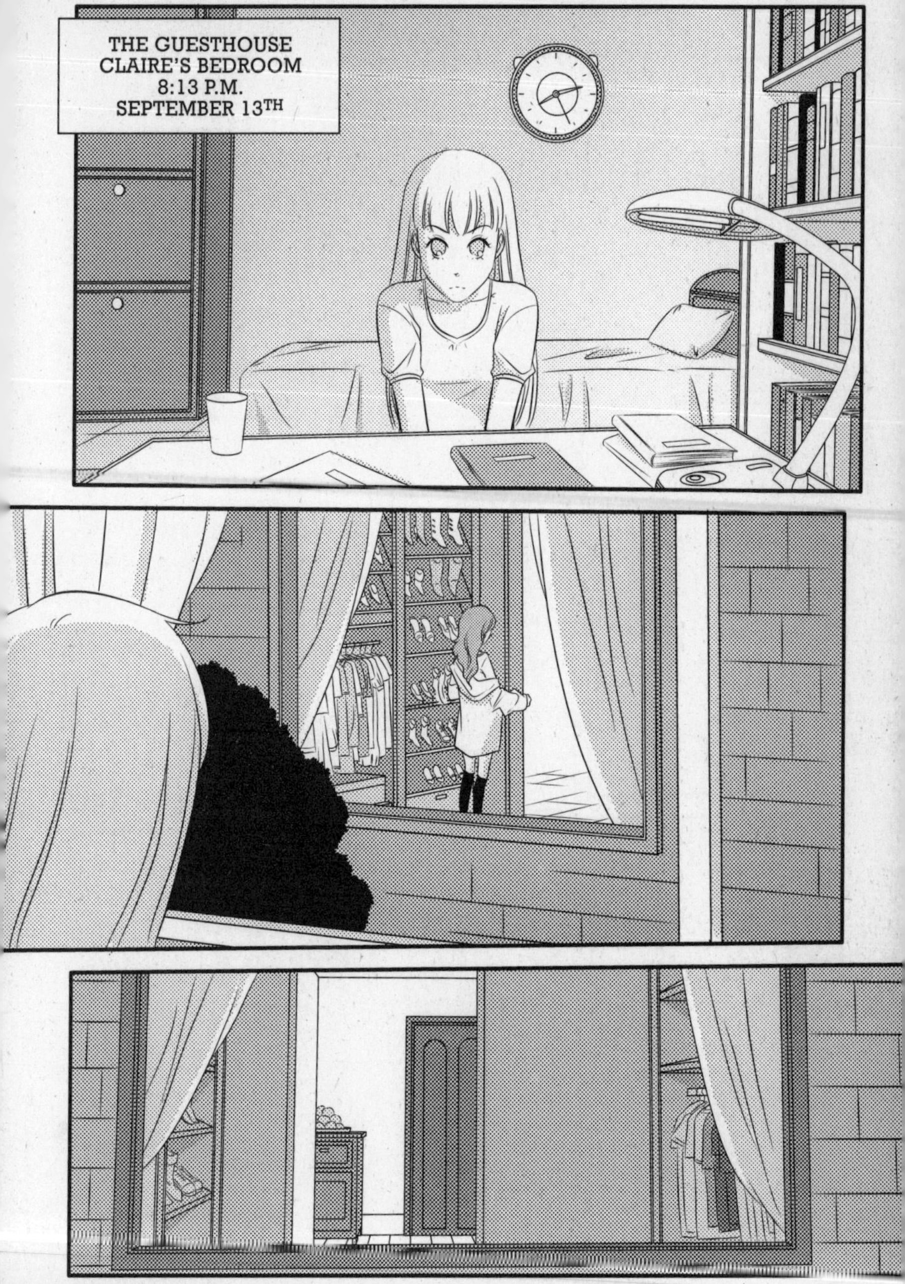
THE GUESTHOUSE
CLAIRE'S BEDROOM
8:13 P.M.
SEPTEMBER 13TH

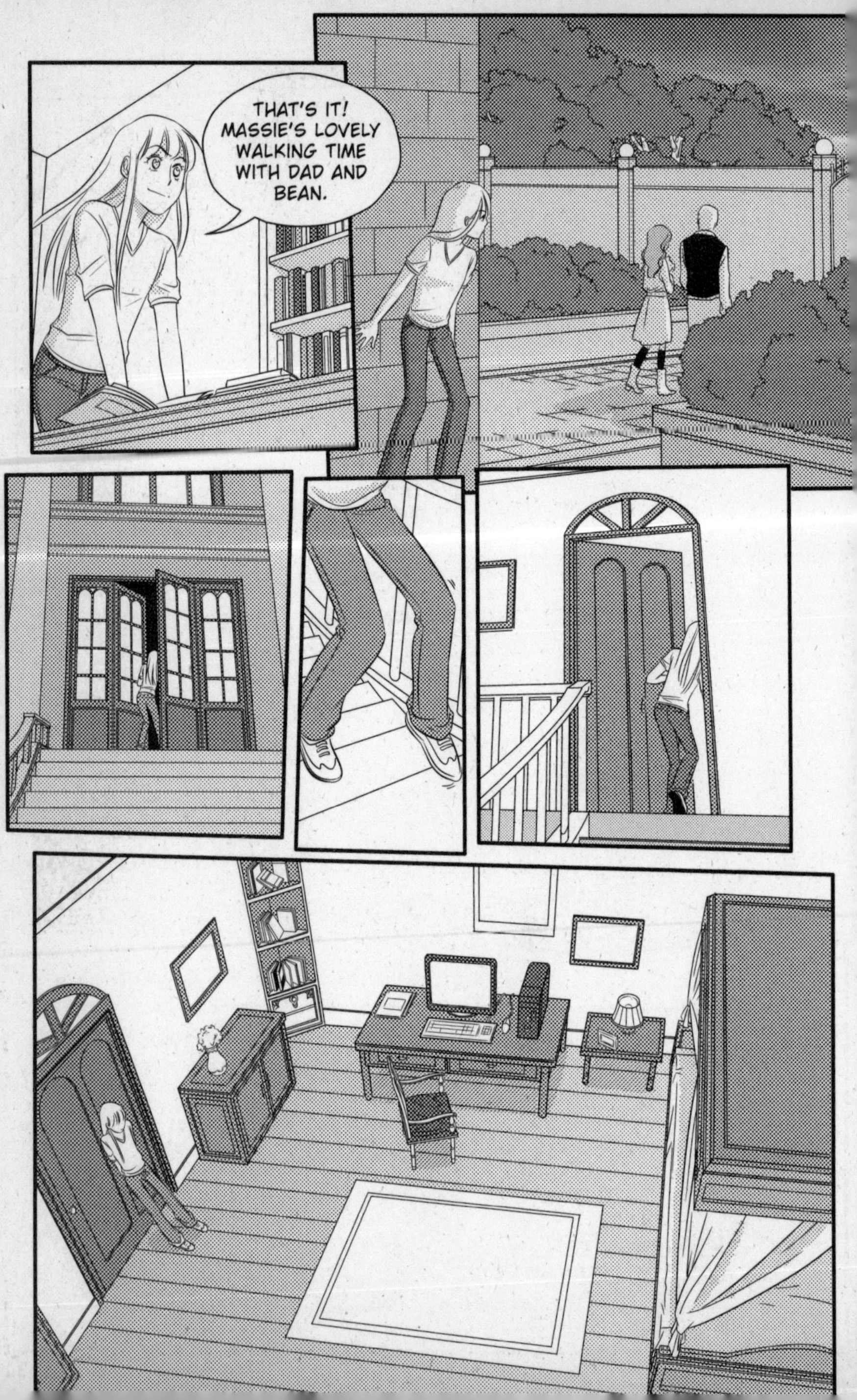
THAT'S IT! MASSIE'S LOVELY WALKING TIME WITH DAD AND BEAN.

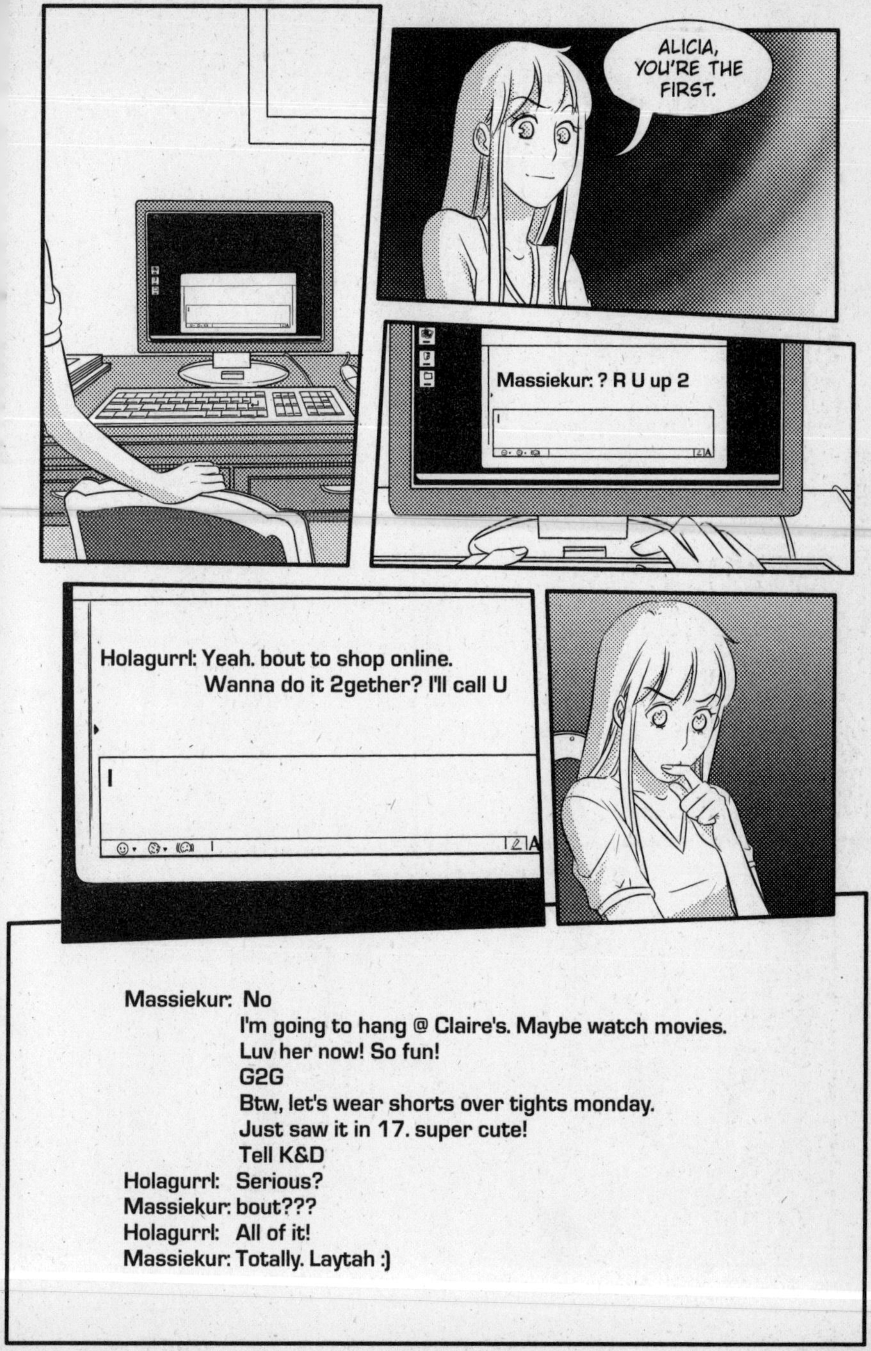
ALICIA, YOU'RE THE FIRST.
Massiekur: ? R U up 2
Holagurrl: Yeah. bout to shop online.
Wanna do it 2gether? I'll call U
Massiekur: No
I'm going to hang @ Claire's. Maybe watch movies.
Luv her now! So fun!
G2G
Btw, let's wear shorts over tights monday.
Just saw it in 17. super cute!
Tell K&D
Holagurrl: Serious?
Massiekur: bout???
Holagurrl: All of it!
Massiekur: Totally. Laytah :)

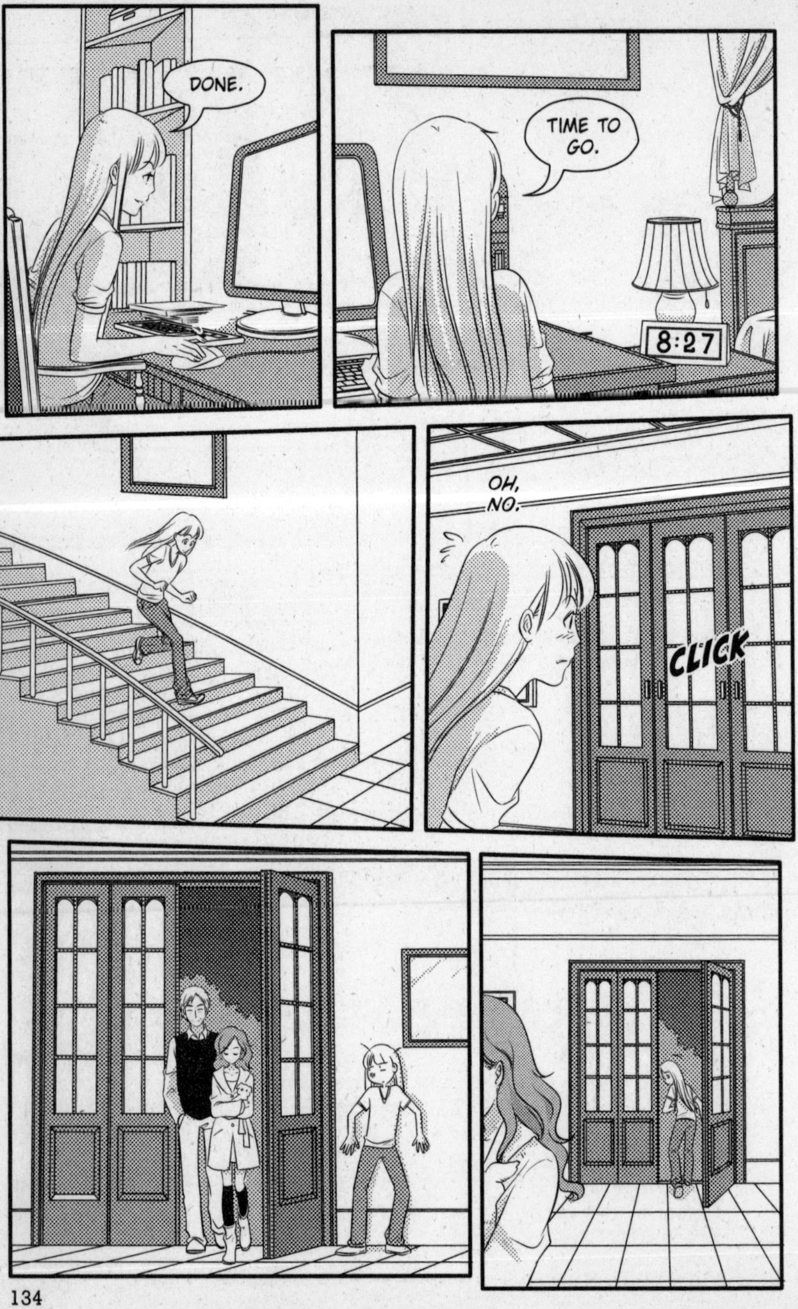
DONE.
TIME TO GO.
8:27
OH, NO.
CLICK

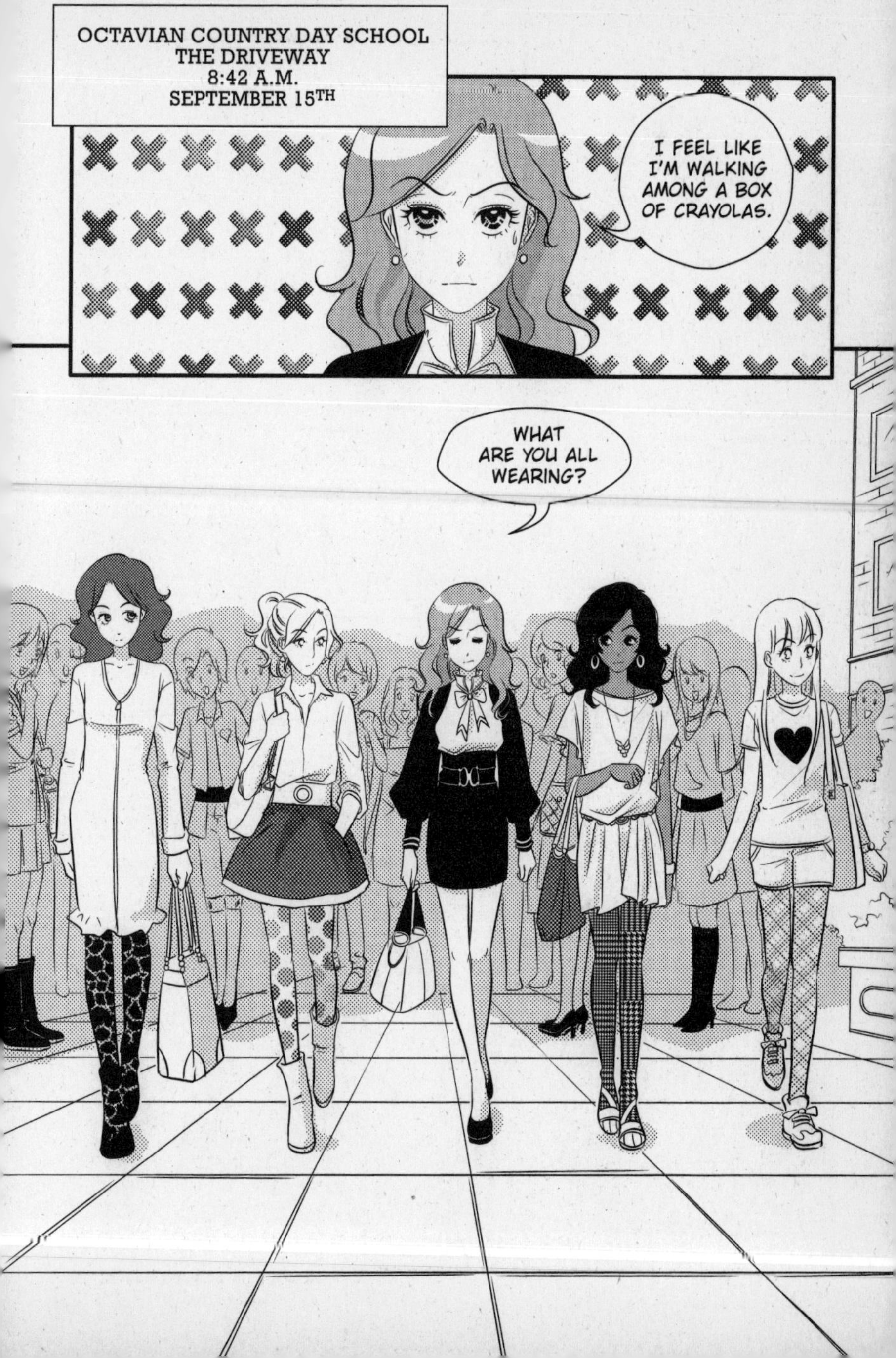
OCTAVIAN COUNTRY DAY SCHOOL
THE DRIVEWAY
8:42 A.M.
SEPTEMBER 15TH
I FEEL LIKE I'M WALKING AMONG A BOX OF CRAYOLAS.
WHAT ARE YOU ALL WEARING?

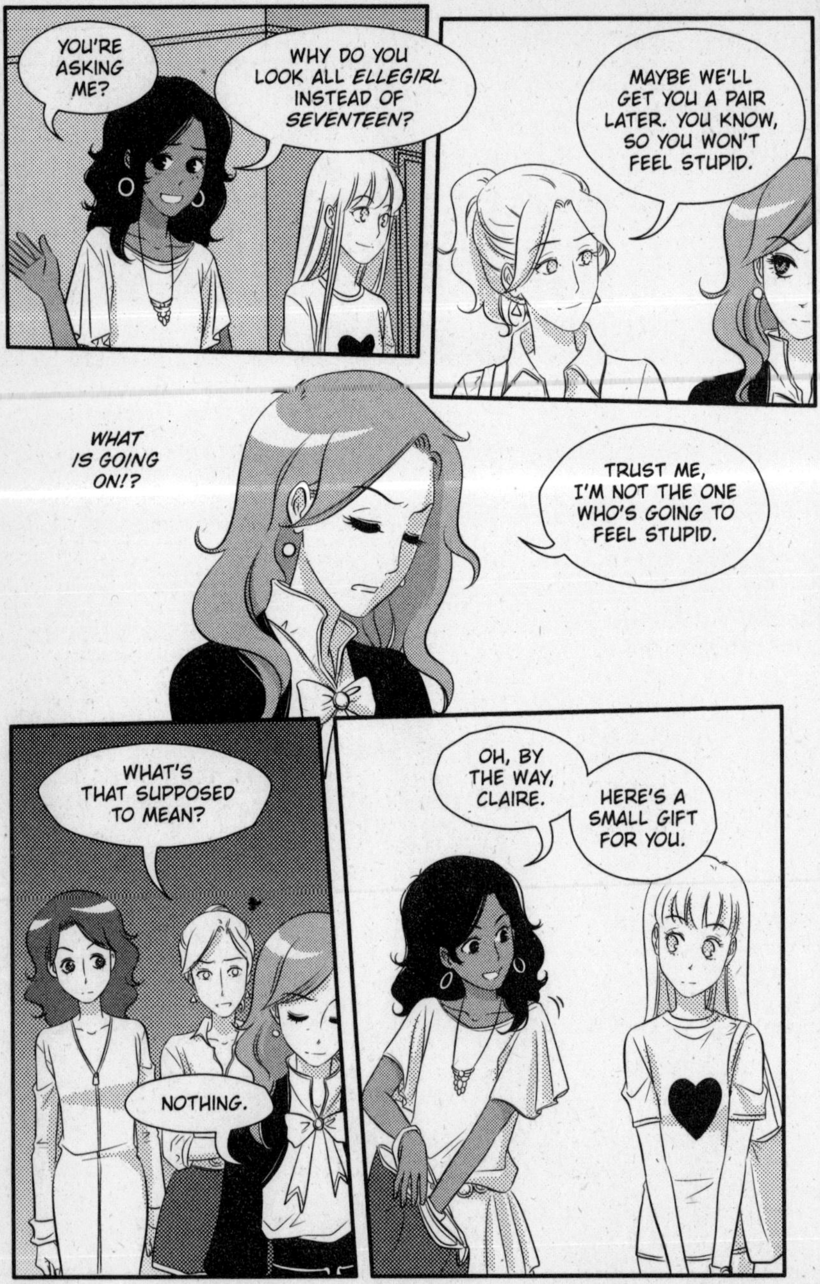
YOU'RE ASKING ME?
WHY DO YOU LOOK ALL *ELLEGIRL* INSTEAD OF *SEVENTEEN*?
MAYBE WE'LL GET YOU A PAIR LATER. YOU KNOW, SO YOU WON'T FEEL STUPID.
*WHAT IS GOING ON!?*
TRUST ME, I'M NOT THE ONE WHO'S GOING TO FEEL STUPID.
WHAT'S THAT SUPPOSED TO MEAN?
NOTHING.
OH, BY THE WAY, CLAIRE.
HERE'S A SMALL GIFT FOR YOU.

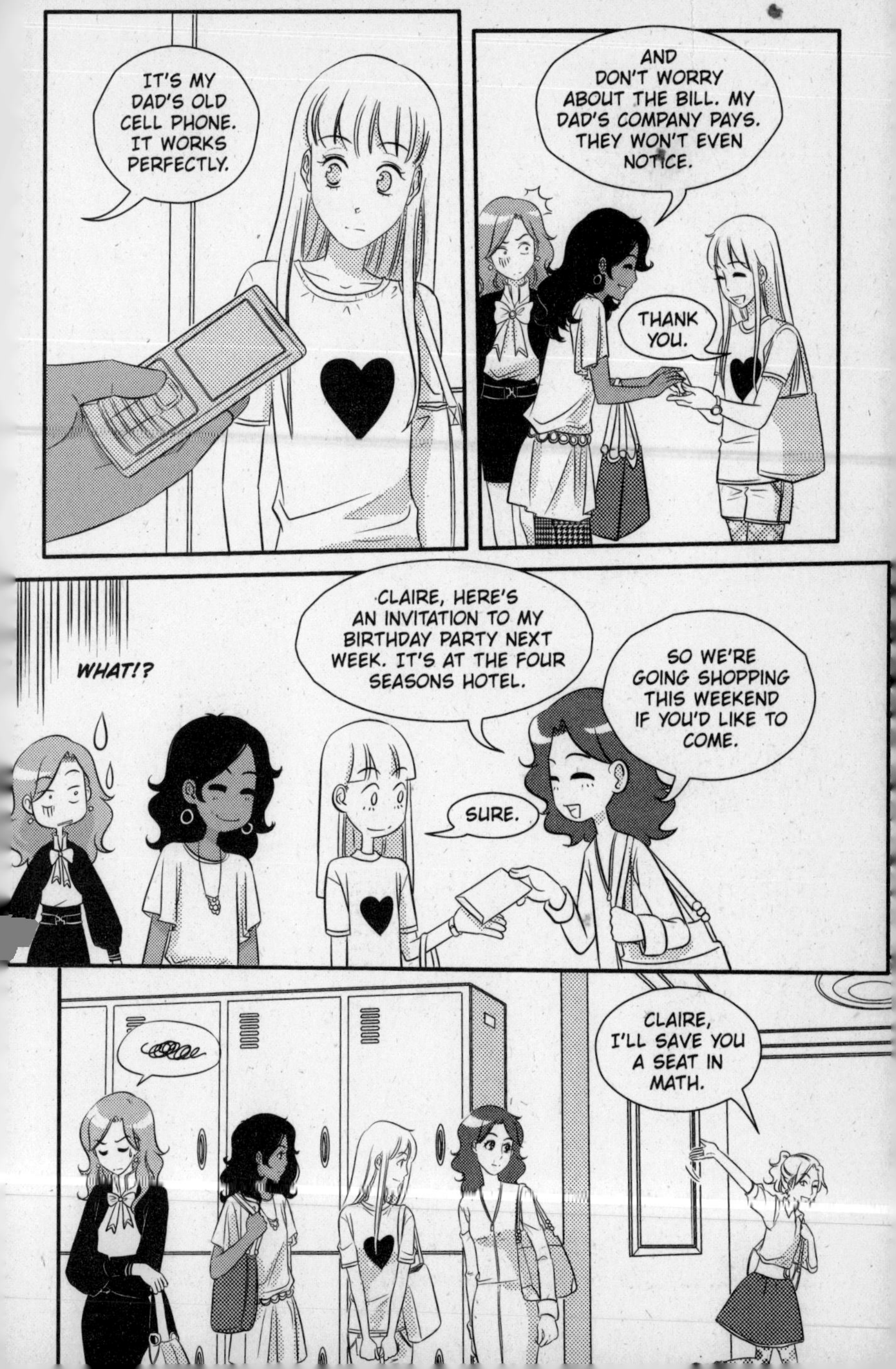
IT'S MY DAD'S OLD CELL PHONE. IT WORKS PERFECTLY.
AND DON'T WORRY ABOUT THE BILL. MY DAD'S COMPANY PAYS. THEY WON'T EVEN NOTICE.
THANK YOU.
WHAT!?
CLAIRE, HERE'S AN INVITATION TO MY BIRTHDAY PARTY NEXT WEEK. IT'S AT THE FOUR SEASONS HOTEL.
SO WE'RE GOING SHOPPING THIS WEEKEND IF YOU'D LIKE TO COME.
SURE.
CLAIRE, I'LL SAVE YOU A SEAT IN MATH.

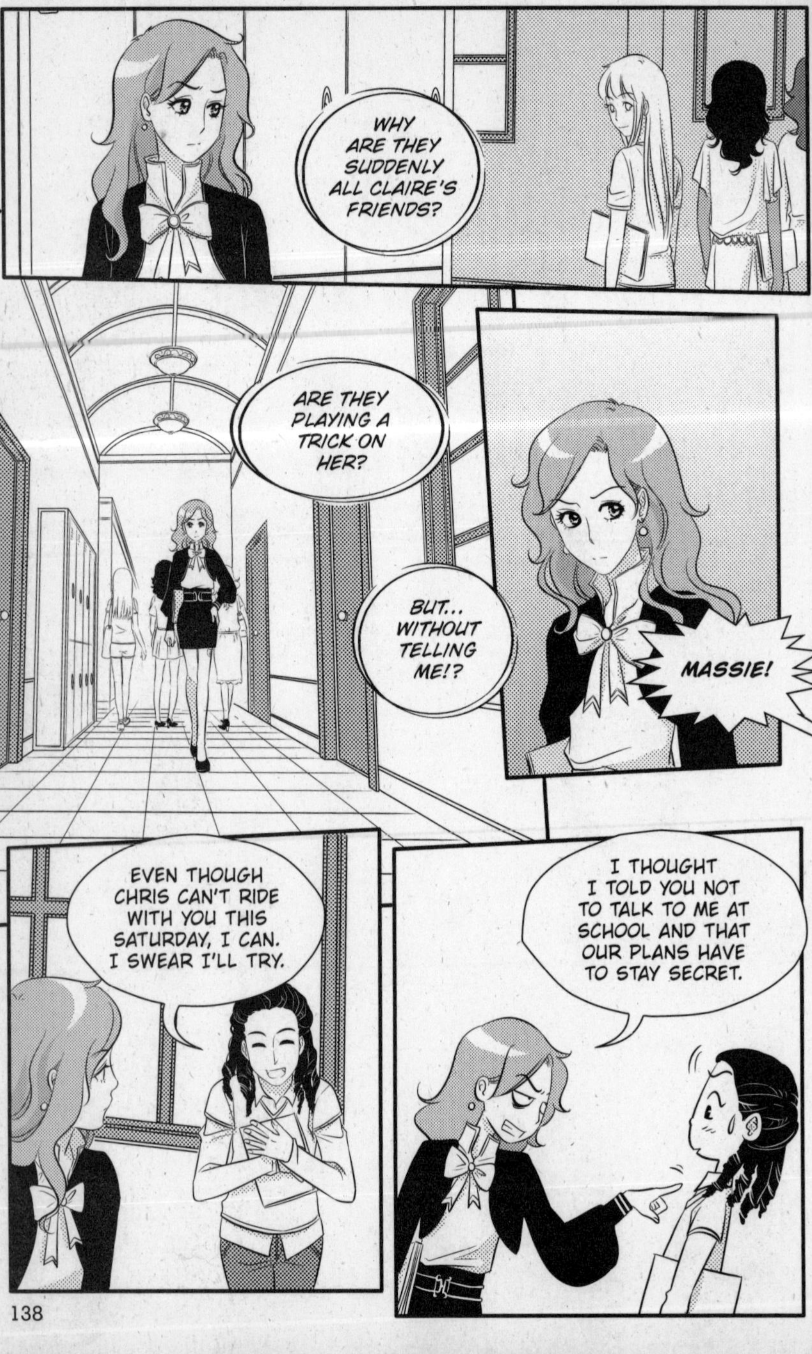
WHY ARE THEY SUDDENLY ALL CLAIRE'S FRIENDS?
ARE THEY PLAYING A TRICK ON HER?
BUT... WITHOUT TELLING ME!?
MASSIE!
EVEN THOUGH CHRIS CAN'T RIDE WITH YOU THIS SATURDAY, I CAN. I SWEAR I'LL TRY.
I THOUGHT I TOLD YOU NOT TO TALK TO ME AT SCHOOL AND THAT OUR PLANS HAVE TO STAY SECRET.

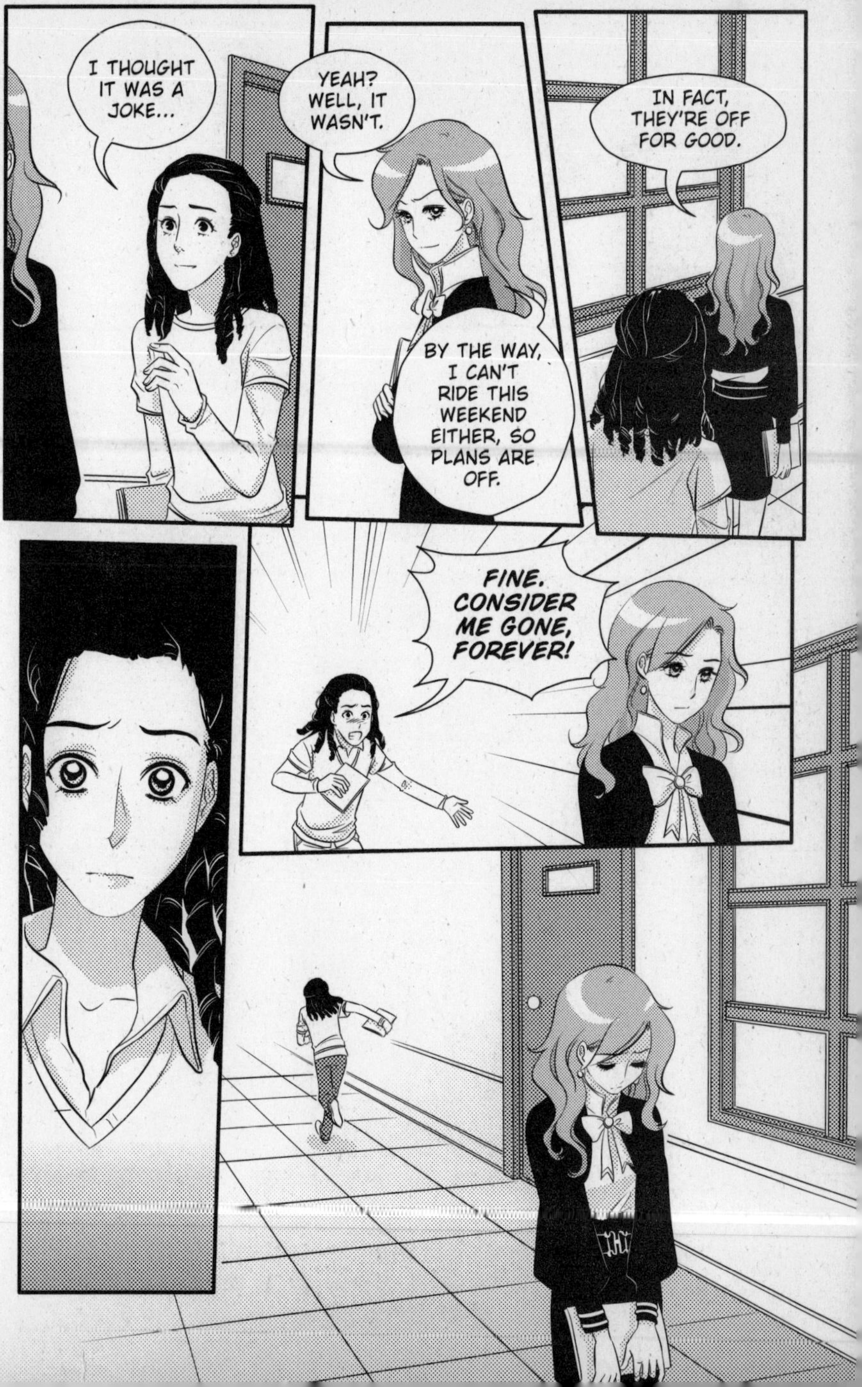
I THOUGHT IT WAS A JOKE...
YEAH? WELL, IT WASN'T.
BY THE WAY, I CAN'T RIDE THIS WEEKEND EITHER, SO PLANS ARE OFF.
IN FACT, THEY'RE OFF FOR GOOD.
FINE. CONSIDER ME GONE, FOREVER!

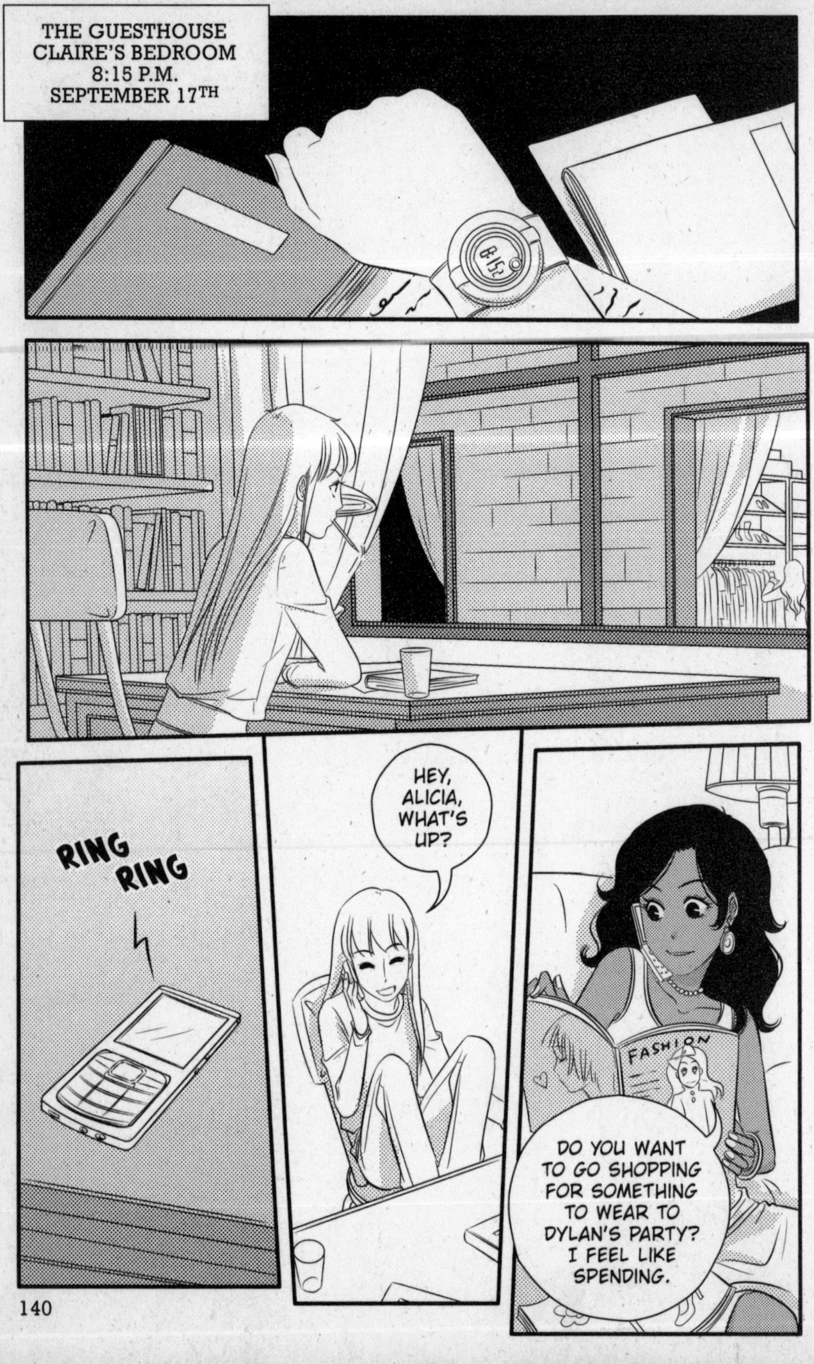
THE GUESTHOUSE
CLAIRE'S BEDROOM
8:15 P.M.
SEPTEMBER 17TH
RING RING
HEY, ALICIA, WHAT'S UP?
FASHION
DO YOU WANT TO GO SHOPPING FOR SOMETHING TO WEAR TO DYLAN'S PARTY? I FEEL LIKE SPENDING.

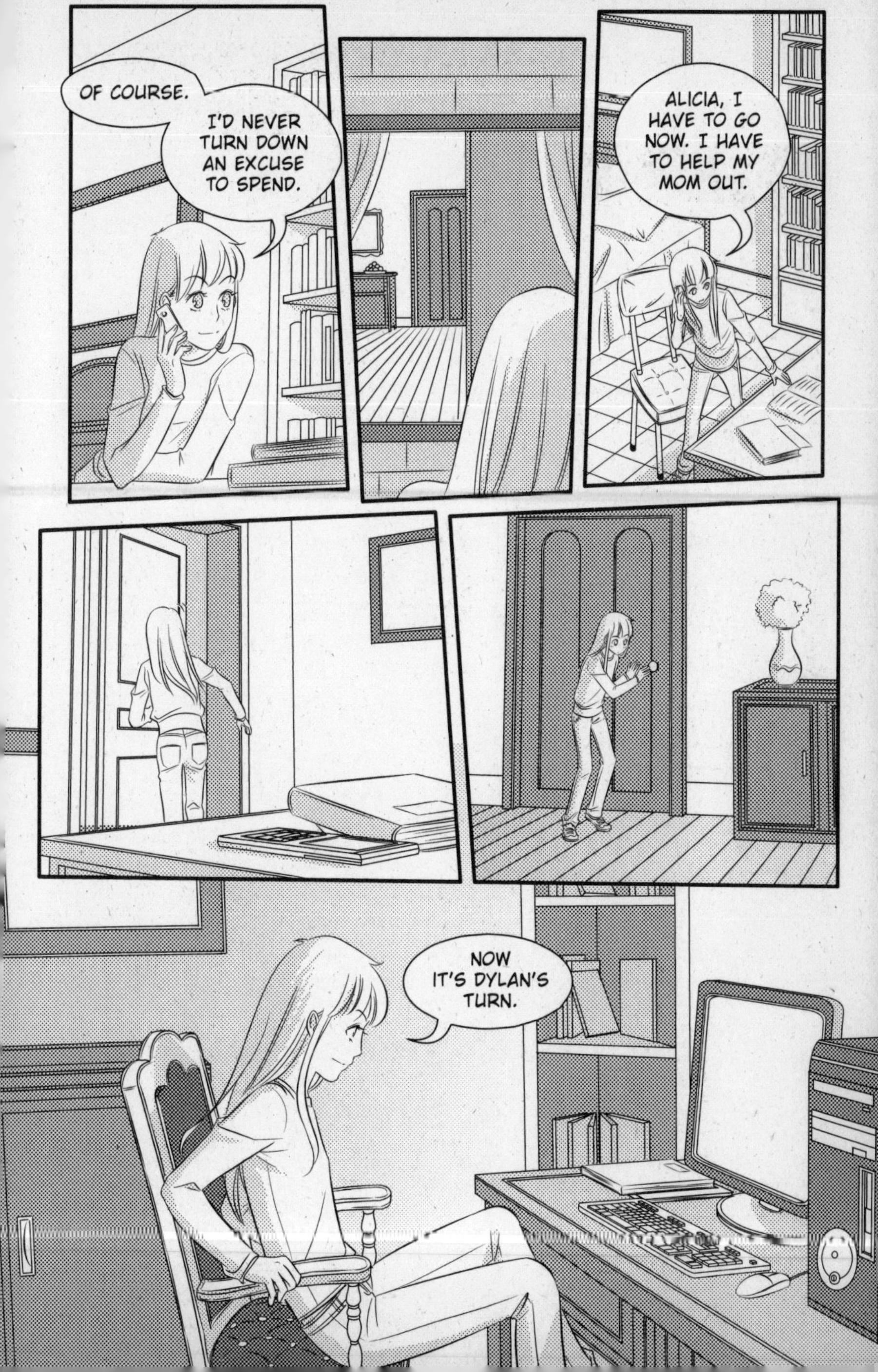
OF COURSE.
I'D NEVER TURN DOWN AN EXCUSE TO SPEND.
ALICIA, I HAVE TO GO NOW. I HAVE TO HELP MY MOM OUT.
NOW IT'S DYLAN'S TURN.

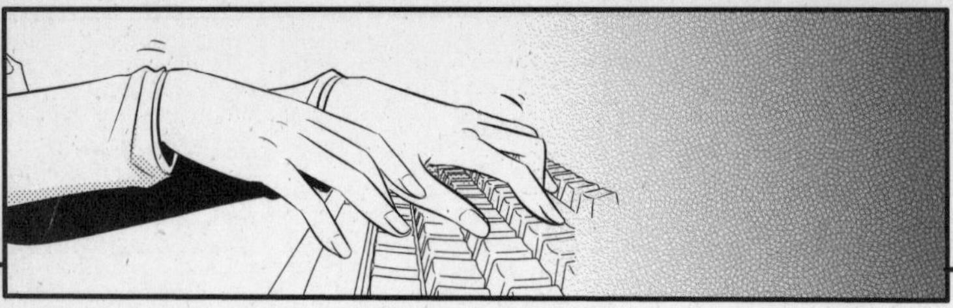

Massiekur: Whats up?
Bigredhead: Biology homework : (
Massiekur: What R U wearing to your party?
Bigredhead: Maybe a suede mini from barney's catalog, PG23
Massiekur: Think your legs will look good in a mini?
Bigredhead: Why?
Massiekur: Just asking.
G2G, claire just stopped by
Bigredhead: What, do you think I have fat legs?????????

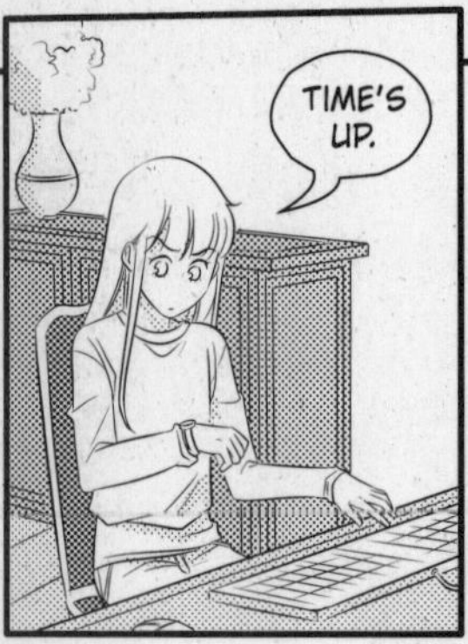
TIME'S UP.

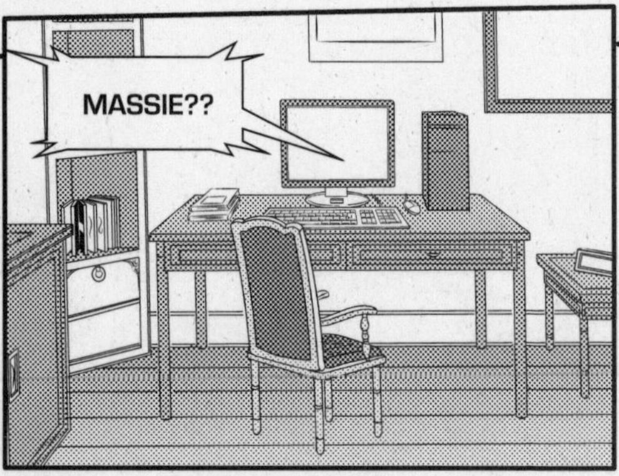
MASSIE??

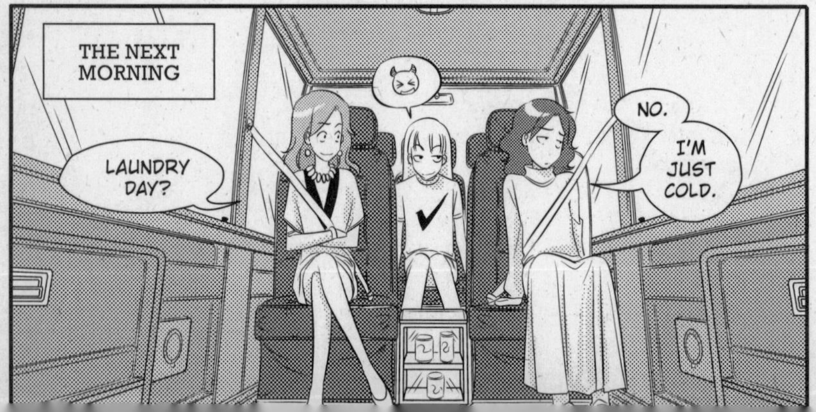
THE NEXT MORNING
LAUNDRY DAY?
NO.
I'M JUST COLD.

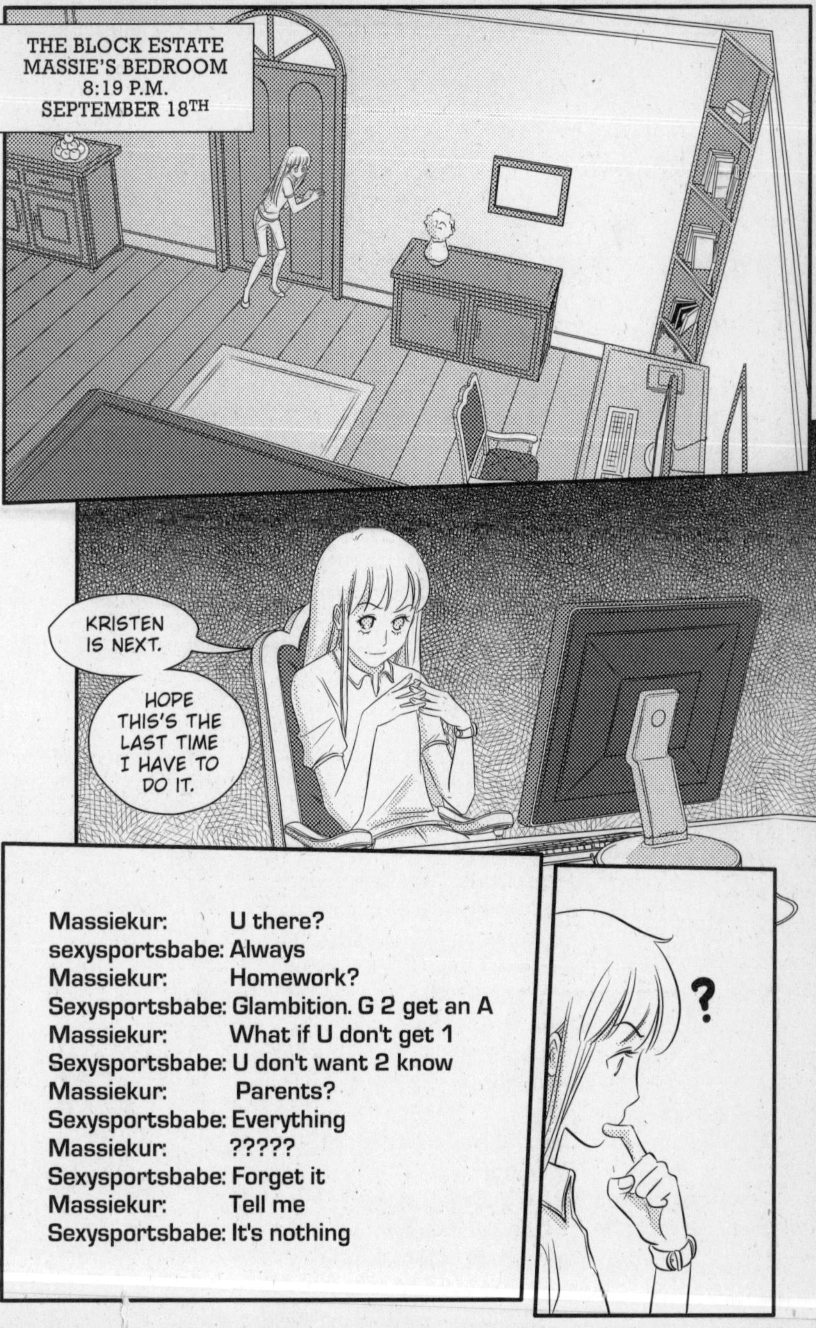
THE BLOCK ESTATE
MASSIE'S BEDROOM
8:19 P.M.
SEPTEMBER 18TH
KRISTEN IS NEXT.
HOPE THIS'S THE LAST TIME I HAVE TO DO IT.
Massiekur: U there?
sexysportsbabe: Always
Massiekur: Homework?
Sexysportsbabe: Glambition. G 2 get an A
Massiekur: What if U don't get 1
Sexysportsbabe: U don't want 2 know
Massiekur: Parents?
Sexysportsbabe: Everything
Massiekur: ?????
Sexysportsbabe: Forget it
Massiekur: Tell me
Sexysportsbabe: It's nothing
?

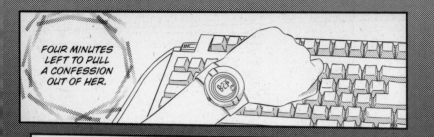

FOUR MINUTES LEFT TO PULL A CONFESSION OUT OF HER.

| | |
|---|---|
| Massiekur: | Secret 4 a secret? I have something I haven't told anyone. |
| Sexysportsbabe: | Swear? |
| Massiekur: | Swear |
| Sexysportsbabe: | K, U 1st |
| Massiekur: | U know how I've been hanging out with C.A. every weekend |
| Sexysportsbabe: | Yeah, I've noticed |
| Massiekur: | LOL<br>Layne has been with us every time |
| Sexysportsbabe: | OMG :p |
| Massiekur: | I've also taken her for mani/pedis and fro yo after school. I actually like her |
| Sexysportsbabe: | OMG x2 |

| | |
|---|---|
| Massiekur: | Your turn |
| Sexysportsbabe: | K but you can't tell<br>U know how I'm always worried about my grades? it's not just cuz I have <u>strict</u> parents. it's because I have <u>poor</u> parents. |
| Sexysportsbabe: | I'm on scholarship at OCD |
| Massiekur: | OMGx3<br>I thought your dad was a rich art dealer |
| Sexysportsbabe: | Was |
| Massiekur: | But you live in the Montdor Building! |
| Sexysportsbabe: | Apt. building next door. |
| Sexysportsbabe: | You better not tell! not even for gossip points. K? |

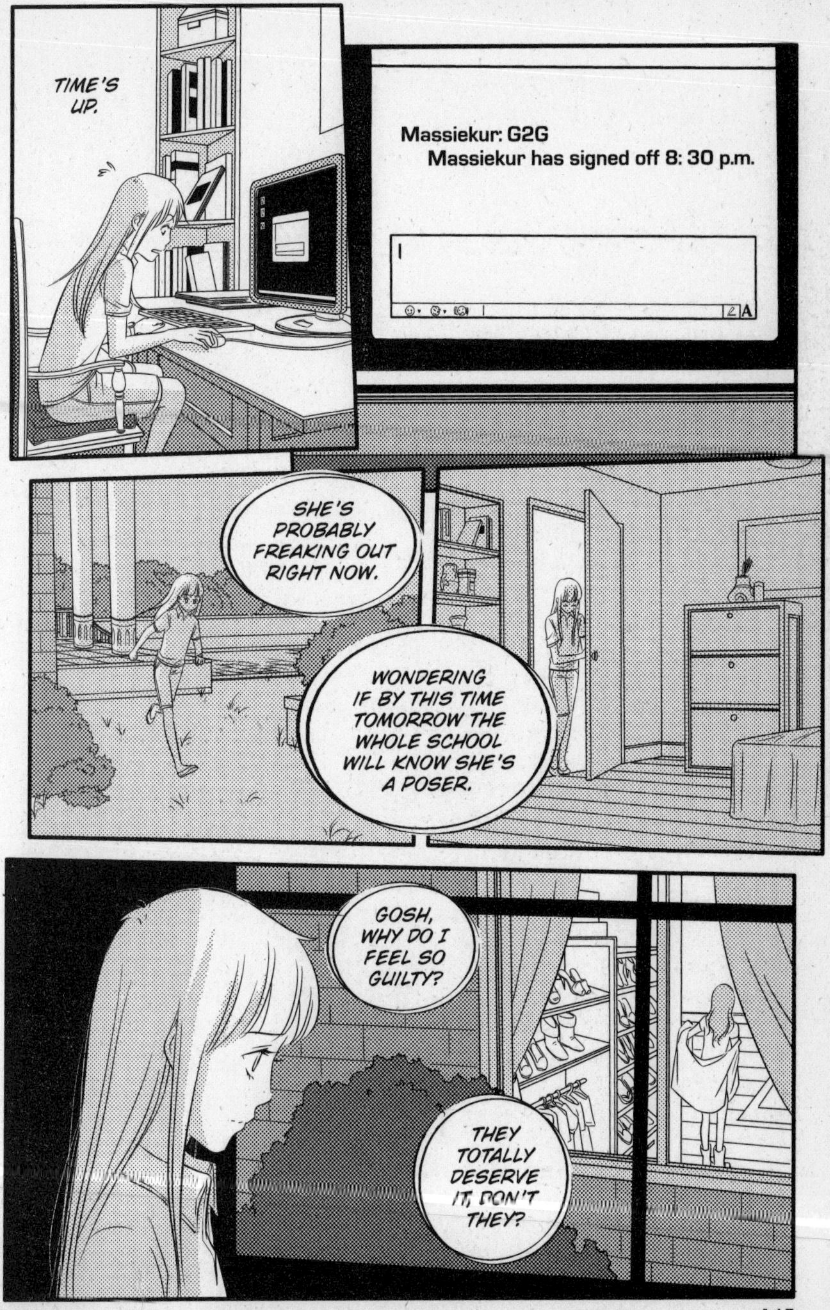
TIME'S UP.
Massiekur: G2G
Massiekur has signed off 8: 30 p.m.
SHE'S PROBABLY FREAKING OUT RIGHT NOW.
WONDERING IF BY THIS TIME TOMORROW THE WHOLE SCHOOL WILL KNOW SHE'S A POSER.
GOSH, WHY DO I FEEL SO GUILTY?
THEY TOTALLY DESERVE IT, DON'T THEY?

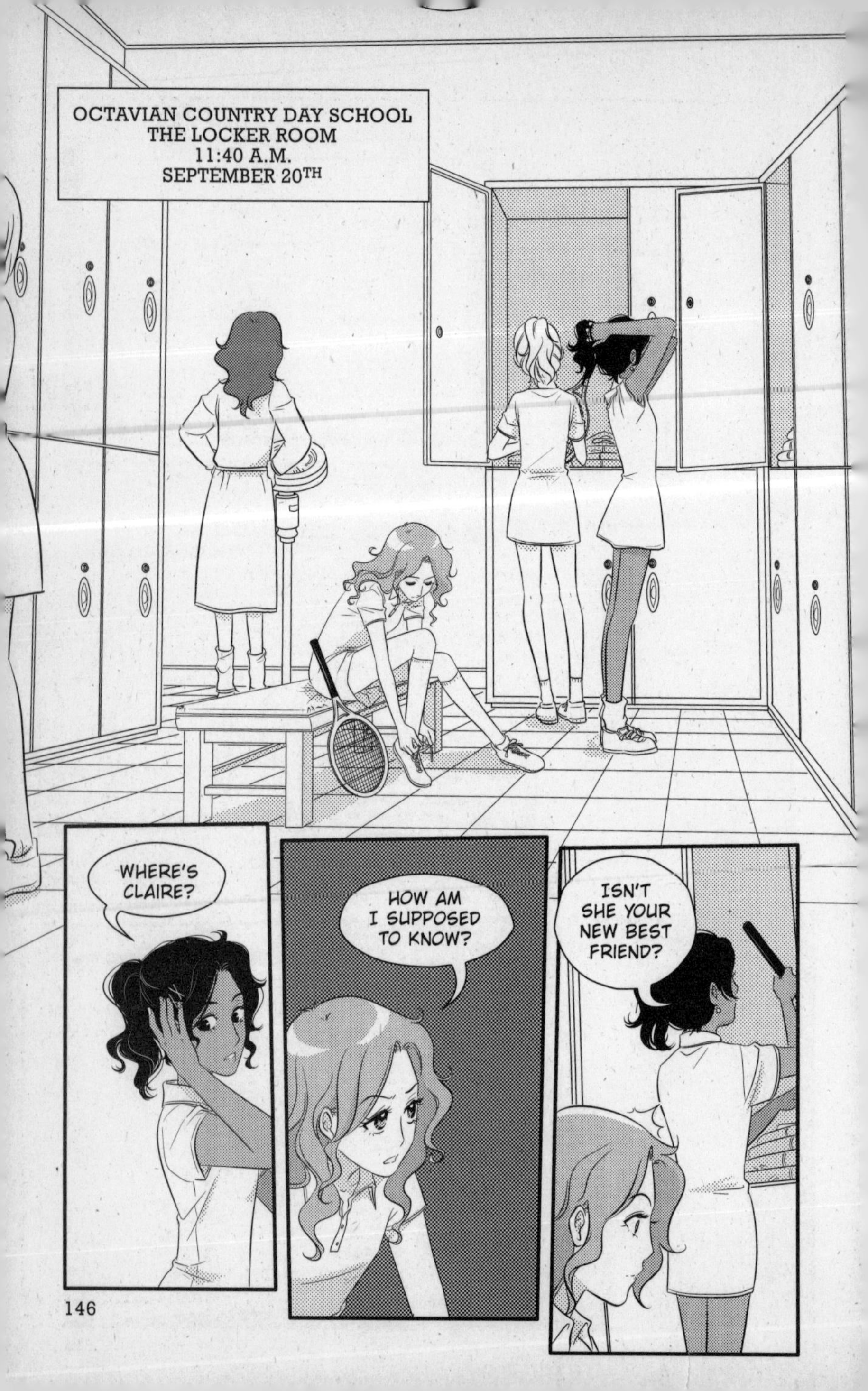
OCTAVIAN COUNTRY DAY SCHOOL
THE LOCKER ROOM
11:40 A.M.
SEPTEMBER 20TH
WHERE'S CLAIRE?
HOW AM I SUPPOSED TO KNOW?
ISN'T SHE YOUR NEW BEST FRIEND?

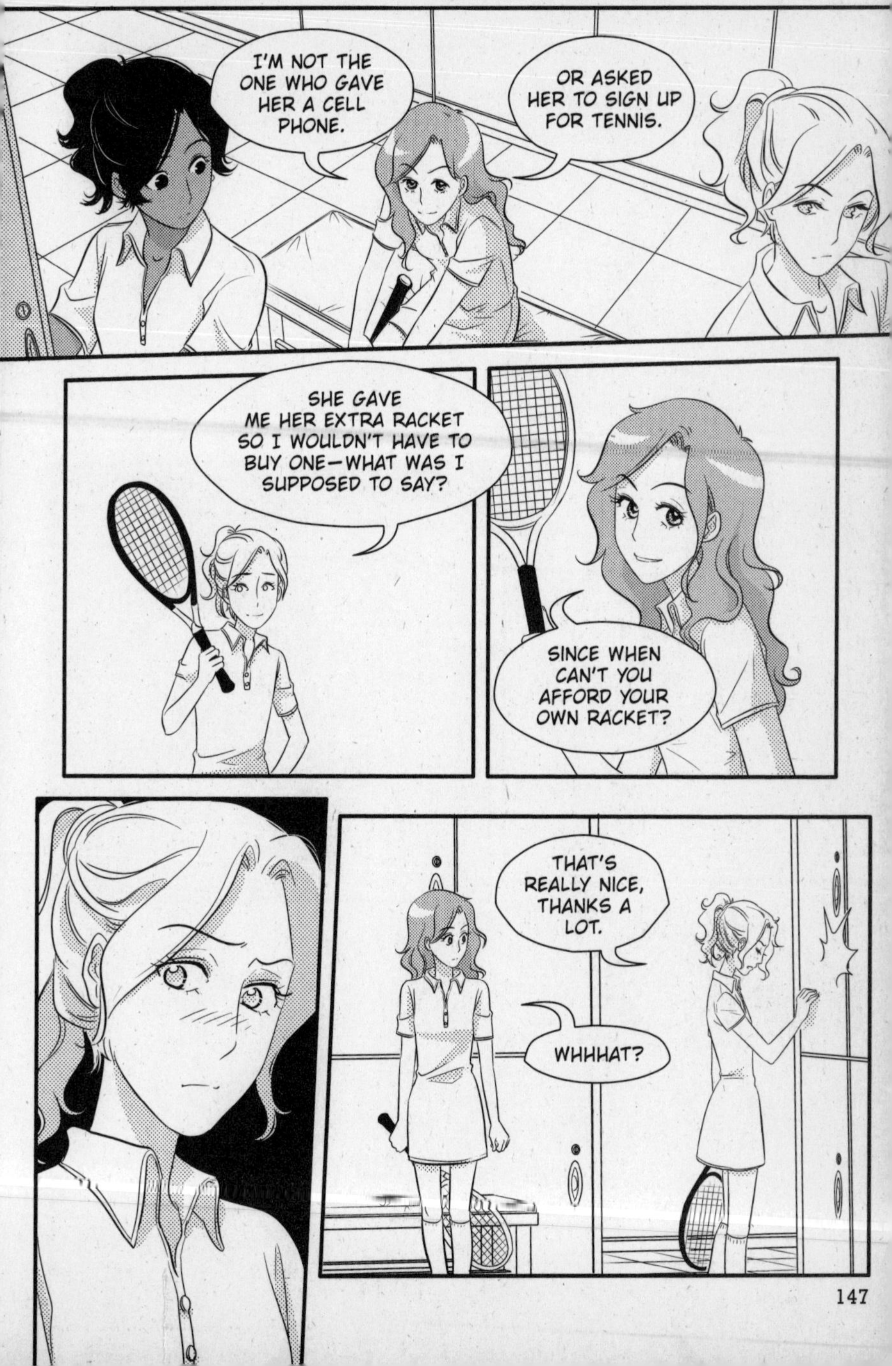
I'M NOT THE ONE WHO GAVE HER A CELL PHONE.
OR ASKED HER TO SIGN UP FOR TENNIS.
SHE GAVE ME HER EXTRA RACKET SO I WOULDN'T HAVE TO BUY ONE—WHAT WAS I SUPPOSED TO SAY?
SINCE WHEN CAN'T YOU AFFORD YOUR OWN RACKET?
THAT'S REALLY NICE, THANKS A LOT.
WHHHAT?

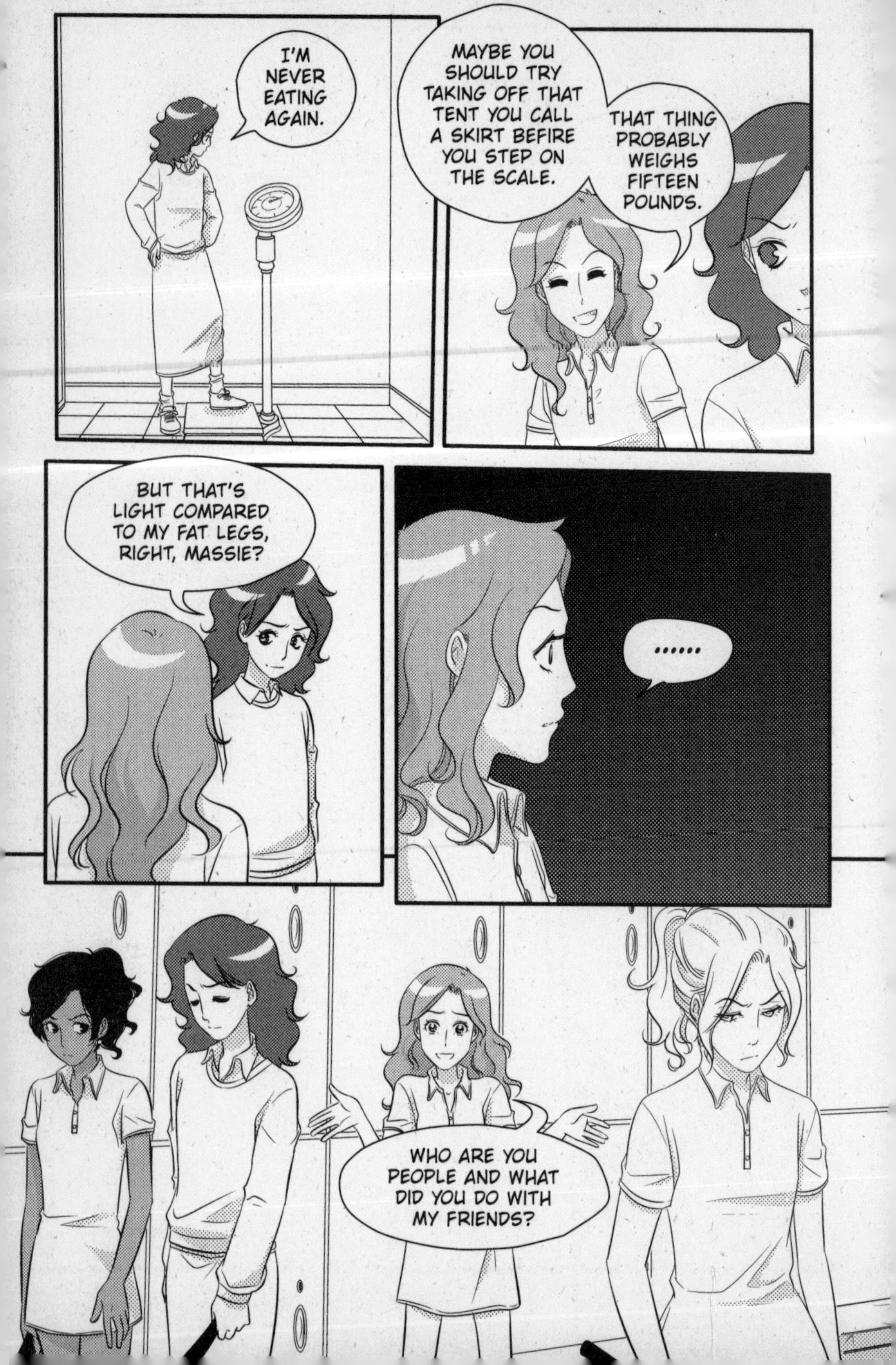
I'M NEVER EATING AGAIN.
MAYBE YOU SHOULD TRY TAKING OFF THAT TENT YOU CALL A SKIRT BEFIRE YOU STEP ON THE SCALE.
THAT THING PROBABLY WEIGHS FIFTEEN POUNDS.
BUT THAT'S LIGHT COMPARED TO MY FAT LEGS, RIGHT, MASSIE?
......
WHO ARE YOU PEOPLE AND WHAT DID YOU DO WITH MY FRIENDS?

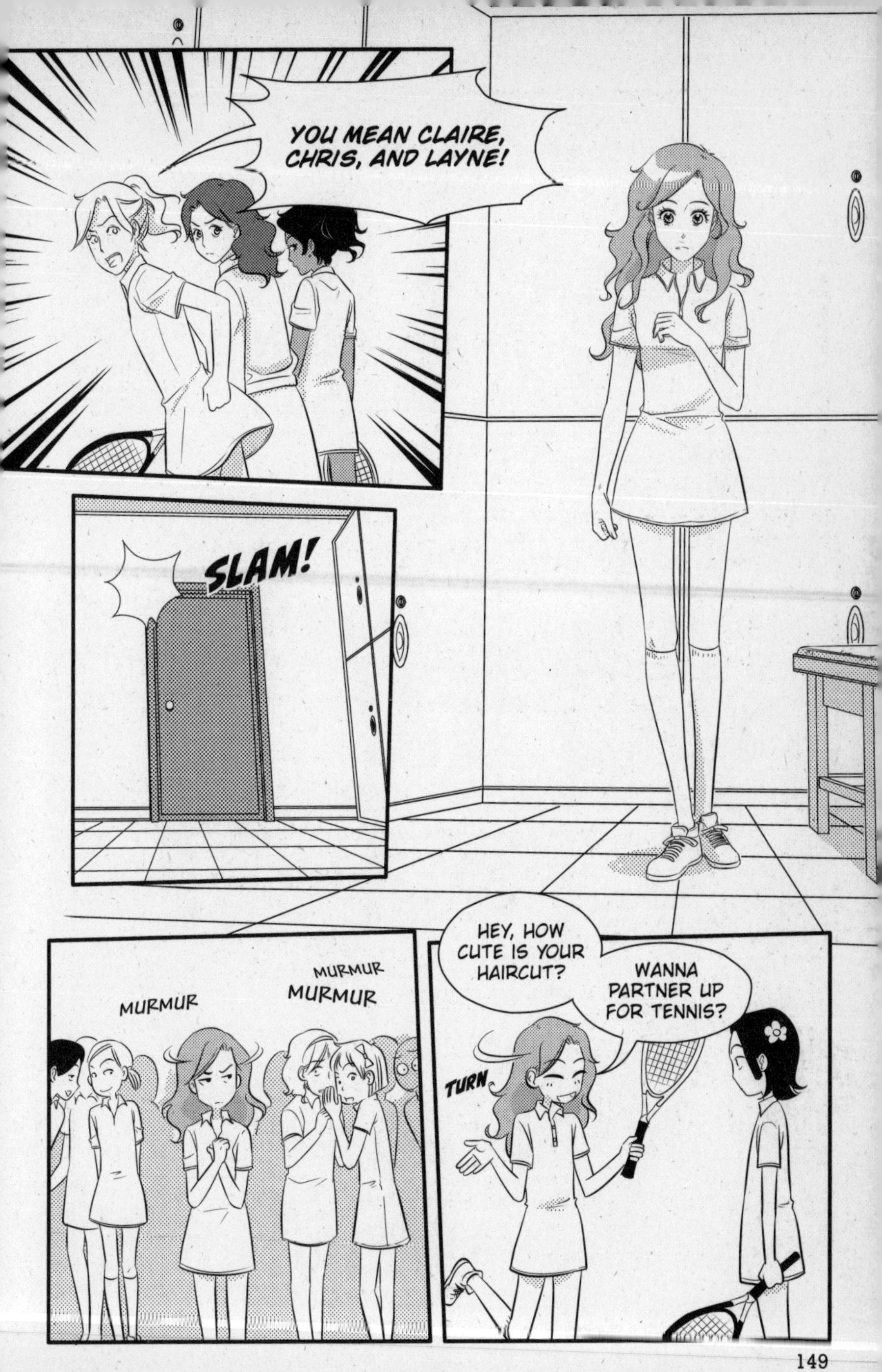
YOU MEAN CLAIRE, CHRIS, AND LAYNE!
SLAM!
MURMUR
MURMUR
MURMUR
HEY, HOW CUTE IS YOUR HAIRCUT?
TURN
WANNA PARTNER UP FOR TENNIS?

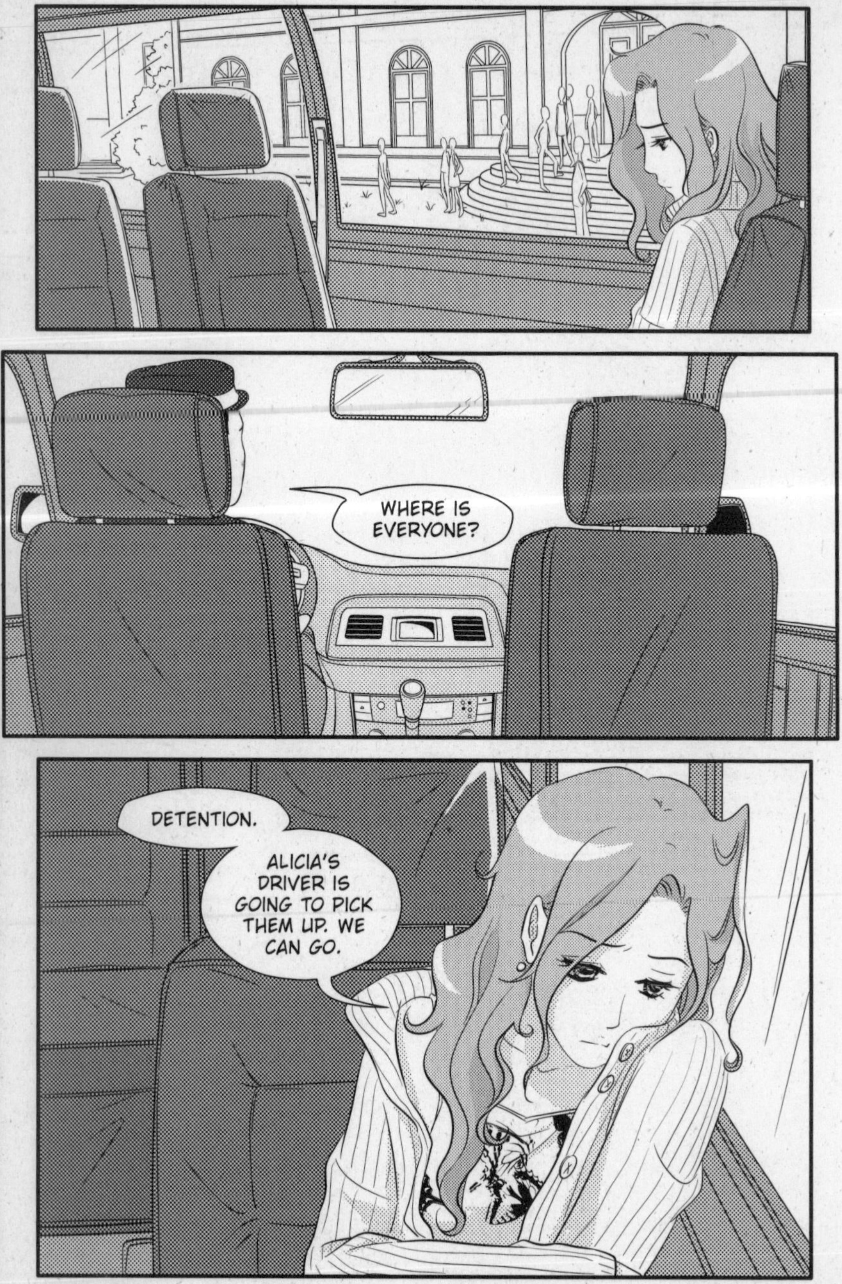
WHERE IS EVERYONE?
DETENTION.
ALICIA'S DRIVER IS GOING TO PICK THEM UP. WE CAN GO.

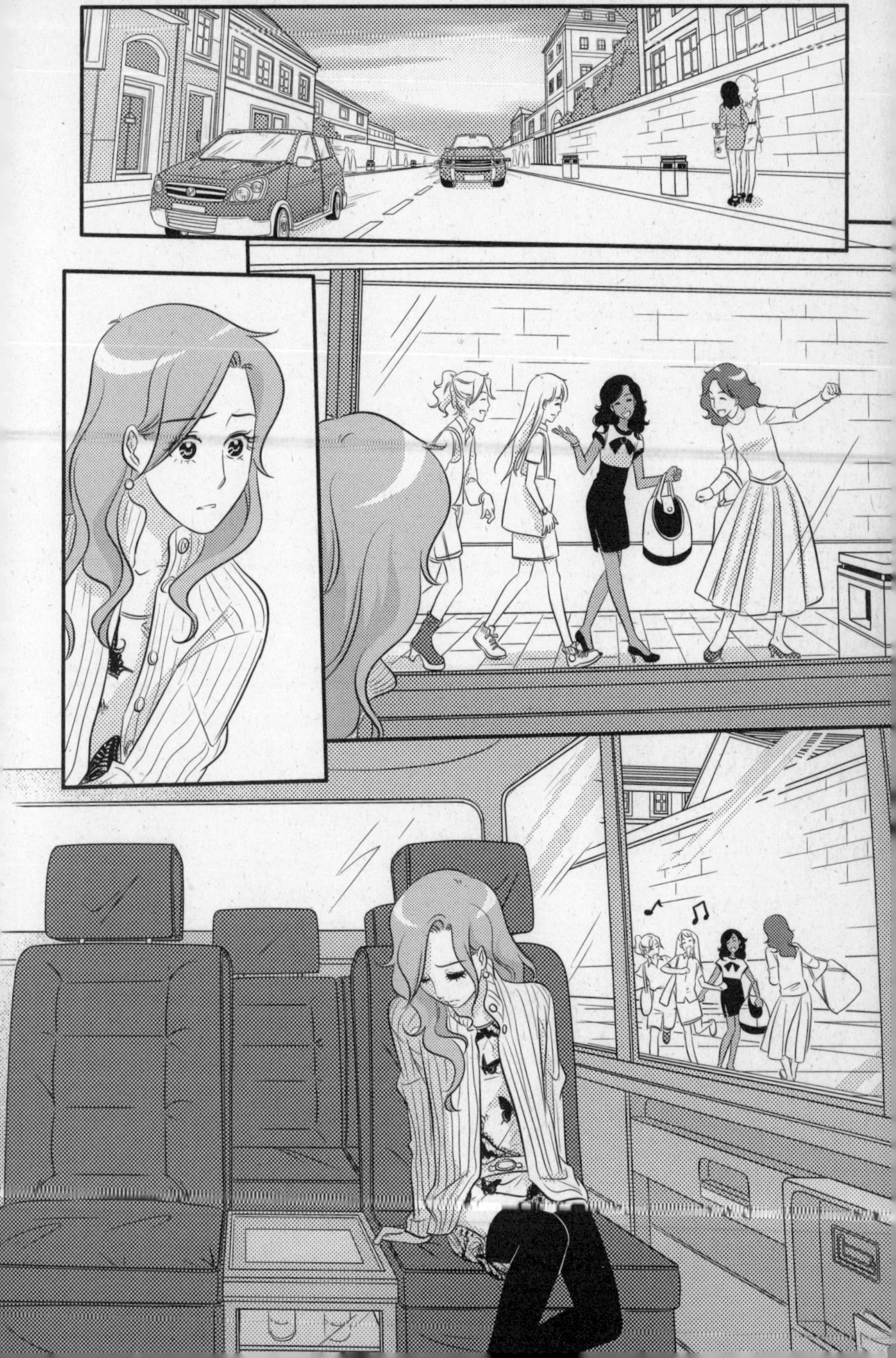

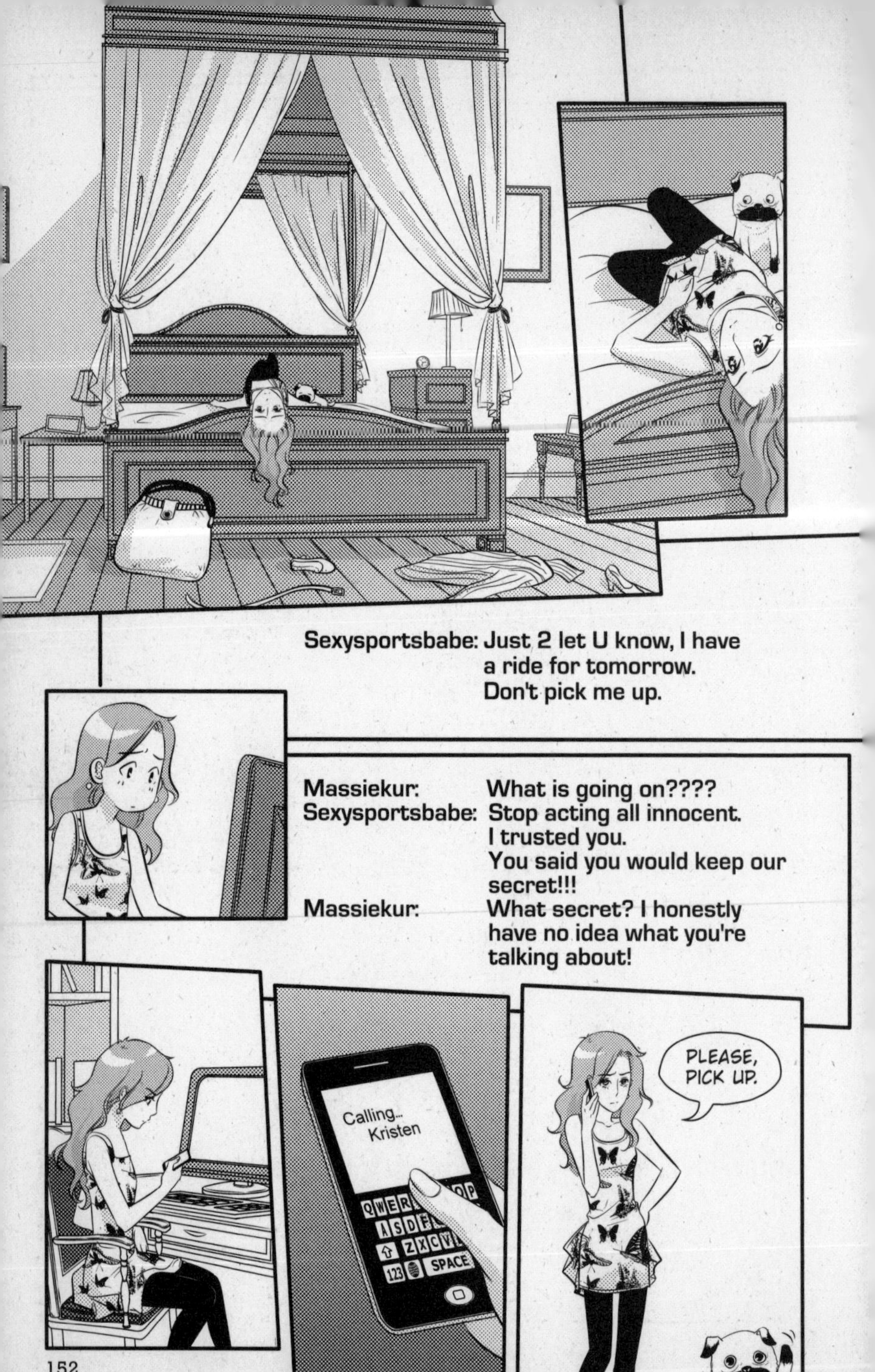
Sexysportsbabe: Just 2 let U know, I have a ride for tomorrow. Don't pick me up.
Massiekur: What is going on????
Sexysportsbabe: Stop acting all innocent. I trusted you. You said you would keep our secret!!!
Massiekur: What secret? I honestly have no idea what you're talking about!
Calling... Kristen
PLEASE, PICK UP.

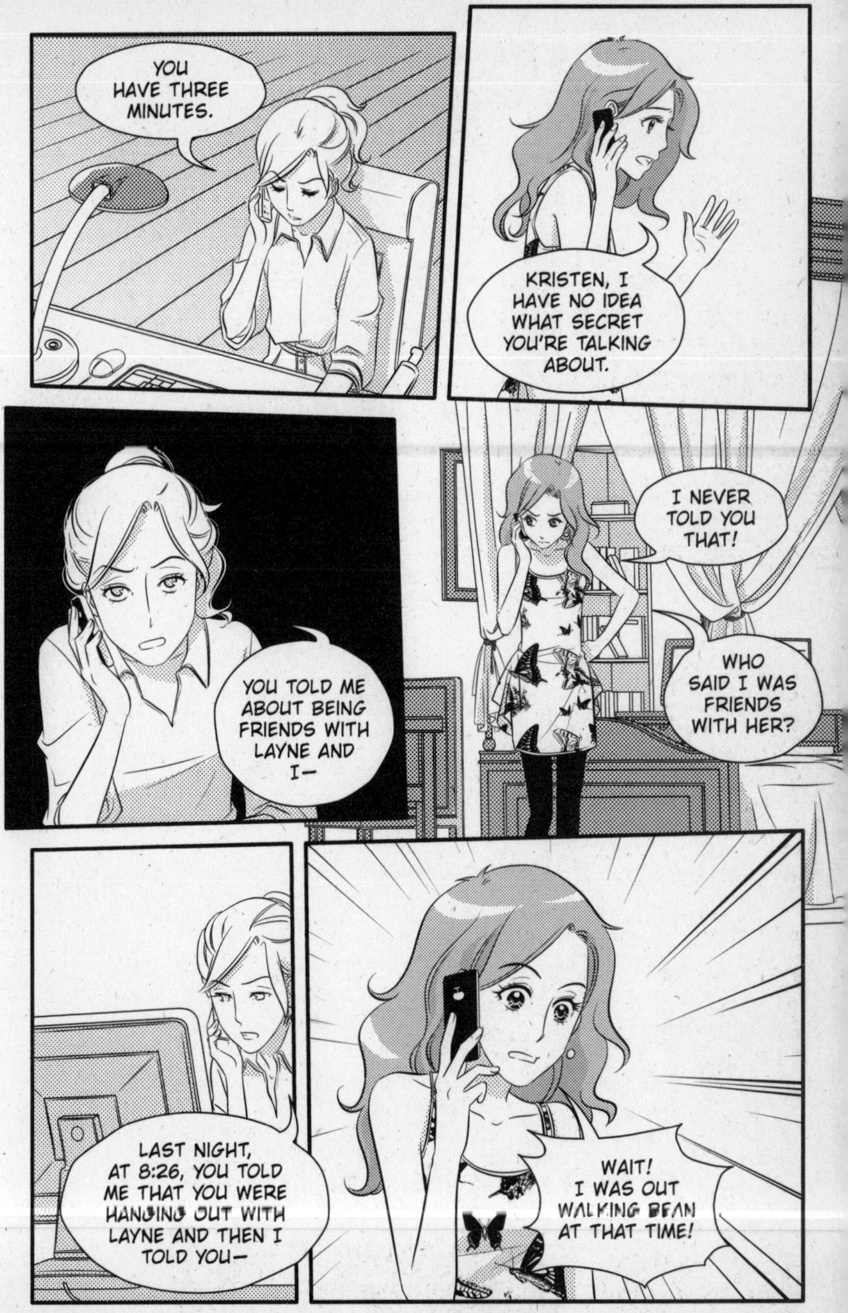
YOU HAVE THREE MINUTES.
KRISTEN, I HAVE NO IDEA WHAT SECRET YOU'RE TALKING ABOUT.
YOU TOLD ME ABOUT BEING FRIENDS WITH LAYNE AND I—
I NEVER TOLD YOU THAT!
WHO SAID I WAS FRIENDS WITH HER?
LAST NIGHT, AT 8:26, YOU TOLD ME THAT YOU WERE HANGING OUT WITH LAYNE AND THEN I TOLD YOU—
WAIT! I WAS OUT WALKING BEAN AT THAT TIME!

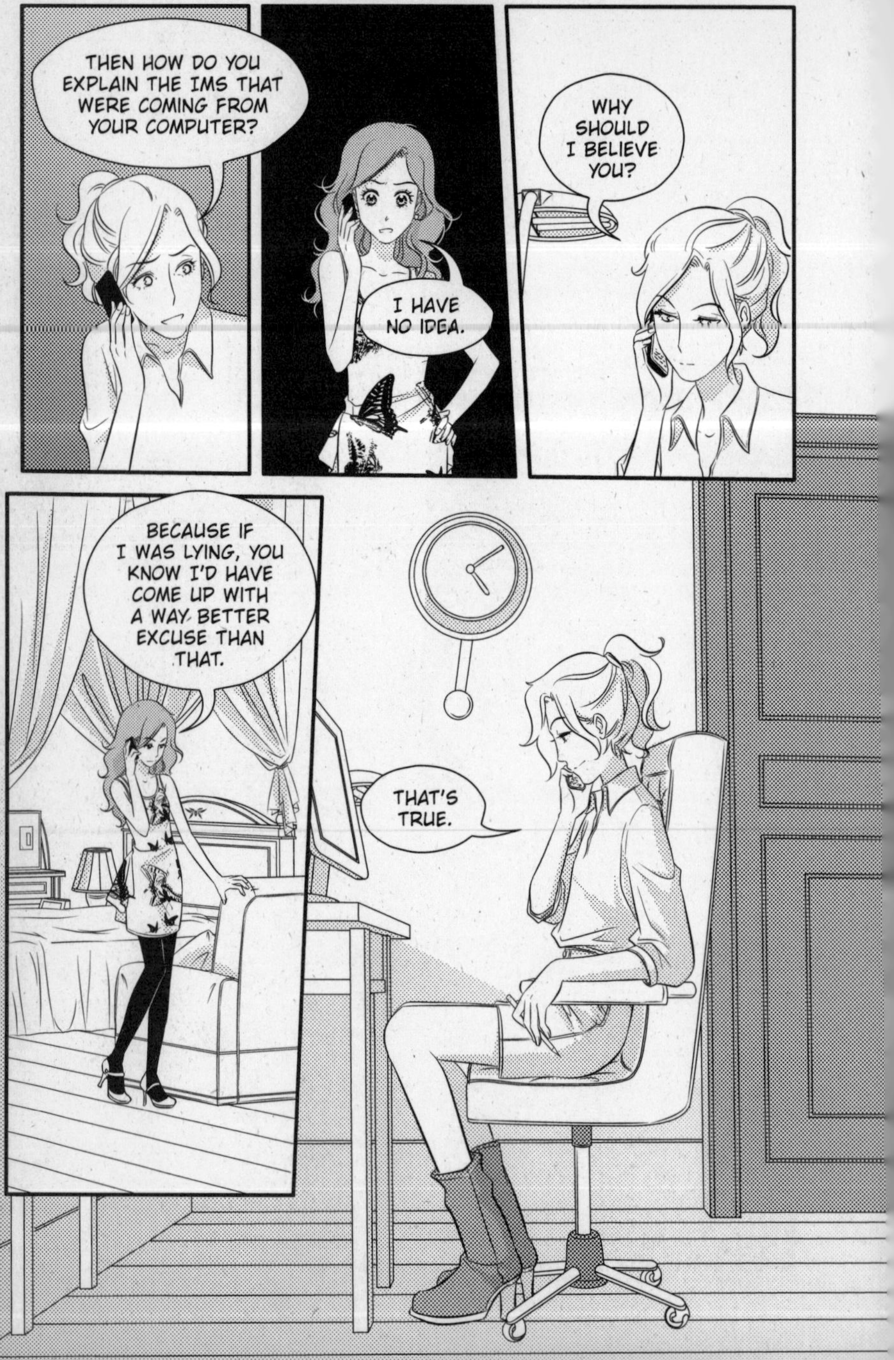
THEN HOW DO YOU EXPLAIN THE IMS THAT WERE COMING FROM YOUR COMPUTER?
I HAVE NO IDEA.
WHY SHOULD I BELIEVE YOU?
BECAUSE IF I WAS LYING, YOU KNOW I'D HAVE COME UP WITH A WAY BETTER EXCUSE THAN THAT.
THAT'S TRUE.

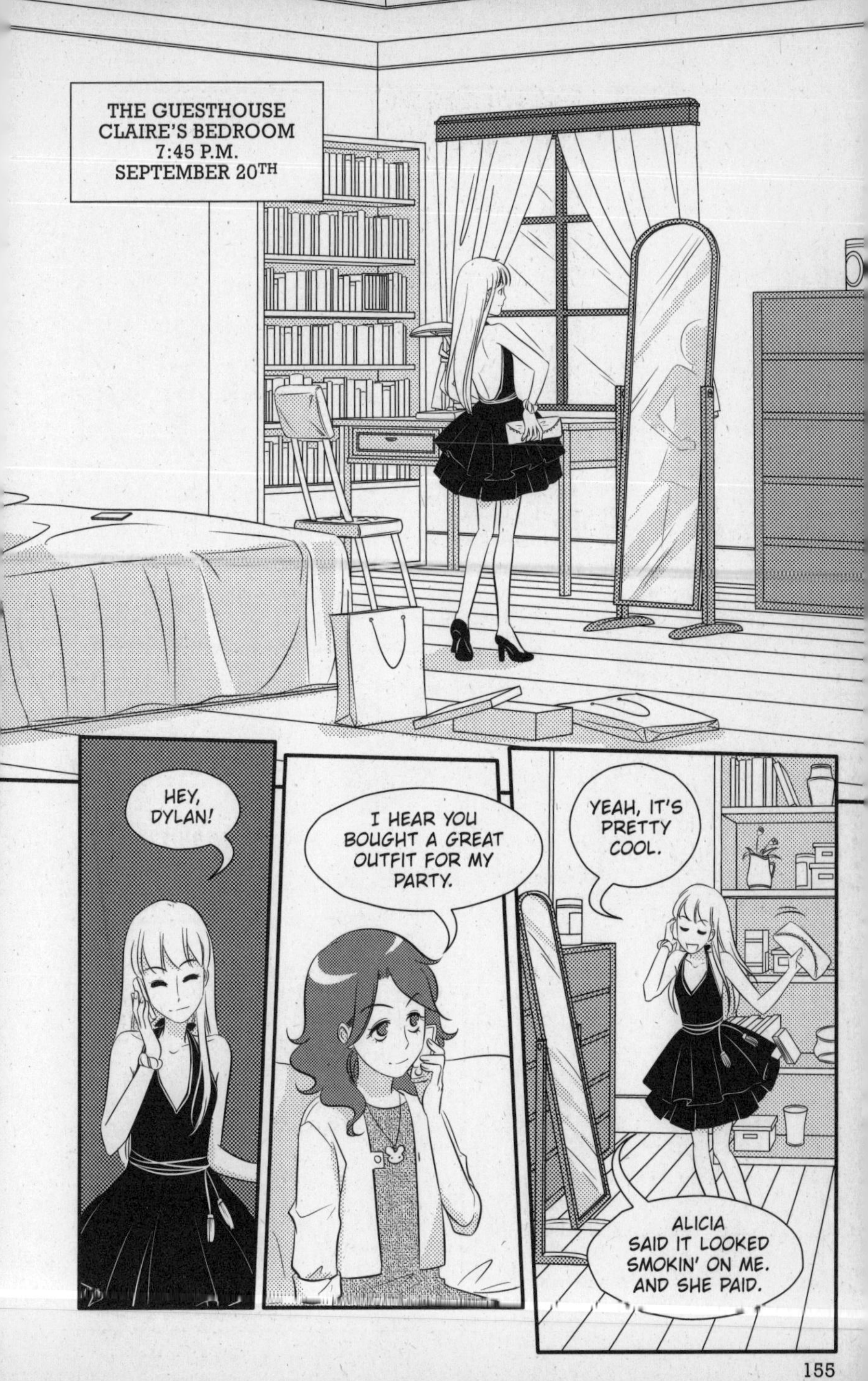
THE GUESTHOUSE
CLAIRE'S BEDROOM
7:45 P.M.
SEPTEMBER 20TH
HEY, DYLAN!
I HEAR YOU BOUGHT A GREAT OUTFIT FOR MY PARTY.
YEAH, IT'S PRETTY COOL.
ALICIA SAID IT LOOKED SMOKIN' ON ME. AND SHE PAID.

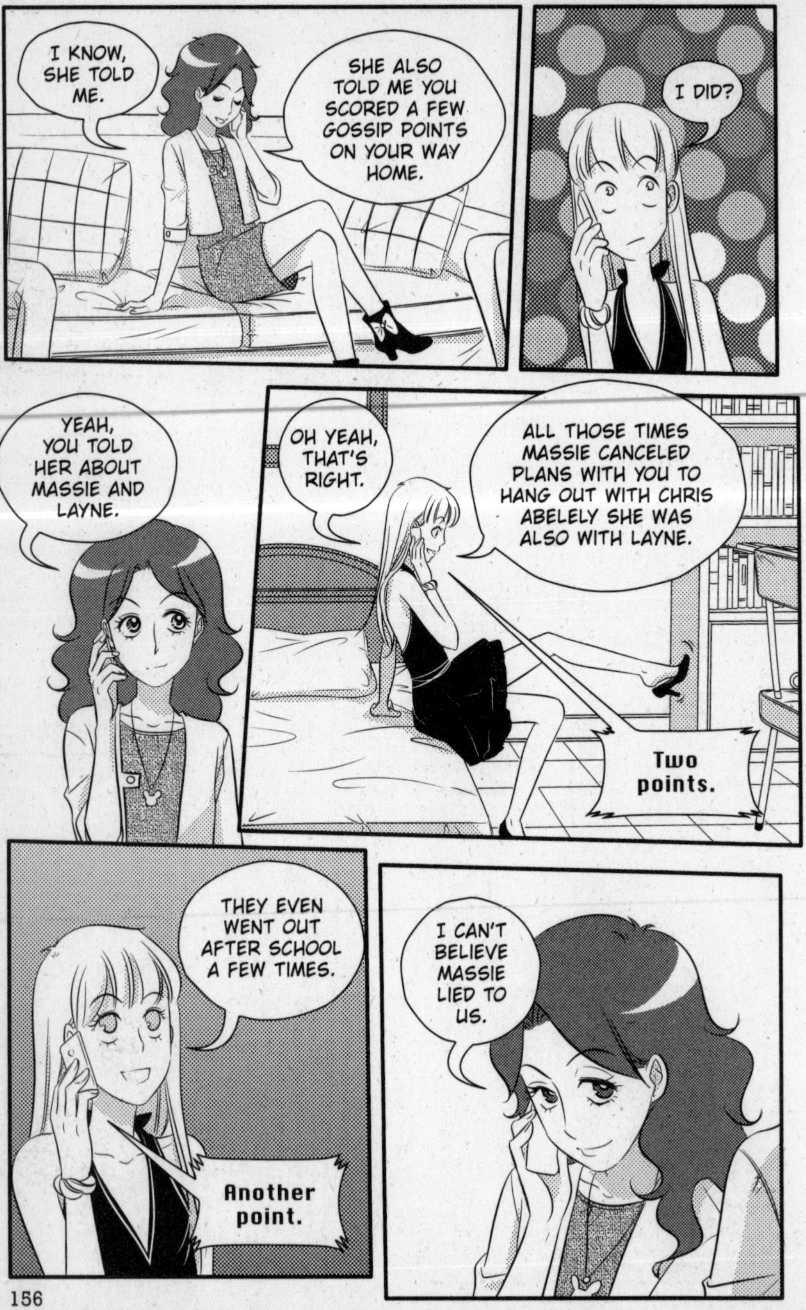

I KNOW, SHE TOLD ME.
SHE ALSO TOLD ME YOU SCORED A FEW GOSSIP POINTS ON YOUR WAY HOME.
I DID?
YEAH, YOU TOLD HER ABOUT MASSIE AND LAYNE.
OH YEAH, THAT'S RIGHT.
ALL THOSE TIMES MASSIE CANCELED PLANS WITH YOU TO HANG OUT WITH CHRIS ABELELY SHE WAS ALSO WITH LAYNE.
Two points.
THEY EVEN WENT OUT AFTER SCHOOL A FEW TIMES.
Another point.
I CAN'T BELIEVE MASSIE LIED TO US.

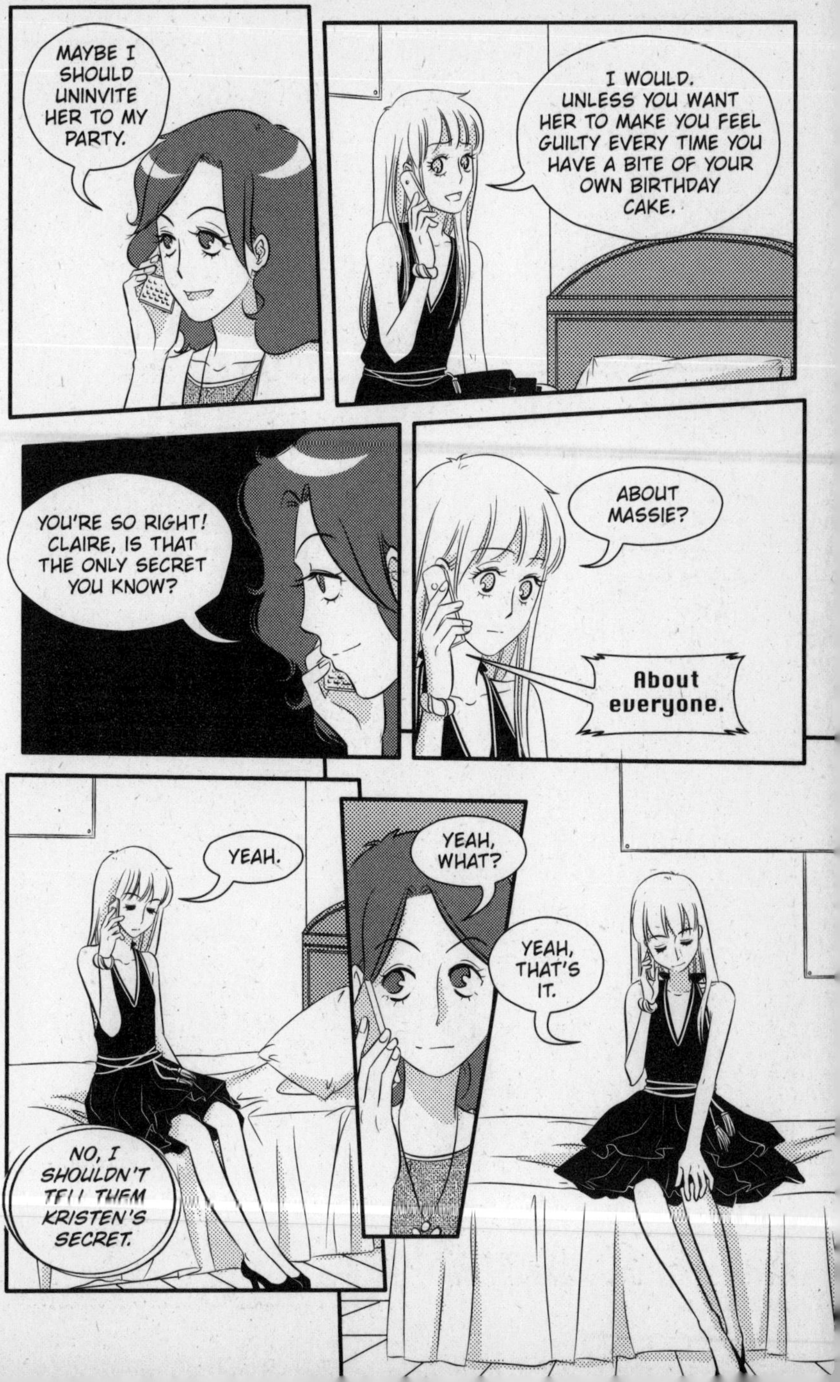
MAYBE I SHOULD UNINVITE HER TO MY PARTY.
I WOULD. UNLESS YOU WANT HER TO MAKE YOU FEEL GUILTY EVERY TIME YOU HAVE A BITE OF YOUR OWN BIRTHDAY CAKE.
YOU'RE SO RIGHT! CLAIRE, IS THAT THE ONLY SECRET YOU KNOW?
ABOUT MASSIE?
About everyone.
YEAH.
NO, I SHOULDN'T TELL THEM KRISTEN'S SECRET.
YEAH, WHAT?
YEAH, THAT'S IT.

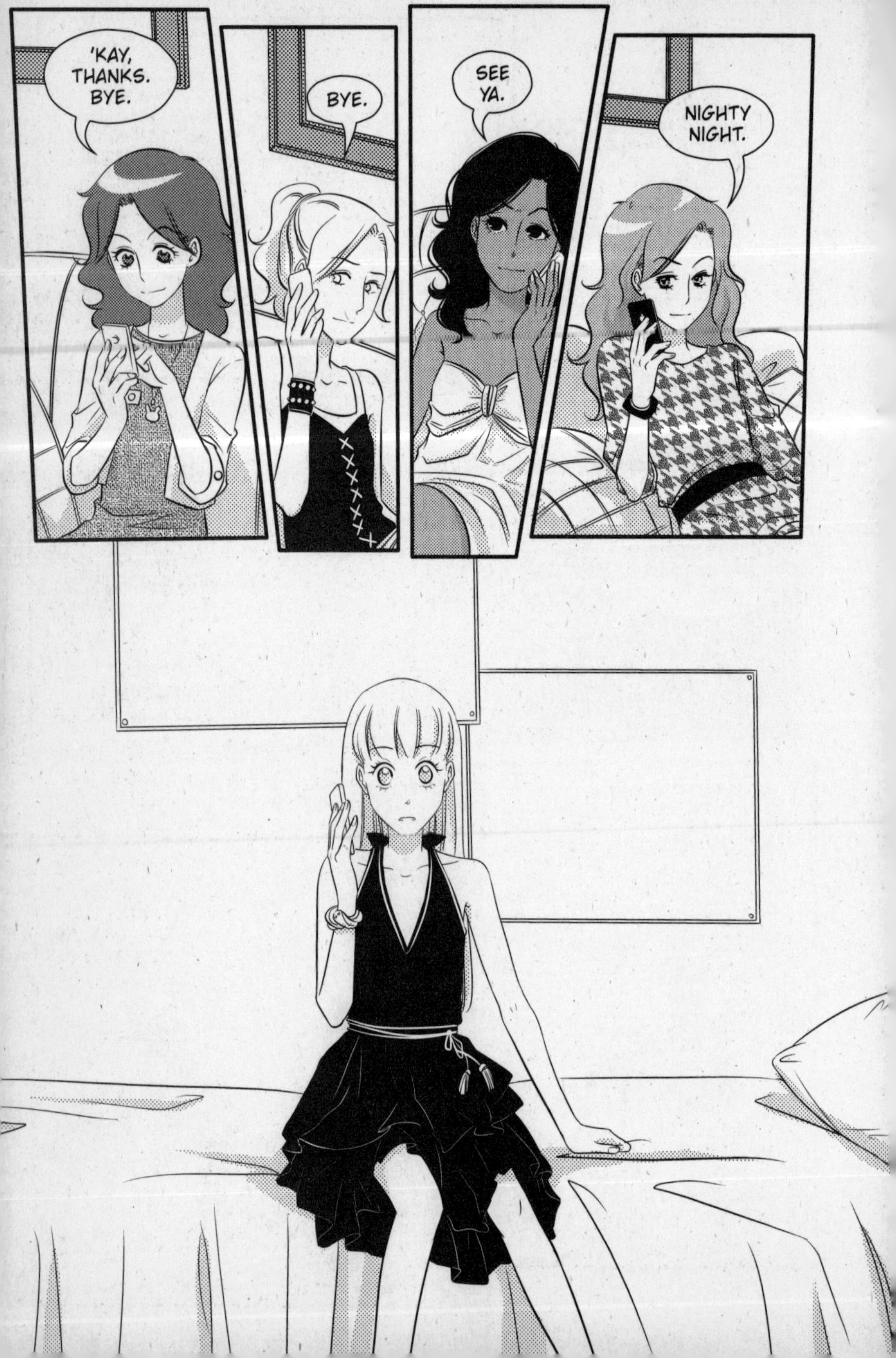

'KAY, THANKS. BYE.
BYE.
SEE YA.
NIGHTY NIGHT.

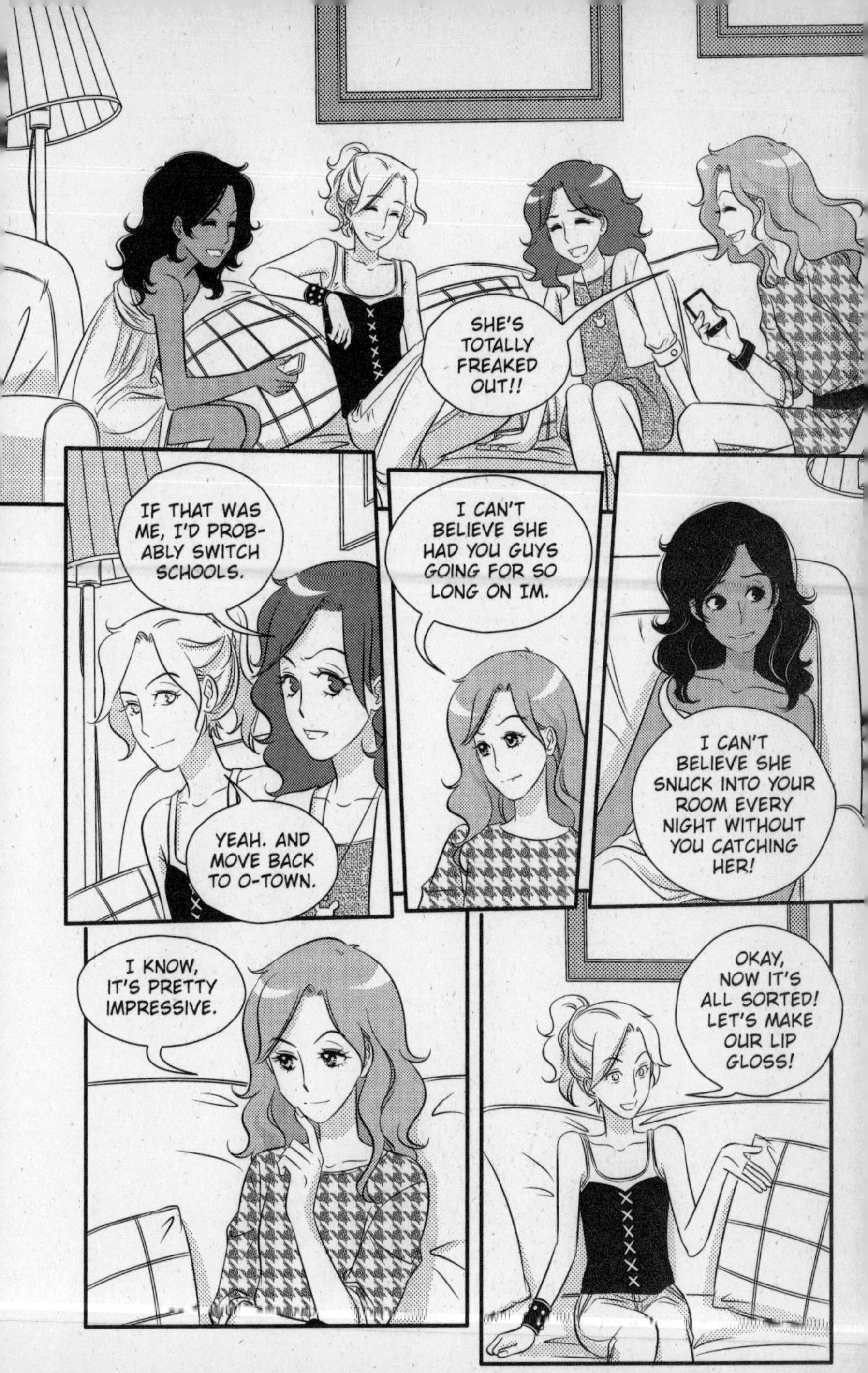
SHE'S TOTALLY FREAKED OUT!!
IF THAT WAS ME, I'D PROB-ABLY SWITCH SCHOOLS.
YEAH. AND MOVE BACK TO O-TOWN.
I CAN'T BELIEVE SHE HAD YOU GUYS GOING FOR SO LONG ON IM.
I CAN'T BELIEVE SHE SNUCK INTO YOUR ROOM EVERY NIGHT WITHOUT YOU CATCHING HER!
I KNOW, IT'S PRETTY IMPRESSIVE.
OKAY, NOW IT'S ALL SORTED! LET'S MAKE OUR LIP GLOSS!

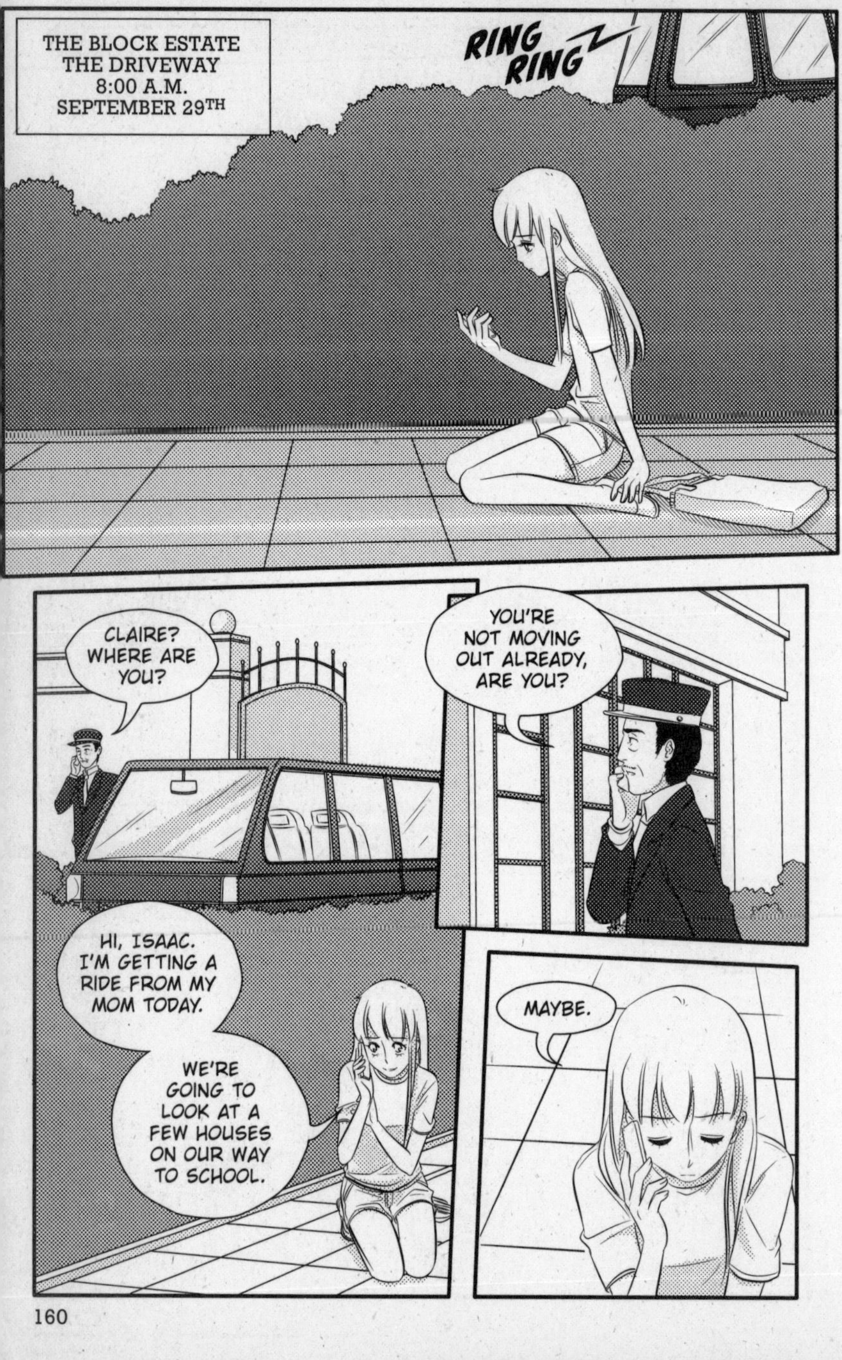
THE BLOCK ESTATE
THE DRIVEWAY
8:00 A.M.
SEPTEMBER 29TH
RING RING
CLAIRE? WHERE ARE YOU?
YOU'RE NOT MOVING OUT ALREADY, ARE YOU?
HI, ISAAC. I'M GETTING A RIDE FROM MY MOM TODAY.
WE'RE GOING TO LOOK AT A FEW HOUSES ON OUR WAY TO SCHOOL.
MAYBE.

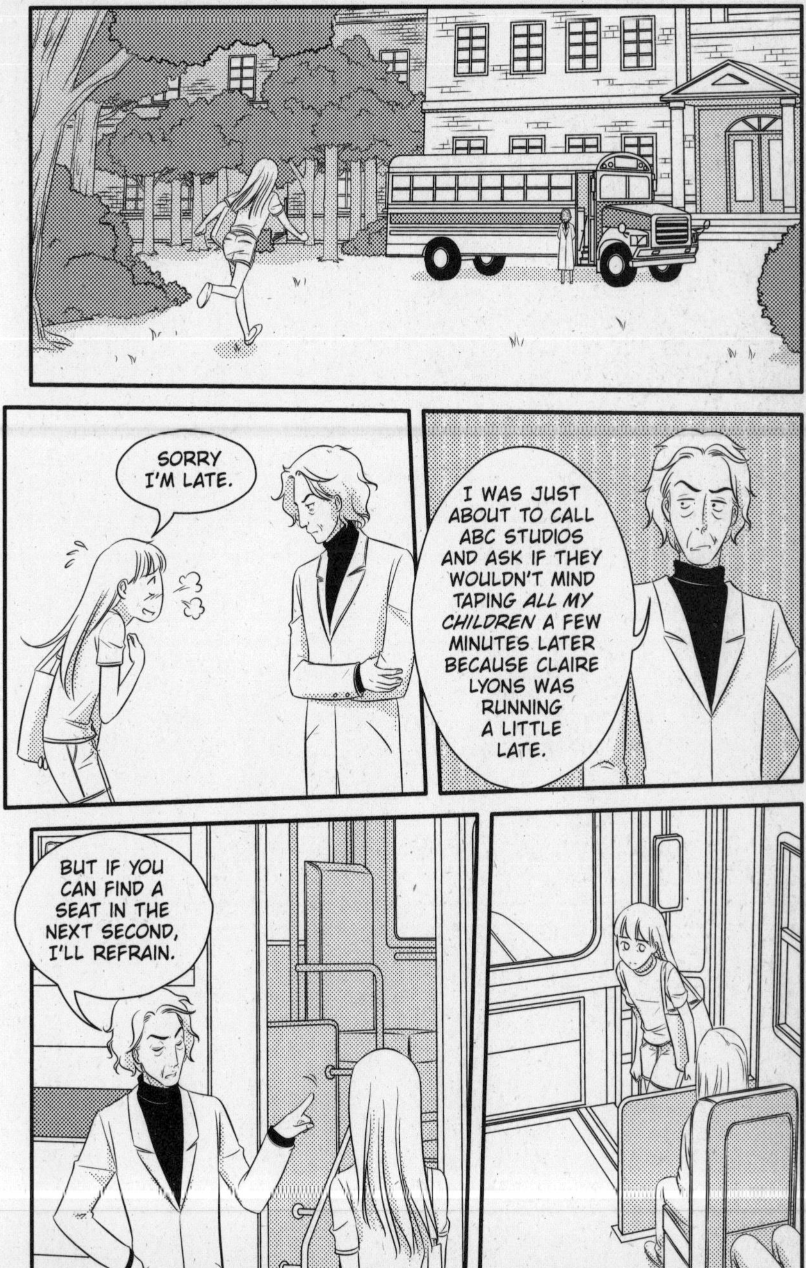
SORRY I'M LATE.
I WAS JUST ABOUT TO CALL ABC STUDIOS AND ASK IF THEY WOULDN'T MIND TAPING *ALL MY CHILDREN* A FEW MINUTES LATER BECAUSE CLAIRE LYONS WAS RUNNING A LITTLE LATE.
BUT IF YOU CAN FIND A SEAT IN THE NEXT SECOND, I'LL REFRAIN.

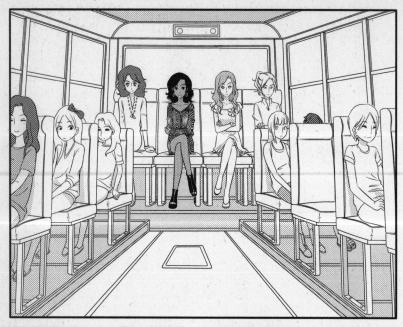

ALICIA, MAYBE YOU CAN BUY CLAIRE SOMEONE TO SIT BESIDE.

CLAIRE, I'D OFFER YOU A SEAT BACK HERE IF DYLAN'S FAT LEGS DIDN'T TAKE UP SO MUCH ROOM.

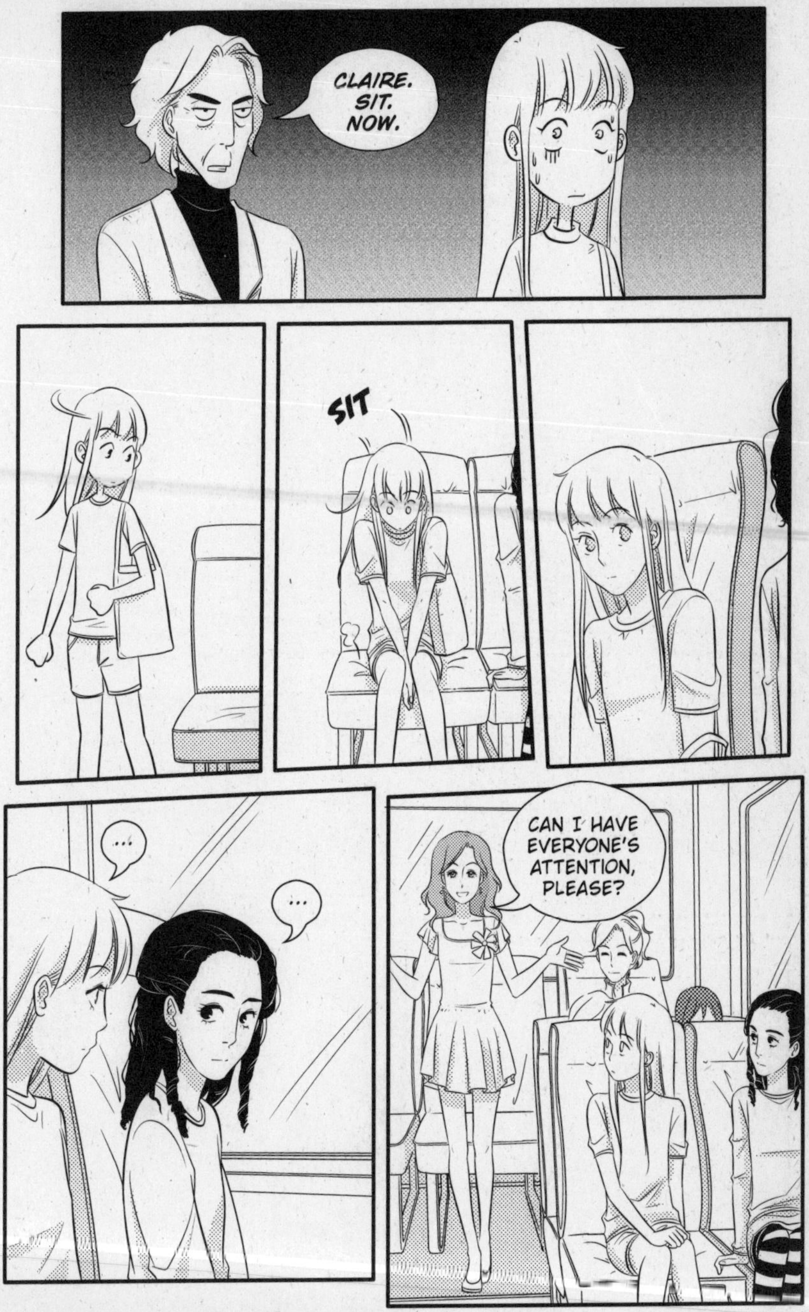
CLAIRE.
SIT.
NOW.
SIT
...
...
CAN I HAVE EVERYONE'S ATTENTION, PLEASE?

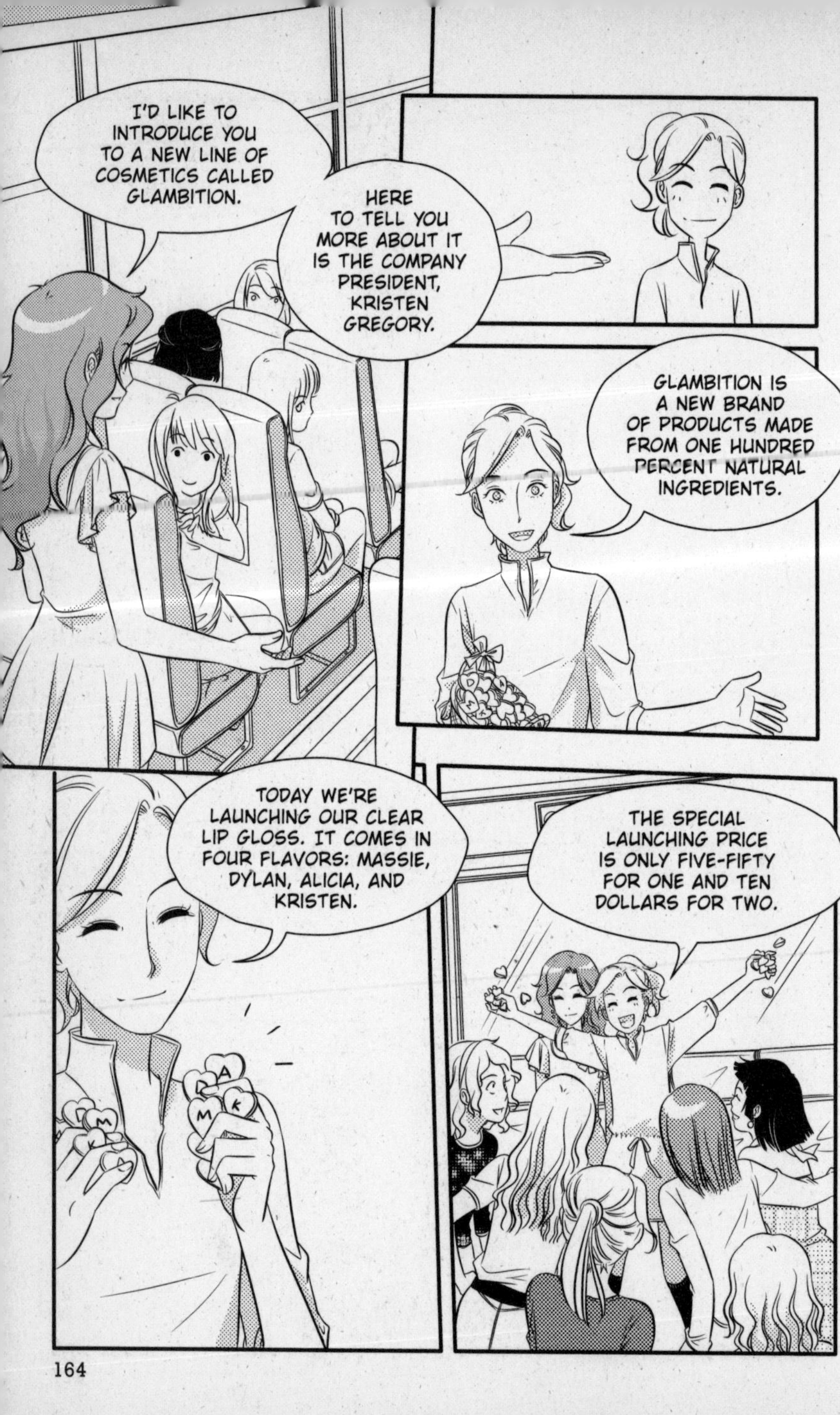
I'D LIKE TO INTRODUCE YOU TO A NEW LINE OF COSMETICS CALLED GLAMBITION.
HERE TO TELL YOU MORE ABOUT IT IS THE COMPANY PRESIDENT, KRISTEN GREGORY.
GLAMBITION IS A NEW BRAND OF PRODUCTS MADE FROM ONE HUNDRED PERCENT NATURAL INGREDIENTS.
TODAY WE'RE LAUNCHING OUR CLEAR LIP GLOSS. IT COMES IN FOUR FLAVORS: MASSIE, DYLAN, ALICIA, AND KRISTEN.
THE SPECIAL LAUNCHING PRICE IS ONLY FIVE-FIFTY FOR ONE AND TEN DOLLARS FOR TWO.

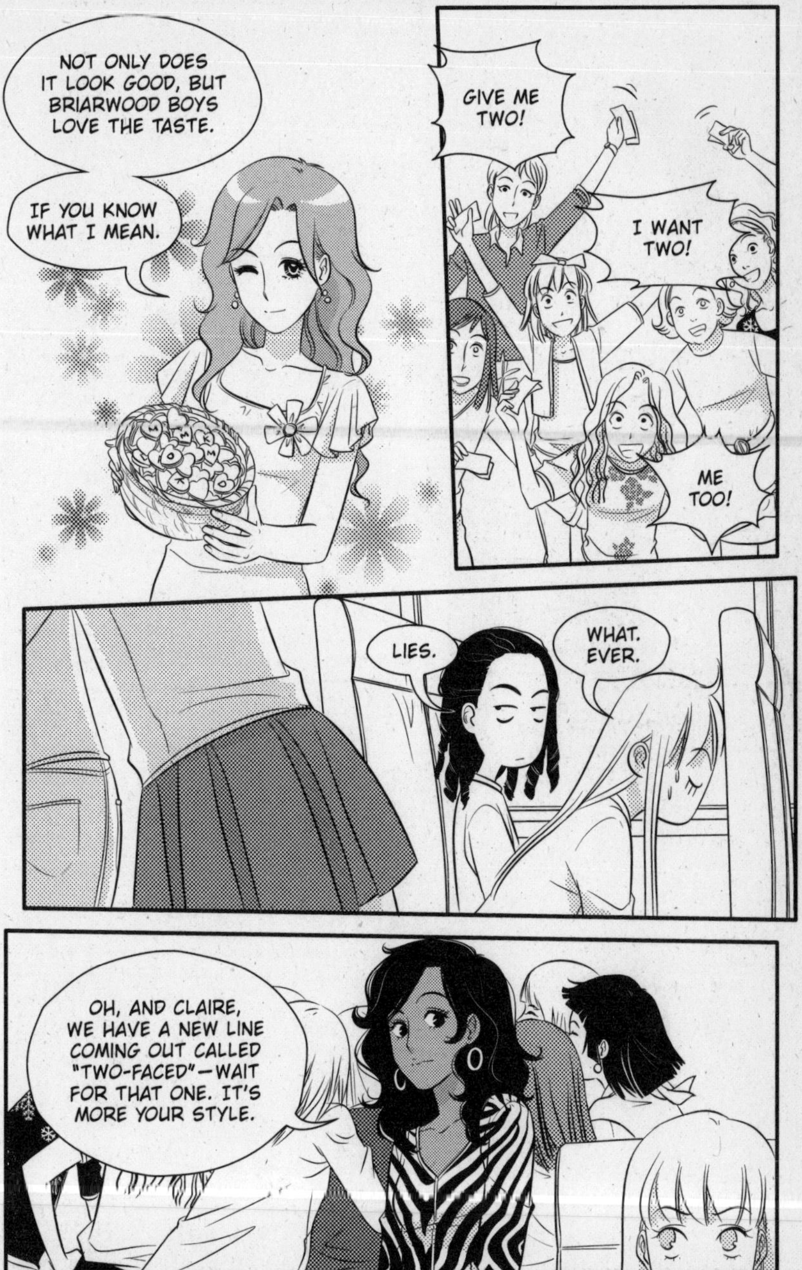
NOT ONLY DOES IT LOOK GOOD, BUT BRIARWOOD BOYS LOVE THE TASTE.
IF YOU KNOW WHAT I MEAN.
GIVE ME TWO!
I WANT TWO!
ME TOO!
LIES.
WHAT. EVER.
OH, AND CLAIRE, WE HAVE A NEW LINE COMING OUT CALLED "TWO-FACED"—WAIT FOR THAT ONE. IT'S MORE YOUR STYLE.

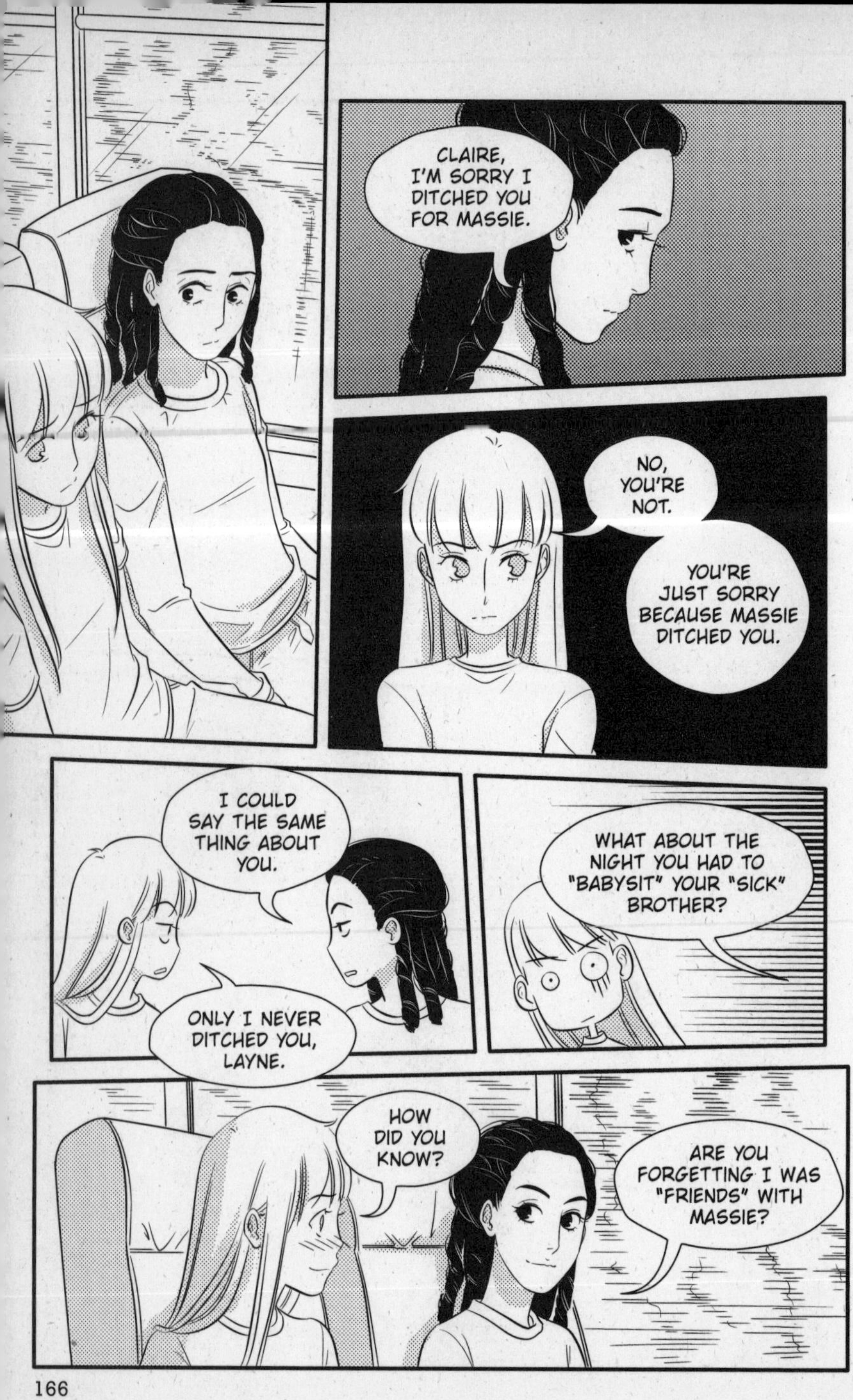
CLAIRE, I'M SORRY I DITCHED YOU FOR MASSIE.
NO, YOU'RE NOT.
YOU'RE JUST SORRY BECAUSE MASSIE DITCHED YOU.
I COULD SAY THE SAME THING ABOUT YOU.
ONLY I NEVER DITCHED YOU, LAYNE.
WHAT ABOUT THE NIGHT YOU HAD TO "BABYSIT" YOUR "SICK" BROTHER?
HOW DID YOU KNOW?
ARE YOU FORGETTING I WAS "FRIENDS" WITH MASSIE?

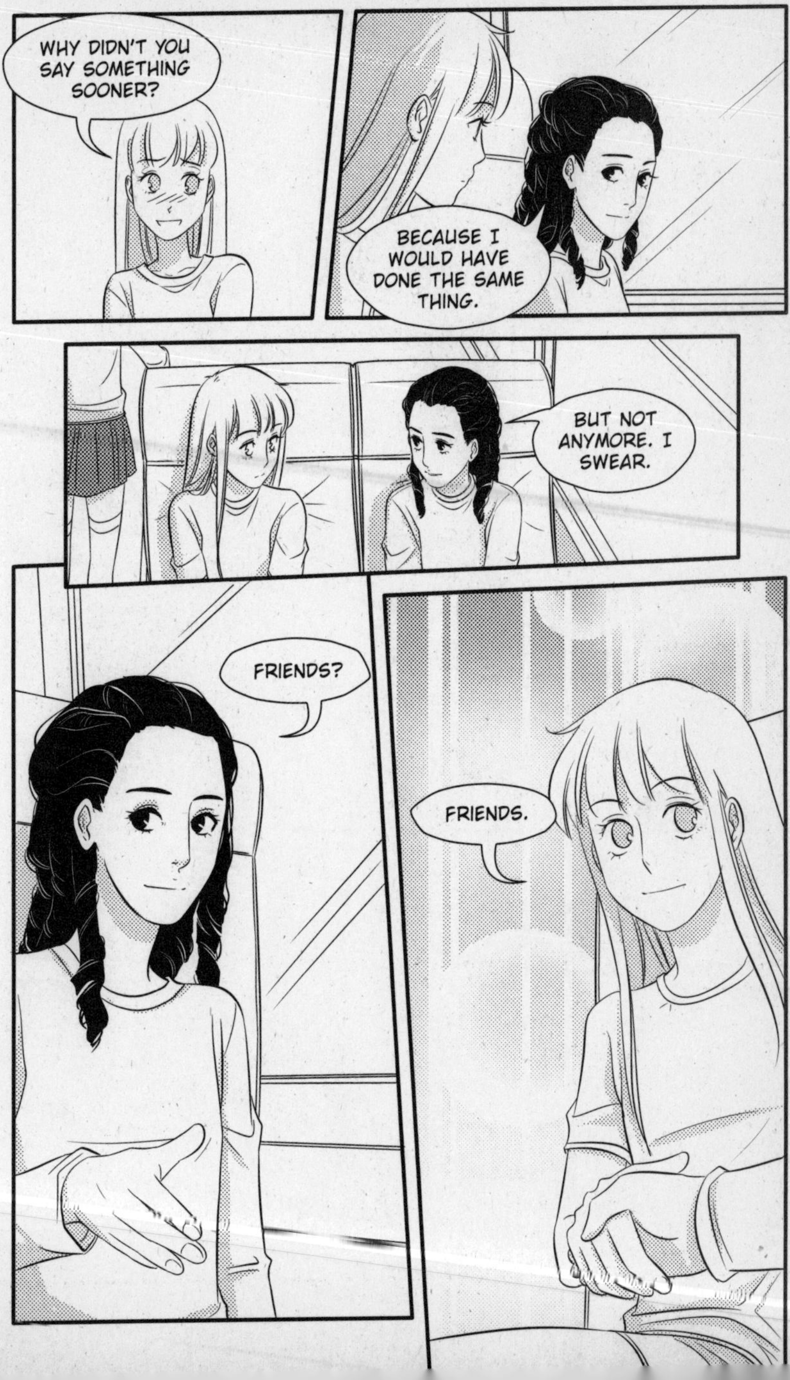
WHY DIDN'T YOU SAY SOMETHING SOONER?
BECAUSE I WOULD HAVE DONE THE SAME THING.
BUT NOT ANYMORE. I SWEAR.
FRIENDS?
FRIENDS.

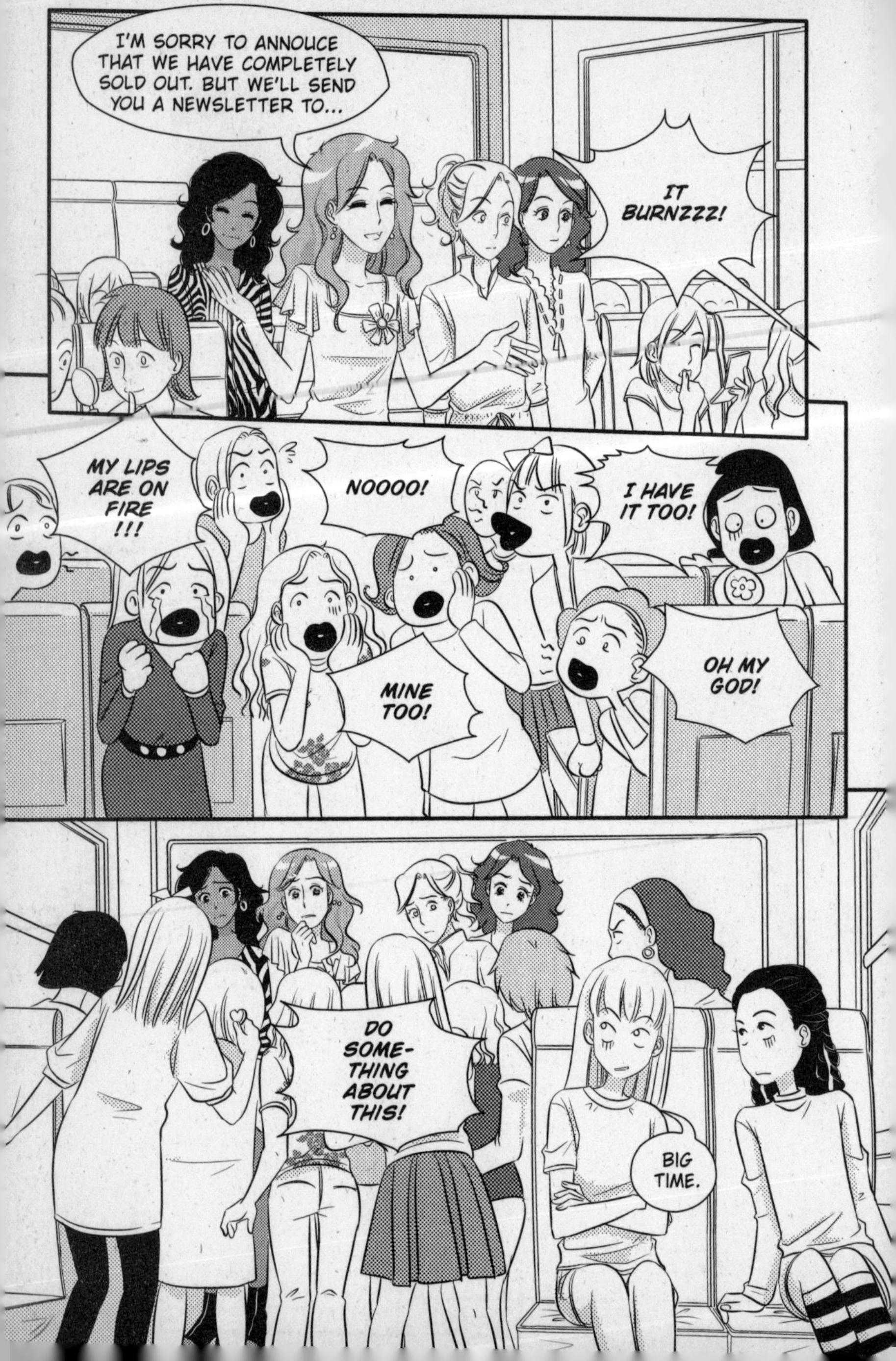

I'M SORRY TO ANNOUCE THAT WE HAVE COMPLETELY SOLD OUT. BUT WE'LL SEND YOU A NEWSLETTER TO...
IT BURNZZZ!
MY LIPS ARE ON FIRE !!!
NOOOO!
I HAVE IT TOO!
MINE TOO!
OH MY GOD!
DO SOME-THING ABOUT THIS!
BIG TIME.

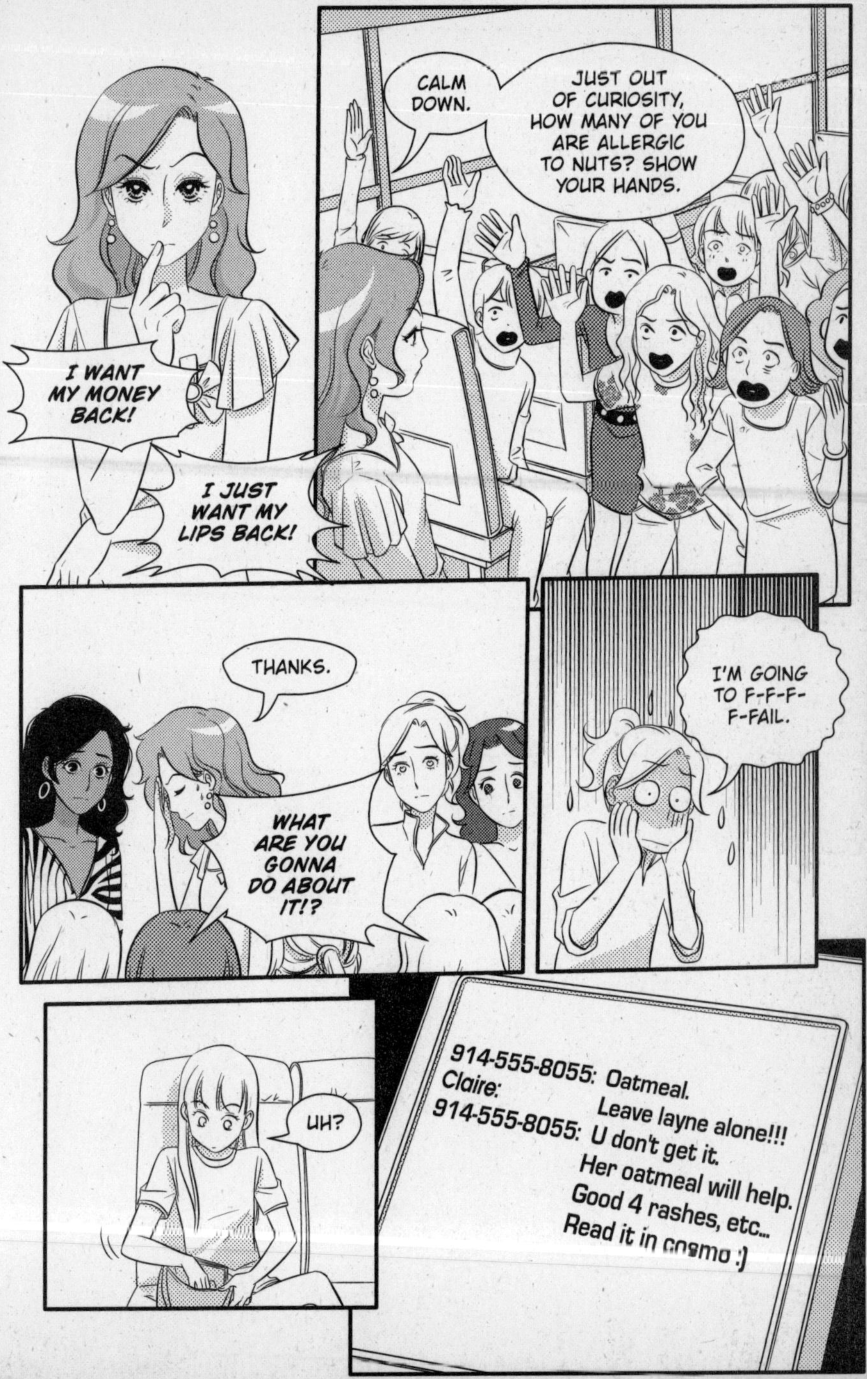
I WANT MY MONEY BACK!
I JUST WANT MY LIPS BACK!
CALM DOWN.
JUST OUT OF CURIOSITY, HOW MANY OF YOU ARE ALLERGIC TO NUTS? SHOW YOUR HANDS.
THANKS.
WHAT ARE YOU GONNA DO ABOUT IT!?
I'M GOING TO F-F-F-F-FAIL.
UH?
914-555-8055: Oatmeal.
Claire: Leave layne alone!!!
914-555-8055: U don't get it.
Her oatmeal will help.
Good 4 rashes, etc...
Read it in cosmo :)

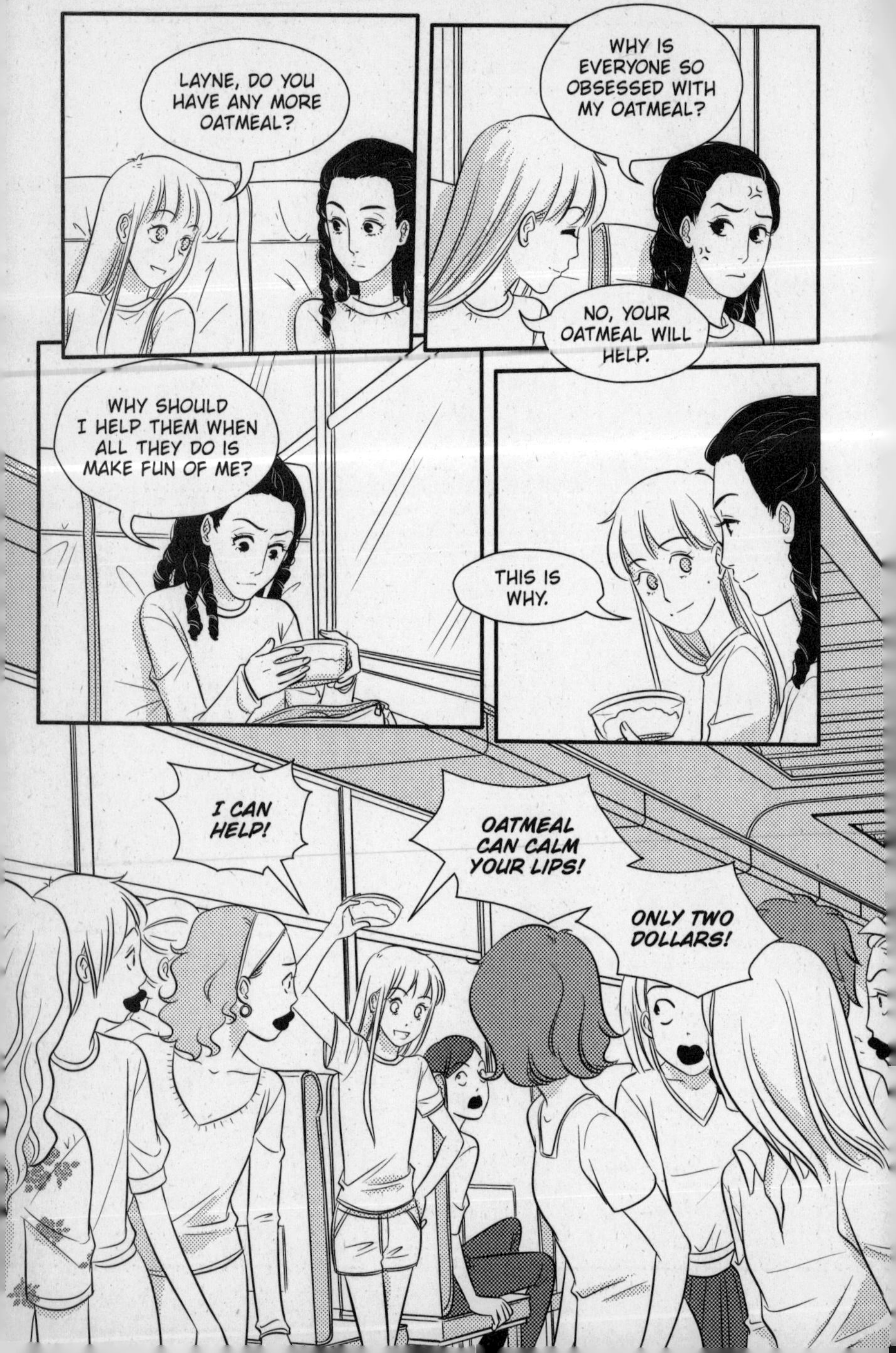
LAYNE, DO YOU HAVE ANY MORE OATMEAL?
WHY IS EVERYONE SO OBSESSED WITH MY OATMEAL?
NO, YOUR OATMEAL WILL HELP.
WHY SHOULD I HELP THEM WHEN ALL THEY DO IS MAKE FUN OF ME?
THIS IS WHY.
I CAN HELP!
OATMEAL CAN CALM YOUR LIPS!
ONLY TWO DOLLARS!

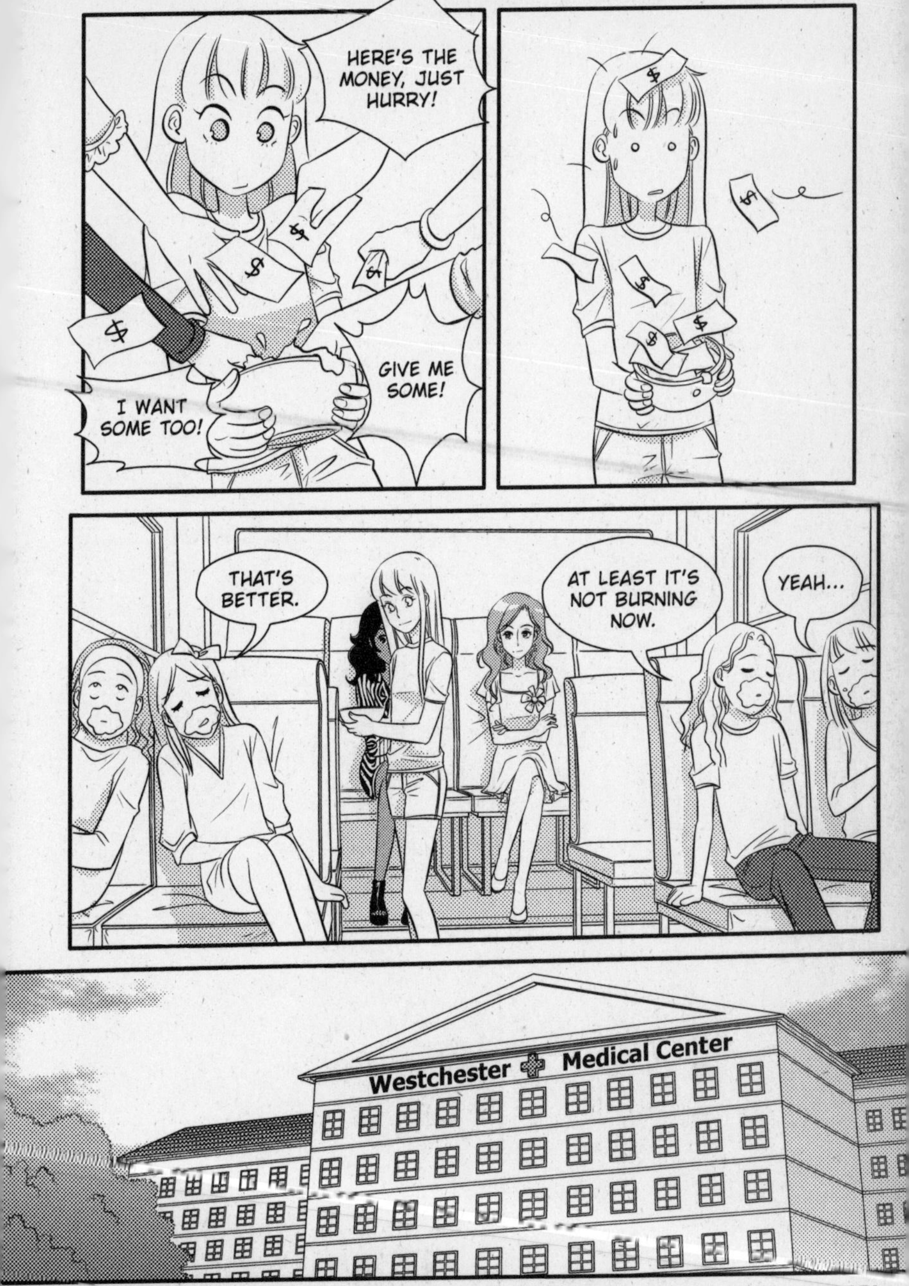
HERE'S THE MONEY, JUST HURRY!
I WANT SOME TOO!
GIVE ME SOME!
THAT'S BETTER.
AT LEAST IT'S NOT BURNING NOW.
YEAH...
Westchester Medical Center

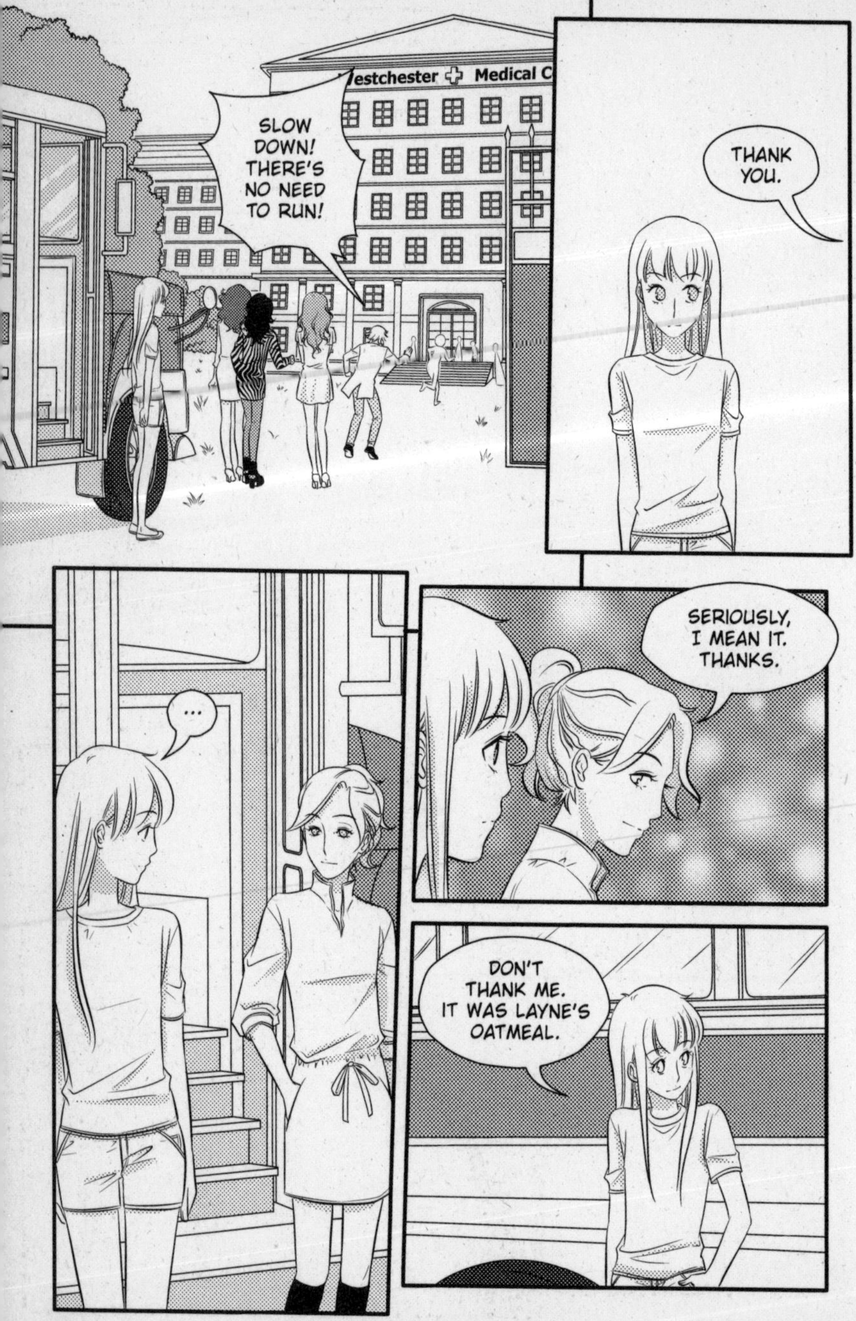
Westchester Medical C
SLOW DOWN! THERE'S NO NEED TO RUN!
THANK YOU.
...
SERIOUSLY, I MEAN IT. THANKS.
DON'T THANK ME. IT WAS LAYNE'S OATMEAL.

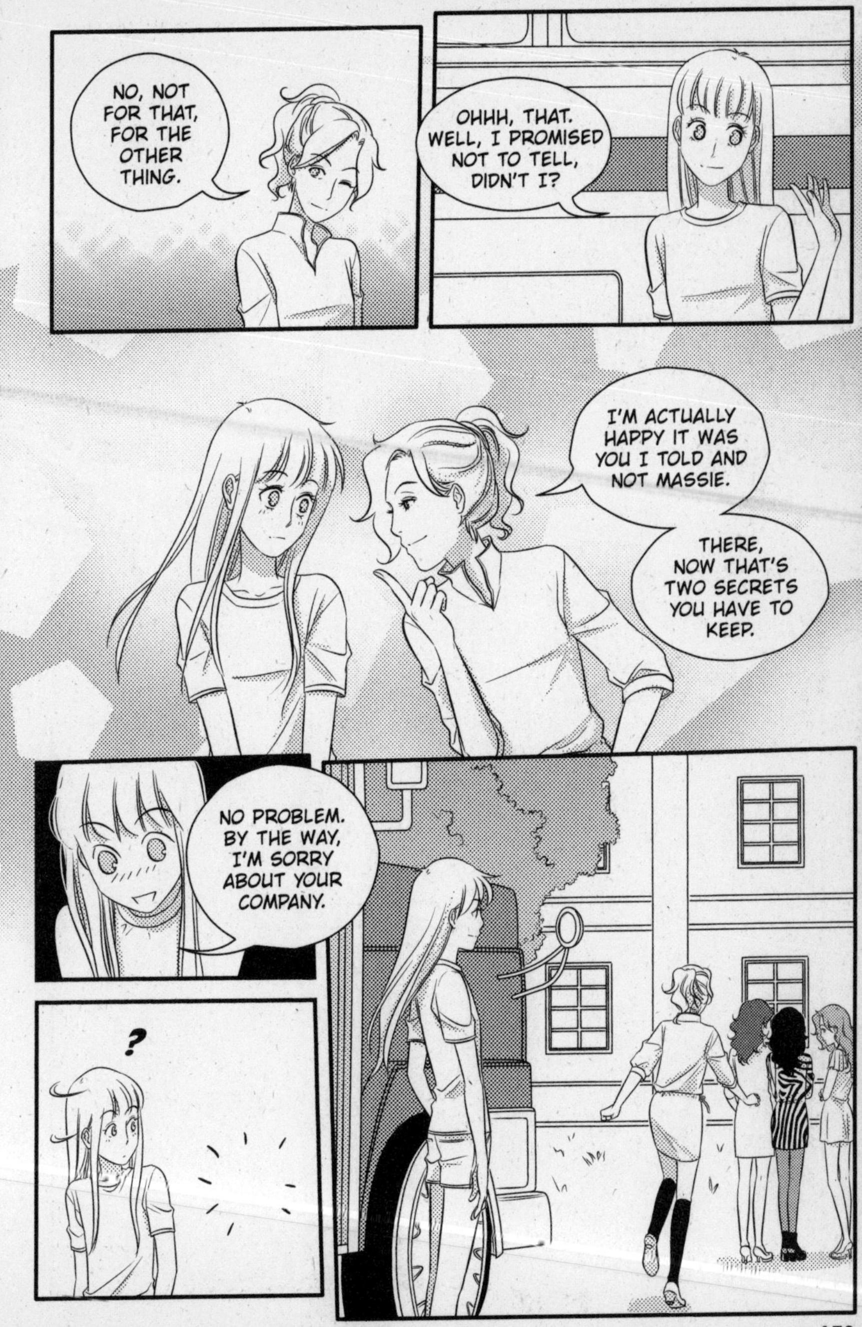
NO, NOT FOR THAT, FOR THE OTHER THING.
OHHH, THAT. WELL, I PROMISED NOT TO TELL, DIDN'T I?
I'M ACTUALLY HAPPY IT WAS YOU I TOLD AND NOT MASSIE.
THERE, NOW THAT'S TWO SECRETS YOU HAVE TO KEEP.
NO PROBLEM. BY THE WAY, I'M SORRY ABOUT YOUR COMPANY.
?

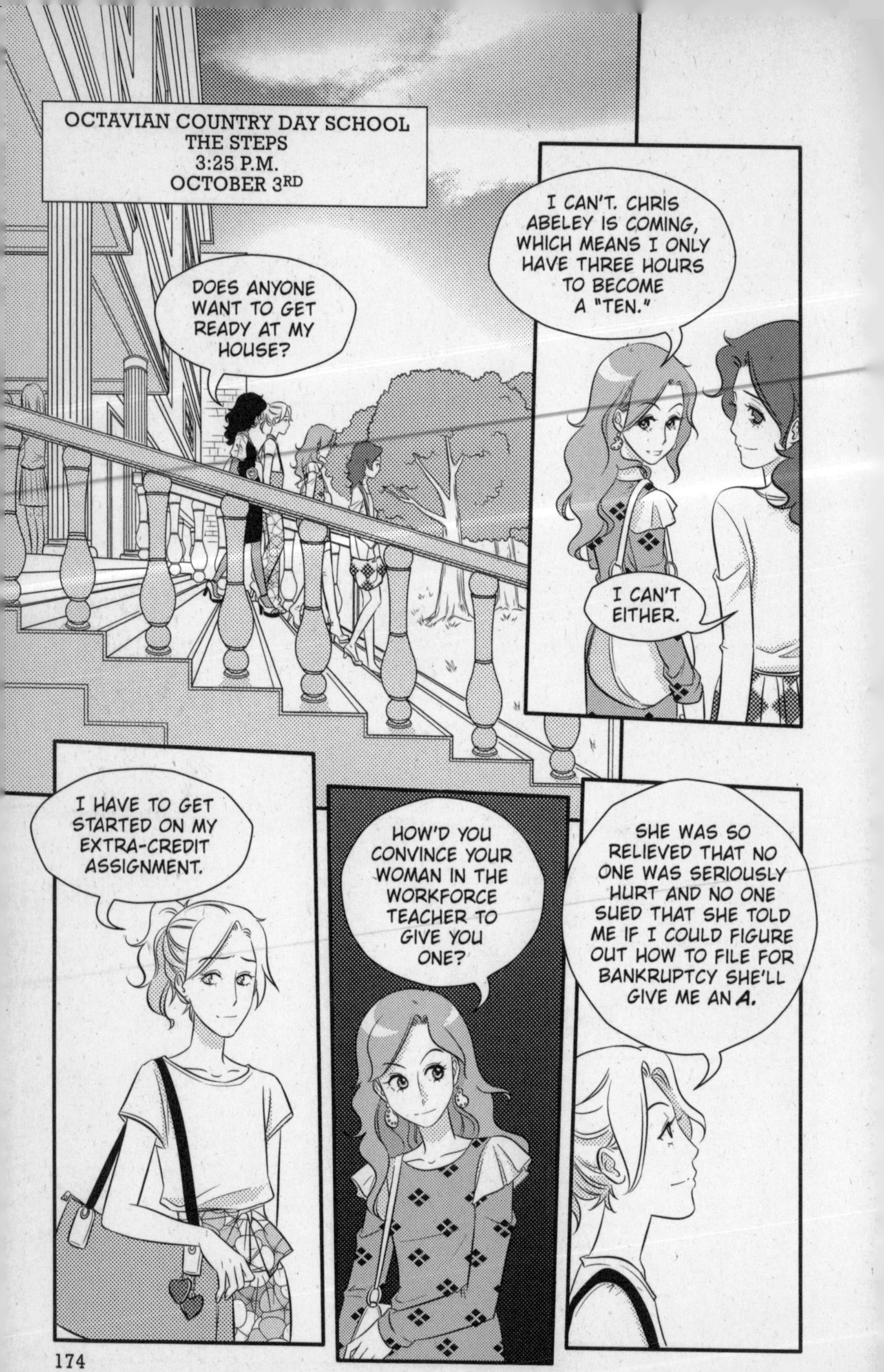
OCTAVIAN COUNTRY DAY SCHOOL THE STEPS 3:25 P.M. OCTOBER 3RD
DOES ANYONE WANT TO GET READY AT MY HOUSE?
I CAN'T. CHRIS ABELEY IS COMING, WHICH MEANS I ONLY HAVE THREE HOURS TO BECOME A "TEN."
I CAN'T EITHER.
I HAVE TO GET STARTED ON MY EXTRA-CREDIT ASSIGNMENT.
HOW'D YOU CONVINCE YOUR WOMAN IN THE WORKFORCE TEACHER TO GIVE YOU ONE?
SHE WAS SO RELIEVED THAT NO ONE WAS SERIOUSLY HURT AND NO ONE SUED THAT SHE TOLD ME IF I COULD FIGURE OUT HOW TO FILE FOR BANKRUPTCY SHE'LL GIVE ME AN A.

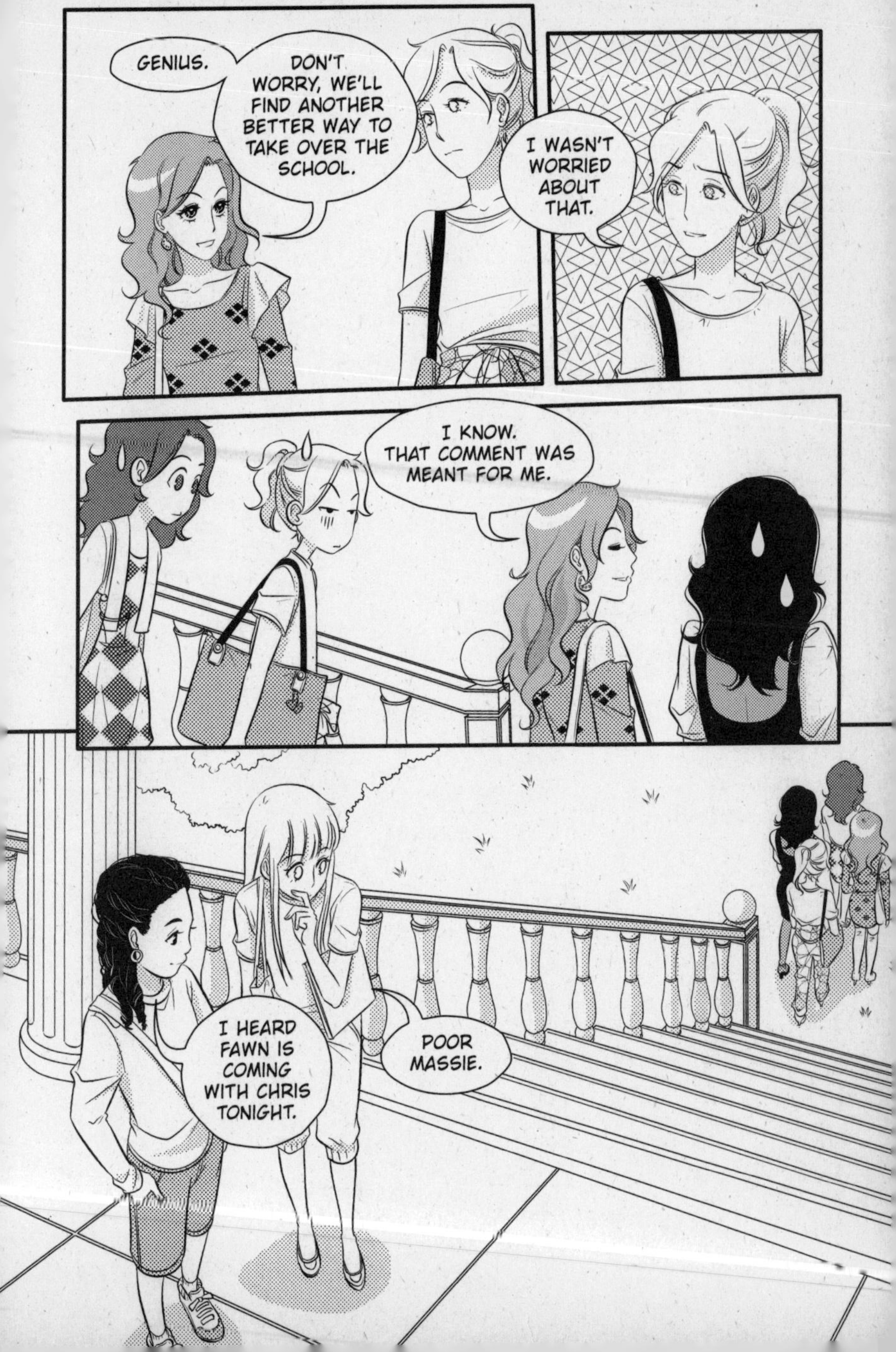
GENIUS.
DON'T WORRY, WE'LL FIND ANOTHER BETTER WAY TO TAKE OVER THE SCHOOL.
I WASN'T WORRIED ABOUT THAT.
I KNOW. THAT COMMENT WAS MEANT FOR ME.
I HEARD FAWN IS COMING WITH CHRIS TONIGHT.
POOR MASSIE.

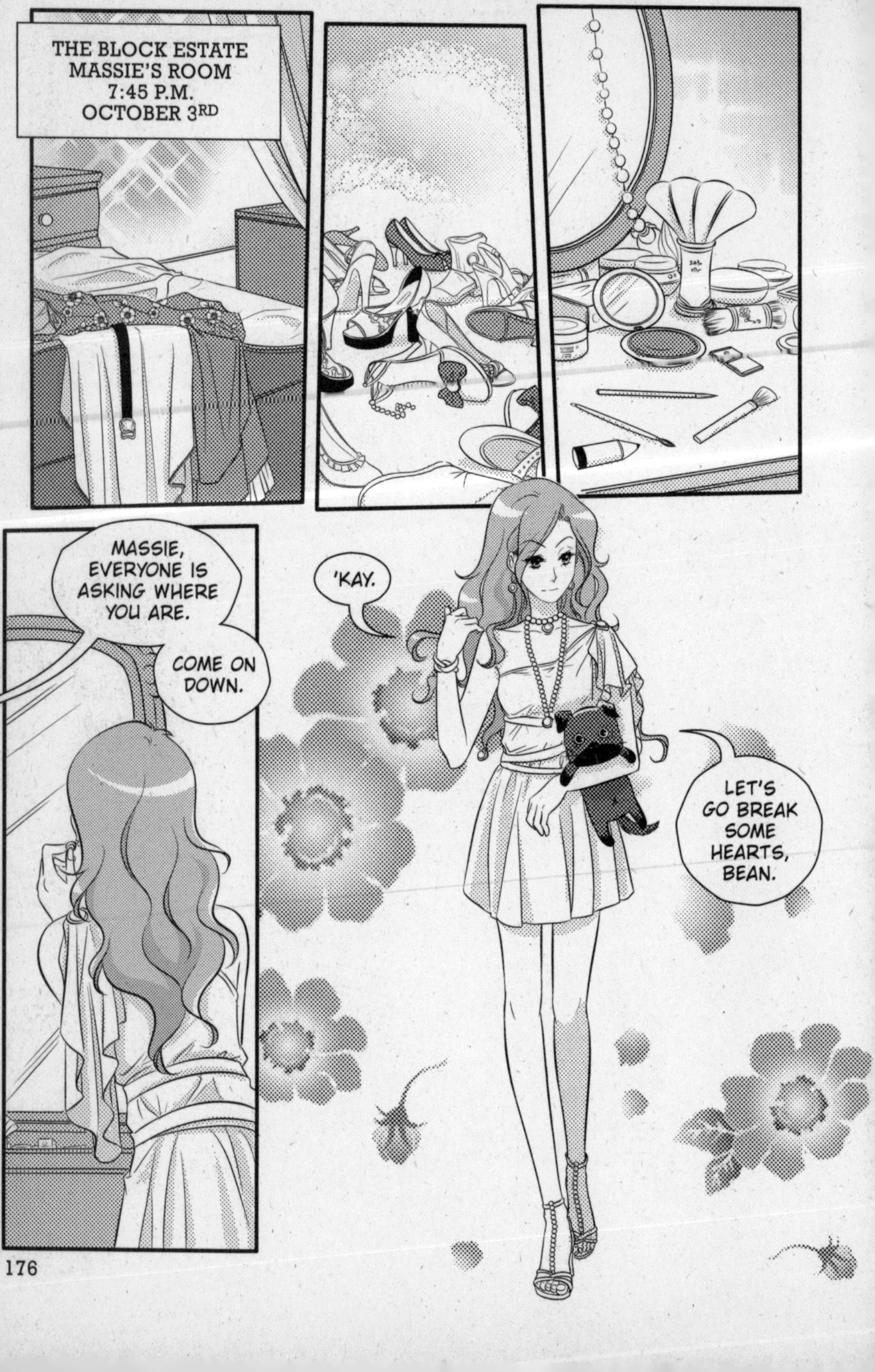
THE BLOCK ESTATE
MASSIE'S ROOM
7:45 P.M.
OCTOBER 3RD
MASSIE, EVERYONE IS ASKING WHERE YOU ARE.
COME ON DOWN.
'KAY.
LET'S GO BREAK SOME HEARTS, BEAN.

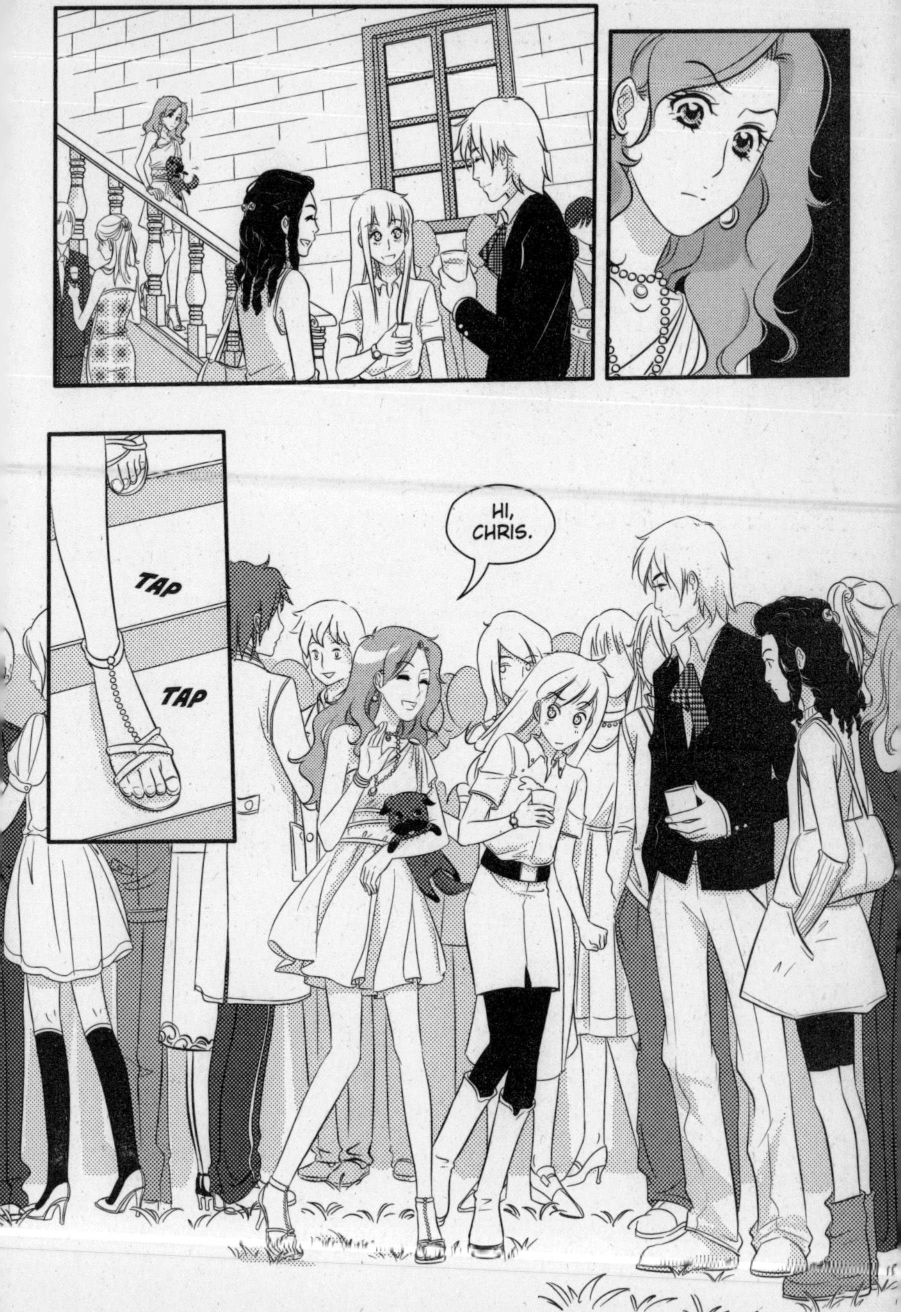
TAP
TAP
HI, CHRIS.

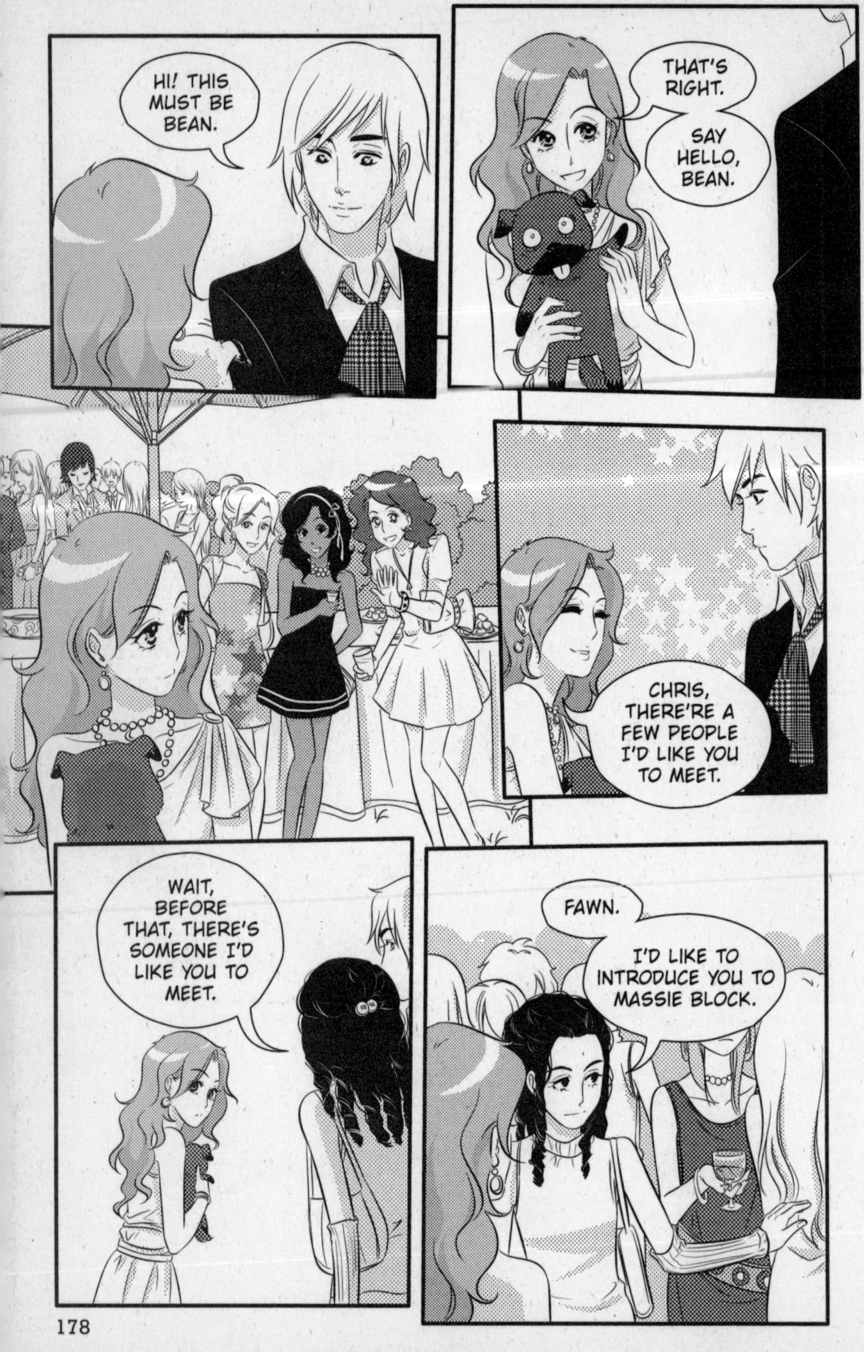
HI! THIS MUST BE BEAN.
THAT'S RIGHT.
SAY HELLO, BEAN.
CHRIS, THERE'RE A FEW PEOPLE I'D LIKE YOU TO MEET.
WAIT, BEFORE THAT, THERE'S SOMEONE I'D LIKE YOU TO MEET.
FAWN.
I'D LIKE TO INTRODUCE YOU TO MASSIE BLOCK.

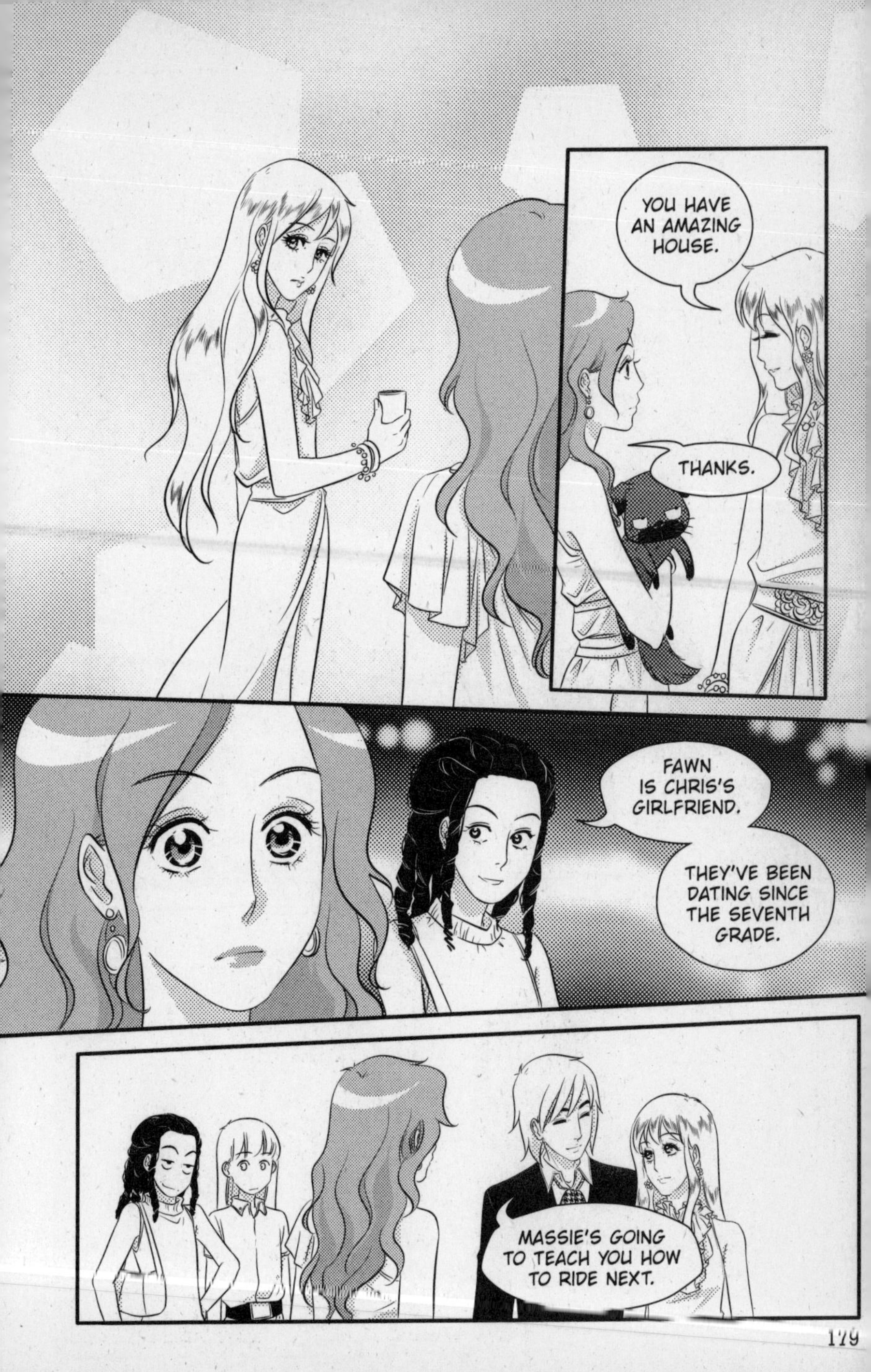
YOU HAVE AN AMAZING HOUSE.
THANKS.
FAWN IS CHRIS'S GIRLFRIEND.
THEY'VE BEEN DATING SINCE THE SEVENTH GRADE.
MASSIE'S GOING TO TEACH YOU HOW TO RIDE NEXT.

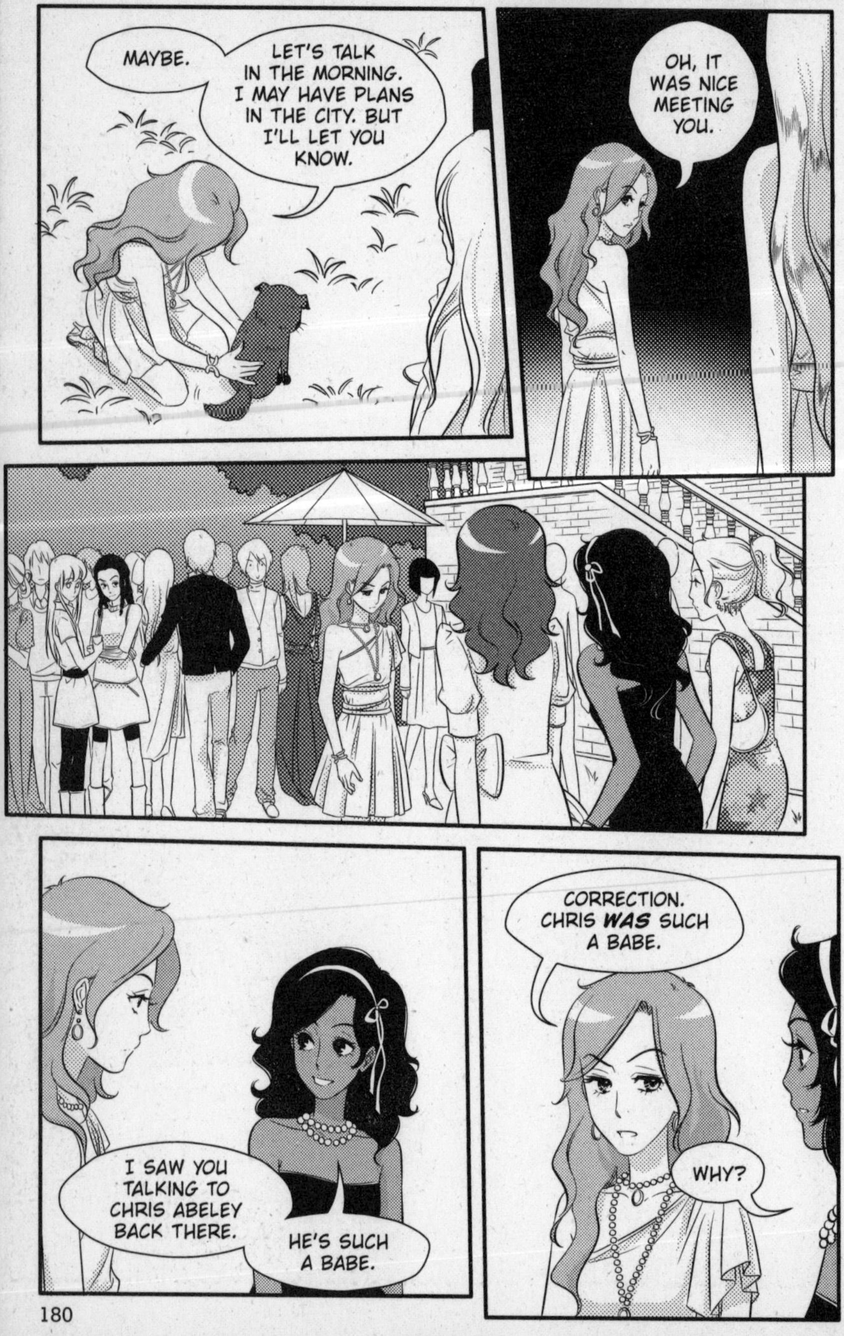

MAYBE.
LET'S TALK IN THE MORNING. I MAY HAVE PLANS IN THE CITY. BUT I'LL LET YOU KNOW.
OH, IT WAS NICE MEETING YOU.
I SAW YOU TALKING TO CHRIS ABELEY BACK THERE.
HE'S SUCH A BABE.
CORRECTION. CHRIS WAS SUCH A BABE.
WHY?

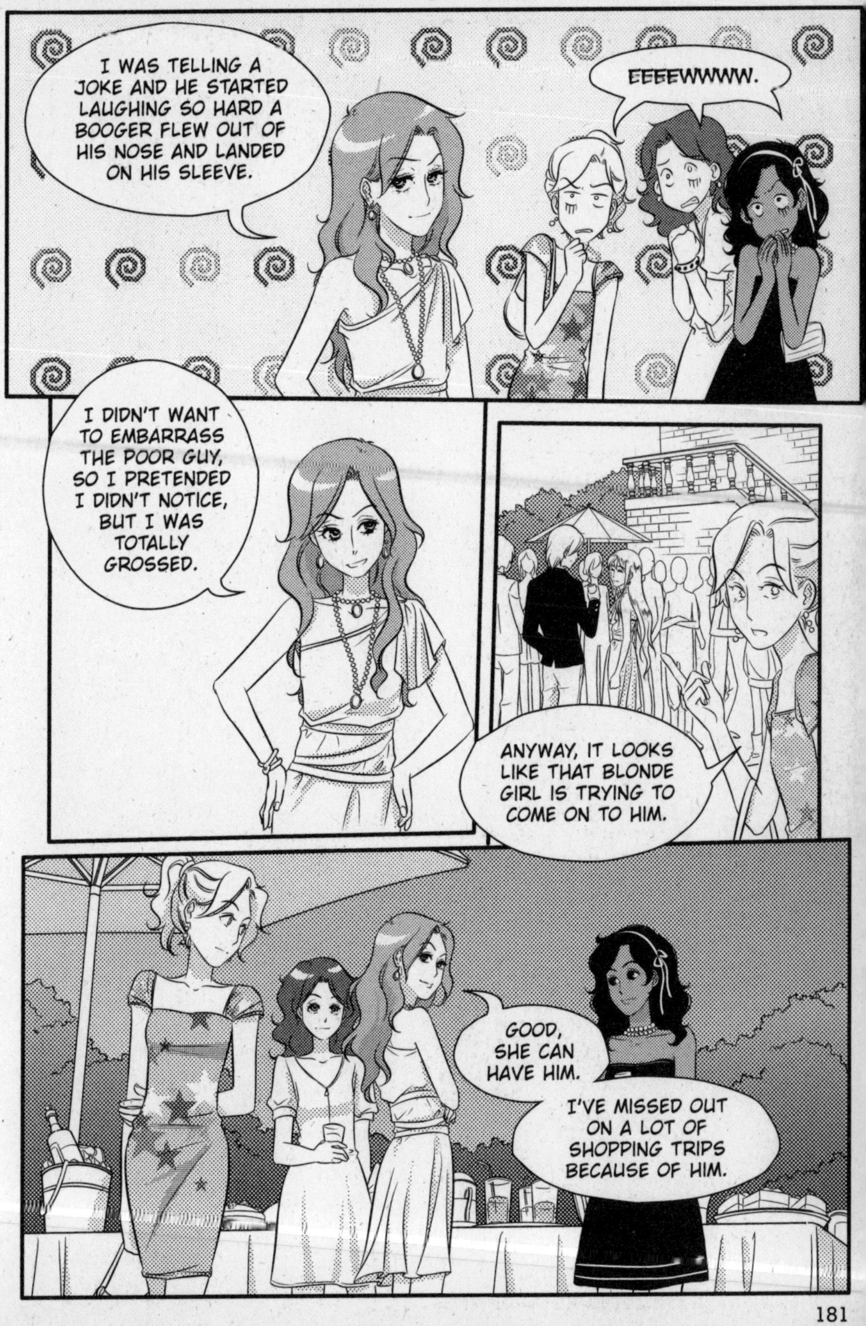

I WAS TELLING A JOKE AND HE STARTED LAUGHING SO HARD A BOOGER FLEW OUT OF HIS NOSE AND LANDED ON HIS SLEEVE.
EEEEWWWW.
I DIDN'T WANT TO EMBARRASS THE POOR GUY, SO I PRETENDED I DIDN'T NOTICE, BUT I WAS TOTALLY GROSSED.
ANYWAY, IT LOOKS LIKE THAT BLONDE GIRL IS TRYING TO COME ON TO HIM.
GOOD, SHE CAN HAVE HIM.
I'VE MISSED OUT ON A LOT OF SHOPPING TRIPS BECAUSE OF HIM.

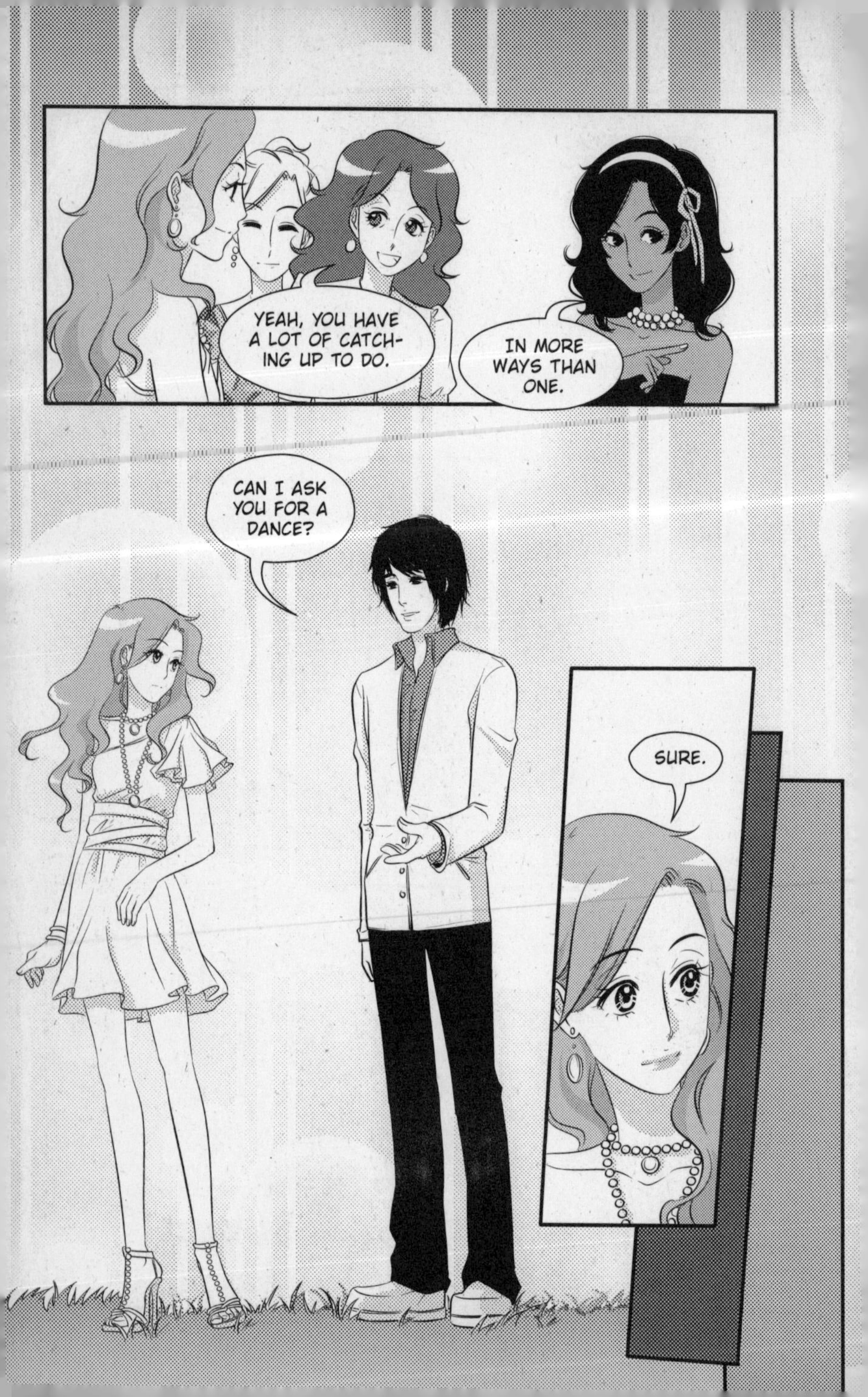
YEAH, YOU HAVE A LOT OF CATCH-ING UP TO DO.
IN MORE WAYS THAN ONE.
CAN I ASK YOU FOR A DANCE?
SURE.

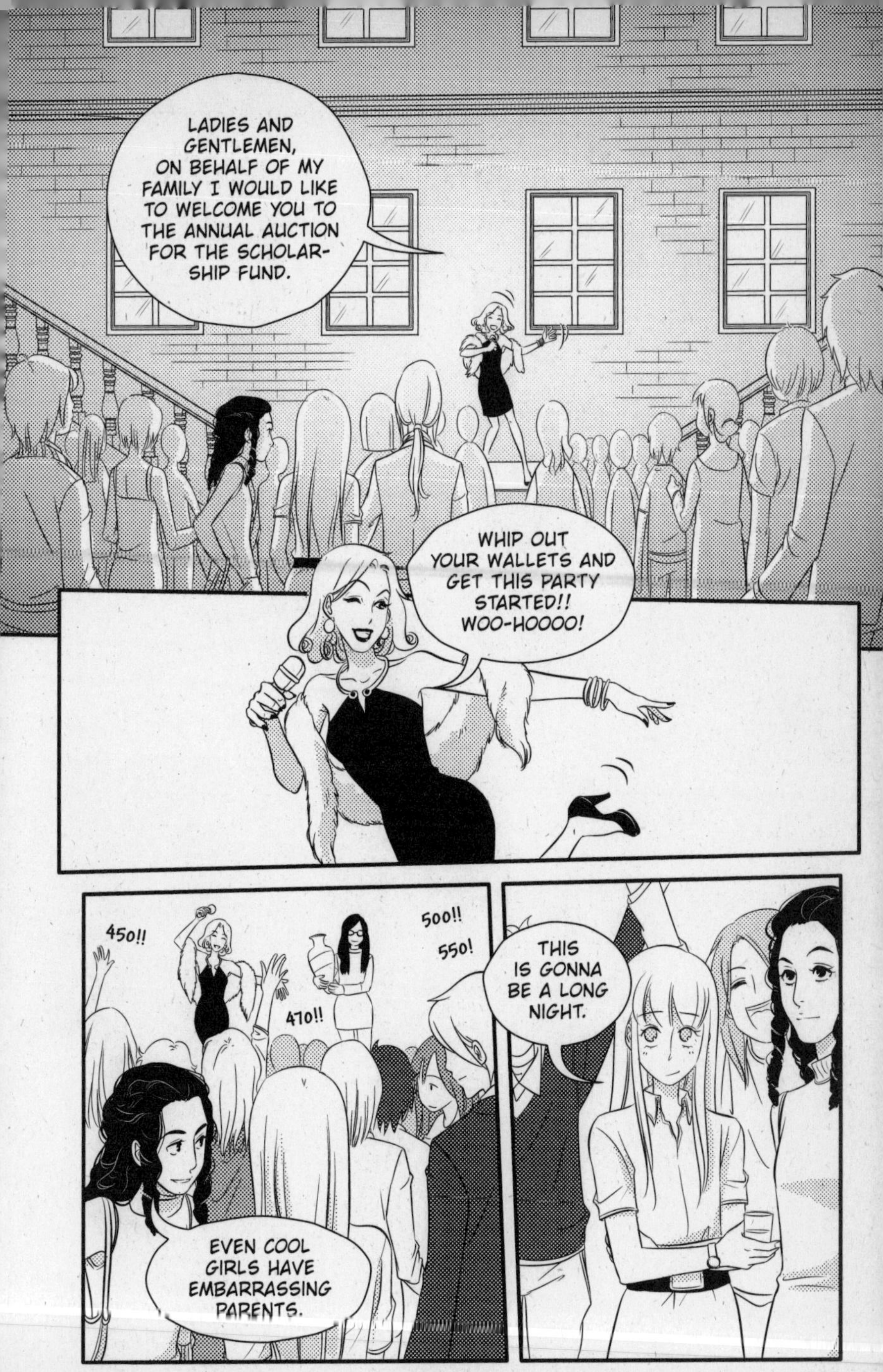
LADIES AND GENTLEMEN, ON BEHALF OF MY FAMILY I WOULD LIKE TO WELCOME YOU TO THE ANNUAL AUCTION FOR THE SCHOLAR-SHIP FUND.
WHIP OUT YOUR WALLETS AND GET THIS PARTY STARTED!! WOO-HOOOO!
450!!
470!!
500!!
550!
EVEN COOL GIRLS HAVE EMBARRASSING PARENTS.
THIS IS GONNA BE A LONG NIGHT.

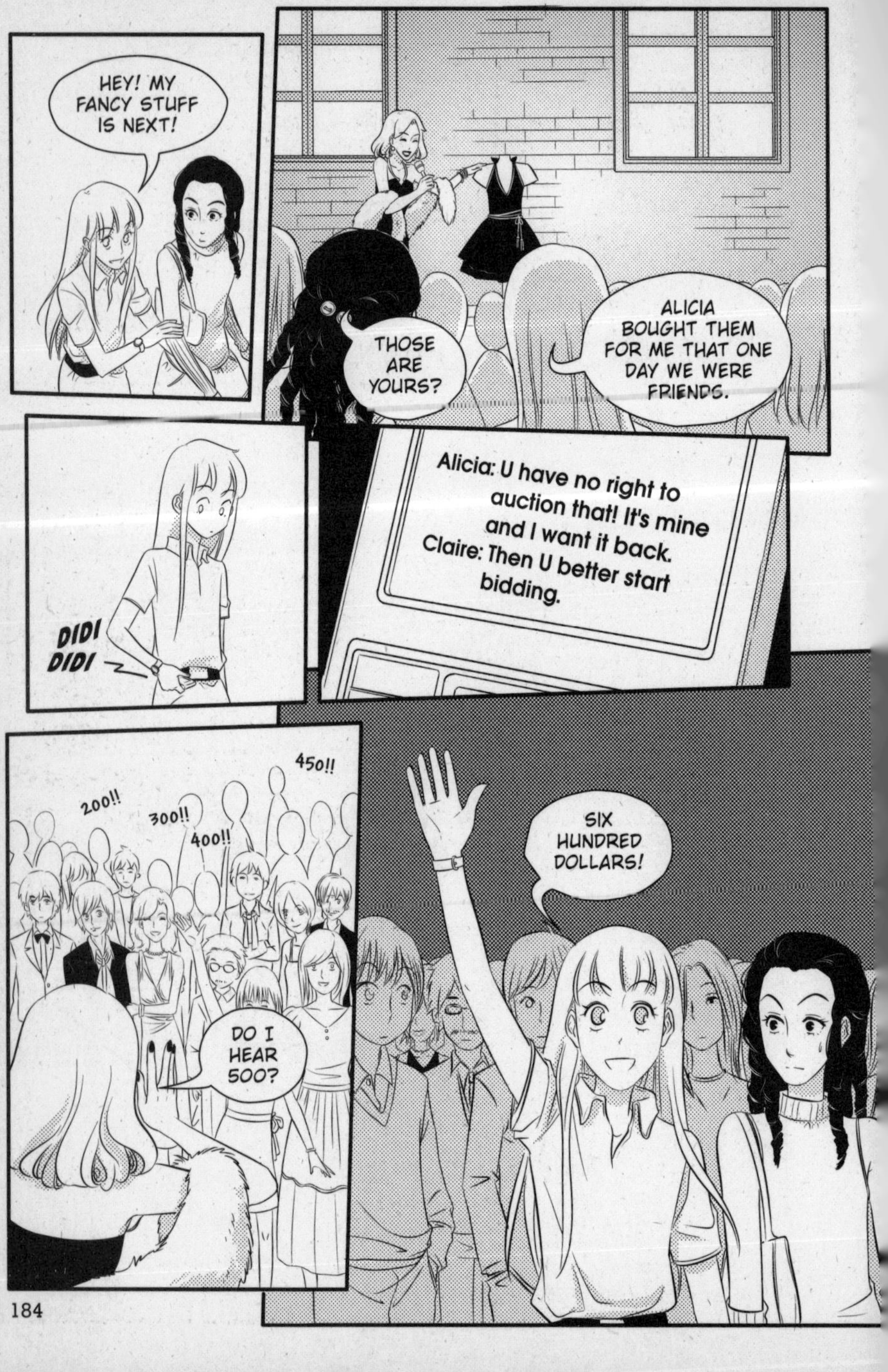
HEY! MY FANCY STUFF IS NEXT!
THOSE ARE YOURS?
ALICIA BOUGHT THEM FOR ME THAT ONE DAY WE WERE FRIENDS.
DIDI DIDI
Alicia: U have no right to auction that! It's mine and I want it back.
Claire: Then U better start bidding.
200!!
300!!
400!!
450!!
DO I HEAR 500?
SIX HUNDRED DOLLARS!

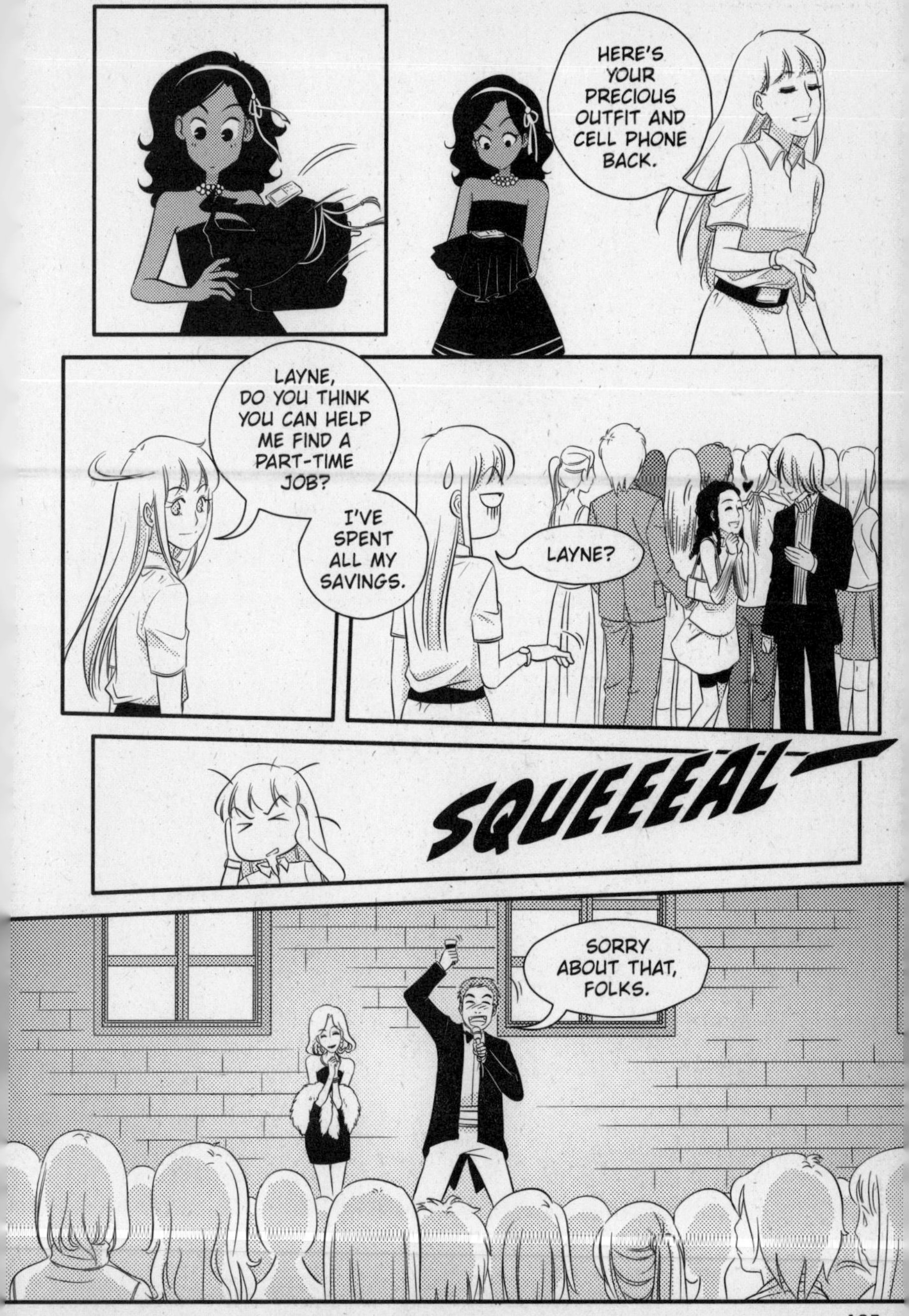
HERE'S YOUR PRECIOUS OUTFIT AND CELL PHONE BACK.
LAYNE, DO YOU THINK YOU CAN HELP ME FIND A PART-TIME JOB?
I'VE SPENT ALL MY SAVINGS.
LAYNE?
SQUEEEAL
SORRY ABOUT THAT, FOLKS.

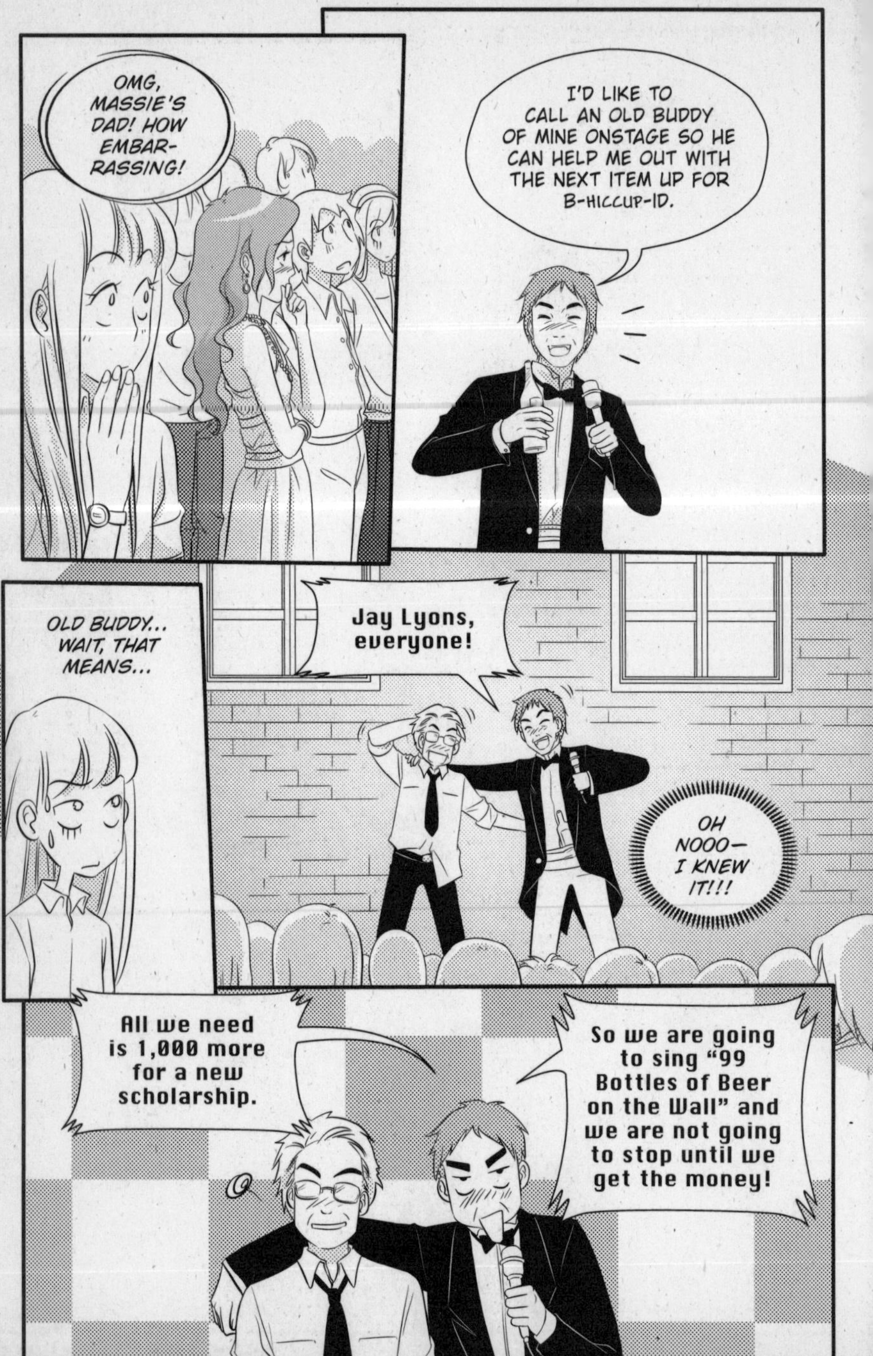
OMG, MASSIE'S DAD! HOW EMBAR-RASSING!
I'D LIKE TO CALL AN OLD BUDDY OF MINE ONSTAGE SO HE CAN HELP ME OUT WITH THE NEXT ITEM UP FOR B-HICCUP-ID.
OLD BUDDY... WAIT, THAT MEANS...
Jay Lyons, everyone!
OH NOOO— I KNEW IT!!!
All we need is 1,000 more for a new scholarship.
So we are going to sing "99 Bottles of Beer on the Wall" and we are not going to stop until we get the money!

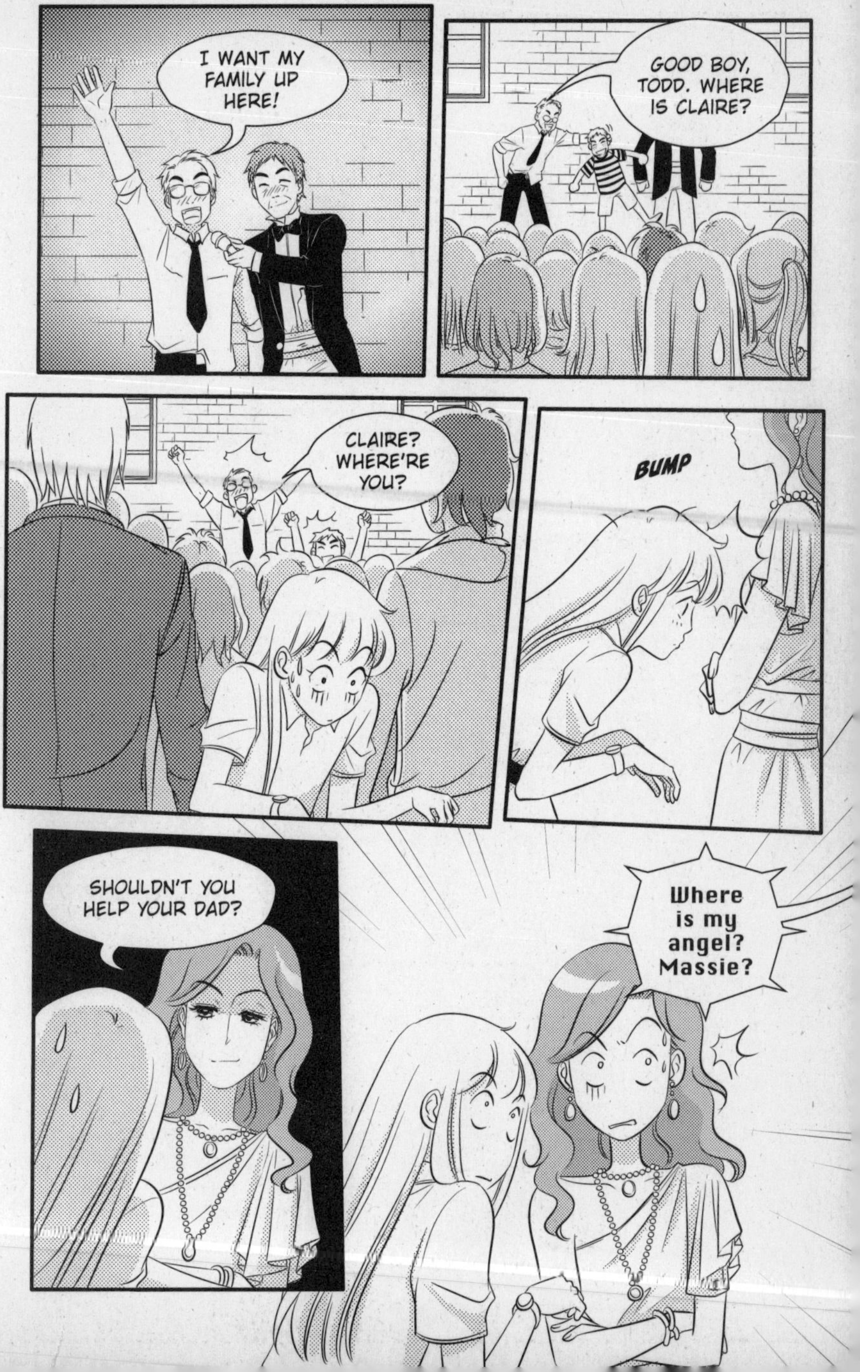
I WANT MY FAMILY UP HERE!
GOOD BOY, TODD. WHERE IS CLAIRE?
CLAIRE? WHERE'RE YOU?
BUMP
SHOULDN'T YOU HELP YOUR DAD?
Where is my angel? Massie?

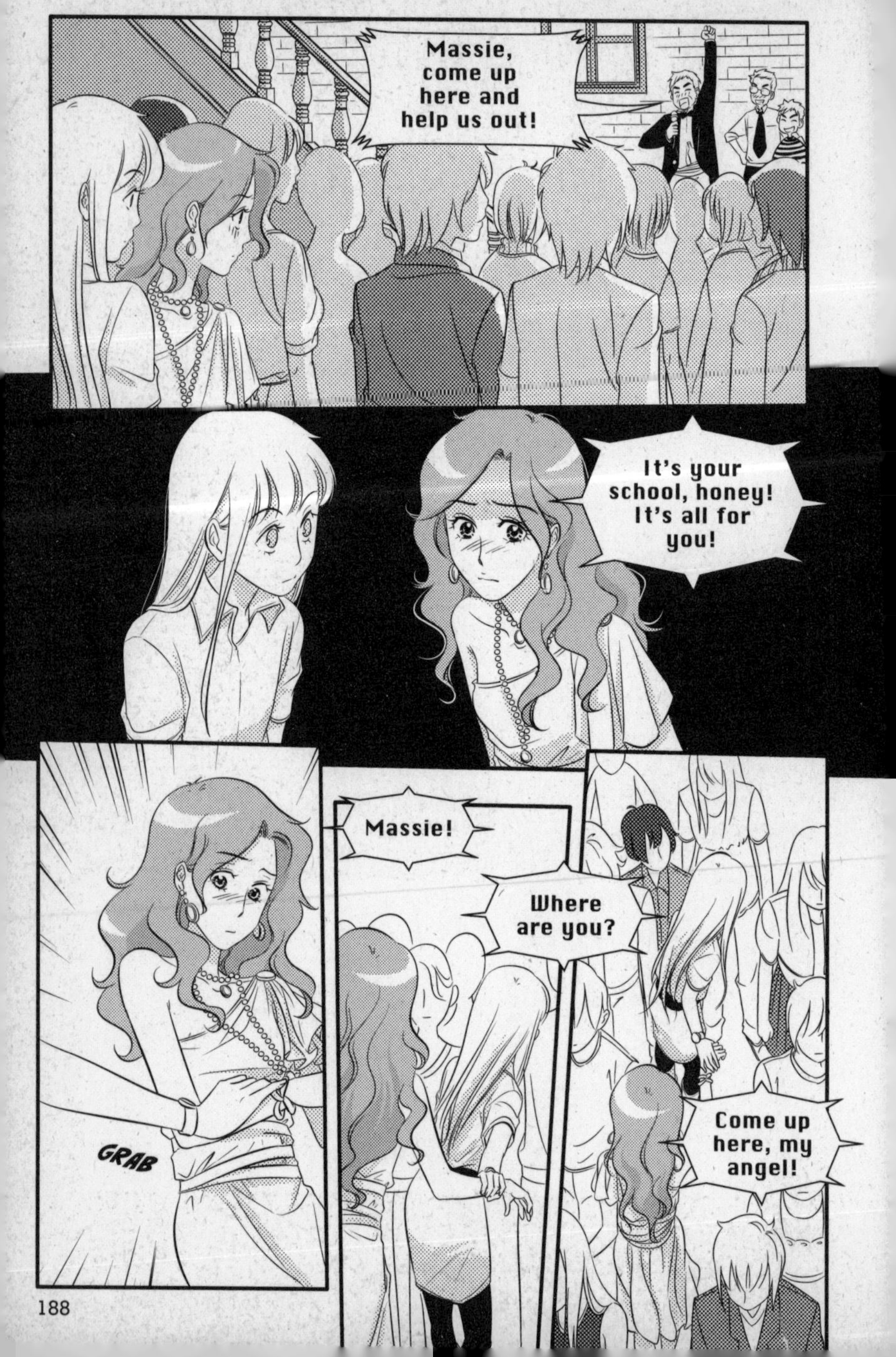
Massie, come up here and help us out!
It's your school, honey! It's all for you!
GRAB
Massie!
Where are you?
Come up here, my angel!

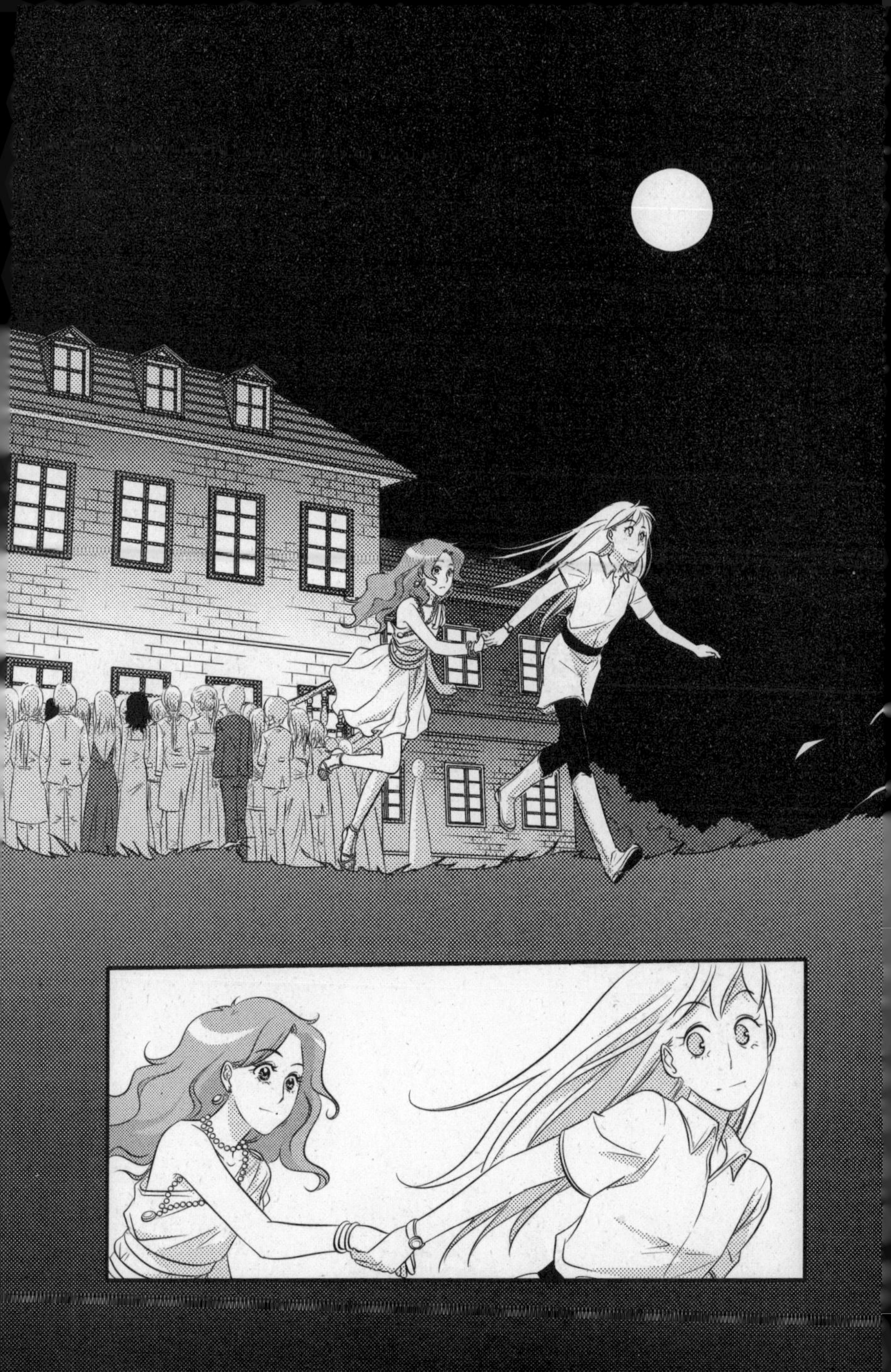

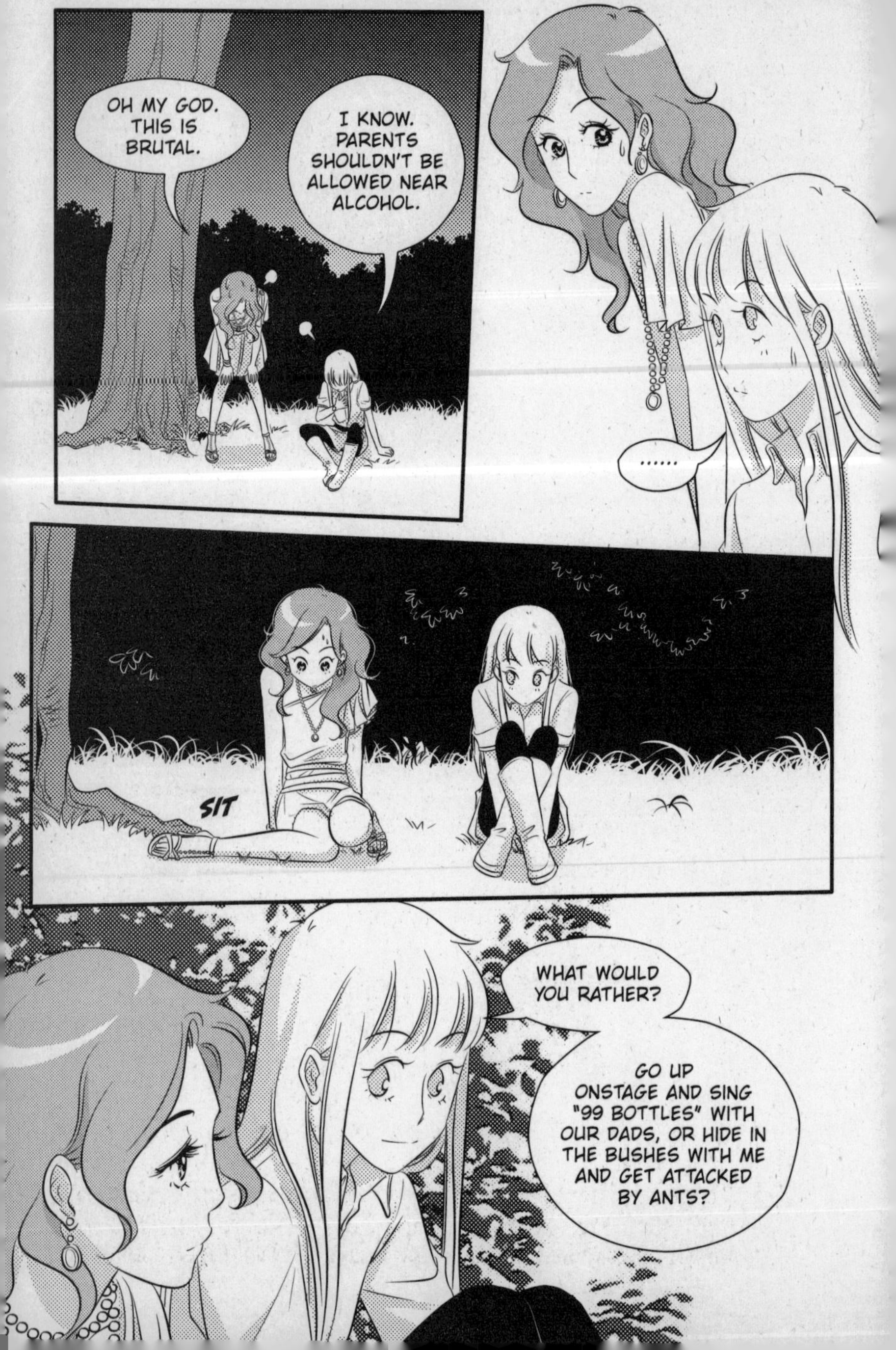
OH MY GOD. THIS IS BRUTAL.
I KNOW. PARENTS SHOULDN'T BE ALLOWED NEAR ALCOHOL.
......
SIT
WHAT WOULD YOU RATHER?
GO UP ONSTAGE AND SING "99 BOTTLES" WITH OUR DADS, OR HIDE IN THE BUSHES WITH ME AND GET ATTACKED BY ANTS?

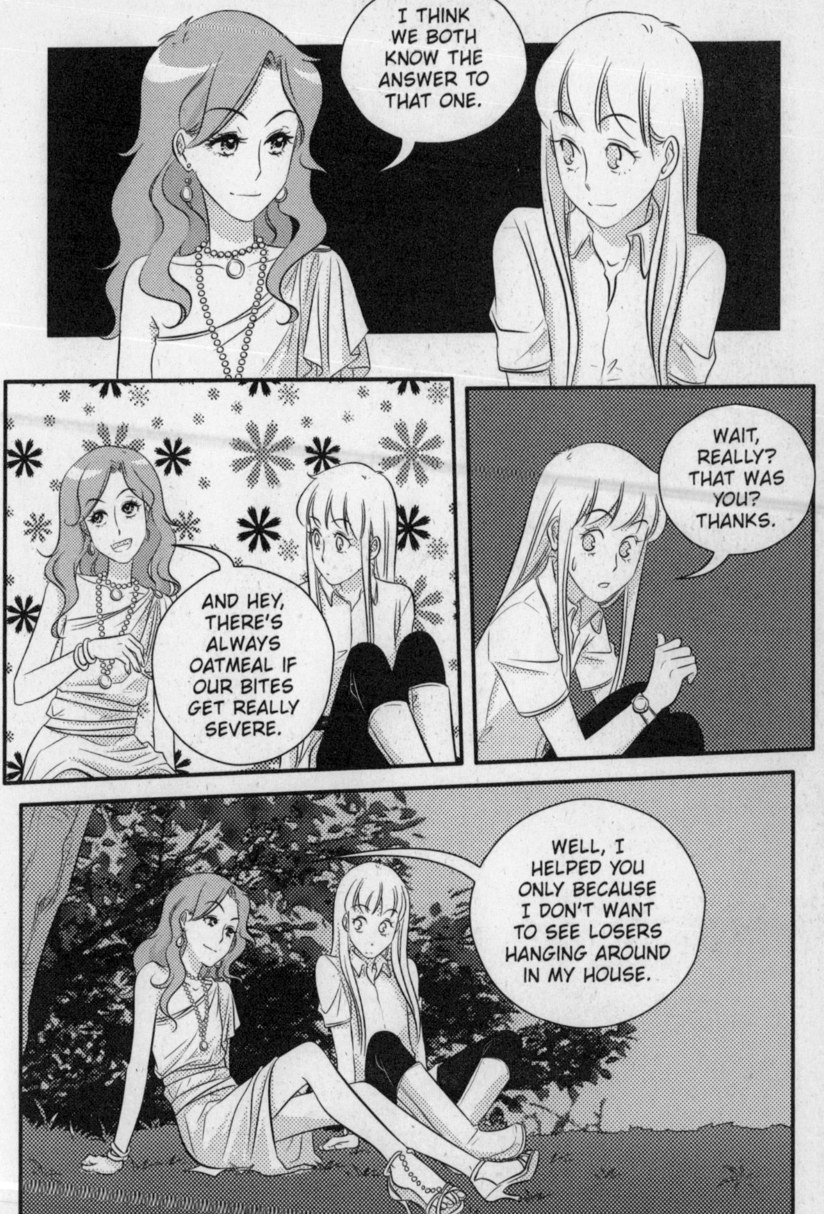
I THINK WE BOTH KNOW THE ANSWER TO THAT ONE.
AND HEY, THERE'S ALWAYS OATMEAL IF OUR BITES GET REALLY SEVERE.
WAIT, REALLY? THAT WAS YOU? THANKS.
WELL, I HELPED YOU ONLY BECAUSE I DON'T WANT TO SEE LOSERS HANGING AROUND IN MY HOUSE.

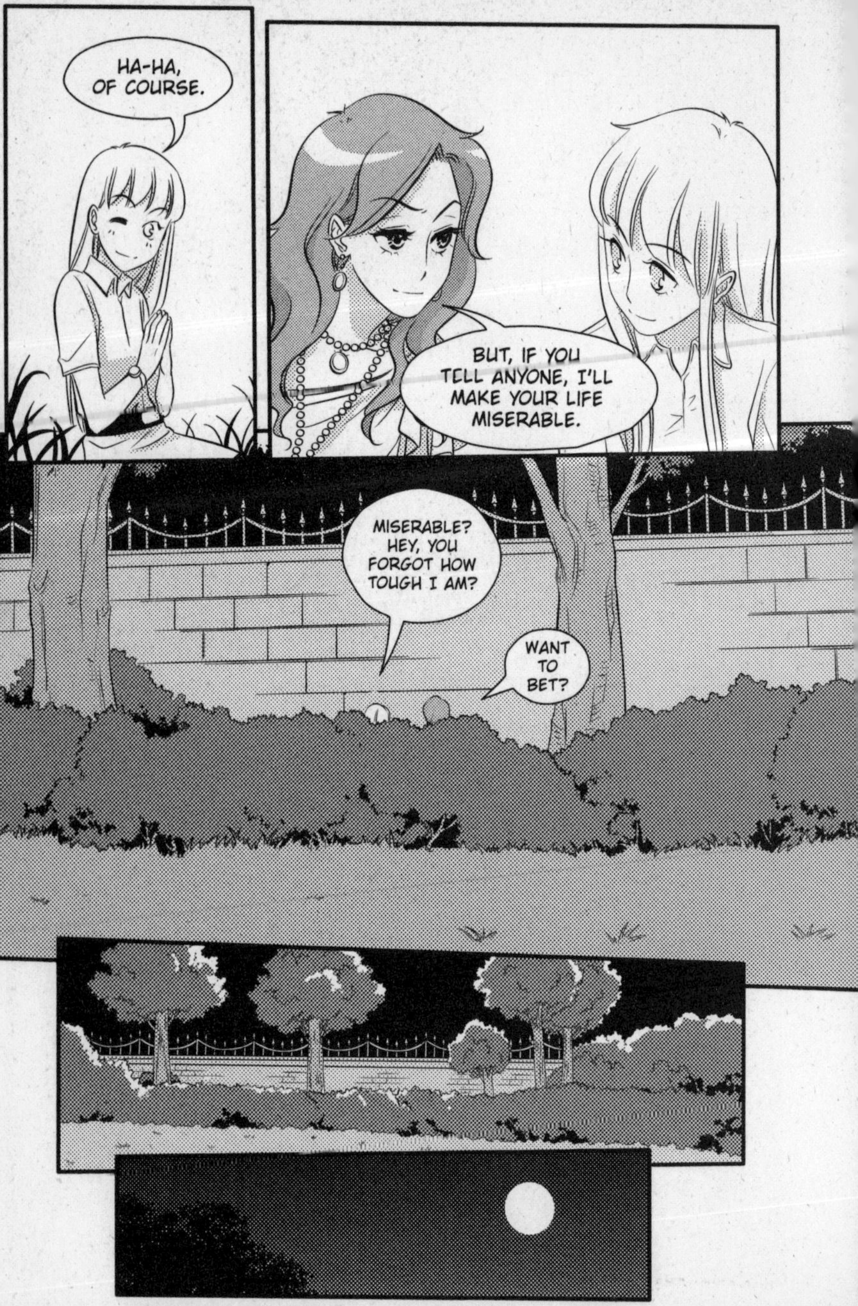
HA-HA, OF COURSE.
BUT, IF YOU TELL ANYONE, I'LL MAKE YOUR LIFE MISERABLE.
MISERABLE? HEY, YOU FORGOT HOW TOUGH I AM?
WANT TO BET?

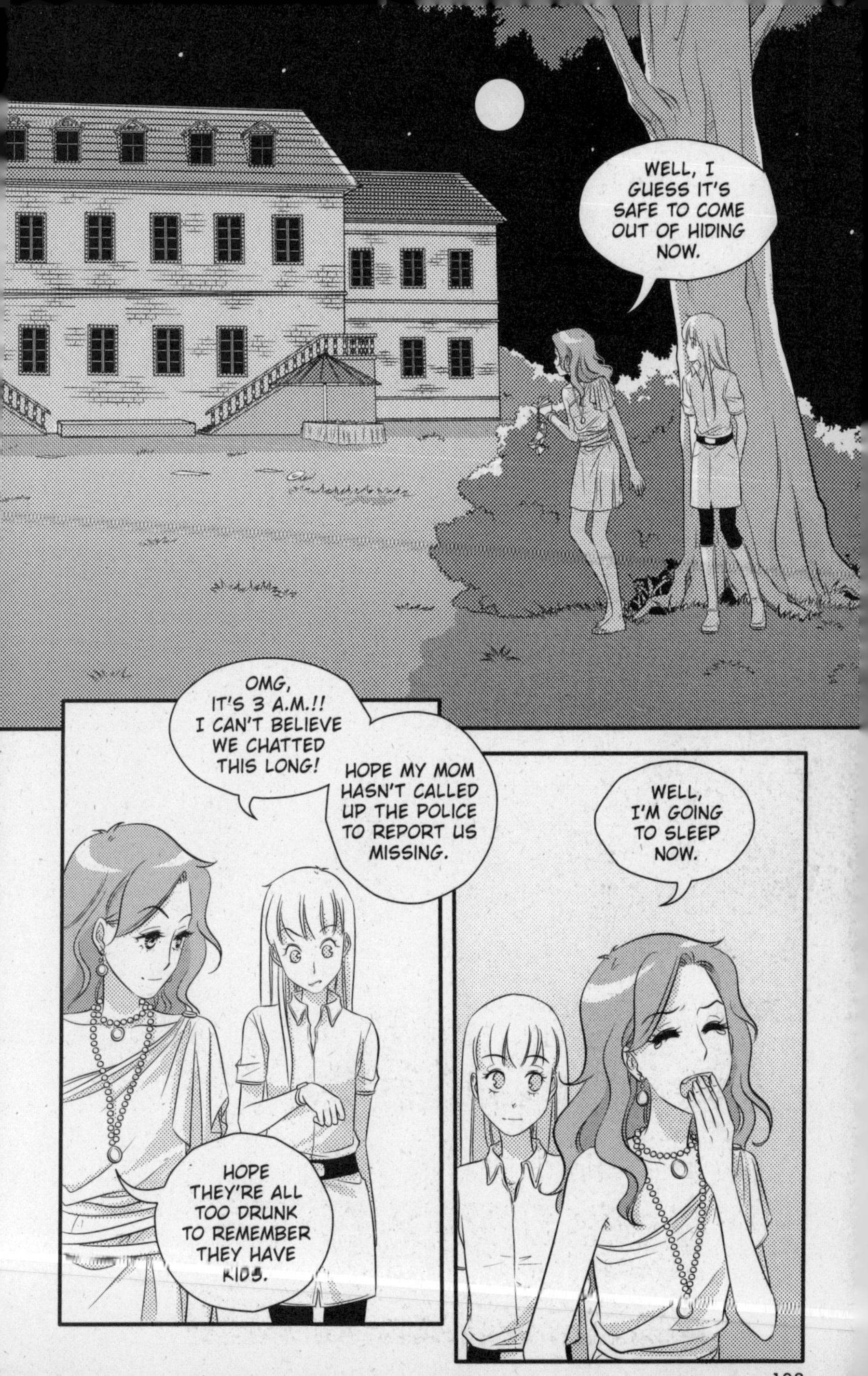
WELL, I GUESS IT'S SAFE TO COME OUT OF HIDING NOW.
OMG, IT'S 3 A.M.!! I CAN'T BELIEVE WE CHATTED THIS LONG!
HOPE MY MOM HASN'T CALLED UP THE POLICE TO REPORT US MISSING.
HOPE THEY'RE ALL TOO DRUNK TO REMEMBER THEY HAVE KIDS.
WELL, I'M GOING TO SLEEP NOW.

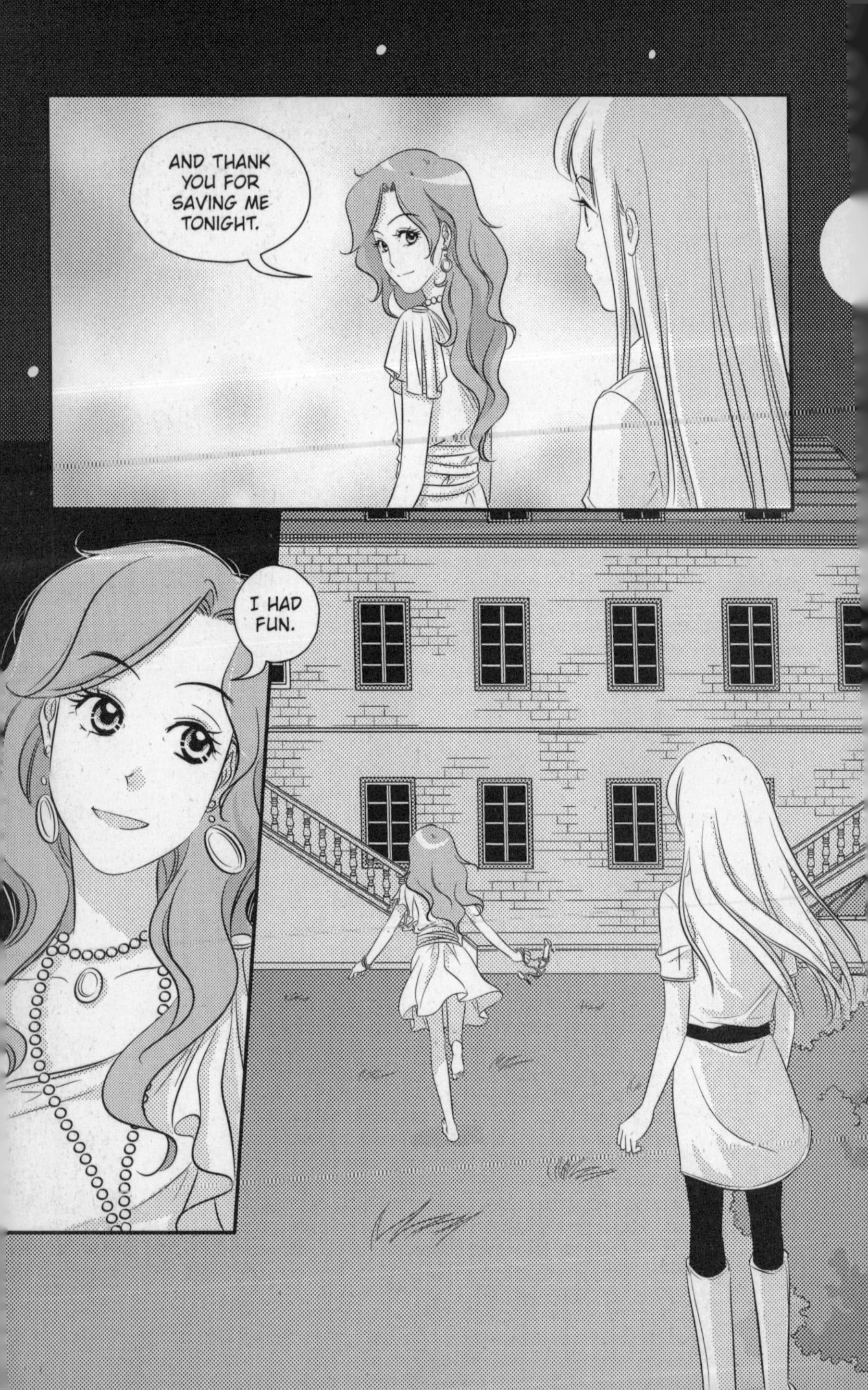
AND THANK YOU FOR SAVING ME TONIGHT.
I HAD FUN.

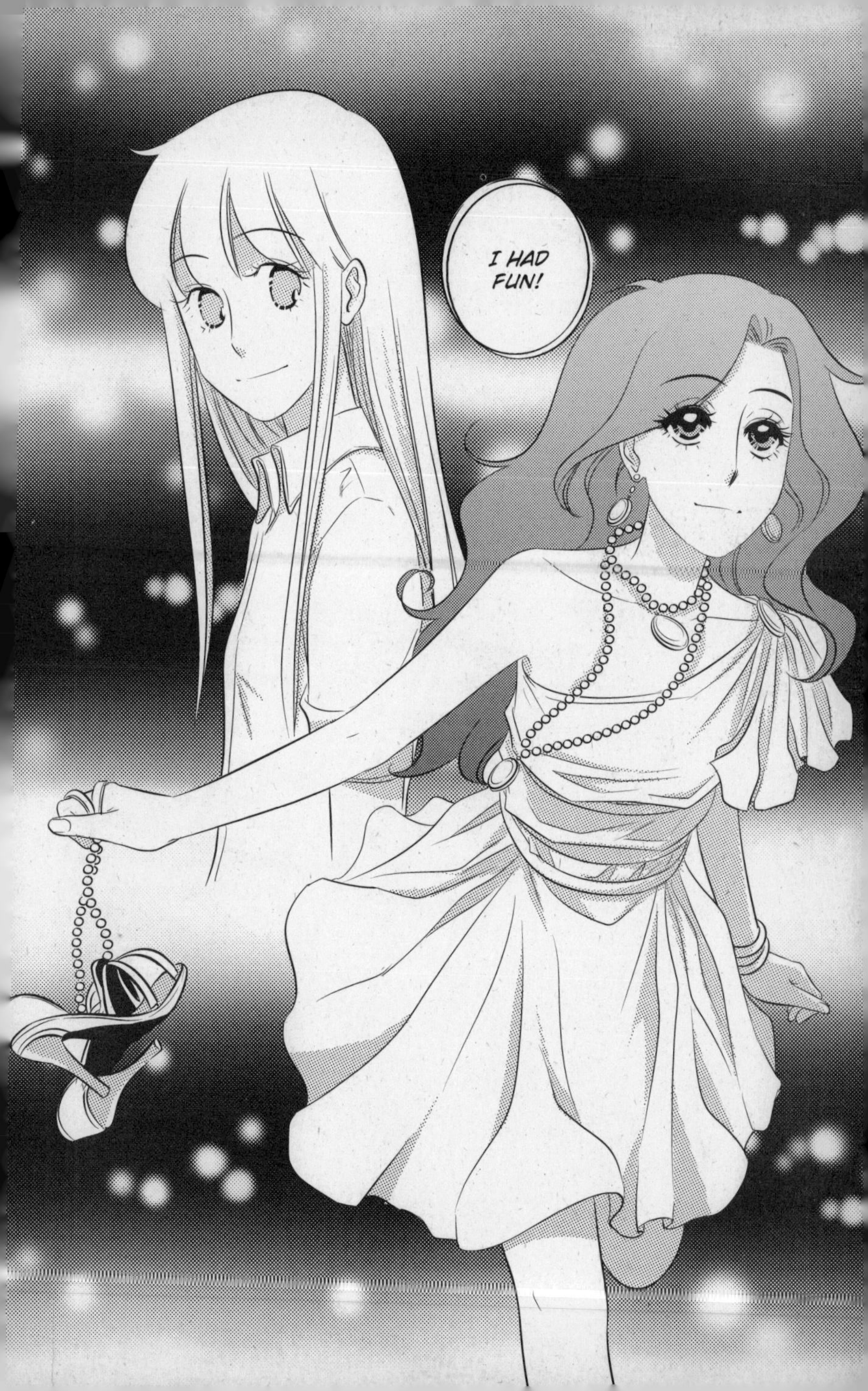
I HAD FUN!

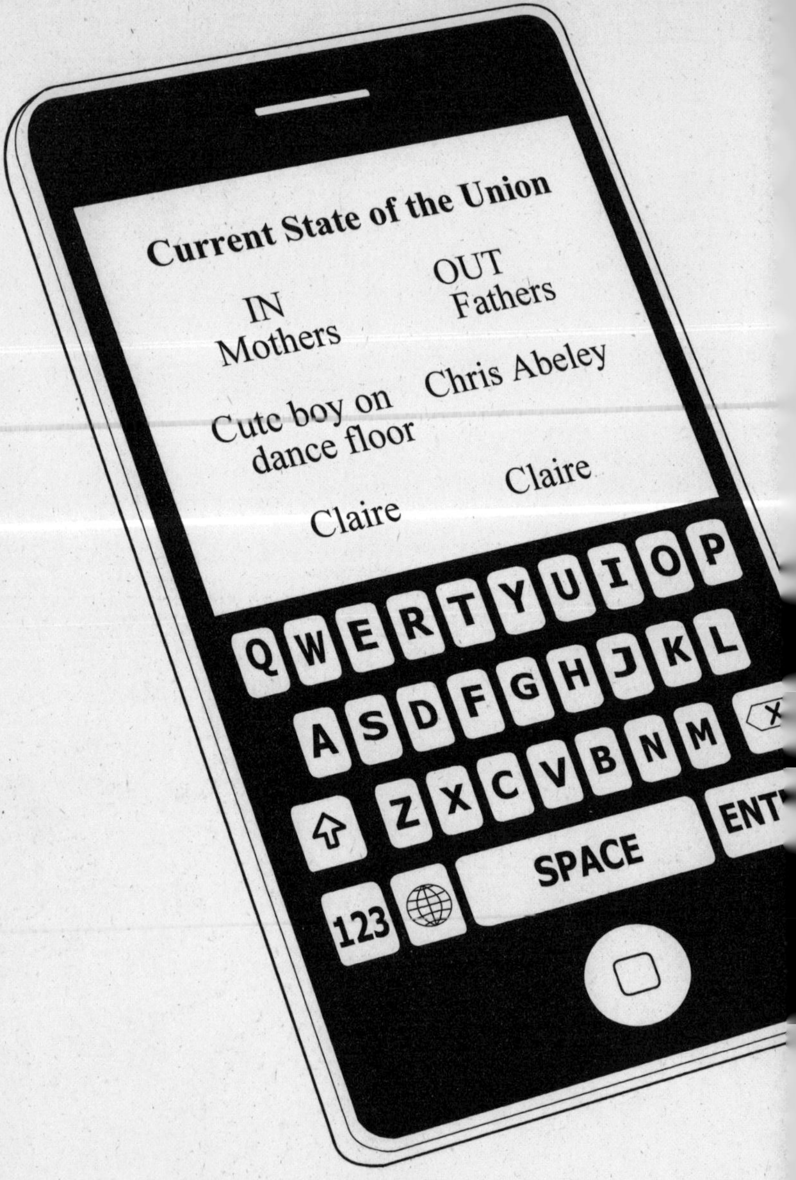
Current State of the Union
IN
Mothers
OUT
Fathers
Cute boy on dance floor
Chris Abeley
Claire
Claire
QWERTYUIOP
ASDFGHJKL
ZXCVBNM
SPACE
123

THE END.

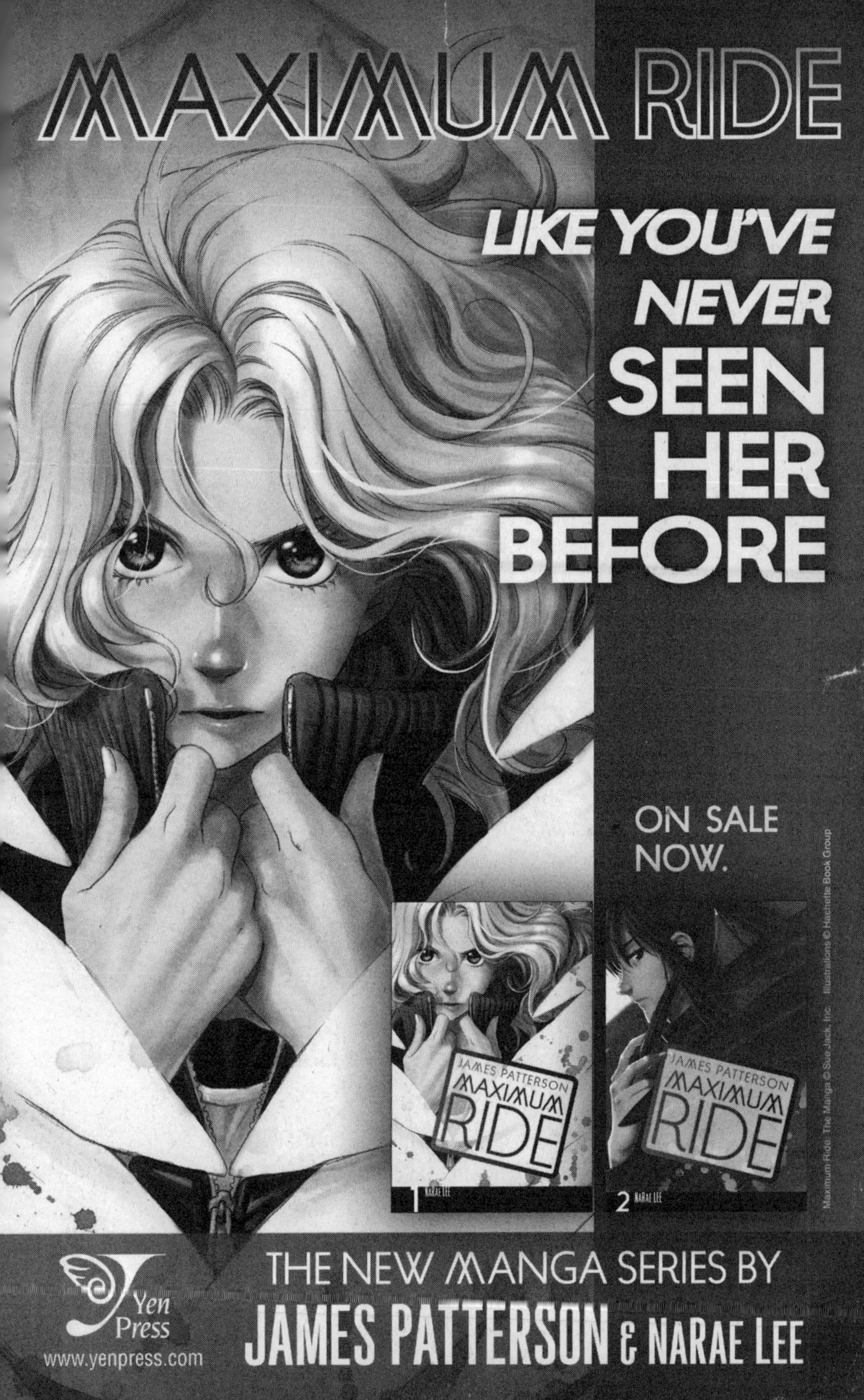
MAXIMUM RIDE
LIKE YOU'VE NEVER SEEN HER BEFORE
ON SALE NOW.
JAMES PATTERSON
MAXIMUM RIDE
1 NARAE LEE
JAMES PATTERSON
MAXIMUM RIDE
2 NARAE LEE
Maximum Ride: The Manga © Sue Jack, Inc. Illustrations © Hachette Book Group
Yen Press
www.yenpress.com
THE NEW MANGA SERIES BY
JAMES PATTERSON & NARAE LEE

# THE CLIQUE
## THE MANGA

Based on THE CLIQUE novels
written by Lisi Harrison

Art and Adaptation: Yishan Li

Lettering: Hope Donovan

Text Copyright © 2010 by Alloy Entertainment
Illustrations Copyright © 2010 by Hachette Book Group, Inc.

Yen Press
Hachette Book Group
237 Park Avenue
New York, NY 10017

www.HachetteBookGroup.com
www.YenPress.com

Yen Press is an imprint of Hachette Book Group, Inc. The
Yen Press name and logo are trademarks of Hachette Book
Group, Inc.

alloyentertainment

151 West 26th Street, New York, NY 10001
alloyentertainment.com

First Yen Press Edition: July 2010

ISBN: 978-0-7595-3029-4

10 9 8 7 6 5 4 3 2 1

CW

Printed in the United States of America